PLAIN AND
AMISH

PLAIN AND AMISH

An Alternative to Modern Pessimism

Bernd G. Längin

Die Amischen
Revised by Bernd G. Längin
Translated by Jack Thiessen

HERALD PRESS
Scottdale, Pennsylvania
Waterloo, Ontario

Library of Congress Cataloging-in-Publication Data
Längin, Bernd G., 1941-
[Amischen. English]
 Plain and Amish : an alternative to modern pessimism / Bernd G.
Längin ; revised by Bernd G. Längin ; translated by Jack Thiessen.
   p.   cm.
 Includes bibliographical references and index.
 ISBN 0-8361-3665-9
   1. Amish—Indiana—Allen County—Social life and customs.
2. Allen County (Ind.)—Social life and customs. 3. Amish—Social life
and customs. I. Title.
F532.A4L36   1994
977.2'74043'088287—dc20   94-8324
                                                             CIP

The paper used in this publication is recycled and meets the minimum
requirements of American National Standard for Information Sciences—
Permanence of Paper for Printed Library Materials, ANSI Z39.48-1984.

Scripture is from Martin Luther's German translation, *Die Bibel,* or
adapted from *The Holy Bible, King James Version.*

The Amish did not pose for any of the photos in this book. Unless
otherwise noted, the photos are by Bernd G. Längin, who holds the
copyright © 1994 for them.

Plain and Amish is the author's revision of his book *Die Amischen: Vom
Geheimnis des einfachen Lebens* (Paul List Verlag, 1990), translated by Jack
Thiessen.

To Christiane

Contents

Love not the world, neither the things that are in the world.
If any one loves the world, the love of the Father is not in him.
For all that is in the world,
the lust of the flesh, and the lust of the eyes, and the pride of life,
is not of the Father, but is of the world.
And the world passes away, and the lust thereof;
but whoever does the will of God abides for ever.

—1 John 2:15-17

Foreword

"Solitude without community is merely loneliness."
—Robert N. Bellah

Most of us in the Western world know of the Amish only through newspaper features on Amish barn raisings or spring plowing. Many among us have seen the film, *Witness*, or one or more documentaries on the Amish. A few of us have needed to slow down behind one of those "horse-drawn vehicles," of which the road signs warn us in Amish areas.

Journalist Bernd Längin took it upon himself to go further in attempting to discover the Amish world in depth. He took the time to rub shoulders with the Amish, stepping into their world and living there as possible for months on end. The result is this book, describing virtually every aspect of Amish life and faith, hope and vision.

Plain and Amish is unique among books on the Amish. The author has found a way to help the reader enter into the life of an Amish community—experience with them their special moments at home, at work, in school, in worship: their hopes and fears, their fortitude and foibles, their keen wisdom and admonitions, their conclusions about the whirlwind and insatiable society of modernity.

The book's subtitle, *An Alternative to Modern Pessimism,* is appropriate for those of us who feel caught in the modern web of manipulation and the machinations of current society. For example, the Amish in general have not lost the art of conversation. They hold tenaciously to the vision of placing human relations above money and possessions and power.

Längin returns again and again to three motifs of the Amish

9

essence—the realities of community, love, and peace: "Amish life rarely rotates around the 'I' but almost invariably around the seriously meant 'We.' " "The earmark that continues to distinguish the true Amish community is its effort further to apply a relevant word of Christ, to 'have love for one another' (John 13:35)." "These Amish were pacifists out of deepest convictions. . . . They saw war as the highest expression of brutality."

The Amish have something hopeful and special to offer their neighbors in the modern industrialized, commercialized, and media-satiated world. The land and people provide relief from the all-embracing societal influence of self-absorption and selfish individualism which has taken such a fierce hold upon most of us moderns.

William Leach in *Land of Desire*. . . and Robert N. Bellah (et al.) in *Habits of the Heart*. . . continue to interpret the tremendous impact that such forces have dealt within the past century to individuals within Western society. Modern culture has weakened the reality of community and manipulated people with great success to consume in ever-greater proportions.

For such reasons, the Amish have attracted much attention, inquiry, and research. Sociologists especially have expended great energy in analyzing the Amish, with John A. Hostetler (since the 1940s) and Donald B. Kraybill (since the 1980s) at the forefront of such studies. In 1993, the tricentennial of the Amish Division within Anabaptism, three conferences were held on the theme of the Amish. From them further research by dozens of scholars will find its way into print. Despite all this, there is still thus far nothing in the English language that brings together contextually at one fell swoop the history, the faith, the culture—in short, the "inside story"—of the Amish.

Unknown to most North Americans, such a book was published in German in 1990. *Die Amischen: Vom Geheimnis des einfachen Lebens* (The Amish: Concerning the secret/mystery of the simple life) was written by Bernd G. Längin, the well-known interpreter of German cultural groups living outside Germany. Längin's approach fascinated me to such a degree that I read the volume twice and decided to recommend that it be translated into English and published as soon as possible.

Herald Press took on the project, and the author found a translator equal to the task of transforming a creative and lively German into its English equivalent—in this case, no easy assignment. What has emerged is by far the best semipopular volume written on the Amish. Several factors combine to make this volume readable and authoritative: Längin's previous research on sister groups to the Amish (such as the Hutterites), his mother tongue being German (with a dialect close to that of many Amish), and his exacting attention to past scholarship on the Amish.

Only a German could have gleaned certain of the deep insights into the Amish lifestyle that Längin describes on almost every page. His journalistic approach makes the volume inviting to read. Here is an author who has lived and breathed the Amish air and has complemented this in-depth experience with careful background research in North America as well as in Europe.

Längin combines history and current life, utilizing the best sociological scholarship, but with all the life and spirit of the Amish way left in. Religious ideas end up a living faith. Yet utter reality is always at hand: the fact that the Amish way is a down-to-earth, dawn-to-dusk experience as they step through life "by the sweat of the brow."

The author does not make the mistake of some scholars who analyze one Amish district and then generalize to give the impression that all Amish are alike. Längin sets the one Amish community he is describing (located in Allen County, Indiana) within the larger historical and social context. The reader is always aware that here is an in-depth interpretation of *one* Amish community, occasionally compared with customs in other Amish settlements.

Längin's choice of the seasons of the year as the basic pattern behind the volume is in keeping with the Amish rhythm of life itself. The book ends, majestically, almost poetically, on the note of community—that elusive element that has almost been squeezed out of our modern-world existence, but which continues so strongly as the centerpiece of the Amish way.

Bernd Längin interprets for us, vividly and profoundly, the Amish communal alternative to modern pessimism, lived out in simplicity and humility. At the heart of the Amish secret to life lies that close, meaningful community of individuals, who together strive to strengthen the art of relating one to another in love.

This volume will appeal to a broad spectrum of creative readers in general as well as to academics within the college and university settings.

—Leonard Gross
Mennonite Historian
Goshen, Indiana
December 1993

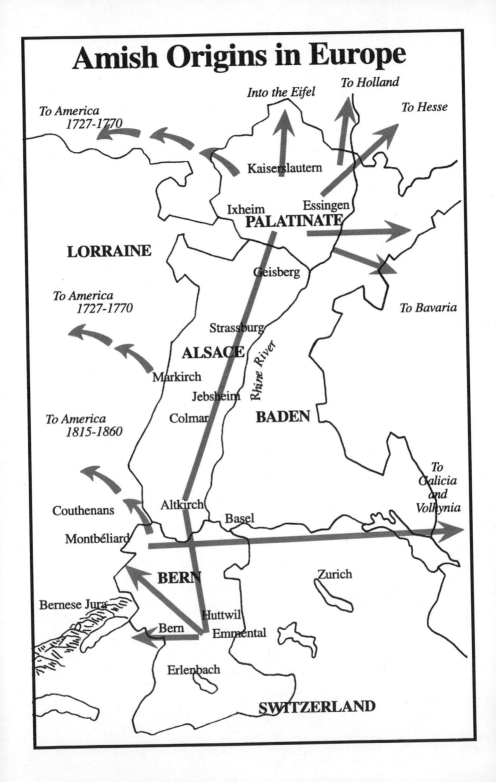

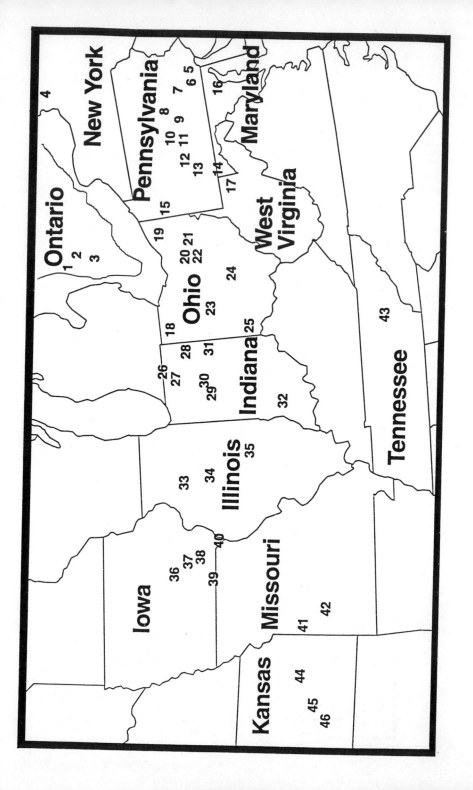

Major Amish Settlements to 1900

O Mostly from immigrants of 1700s
◆ Mostly from immigrants of 1800s
∅ Mixture of both
M Amish mingling with Mennonites

Ontario
1. Zurich ◆
2. Waterloo-Perth Cos. ◆
3. Perth Co. ◆

New York
4. Lewis Co. ◆

Pennsylvania
5. Chester Co. O
6. Lancaster Co. O
7. Lebanon-Berks Cos. O
8. Union Co. O
9. Juniata Co. O
10. Mifflin-Huntingdon Cos. O
11. Mifflin Co. O
12. Cambria-Somerset Cos. O
13. Somerset Co. O
14. Somerset Co. O
15. Mercer Co. O

Maryland
14. Garrett Co. O
16. Baltimore Co. O

West Virginia
17. Preston Co. O

Ohio
18. Williams-Fulton Cos. ◆
19. Geauga Co. ◆
20. Wayne Co. ∅
21. Stark Co. ◆
22. Holmes-Wayne-Tuscarawas Cos. ◆
23. Logan-Champaign Cos. O
24. Fairfield Co. O
25. Butler Co. ◆

Indiana
26. Elkhart-LaGrange Cos. O
27. Elkhart-St. Joseph-Marshall Cos. O
28. Allen Co. ◆
29. Clinton Co. O
30. Howard-Miami Cos. O
31. Adams Co. ◆
32. Daviess Co. ◆

Illinois
33. Bureau Co. ◆
34. Woodford & neighboring Cos. ◆
35. Douglas-Moultrie Cos. ◆

Iowa
36. Iowa-Johnson Cos. O
37. Washington Co. ◆
38. Henry Co. ◆
39. Davis Co. ◆
40. Lee Co. ◆

Missouri
41. Cass Co. ◆
42. Hickory Co. ∅

Tennessee
43. Knox Co. ◆

Kansas
44. Lyon Co. ◆
45. McPherson-Harvey Cos. M
46. Reno Co. ◆

Dramatic Expansion

Some of the Major Amish Settlements shown on pages 14-15 died out in the 1900s, such at Malvern in Chester County, Pennsylvania; and in Bureau, Woodford, and neighboring counties of Illinois. In the 1900s, the Amish established new settlements here and there. Counties to the west and northwest of Lancaster County, Pennsylvania, were especially favored with many new settlements. So were Ohio counties surrounding Holmes County. In 1993, Ohio had 255 districts (congregations), Pennsylvania 227, Indiana 166, Missouri 32, New York 28, Iowa 25, Illinois 19, Ontario 18, and 6 each in Kansas, Maryland, and Tennessee.

Amish also migrated to other states in the 1900s. Some of these settlements died out, but many survived. By 1993, in Wisconsin were 47 districts, Michigan 40, Kentucky 17, Minnesota 9, Delaware 8, Okalahama 4, and 1 each in Florida, Montana, North Carolina, Oklahoma, Texas, and Virginia. Michigan and Wisconsin proved to be quite attractive. For the most up-to-date record, see Raber's *Almanac*. Also listed in the Bibliography are helpful books by David Luthy, John A. Hostetler, and Stephen Scott.

Luthy gives several reasons for Amish migration: Search for cheaper farm land, to have a plainer *or* a more modern discipline, to escape church problems *or* military draft (by moving to Ontario), to improve youth standards, to avoid urban crowding and regulations (such as those about schools, milk cooling, and septic systems), and to better the family financially.

What Took Me
to Allen County

Galatians 6?

Galatians 6!

John, the dyed-in-the-wool Amishman, eyed me unmercifully as he shoved his Bible toward me. It was marked by well-thumbed pages. "Here, read this! What does it mean?" He did not really expect a profound theological interpretation from me; a Bible-based response would have been quite good enough. After all, what can one expect of a man of the world who has drifted into the company of the devout? And yet, some response was expected of me.

Galatians 6. Everybody was talking about this passage—except me.

There I was among the Allen County (Indiana) Amish, standing before a large, typical seventh- and eighth-grade class. I was the nobody from the outside who once again had laid aside the pinstripes of the business world, trying to adjust to a world of yesteryear, to people who at first glance seemed more like relics of a bygone era than of a contemporary age. It's not that easy! There I was, one who in Old Europe had received a bit of religious nourishment in school. Upon confirmation as a Lutheran in my early teens, I was given a motto, the Golden Rule from Matthew (7:12) as a guide to life's way. I knew Galatians only by the table of contents from the Bible. In short, I was ill-equipped for today's test in the schoolhouse on Cuba Road. All the while I bought time while musing, "Matthew, Mark, Luke, John, plus Acts, the New Testament so begins; then Romans, the two Corinthians, Galatians, and Ephesians: Paul's prescription for overcoming sins. . . . " That was pretty well it.

Galatians 6: "For he that sows to the flesh shall of the flesh reap corruption."

Well, *was meint's* (what does it mean)?

Before me sat some forty pupils segregated according to age but not conviction; their belief was as uniform as their dress. The Amish youngsters were in a church-run school designed to keep the rising Amish generation of biblical Christians on course. The children of America's most conservative society were becoming part of an educational system that rejects the rational-scientific views of the world (my world!) whenever these come into conflict with biblical doctrine—or with the tried and proven world of the old, the traditional, the faith of their fathers. It was a class of *Mädli* and *Buwe* (girls and boys) who would rather hearken to the clackety-clack of horses' hooves than to the clickety-click of modern gadgetry. They eyed me, the representative of the world of lusting eyes, selfishness, and pride. I was held highly suspect even though this very morning I had already milked a cow, recited the Lord's Prayer in German, and given a hand to harnessing a horse.

At my side, John Zehr stretched himself. He was the chief shepherd of the flock here assembled. Behind me hung a huge blackboard with sprawling children's script, reminding me of Sütterlin's scrawl, the penmanship models from the old German master. In the corner roared the Amish *Hitzer* (woodstove made by the Hitzer Company of Berne) on which merrily bubbled foil-wrapped lunches for teachers and pupils alike. On the sidewall hung a plaque with the Christmas message, "And the angel said . . . " (Luke 2:10). Everywhere stood oldish brown furniture and worn school desks, taking me back in memory to the penury of postwar Germany.

"Was meint's?"

John was stoking the furnace with wood while my mind was a blank. Why did we not instead read 1 Peter 2:9? "You are a chosen generation, a royal priesthood, a holy nation, a peculiar people." Ever since I came here, I had been prepared to discuss this verse simply because it corresponded so well with those thoroughly Amish, like John and his students.

Then to the pupils I simply would have gathered from 1 Peter 2 reasons why their parents regarded themselves as a "holy nation." The children before me were on four rows of school benches and eagerly and piously poring over the text of Galatians 6 in Luther's German Bible. What made them members of the most conservative, anti-Roman Catholic Anabaptists in the New World? I could have repeated what their faithful Preacher Joseph regarded as true Christianity. The pupils were certainly informed on the subject because they all knew Joseph well, and many were related to him.

Here it was usual and acceptable to repeat something a thousand times, and surely it was better to utter a little something than nothing at all. Given the chance, I would have stated why I regarded the brothers and sisters of this larger community as one of the last living Swiss-German cultural monuments to earlier centuries. Unlike many other immigrants in the United States of America (USA), these Amish managed to survive the infamous effects of the melting pot through their religiously based tenacity. But this, too, was of no great interest to anyone except John.

Yet the Amish of Allen County are not the only ones in the New World who, on this very morning, pray to be counted as a holy generation. After all, other groups of radical Christians of Anabaptist persuasion exist as well. Among them are many diluted versions, including those of synthetic "instant" traditions. The Amish, however, together with the Hutterites and traditional Mennonites such as the Old Order and Old Colony, certainly represent a most authentic continuation of the original Anabaptists whose left-wing position during the Reformation shook the world of Luther's Germany and Zwingli's Switzerland. The word *Anabaptist* (from Greek roots) means "rebaptizer." Anabaptists went around rebaptizing, upon confession of faith, those who had been baptized as infants. These Anabaptist pioneers, on account of their religious convictions, were murdered or executed by the thousands. Some managed to find in America what their homelands had emphatically denied them: freedom to practice their faith.

In the ranks of the more culturally conservative heirs of the Anabaptist tradition, we find the full-bearded Hutterites on the prairies. Roughly sketched through the eyes of the historian, they are Austria's contribution to the Reformation. The Hutterites practiced community of goods and found refuge in Moravia and

Slovakia and elsewhere in Europe before emigrating to America in the 1870s. The Old Colony Mennonites (of Canada and Mexico) are heirs of the Dutch and Prussian Anabaptists, while the Old Order Mennonites and the Amish are descended from the Swiss Brethren Anabaptists. Beards are a gauge of their distance from the world, fuller beards for the more traditional. The Amish are outwardly distinguished not only by their clothing. In accord with church order and to part company with the military of Old Europe, the men shave off their mustaches like the Old Colony and Old Order Mennonites but wear beards on the chin and cheek like the Hutterites. The Old Colony men wear stubble, and the Old Order Mennonites wear no beards.

All these conservative Anabaptist groups, heirs of identical church reformers, represent something similar to the medieval monastic system of the Catholic church. Transplanted into colonial America, they have persevered in living a Protestant ascetic alternative—but without the vow of celibacy. They regard their hour of birth in Reformation times to be like the gift of the Spirit on the first Christian Pentecost in Jerusalem, from which blossomed the apostolic church. For their language of communication and worship, these groups use the old German of Luther's Bible or an antiquated German dialect. Hutterites, Amish, and Old Order and Old Colony Mennonites share early martyrs, Anabaptist hymns, and teachings. They recite innumerable stories of the past from common sources such as *Martyrs Mirror*, telling of times when executioners solidified the power base of the state churches in the sixteenth and seventeenth centuries.

Here are reasons enough for these conservative church groups to bear the common burden of being different in an alien world. While still on earth in their countercultural Anabaptist peace, they invest their life to receive a place at the table of the Lord. However, their respective stories and histories and a whole range of beliefs divide these Anabaptists theologically in a way confusing to an outsider. Thus, their groups and subgroups, like the fractures of Europe in Reformation days, constitute some forty church fellowships. While these numbers have decreased, today they believe, as they did two or three hundred years ago, that they are called to be God's chosen people, God's second choice after the Old Testament Israelites. They pray to be in favor with the Lord, who will return one day to claim them.

To them, God seems to be like the Hutterite, Amish, or Old Order or Old Colony Mennonite Anabaptists, and German-speaking to boot. After all, their Bible tells them they are made in God's image and that God called out to Adam, *"Wo bist du* (where are you)?" Even if these conservative Anabaptist groups are not in church fellowship with each other, they maintain friendly relations and live in historical and sometimes geographic proximity. They have similar apocalyptic expectations of paradise, but their ideas on the right way toward that destination differ greatly. Thus one may wonder which of the radical Anabaptist groups of the German-speaking Reformation, in the vale of sin in America, most closely personifies The Way.

Anabaptists believed it was the right of every believer, not just the clergy, to explain the Holy Bible and share in discerning God's will for the faith community. Their interpretations outlined many characteristics for the saints to live out during their temporary sojourn on earth. However, years of pondering and hoping against head winds of history and in worldwide migrations also left room for human enterprise and the natural growth of individuality. The Hutterite experience strengthened the zeal of their early communism, which they practice in the grim-gray waiting-room atmosphere of their colonies, physically and spiritually secured from the cradle to the grave. The Hutterites counter the sinful world with a dark pessimism. An awareness of their own mortality overshadows their lives. On the other hand, persecution and migration forced the Old Order Mennonites and the Amish to discipline their emotions but left them with a little more life before death.

Nevertheless, a certain consensus exists among all of them, be they Christian-communist Hutterites or the money-wise Amish and Old Order and Old Colony Mennonites: there is more doubt about the worldly—those out there, like me—inheriting eternal life, but they leave us in God's hands. A beam of heaven's light might fall my way to pierce through the outer darkness. So they tend to keep a respectable distance from those baptized as children. For them, infant baptism suggests outcasts, who indulge in works of the flesh listed by the apostle Paul: "adultery, fornication, uncleanness, lasciviousness, idolatry . . ." (Gal. 5:19-21).

21

In this context I first met John, an Anabaptist teacher, a fellow with one of the fullest beards in Allen County, whose handshake makes a man out of a boy. We stood side by side, one as solid as a boxer and the other an urbanite believer-philosopher, three centuries at one glance. I was the apparently enlightened man of the world who wasn't quite sure why I referred to myself as Protestant, who thought such matters are accidents of birth, like being born American or French, black or white, man or woman. I was tempted to count Noah's ark or the Tower of Babel as ancient legend, and I had difficulty understanding such doctrines as the virgin birth and resurrection.

In short, I was still searching and weighing the difference between faith and knowledge. I wanted to get to know people who seemed literally to carry truth around with them hour by hour. I wanted to take a closer look at these Amish characters, monuments of a whole era supposedly past. Each one through adult baptism had been poured into a Christian mold and thus appeared permanent in a temporal world. In short, I wanted to communicate with those who seemed to have real knowledge of heaven.

Here were John of Allen County and I, whose church and worldly value system seemed light years apart. However, it was of secondary importance that I, the city man, had no experience of Amish agriculture and cattle breeding and kept a respectable distance from Amish animals. I was afraid they might be shy of anyone not wearing a black hat on a masculine tousled head, or an organdy bonnet over feminine hair parted in the center. Only one fact caused him to take an interest in me: I was, after all, a *Dütscher*, a *Deitschländer* (German), in the ethnic and cultural sense of the word, like the teacher himself, and therefore no *Englischer*. John and the brothers and sisters of Allen County shared this curiosity about me.

But this morning in the schoolhouse on Cuba Road, no word was spoken about the holy nation in Peter or shunning in Corinthians. We spoke about sinful flesh in Galatians. In Galatians 6.

"As many as desire to make a fair show in the flesh, they constrain you to be circumcised. . . ."

"Well, what do you think? If you have anything to say, now is the time."

22

Flesh, healthy flesh, sick flesh, sinful flesh. Circumcision, round incisions, cutting off, cutting away, circumcision as sacramental sign of belonging to the people of God in ancient Israel. My only hope was that my language, High German, would be as difficult for pupils and teacher to understand as their old-fashioned Swiss German was for me. But suddenly I heard from one of the pupils, "You talk like our minister," meaning the German of the Luther Bible, the language used in Amish worship services.

I could have answered John in the Baden dialect, since we both used Alemannic (dialects of German spoken in the Alsace of France, in Switzerland, and in southwestern Germany). Just like John, I knew full well that *Grummbiere* (ground pears) are potatoes or *Gschmier* is jelly and *Rübli* are carrots, that a *Kaschte* is a chest or *de Buckel nuff* means up the hill. In my dialect I would have run the risk of being understood in the Amish school—exactly what I didn't want. At least not when discussing Galatians 6.

"For in Christ Jesus neither circumcision avails anything, nor uncircumcision."

It was getting close to lunchtime. The foil packages on the *Hitzer,* warmed-up goodies from the day before, were bubbling ever more merrily. The overpowering aroma of it all pervaded the schoolhouse on Cuba Road. Some now asked for permission to make a quick exit to the *Kackhisli* (outhouse), meaning noon had come.

"What is meant by circumcision and by uncircumcision?"

John was merciless, the pupils more so. In these parts, nothing was normal to me, not a single thing. But had I not become accustomed to this state of things among the Amish long ago? We went through the winter in an open carriage at minus 22 Fahrenheit, sweltered in the greenhouse heat of Elam Graber's farmhouse, sat under one of Tobi's milk cows, or basked at midday in the gold of a grainfield.

As others count sheep, last night while going to sleep I again stitched together a tapestry of odd designs declaring the shalt-nots of Amish Christians. People like John were not to forget them for even a second: (1) no belt, (2) no napkin, (3) no electricity, (4) no kind of ornament, (5) no sweaters, (6) no garish colors, (7) no radios, (8) no large mirrors, (9) no pictures on the walls, (10) no pointed shoes, (11) no flush toilets, (12) no cars, (13) no lightning rods, (14) no musical instruments, (15) no outside pockets on jackets, (16) no trousers with zippers, (17) no cross-breeding horses and donkeys, (18) no mascara on eyes, (19) no. . . .

At the end of the list, I intended to add activities allowed, such as praying and working, eating, working, and then praying and sleeping. But then, in the middle of all that thinking, I must have dozed off.

I might now have explained to John and his pupils what I thought of their index of taboos. But that did not really fit the passage in Galatians. It would instead have taken us to Ephesians, Peter, or Corinthians. The young set would then have fairly countered that these were the very things that showed they were called to be the "church without spot or wrinkle" (Eph. 5:27), the "bride adorned to meet her husband" (Rev. 21:2), and the "light of the world" (Matt. 5:14). That left me as an outsider, a castaway deserving their pity.

This is exactly the approach the children would use toward me. I had no reason at all to doubt their self-confidence. As customary among religious sectarians, these plain people have a long-standing suspicion of anything that waters down their faith and could lead them to doubt their Amishness.

Galatians was about to strike at a weak spot in my worldliness. I knew well enough what was acceptable to this devout community. I did not want to try to interfere with their theology, so I preferred to make no more blunders when dealing with them. In recent years I had managed to come to terms with the spectrum of their life, with their gracious assistance. I have every reason to tip my large Amish hat to a goodly number of them: in the USA, to the widely dispersed Grabers family living around Grabill, Indiana, and especially to Preacher Joseph Graber and his sons-in-law Elam Graber and David Nolt, who so often extended every hospitality in their homes and harnessed many a horse for me. Through them I discovered secrets of plain living.

Brothers instructed me in understanding the present tense of the past in the vicinity of Berne, Indiana: Daniel Wengerd, Menno Neuenschwand, and the Amish healer Solomon J. Wickey; in Shipshewana, Indiana: Eli Gingerich and Alvin Miller; in Ohio: David Kline, Jr. (known as the Birdman), Atlee D. Miller, and Ben J. Raber; in Pennsylvania: Christian Newswanger/ Neuschwander, Jacob L. Smucker, Gideon L. Fisher, Sylvan Blank, and Bennie C. Yoder (at Springs, in the "Amish Alps"); in Florida: Levi Miller and Christian Kurtz; in Minnesota: Bishop Atlee J. Shetler and the "jaywalker" Gideon Hershberger; in Wisconsin: Omar B. Bontrager from the Cashton area; in Kansas: the Amish Schrocks and Yoders families; in Iowa: the Stutzmans and Bontragers around McIntyre; in Paraguay: Laban Eichorn of the Beachy Amish in Luz y Esperanza Colony. Atlee Miller and David Kline conducted a "mission impossible" by tracking the trail of their forebears together with me for weeks on end through Europe.

What about the Hutterites? Preacher Peter Tschetter of South Dakota and John Hofer and Jacob Gross of Manitoba introduced me to the basics of an old faith in the New World. In researching sources about the triumphs and tragedies of the European Anabaptists, I received assistance from Gary Waltner of the Mennonite Research Center at the Weierhof, Palatinate (Germany), and Dr. Leonard Gross of Goshen, Indiana. In Switzerland, I would like to thank the Mennonite elder Hans Rüfenacht of Emmenmatt as well as the members of his church in the Emmental (valley of the Emme), the Fankhausers family of Hinter-Hütten (an old Anabaptist estate), the family of Anabaptist martyr Hans Haslibacher in Haslenbach, Preacher Ulrich Gerber of Überbalm, and Hans Rudolf Lavater, Reformed minister of Bern. I give thanks to several in France: Mennonite Preacher Jacques Graber of Seppois-le-Bas and the members of his church, the Hückel-Graber family in Couthenans, and Ives and Monique Jeanroy of an old Anabaptist estate at Markirch (now Sainte Marie-aux-Mines).

My gratitude is also extended to the historian Robert Baecher of Pfastatt for many insights into the life of the first Amish church in Alsace; and to Peter Klassen, superintendent of schools in the Mennonite Chaco colony of Fernheim, for providing me with information regarding the role of the Amish in Paraguay. In the search for paradise, many brothers and sisters from the Grabill churches and from touristic Lancaster County (Pa.) escorted me, even though during my "apprenticeship" I deeply and continuously frightened them with my camera. Amos Zehr of Fort Wayne first directed my way to the Amish of Allen County. Werner Lanz, secretary of police of Huttwil in the canton of Bern, pointed out many tracks leading to the original Grabers. One of these finally led to the old Anabaptist estate at Huttwil-Nyffenegg and then to the Swiss highlanders, who still have much to say about the comings and goings of the early Anabaptist church.

******

This very morning I had awakened to a scene reminiscent of some old black-and-white movie on TV, in the midst of a houseful of lively humanity, pervaded by the religious breeze of previous centuries. Soon after the first cock's crow, there was the glow of a kerosene lamp, the recitation of the Lord's Prayer, the rattling of milk cans, and the rumbling of fire in the woodstove. These all merged into a wide stream of blessings at dawn. Then there was the swish of well water which I pumped into the basin for morning ablutions in the washroom beside the master bedroom.

It was as if time itself trotted at a different pace, with a new and strange sound to it, affecting even the taste of the *Morgeessen* (breakfast). The people were different, too, with rolled-up sleeves, and additional suspension of time in their suspenders. Yet they seemed more natural and certainly more carefree and genuine than most other human beings. Considering the whole setting, I felt their world to be confining, possibly forgotten, but never alien or rejecting.

To rid myself completely from the last traces of city life, I had tried my luck at a cow's udder, given a sick calf to drink from a milk bottle, and then assisted the girls in harnessing Judy. This hybrid with giant fearful eyes, half Belgian, half pony, had drawn our sleigh along the well-traveled tracks on a dove-gray, snowy Indiana morning all the way up to the schoolhouse on Cuba Road. Ben was in charge of the reins, while I managed the large, black umbrella with a plastic peephole that protected us from the icy wind. The Allen County Amish have a church ban against roofs over sleighs—even in subzero weather.

A winter's day like this one posed many questions. Why had I landed, of all places, on the flat country around Grabill? Granted, Grabill in Indiana is to the USA what Ringelbach or Hasselberg is to Germany: a real one-horse town, where everyone knows everyone else or at least has seen them often. It is a place in a certain sense remote, but there family, decency, school, and church are still traditional institutions, and their world is well ordered.

However, Grabill for me was more than just small-town America. For one, it had that homey ring of dialect, for in its name I sensed the Alemannic *Krähenbühl* (crows' hill). With regard to the Amish, I had simply staked my last hope on Grabill and the surrounding Allen County. There were, of course, many better-known Amish communities in North America, some of them large areas where shrewd businessmen ruthlessly exploited the piety of the believers with catchy advertisements.

Lancaster (Pa.), for example, with more than ninety church districts, is known as the "Amish capital of America," but it is also a haven for vacationing romantics. Even more Amish live around Berlin and Sugarcreek in Ohio, in Holmes, Wayne, Stark, Tuscarawas, and other counties. In Ohio they are still regarded as the "second largest tourist attraction," but in Indiana their communities around Shipshewana have for long been the biggest draw for the tourist trade.

I had met Amish in Minnesota and Iowa, in Ohio, Pennsylvania, Wisconsin, Florida, Kansas, Michigan, Kentucky, Tennessee, Illinois, in the state of New York, in Ontario, and in Paraguay, but I never managed to establish such intimate contact as around Grabill. All the other Amish, who call themselves brothers and sisters in homely fashion, regarded me with some degree of suspicion and sent me either here or there, mainly to other groups, and generally intending to get rid of me. The best place was always "down the road."

I also received little support from others of the world who were acquainted with the Amish. Yet I had never met anyone who knew the Amish and remained indifferent to them. Some loved them, others hated them; some ridiculed the group, others simply felt sorry for them. Almost all viewed these Anabaptists as hopelessly backward, Germanic, mothballed conservatives, doomed to extinction. Invariably their stereotyped impression was of a man with a beard, a hat, at least half a dozen horses, and a wife with a white bonnet, about a dozen children, and another hidden beneath her apron. That was all.

Yet today, in the USA and in Canada, live about 150,000 Old Order Amish bearing some one hundred family names, including the unbaptized children and teenagers who constitute over half their number. However, these brothers and sisters only roughly estimate their numbers since they object to the "numbering of the people," as in King David's census, punished by a plague (2 Sam. 24). God knows their number and has counted them, not missing a soul. The world need not be concerned about how many Amish there are. Yet since the government has a fetish to enumerate, the Amish do not obstruct an official census.

However, to speak of the Amish in such a general way is risky. In Amish country, what counts is the plurality of things. Congregations divide time and again when groups become too large to meet in a farmhouse. Yet they manage not to commit suicide. These churches have sorted themselves out by how closely they hold to their own age-old sustaining traditions.

All the church districts have corners, angles, and edges just like the Emmental of Switzerland, from which most of the Amish forebears originally came. But not all came from there. The original ancestor of the Stoltzfus (Stolzfus) family, for example, was a Saxon; the Brandenbergers probably came from Cologne; the Delagranges are former Huguenots. Even Old Europe never managed to bring its Alemannics under one crown, and many of the brothers and sisters have remained arch-Alemannics of original cast.

The differences in their congregations can be determined by the breadth of a hat brim, whether pants are held up by one or two suspenders or none, whether the brothers already wear belts or even jeans, whether or not they upholster their chairs, whether they marry in autumn or winter, or whether the driver uses blinders on his horses. These plain people even remember whether their Anabaptist ancestors came as old-evangelical farmers directly from Switzerland (*Töfer*), or as day laborers from Alsace (*Tüfer*), whether they originally were lumberjacks from Bavaria (*Täufer*), Hessian Amish from Waldeck, or estate managers from the region of Kaiserslautern in the Palatinate.

One factor distinguishing groups is how long it takes a congregation to sing the *Lobliedli* (the praise hymn), whether they use the *langsam Weis* (slow style) and draw the singing of its four verses out to twenty-five minutes (more orthodox), or only use eleven minutes (more adaptive). If ever a common Amish national anthem were chosen, it would definitely be this *Loblied*, number 131 in the *Ausbund*. It is the first hymn sung at *Ordnungsgemee* (counsel meeting) and *Grossgemee* (communion service) and the second hymn sung in other Amish worship services.

There are so-called Amish who exchange the blizzards of Indiana for the palms of Florida and ride bicycles or perhaps even board airplanes on the way south. Some have been overtaken by the automobile and are no longer regarded as true brothers and sisters of the Allen County Amish. There are congregations like the one at Guthrie, Kentucky, whose members prefer to pull their "buggies" during the week with Ford 2810 tractors and only on Sundays with horses. Other Old Order communities might challenge it, but the Yoders, who run a country story at the corner of Kentucky highways 848 and 181 still insist that their "horseless carriages" don't hinder them from being true Amish. And there are also church districts like the one near Lobelville, Tennessee, where plain people live totally according to the Old Order lifestyle but won't call themselves Amish or Mennonite.

The farther west one goes, the more conservative the North American Amish seem to become, although this may be too simple an observation. Probably the incomprehensible vastness of the western horizon and increased isolation cause the Amish to turn into themselves more deeply as they head in the direction of sundown. Once one is west of the Mississippi, the brothers and sisters occasionally are so strictly bound to tradition that, until actually visiting with them, one could mistakenly imagine that they are hostile.

The forebears of most of the Amish left Europe in the eighteenth century. Others departed a hundred years later. Between these immigrations lay a space of time in which new customs and orders developed on both sides of the Atlantic. This explains, for example, why some Amish prefer a higher standard of draft horses and others are prepared to make do with more modest mules. The Amish community of Allen County firmly rejects the mule as a hybrid since they regard it as un-Christian to interbreed God's creatures, like horses and donkeys. Other communities prefer mules for the simple reason that they consume less feed than horses. Around Lancaster, where the Amish of the New World have been established longest, they claim to have the finest horses, the best-tended gardens, and the best-scrubbed children. But they also use milking machines and have indoor plumbing, which those of Allen County do not regard as pleasing to the Lord.

Their range of religious scruples prevents Amish from being interchangeable. In some areas groups differ so radically from each other that one can best describe them as individual trees instead of a forest community. This variety depends chiefly on how strictly they regard the Bible and how closely they adhere to certain verses of Scripture as explicit direction for their path of life. A *typical* Amish person, who follows Jesus' command to be "in the world, but not of the world" (John 17), simply does not exist. In spite of their uniformity in basic faith understanding and view of the world and its ways, the brothers and sisters vary in a whole spectrum of items, and even in the cliché imposed on them by the world. What they all have in common is that they obey God more than human authority (Acts 5:29), and yet one cannot reach a general consensus defining the obedience of the Fishers, Beilers, and Stoltzfuses of Pennsylvania; or the Yoders and Millers of Ohio; or the Bontragers, Grabers, and Zehrs of Indiana.

There are also apparent differences in the style of their interaction with the worldly, such as me. Many of the Amish I had previously met were friendly but reserved, while others were skeptical and leery of outsiders. To establish personal contact with a really rigid brother is invariably hard work, sometimes even impossible. Their faith leads them to a peculiar way of thinking and a unique manner of communication with the worldly. The Amish are fashioned out of primeval Germanic rock and therefore can seem to be curt, contrary, and difficult. At times I got an American "hi" here, a "hi" there, and then the high-level conference was over. Not so the brothers of Allen County. Therefore, I knew full well why I had landed in their midst.

Around Grabill are twelve congregations of so-called traditional Amish, making a numerically respectable group. In this sample community of Amish, the majority derive from European immigrants of the nineteenth century. They share a similar legacy of suffering and group characteristics, and they attempt as much as possible to hang onto established, time-honored customs. They all come out of a movement which managed to survive as the Swiss Brethren even though the world around them collapsed several times. Their forebears had converted to the old-evangelical Anabaptists, some joining the original founding church, others uniting with them later. In their day these Swiss Brethren were known in Europe as believers of strictest observance. The plain people of Allen County are not far behind. As a result, they can be visually recognized by the fact that they still reject the *Dachwägeli* (roofed buggy) of other Amish congregations right up to this very year of our Lord. They also reject the solid rubber strips on wheels, now quite common a few miles away on conservative carriages of fellow believers.

A further tie between the Swiss Brethren and Allen County is, finally, the role of the Grabers, a country clan both faithful and fruitful ever since they appeared in the history of this church. The Grabers originally hail from the forested mountain area of Huttwil in Switzerland, as I was able to establish by research in the canton of Bern, in Alsace, and in the area surrounding Montbéliard. While at Huttwil, they were united with the Anabaptist martyrs' church. They were always known as upright people, and as such their names can early be found in the records of the "heretics."

In those days, the Swiss had established an official church pattern enforced by the morality squad of the police. Memory of this is deeply anchored in the history of the Swiss Brethren, who were regarded as cancerous carbuncles of the Reformation. They were people who spoke to God, died trusting in God, and certainly over the long haul demonstrated more consistency than their torturers. Thereby the Swiss Brethren came to be recognized as a symbol of the steadfastness of the Anabaptists.

These Grabers were—and have largely remained so to this day—a solid human caste of *Menschen* (a people), as substantial as their national dish, the traditional Bernese *Platte*. In 1671—hardly a hundred years after the first Grabers were called to face the Committee of the Gentry on account of their Anabaptist persuasions—one of the original Grabers just barely managed to escape the canton of Bern with his family before the city council decreed to have him "chained in iron for Venetian galley service." Such a decree was meant "to instill fear into the Anabaptist hordes." Obviously some of the Grabers who had not converted to Anabaptism or who had returned to the established Reformed Church remained in Switzerland at that time.

In his day, one Graber became president of the Swiss Confederation, another barely escaped the guillotine, while another bred the now-famous Montbéliard, the "Mennonite cow." One branch of the family introduced the potato to the region of Mömpelgard (later called Montbéliard), at that time belonging to the German duchy of Württemberg. One Graber is today the elder of the (previously Amish) Mennonite Birkenhof-Altkirch congregation in Alsace, only a stone's throw from the Swiss border, while another Graber is a bishop in Allen County in America.

The Grabers of USA have remained a blessed family in every respect. The above-mentioned couple fled from Switzerland to the Alsace, from there to Mömpelgard/Montbéliard, and today the family counts ten thousand descendants in the USA and another twenty thousand in Europe. All of them stem from one Anabaptist family of Huttwil, which once testified before God and to the world that the state churches should cast the devil out of infants during baptism free of charge since there was simply no room in the little ones for the devil anyhow. This Graber family of Huttwil belonged to a people that practiced believers baptism and therefore were called *Wiedertäufer* (Rebaptizers), *Täufer* (Baptizers, Anabaptists), or *Taufgesinnte* (Baptism-inclined or Baptism-minded). These three terms were used to designate those who stood for a revolution of the church. When necessary in making this stand, they were as vehemently opposed to worldly authorities as to spiritual authorities. Yet neither realm ever managed to rid itself of the conservative Graber clan. God knows the long-term attempts to extinguish them!

In a nutshell, that's what took me to Allen County and thus to the seventh and eighth grades of the Amish school on Cuba Road. There I was, packaged in a slate-gray outfit of winter clothes, still red-cheeked on a cold January winter morning. The pupils before me, spiritually tuned, were waiting to hear about the theme of fleshliness from one "disposed to be fleshly," dubious of learning from an unholy one more about the topic than they already knew. I was pondering and reflecting for all I was worth what Galatians really and actually "meant." How could I best explain to a group

32

of Anabaptist children what the Jewish ritual of circumcision was all about, without going into detail? I was a German journalist who for years had given much attention to the Amish and felt rather well if once in a while I smelled of the perfume of barn and stable. Yet I was no Amishman and certainly lacked the strength ever to become plain and Amish.

Galatians 6: "For what a man sows, that shall he also reap."

"*Was meint's?*"

Now I could have struck fire. To sow and to reap was a theme also understood by a thorough urbanite. But to sow and to reap was a topic which John, close to nature as he was, preferred not to have interpreted by a worldly man. Whatever I answered, he could use it as a foil, as a contrast to his own Amish insight. After all, the young people before me today were reaping what their mighty forebears of yesteryear had once sowed for them in the historical-hysterical days of the Old World. On that religious field, their parents and their congregation still worked day by day.

The blood of the old martyrs as the seed of the Amish church was also the wick which kept the lamp of the plain folks of Allen County burning until today, even though time and again it was almost extinguished by the typically Germanic thoroughness of the authorities. The very fact that wicks and lamps existed until this very day was the reason I always felt drawn to this Bible Belt in the state of Indiana. I came thus to a group of believers who humanly speaking had no business existing and yet managed to exist four thousand martyrs after Luther nailed his theses to a church door in the year of our Lord 1517, nearly five centuries ago.

Galatians 6 was unhitched. John had recognized me to be a hopeless case when it came to explaining new dimensions of faith to his pupils. But then, possibly, he had something else up his sleeve. Religious studies as a subject in school is unknown to the Amish. Anyone who grows up in the community of the faithful knows about the Bible. Anyone who comes from outside supposedly knows nothing, as shown by the question-and-answer children's game the teacher started with the worldly man. I was well acquainted with this tactic from my innumerable visits to the Amish. It typically begins with subjects far removed from the Bible, such as their seemingly inexhaustible curiosity regarding the German *Autobahn* (expressway).

33

For the Amish of Allen County, Germany above all is the land of their forebears, the founding of the church, and the Reformation. Immediately following, it is the land of the autobahn, then of sauerkraut, the yodelers, and also home of the Volkswagen. What about Goethe or Beethoven, Hamburg or Berlin? There had never been any interest about them in these parts. Only after the autobahn has been resolved, yet again, do they come to ask whether the "Old Country" still knows what a *Gaul* (a horse) is, whether the Negroes in Germany are black, whether there are also Jews in that country, and whether the *Dütsche* dollar (deutsche mark) is worth as much as the U.S. dollar.

The bearded teacher was capable of becoming a trifle indignant if one of the pupils spoke a little too softly to me. "There's a German in the classroom," he rebuked the questioner, "and you have to show him due respect by speaking up loudly and clearly!"

Finally the lunches on the *Hitzer* were warmed and ready to eat. John, whose knowledge of German, with few exceptions, was equivalent to the vocabulary of the Gospel of John in Luther's Bible, embarked on a rather sly interrogation as if to redeem my visit to his school on Cuba Road. "In Germany there are certainly a lot of Volkswagens." I agreed with his statement. "In Germany there are also suicides." I nodded. "And in Germany there are certainly a lot of people who commit suicide due to inhaling exhaust pollution." Again I answered in the positive.

That's what John, a veteran in his field, was waiting for. This was teachable material which every child could easily grasp. Deaths by exhaust pollution could only be understood as yet another proof of a satanic principle in modern technology. Its lightning rods and running water, telephones and automobiles threatened the classic way of life among the Amish of Allen County. Now the Anabaptist teacher with the untrimmed beard frankly and freely promoted Amish standards to his pupils. I wondered if he intended to coat their bitter pill of being different with a bit of sweet icing. "Look here," he announced, staunch in his cause, "it is not only the alcohol behind the steering wheel, or the heavy foot on the accelerator which can kill people, but also the exhaust of a car." Now this was something to which none of these children had yet given a thought. The moral of the story was sowing and reaping: a car is antinature, and its exhaust kills; but the exhaust of a horse does no such thing. Conclusion? The horse is God-given, the car obviously is not. Such is according to John of Allen County.

This morning in the schoolhouse on Cuba Road, the discussion about Galatians, sinful flesh, flesh in general, circumcision, autobahn, and car exhaust had resulted in a score of 2—0, in favor of the bearded brother. John well knew in his teaching how to mix the good of the Amish with the bad of the non-Amish. But I had long since become accustomed to his way of refereeing the game of life and therefore the inevitable final score of games played on his turf. Upon reflection, I had been experiencing that ever since the day I first managed to jump across the ditch to the Graber household, to that-foreign-to-the-world island of the pious plain people of Allen County, separated from the mainland of the lost . . . and the rest of the world.

1

The Buckboard Still

On warm summer days, a string of light carriages and fast horses extends along the paved road leading to Grabill. The buckboard still rolls here. It is barely an hour's distance by trotting time as the buggies stream past the many fences, erected to keep the cows in. The fences remind one of Amish church rules, dividing between members and the world. Once in Grabill and in front of life's many abominations like the automatic car-washes, the Chevrolet dealership, and the Sunoco gas station, the long line of carriages assembles as a body before an ice-cream parlor. "Healthy flesh has its urges," explain the men and women, all in uniform Amish dress.

Here they meet after long summer days, conveyed by one-horse power, instead of the hundred-plus horsepower car, from their ghetto community to the parking lots of the Grabill shopping center. Americans call them "the plain people." Among the common lot are always some Grabers, who make up the majority in these parts; Brandenbergers, whose daughters are regarded as the "ladies" among the Amish; Lengachers, who in spite of all linguistic shifts from days long gone still speak an acceptable German; or the Schmuckers, known as highly successful farmers. With them gather the Kauffmans, the Schmidts, or the Eichers, with their swarm of children, each child a copy of the next and of the parents. All the Amish together are copies of simple, deeply religious Alemannic farmers from the seventeenth and eighteenth centuries. On first sight they appear as dark compositions, people from a curio cabinet, who introduce the old costumes of Europe to the streets of America.

The deepest roots of the quietest of the quiet of Allen County are to be found in the Swiss canton of Bern. Here the rigorous sect, which churches and states of the Old World attempted to exterminate, is all but forgotten. The Emmental (Emme-valley) Swiss attribute their world fame to their excellent cheese, not to the Anabaptists. Among them were a group of *"waffen- und rachlosen* (weaponless and revenge-free)" Christians for whom the strict Anabaptist mother church toward the end of the seventeenth century was no longer strict enough. Such believers gathered around Jakob Ammann to return to more conservative principles.

Ammann's followers, the Amish of today, comprised a group of relatives, neither Catholic nor Protestant, who gather for holy communion, to break bread, to ban from their midst what needed to be banned, and to bear each other's burdens in life. In being so different from the world, one might term them the *Homo amischius* of the human species: people who were on the European hit list in their day and are now again regarded as endangered. To join the group means, among other things, to go back a century or two into the history of these people. A further condition is to regard the congregation as "God's planted field" (1 Cor. 3:9), the "body of Christ" (Col. 1:18), "God's people" (1 Pet. 2:10).

The parking lot for the single-horse carriages next to the Grabill shopping mall serves the purpose of exchanging *Neuichkeita* (the latest news) in an Alemannic dialect. This dialect was spoken in its day in Bern but is now so antiquated that it would scare a contemporary Bernese citizen. Conversations abound and bear witness to the power of the devil and the much greater power of God Almighty, as witnessed a hundred times each day. Conversing may also take more mundane turns such as the price of a bushel of wheat, a choice trotter from the downs of Hicksville (Ohio), this or that mare which should be bred by this or that stallion, or simply about a truly universal theme: the weather.

Then talk might turn to some warring escapade among the kingdoms of the world, attempts being made to force Amish to receive agricultural assistance funds, or arguing whether thoroughly sinful America will manage to retain its position as the leading world power. What the Amish fear most is that "the bad boys from overseas"—meaning the old-style Communists in general—one day might just get the upper hand even in Allen County and unleash another era of martyrdom. While the conversation takes many directions and turns, tobacco is squirted, horses scrape and scratch with their hooves, children complain, and babies are comforted. All around is the world's din of sin because Grabill is home not only to Amish moralists. Mennonites, Lutherans, Pentecostals, a few Catholics, and some wayward saints (ex-Amish) also live in proximity. Many of these, however, have long since become average American citizens.

"You can't miss the Amish. They have their buckboards still and apples, horse-made, if you know what I mean." Amos, an *Entlaufener* (renegade from the Amish) had directed me from the edge of the city, Fort Wayne. "Follow the four-wheeled, black single-horse carriages, which they call buggies, and the sails of windmills for pumping water. . . . These signs point to the Amish." As to where their settlement begins and ends, that is a question I would have to direct to some house-Amish, people with ascetic ideals, holy people without a church building, America's most honest puritans, but also its most obvious outsiders. Whether they are harmless misfits of society or the last of the most honest Christians of the world or both—that depends on the eye of the beholder. I might be received by such a group, I was informed, but only "if you have nothing to hide."

Amos is a man of today who remembers the past. He grew up near Grabill, in an Amish congregation living as an alternative community on the U.S. landscape, and had been one of them until he realized he would have to forego many forms of luxury. Thereupon he opted for the luxury of choice, turning his back on the inflexible God of his parents, and yet he was unable to replace God in his life. "He had his hair cut," claimed the brothers and sisters of Amos, meaning that he was no longer one of them. But he would have had a much worse time of it if they were to claim that he had not only had his hair cut, but that he had also become *Englisch* (non-Amish). This would mean that Amos had not only gone against church standards but that he was not even a true believer any more.

"And be sure to tell them that you are a *Dütscher*. Otherwise they will give their horses a 'giddy up' and take off on you." It's a simple fact: the strictly pacifist Amish have no means of defense except a fleet horse hitched to a fast carriage. Members of God's faithful minority do not think much of outsiders who descend upon them like acid rain every year in the tourist season and seek to devour them. There are simply too many snoopy people who are ever ready to stare them into submission and to finish them off with trendy clichés. To the people of the world, the Amish are reputed to be a segment of Anabaptist faith. Yet they are often treated as a spectacle at the zoo, and not only because of their fast horses and rusty traditions.

Many a believer has sustained inner hurts from interaction with the worldly and from the confusing abomination of tourism. Tourists arrived because they believed the Amish would soon die out; in turn, some Amish congregations were threatened with extinction because of the tourist trade. Many of these photogenics in black did not think overly much of the *Englischen*, meaning any and everyone non-Amish and therefore one of the crooked and perverse tribes of the outside world (Phil. 2:15). When the Amish turn away from these worldlings, it is not only reminiscent of former times of bloody persecution; it also by necessity has become a consistent style of their religious life.

Horse apples (droppings) first came into view a few miles northeast of Fort Wayne. During the heat of the midday sun, a little dark object lay on the distant road. I quickly came to associate this with a black Amish ark on high-spoked wheels and the nervy trotter whose gait determines tempo, time, and distance of a radical Christian's everyday life. On the edge of Cuba Road appear the first windmills, carriages standing around on yards, corn spread out to dry, and before the settlements the invariable sign for the tourists, showing a whip-swinging, dark-clothed Amish coachman.

I raised my hand in a friendly wave to the black-clothed driver on the billboard. Amish rarely initiate greetings, but they generally respond, even if casually. When they respond, they do so by upping the German index finger, probably indicating the direction *they* are going one day (heaven above, hell below). The actual, tangible Amishman, with a flowing beard and wrapped in a simple homemade jacket, can in fact be found right by the ice-cream parlor of Grabill. This is hardly coincidence. My first contact with the ice-cream munchers and hamburger wolfers of the holy society quickly gave me a feeling of comfort. While somewhat akin to curiosity and conversation pieces, these Swiss Germans remind one of the neglected widow of the Reformation, a stranger in her fatherland, who looked for and found a new *Heimat* (homeland) worlds away in America. Yet in Grabill, with ice-cream and hamburgers as the essence of the American philosophy of life, we both, the Amish and I, were on the soil of the United States.

This is exactly the way I had imagined my probings leading to the faithful Amish of Allen County. Similar patterns exist among other religious ascetics. Far away to the northwest, the ark of the Hutterian Brethren is anchored on the Canadian and U.S. prairie seas in an attempt to escape worldly sin. Here in front of the Grabill shopping center, these people are friendly in spite of being tightly buttoned-up, right to their collars. Well, not exactly buttoned-up, because buttons are forbidden on their best clothes and hooks and eyes and pins still do the job of keeping them straight and laced in their attire. Also, the Amish wear no collars on their *Wammes* (jackets), for in their day in Old Europe, buttons and collars were first and foremost privileges of the military rather than of poor peasants. And these peace-lovers want no part of the military.

I was greeted with similar questions from the Hutterites and the Amish. "What are you called?" (Their skeptical look shows they think Bernd is no real German name.) "Baptized?" "You Catholic or Christian?" (Perhaps they imply, You'd better look out for those Catholics.) "Really German and truly not from Chicago?" "Married?" "You know where your wife is now?" "Have children?" "One?" (I suspect they are thinking, How can you be so lazy?) "How do you make a living?" ("By writing!" I reply.) "No, what do you *do* for a living? Writing is not for making a living." "You have a sack full of money?" "Are you rich or are you a poor Lazarus?" "Did you make your money, or did you inherit it?" "D'you know Berlin?" ("Yes.") "Then you must know Irene. She was here some years ago." "What do you do for your spiritual health? D'you know the Bible?" And so on and so forth, questions from young and old and in between.

I had learned to know the Hutterites, and now I was entering into the Amish world. It occurred to me that one must have copied from the other in their style of questioning. The only difference is that the Hutterites spoke a Tirolean-Bavarian-Carinthian mixture of dialects, reinforced with numerous English loanwords, while the Amish around Grabill spoke German with an Alemannic accent. Their vocabulary was based on Swiss-German, to which they added some earthy Pennsylvania German expressions and, more recently, an extensive collection of English loanwords.

"They have nags in Germany?" "How about Pepsi-Cola?" "What can you buy with the German dollar?" "You ever been in Rome?" "What do you call a hill? A *Buckel*? That's the mother tongue. We speak it but we don't spell it. You know what a *Henkl* is? A chicken? If you know that, you're a German and no Yankee"—a matter of considerable significance in these parts. Also important is the repeated question regarding yodelers, at least for the Amish. On this query, I disappointed them. While I had a whole series of music cassettes for my car radio, no yodeler was included in the repertoire.

The Amish knew at first glance that I came out of a world different from theirs and thus belonged under the rubric they reserve for hypocrites, the "fleshly-inclined lip Christians." For them, I hailed from a part of the world which was the enemy, the lost ones, and so I symbolized the opposite of what they stood for. The conservative German Anabaptists obviously found this concept necessary to solidify their own position. Thus I could not easily persuade the questioners to accept myself or my plans and aspirations. After all, one's choice of friends reflects one's religious views.

These people glean from the Holy Scriptures and from God's good creation the lesson that what you sow, you reap. Hence, they do not allow a worldly person to win their trust quickly, even if that party responds to their Anabaptist sensitivities with due care. I was not of them, even if I knew the difference between a *Henkl* and a *Buckel* (chicken and hill) and knew many generations of Graber genealogy from the Emmental. For them, I remained a man of the world, a worldly man, who sought his happiness behind the steering wheel of a car and wore buttons on his pants and a ring on his finger. These all were items which the streets of America sold or traded and which these Amish in their Swiss-drawled accents condemned as "works of the devil."

"Know what? We set up a fence around us in order to keep outsiders out. And the people of the world want to poke holes in that fence and come in. They want our women, they want to take pictures of us, and we have had difficult times with all of these matters. They sing whoring songs, and you probably can guess the rest of it. . . . But we will not permit all that. Let us assume that the dear Lord Jesus Christ, the director of our path, would return today. If he did, we would want him to come and live with us Amish. So we have to keep ourselves clean, clean from the world and its sinful people. . . ."

I knew about the self-confident suspicion, the age-old caution of these un-American Americans, their deeply rooted mistrust, which would only be fortified by having contact with me and what I stood for. Even a professed Christian from the outside did not make it by their standards. So what about me? A writer whose weapon was crafting headlines and taking pictures? No way! Except that I was a "genuine German" in the Indiana heart of the USA Bible Belt, one who knew Amos and Switzerland and the family tree of the Grabers with its many branches and leaves. Without all this, they would not have given me a second chance.

"Now, you want to write a story? Are you a *Doktor der Schrift* (doctor of the word)?" But the Amish do not want stories to be written about them. To see their names in print is equivalent to arrogance and could be mistaken for the sin of pride. Does it not say in the Book of books that "our names are written down in heaven" (Rev. 21:27), not by journalists on earth? Publicity for the Amish of Grabill? In America the children of the Amish had been burned too often in their history to believe any good could come of it.

The Amish knew about negative reporting only too well. Detailed studies on them, some important, others less so, have been undertaken over and over again. And yet, America has often written about its conservative Anabaptists in terms inaccurate, false, and misleading. More often than not, journalists have encountered barriers, handmade by the Amish. This led to a variety of distortions in describing these folks. Then instead of straightforward reporting, sensational newspapers aim to tantalize and spotlight things that seem odd to readers. Furthermore, the Amish do no missionary work beyond their own families and congregational fellowship, so a journalist like me could hardly be a mission project for them. The Amish worry about the evil world and its headlong rush to destruction, but they do not expect another book to rescue worldlings. The Bible is already available for anyone to read.

That first summer evening with the Amish, I was in one of their "chariots," carried away and swinging higher rather than lower, being pulled out to the country by a perky trotter. This event was due to the venerable, gray-haired preacher, *Diener zum Wort* (servant of the Word), Joseph Graber, and his son-in-law Elam, both of whom farm on Cuba Road, which leads to Cuba, a few miles east of Grabill, Indiana. One of them had obviously given much thought to Germany and the Germans of the time of the Reformation and right up to the present. He thus proved false someone's comment that the Amish wear blinders like their horses. The other man freely offered me accommodation in the upper quarters of his house. From these actions I concluded that Elam (husband and head to Rachel) and Joseph (head of Rosanna) seriously lived out Jesus' command to "let your light so shine before the people so that they will see your good works and praise your Father who is in heaven" (Matt. 5:16).

After all, what was there to hide from a German? Of course, all this would retroactively be brought before the *Gemee* (congregation), Elam's brothers and sisters in Christ, for their approval. In these parts, if you know where the congregation is, then you also know which end is up among the Amish. The venerable seniors, like Joseph, appeared to be like linden trees of old Germanic villages, centerpieces of faithful living, around which the pious flock gathered. But one needs to look for the sum total of them, their essence of unity in speech, thought, and action. This was up to all, up to each of them. Woe unto the one who excited his neighbor into a spirit of anger by not examining everything by the standard Anabaptist word of Paul's admonition "to prove all things and hold fast to what is good" (1 Thess. 5:21)! This was necessary to guard "lest any root of bitterness springing up trouble you, and thereby many be defiled" (Heb. 12:15).

So it happened. "It will come to pass if nothing stands in the way. . . ." Riding in a buggy or traveling by car, I was to see the country around Grabill in the next day or two. But what I was to see lay exclusively in the hands of my hosts, the Amish of Allen County. I had little to do with decision making in these parts. Of course, I had to take care not to sin, for then they would have unceremoniously booted me out.

Nothing stood in the way, my way, no obstacles hindered the intentions of the doctor of the word, a sinner among the holy, but also a German among Germans.

By some quirk or coincidence or by word-of-mouth common consent, as happens only among old friends, that evening a houseful of guests arrived from the neighborhood, people the Americans refer to as "longhaired Dutchmen," meaning German people of some conservative persuasion. They had come and now were assembled in Elam's huge dwelling. It almost appeared as if each wanted to be first to shake the hand of the "*Auswendigen aus dem aalt Land* (outsider from the Old World Country)."

If anyone had imagined that such Amish meetings happened only in order to moralize or to compare earthly misery with earthy misery, such expectations were quickly dashed. In that farmhouse on Cuba Road, so much of Old Europe was exuding from every living and inanimate pore. Yet to that they added a goodly portion of life in the American style, striking up a happy conviviality, even if it all took place according to the somber ways of the Amish passed down with the genetic code of their Alemannic heritage. The horse carriages and windmills alongside the earthiness of these farmers allowed for no unchristian haste and hurry. Even so, faster than I could follow, my hosts emerged as lively personalities, as though stepping out of gilded calendar pictures of long ago. They turned out to be hearty folk with healthy wit and humor. I took this as a strong contrast to the Hutterites, who in my visits had told me that sadness was one of the prime Anabaptist tasks.

At first I had thought all the Amish at Grabill looked like sacrificial victims, a pitiable remainder of a heavily encrusted societal order and tailor-made for the tourist trade: beard plus horse plus Bible plus wife and a flock of children equals an Amish family and stands for a radically biblical counterculture. However, even if I expected to land on the first step to heaven, I soon came to realize that I was still a pilgrim, with them, on this earth.

I could not really rid myself of the feeling that what I saw here was something like a stage, torn from an outdated picture book or the vision of some filmmaker. Here were bearded men in home-tailored vestments, shirt next to shirt on a ten-seat-long smoothly polished bench. The women or *Weiber* generally outweighed their husbands by more than a pound or two. The teenage daughters wore the customary outfits, outdated by worldly standards, and were sitting along the whitewashed walls of the room. Everyone was perspiring, no doubt from being so thoroughly buttoned-up. Whether overdressed or not, the thermometer outside registered a hundred degrees on the Fahrenheit scale, with a stiff breeze fanning the heat. The temperatures inside reminded me of an efficient hothouse.

The children were whipping around the parents, playing jack-in-the-box, using milk containers of various sizes as receptacles for the balls. Here the patriarchally inclined Amish family was intact. Joseph's *Weib* served up a well-roasted chicken which had registered some two thousand flying hours before landing on the plate via the chopping block. Before us stood the gifts of God in culinary form: *Grundbiere* (potatoes), white and yellow rutabagas, bread and jam or grease (hog-fat), and pears and peaches for dessert.

Elam's Rachel served up cow-warm milk and earth-warm water. The latter was used as an object lesson for right living—"the Lord in heaven be praised and glorified"—and as a warning about the "demon alcohol, the drinking thereof, and refilling." My hosts obviously regarded it necessary to make reference to the potential effects of such drinking since a neighbor Amish congregation near Berne, Indiana, had been visited by the evil one in the form of alcohol, resulting in a bad fight. The Amish refer to a drunk person as being "loaded," and they admonish each other, saying, "Don't look at the wine, for it is red and beautiful in the glass. It flows down smoothly, but then it bites like a snake so that the drunkard in eternity will have to suffer without any cooling" (Prov. 23:31-32).

However, not every Amish person was holy, and not everyone who looked Amish was necessarily a Christian. Chris Graber calls some of them "worldly people dressed like Amish." His circle was always mindful of such possibilities and therefore exhorted one another to be faithful. According to Joseph, the unworthy, drunkards, whoremasters, or killers drank themselves right up to the judgment seat of God. All this was in reference to that other church district. My hosts' congregation, however, was relatively "clean of strong drink and use of tobacco." I use the word *relatively* because a local alcohol vendor later told me about the spirits some of the brothers occasionally purchased from him, presumably to drink in private.

Then for the first time I heard the song of the yodel among the Amish of Allen County. Rosanna suggested, "*Jetzt wollen wir das erste Mal jodeln* (Now let's start with a yodel)." They sang with great dedication. This worldly song is much removed from the Amish melodies of early martyrs in their desperate search for paradise. Yet as a naive song, it is ideally suited for the work under a cow, and the Amish sing it for as long as they milk and sometimes even after the milk has stopped dribbling. However, they also yodel during an amiable evening like tonight in Elam's house.

In Switzerland today there still exist more sophisticated versions of this yodel song: "*Jetzt wollen wir das erste Mal jodeln.*" The children in the formerly Anabaptist valley of Trub (Trubtal) still sing it. I heard only one version among the Amish, and it goes like this: "Now let us first yodela, yodela, yodela, now let us first yodela, yodela, yodela." And then the heartrending yodelers break into musical flourishes as if the echoes of the Swiss Alps were resounding all the way to the flat terrains of the New World. The second verse goes on: "Now let us a second time yodela, yodela, yodela. . . ." And away they go, yodeling, with the next verses following in numerical order and stopping only after the cow has dispensed its load or until the yodeler is tired or bored.

Rosanna, her children, and her children's children sang the individual verses most fervently with their eyes firmly closed as if praying. I was to hear this song and yodel frequently. It became part of my life with the Amish, and long after I had left these Amish yodelers, I heard its merry refrain as my memory slipped that compact disc into my ear. Maybe all this was the result of a bad conscience. On that evening when Rosanna again opened her eyes from her yodel revelry, I did not have the heart to confess to her that not every German is a talented yodeler and that this yodel-song does not necessarily fit in every German repertoire. Somehow I was under the impression that if I were to make such a comment, I would seriously undermine their worldview of the "good German"—which in these parts meant not only Germans but Alsatians and Swiss as well. That was the last thing I wanted to do on this first evening of introductions.

I simply am no yodeler, but then again, not every Amish person is a good one, either. This largely depends on where their ancestors came from and where the course of Anabaptist history scattered them before they arrived in America. In any case, the Grabers of Allen County are experts in yodeling, and so are the Indiana congregations around Geneva and Berne.

Later I was able to compensate for my inability to yodel as a true German; at least I could read like one. Whenever I read Psalm 23 in Wagnerian diction, I was always assured of a round of applause: "*Der Herr ist mein Hirte* (the Lord is my shepherd)," the ABC of the faithful. "I shall not want. He makes me lie down in green pastures. . . ," the evergreen favorite of the Holy Bible. The German inflection always appealed to them. To the circle of the Amish, I was and remained a lightweight, deceived by child baptism, one from the opposite world. "D'ya have to read the twenty-third Psalm? Don't ya know it by heart?" This was one of their many ways of ensuring that I knew I was an outsider. Yet whatever and whenever I read, it was simply High-Germanly beautiful to the ears of the Amish.

When darkness slowly fell, the kerosene lamps were fetched and lit. The Amish to this day make do with the light of a flame, just as Homo sapiens has done for some twenty thousand generations. After *Grundbiere*, chicken, water, many yodelers, and the warning about Satan alcohol, the sisters and brothers obviously felt that the time had come to bring up a topic as inconspicuously as possible. Even though worldly wisdom seemed to them to be an abomination before God, they wanted to pull out of me as much firsthand knowledge as possible regarding their history, the land of their faith and their forebears. For that, they obviously had to turn to one who was suspect and who really ought to have appeared more suspicious to them than they cared to admit at the time and under the circumstances.

They wanted to know all about Germany's south, Switzerland, Alsace-Lorraine, and the French Montbéliard, the area of the old Württemberg's Mömpelgard. No one recognized the names of

47

politicians like Kohl or Schmidt; Germany's Green Party was new to them. However, they knew about the Old Fathers, about the autobahn, and one of them even thought Germany simply liquidates a generation now and then whenever it runs out of space.

What really delighted these people was to establish a relationship "in our language" and "in your language" regarding some words. "What do you call a *Kaschte* (chest)," "a *Leicht* (funeral)," "Mark's *Efangelium* (Gospel)"? They all wanted their words to match the original language of their Amish forebears. Some of them spoke higher German than others, so went the consensus, and higher German here meant Luther's German. If all else failed and my Bernese or Swiss German ceased to communicate and the exaggerated Badenese also did not manage to bridge the gap of understanding, then we resorted to English.

Meanwhile, Joseph time and again observed with heavy regret that all our linguistic difficulties were attributable to man's delusions of grandeur, dating back to the tower of Babel (Gen. 11). To prove this, he served up obvious examples from recent history. I could see that the New World had not succeeded in ridding the Amish of their German language. There was a hint of irony in Joseph's thinking: in the history of Europe, his people had been in conflict with established society, and now current history did not accept them and their language.

This German tongue sets the tone for the Amish household. Whether or not their view of the world is boarded up, it is a place in which German romanticists feel at home. Joseph confirms all this by observing with a smirk that his horse Billy is a polyglot, for in addition to responding perfectly to English, he also has a flawless understanding of German. Thus it goes without saying that Billy is more clever than *Englischers* who know no German.

Germany, according to Amish depictions, is the land where "the blood of the devout witnesses of God was flowing." Yet whatever they know about the Germans is based on hearsay, on grizzly reports, or the literature of lamentations, *The Bloody Theater or Martyrs Mirror of the Defenseless Christians,* the Anabaptists. To be sure, there were some exceptions: they know that certain German lands gave refuge to their ancestors.

A number of non-Amish German immigrants also live in Allen County. Preacher Joseph says that during World War II some

German POWs proved themselves as "good German" farmers around Grabill, by Anabaptist standards. A little German light, after so many English shadows. . . . Yet these Amish folks reveal an astonishingly optimistic memory regarding the "Old Country." Germany was the mother, America the stepmother. Germany was the standard, a permanent column of orientation, as if nothing had changed over there.

A typical Amish reaction to things German is given by David Kline. He belongs to the New Order Amish, called this because their church in Ohio has raised the age of *real* dating for their teenagers, put an end to the practice of bundling, and allowed modernization of agricultural machines. In David's words, "If someone knocks on the door at night and speaks English, the door remains bolted. If, however, such a person speaks only one word of German, the door flies open."

Previous generations gave their descendants a tried and uncompromising confidence in that German language. They lived on the Rhine, the Limmat, the Aare, or the Emme rivers, produced Amish models of faith, wrote their hymns and doctrines, and witnessed with their hearts—and if need be, with their bodies at the stake. It is no longer of great significance to most people that the Anabaptists provided the greatest blood sacrifices of the Christian confessors to the faith in the sixteenth century. Yet neither the Catholics nor the Protestants could overlook the strong Anabaptist community of faith.

While being German did not mean everything to Elam, the master of the house, and to the visitors, Joseph, James and David, Ben and Tobi (Tobias), it definitely ranked higher than many other things on their scale of values. It was not as if they suffered from living in the German diaspora. Even the Jews have prepared for their golden era, far removed from temple and homeland. Through the diaspora, the Lord educates and develops his people.

The original German homeland has remained a source of strength and weakness for the Amish since their emigration. The Amish have been reared and sustained with this emotional tie to the land of their forebears, based not so much on historical experiences as on illusions. For them, "German" does not mean a politically definable space but rather forming and keeping an ideal concept to divert attention away from America. With this aid, the

Amish have been able to retain the culture of the Europe of the sixteenth, seventeenth, and eighteenth centuries like no other Germans living in the world today.

Soon I received a new lesson explaining that almost everything, but then again not exactly everything, was based on reference to Scripture. The older men often asked questions regarding earthly matters which contained built-in answers. Whenever they spoke, their eyes did not wander around the room to seek confirmation. In Elam's house, everyone was of identical opinion regardless of age, sex, or position held in church. Likely this was because they shared the same education, the same upbringing, and the same degree of knowledge and learning in general. In addition, the younger set demonstrated almost unlimited respect toward their elders. The young thought whatever their elders thought, and these in turn thought as *their* elders, in their time, had thought. Among those who stayed in this faith community, I noticed no breakdown in communication between generations, between fathers and sons, between mothers and daughters! They all shared an Amish homemade logic that appeared unshakable.

The women, who in their attire reminded one of deaconesses rather than reincarnations of European peasants, were somewhat withdrawn in matters of discussion. The girls tended to be ever busy killing mosquitoes with flyswatters, squishing them against windowpanes, or simply chewing their fingernails: "Y'know, if your fingernails are too long, the cows kick when milked."

While fresh well water was flowing by the dipper, the talking flowed on to crystallize a negative image of human society. This meant that the worldlings out there, the *Englischers*, were always and had always been an opposing force. One had to be on the lookout for them because, even here in Allen County, they tried to tear apart the ideal picture of life, that of being Amish-German. These Amish were pacifists out of deepest conviction and believed that Germany had never started a war, as the *Englisch* insisted. They saw war as the highest expression of brutality, and "the Germans do no such thing." Such an observation was based on the fact that *the Amish* certainly would not make war. All other claims were based on the malice of *Englischers*, which filled the hearts of the believers around old Joseph with anger, to the extent these Amish were capable of anger.

The big war and all big wars, for that matter, appeared to be a heavy concern for the Amish. When America had entered the war against Hitler's Germany, the heavens above Grabill had turned bloodred. Not only had Preacher Joseph witnessed this heavenly sign with great clarity, but so had many others who could vividly describe this apparition. When it comes to the color red, the Grabill Amish see red. Not a hint of red is allowed to them, starting from red paint on their houses to red on a piece of clothing, to say nothing of rouge on women's faces. Red is the color of Christ's blood and therefore banned, according to the Grabill Amish. Sons knew of this commandment from their fathers, as they knew it from *their* fathers. Already in 1659 Old Flemish Anabaptists had ruled against wearing "crimson linen," as did the 1779 Essingen Amish *Ordnungsbrief* (letter of church rules). This was in line with widespread Anabaptist customs of wearing modest and simple clothing, as shown by Melvin Gingerich in *Mennonite Attire*.

The sum total of all such rules they called *tradition,* and in Amish life, the old represented what was best. No one was capable of presenting a plausible reason for abandoning the best of all worlds and starting afresh with new beginnings. This tradition every day establishes connections to the world of their forebears, to the fathers and mothers of old, whose knowledge and values are handed down subject to the watchfulness of the church, thereby preserving what is good.

As Joseph tells it, the present Germany is a part of the "last earthly kingdom before the end of the world," just as the Bible prophesies. He believes the coming kingdom of the world is to be found in the European Community. The preacher teaches that we are living in the last seconds of our time because of the many ugly wounds which have been inflicted on the face of our planet. For non-Amish like me, there may still be hope because the sense of time is basically different for the Amish than for the world.

Woe unto anyone who would claim in Amish country that our world is more than six thousand years old, thereby sending science and religion on a collision course! As far as these folks are concerned, everything is wrong with the scientific approach. The best example to demonstrate this is man's flight to the moon. Had anyone asked the Amish of Allen County or read the related passages in the Bible, the entire enterprise would have been regarded as superfluous. Nothing, absolutely nothing was to be found up there, since the Bible describes it as "the lesser light." The moon, according to the Amish, serves the purpose of reflecting the sun's rays, nothing more.

The repeated reference to matters of English and *Englischers* had some significance. It was a popular word, even if it had a dual meaning. It certainly did not carry an anti-Yankee sentiment since the Amish are thoroughly loyal citizens of their homeland, as long as this loyalty does not override their obedience to the Word of God. Although they reject many of the privileges of U.S. citizens, their life runs parallel with the non-Amish, with whom they relate for business and casual social transactions—within limits. Only in exceptional cases do confrontations occur. To the Amish, a Yankee is someone who lives outside of Noah's ark, God's protection. A deep abyss yawns between the spiritual worlds of the Yankee and the Amish, and this inevitably affects social relationships across the barrier. The Amish maintain family and church at the cost of considerable isolation from so-called civilization. They know well that too much contact with non-Amish civilization will exact its own high price.

In principle, so the Amish believe, all people "from Adam have been created from one lump" and therefore are the same before God, be they man or woman, count or beggar. What accounts for the difference is the heart. From colonial times in America, *Englisch* represented to the Amish everything in the religious context regarded as evil or at least partially evil. Anyone who began dressing like an *Englischer* was one of the worldly, had therefore betrayed the old faith in the New World, and would go down with it.

Thus *Englischer* (sometimes called "gay") described anyone non-Amish, someone not *"von unsrer Sort Lüt* (one of our kind)" (as here, Alemannic allows *ü* to stand for *eu*). It mattered not at all whether such a person was Italian, Scottish, French, or just a Yankee. Germans lay somewhere between "our kind" and the "other kind." However, there could be absolutely no doubt that an upright Amish was not to be "yoked together with unbelievers," regardless of who that party might be (2 Cor. 6:14). This attitude surfaced repeatedly whenever the Amish spoke to me. Sometimes they changed from their Swiss-German to English in my presence and then apologized, claiming they did so on instinct since a stranger was an *Englischer* and an *Englischer* spoke English.

Just how deeply this idea has taken root among the Amish is something I was to discover a few years later. A most happy circumstance enabled me to travel through Europe with two New Order Amish—David Kline and Atlee Miller from Ohio. These fellows took note of the fact that Germany made do without slums, that the Germans made *Spätzle* (Swabian dumplings) just like they did in Ohio, and that "they dried hay on wooden racks." In an old obscure cemetery, Atlee Miller discovered a gravestone of one of his direct forebears.

However, what was to fascinate these two Amish most of all was the fact that "in Germany the *Englischers* all speak German." The term *Englischers* thus also applied to all Germans who were not Amish. The Germans were no less surprised. Wherever these brothers opened their mouths in the Palatinate, they were certainly understood by the local population. Miller and Kline spoke their Pennsylvania German which, although enriched with various English terms, was obviously a dialectal variation of the Palatinate tongue.

Oh, yes, and what about "*unsre Sort Lüt* (our kind of people)"? They had originated in the "Old Country," according to their *Ausbund*, a "booklet for gracious readers and singers" which starts as follows:

> After the contamination of the latter times had taken the reading of the Holy Scriptures from a larger part of Christianity, these people lay in a deep sleep of ignorance about the holy Gospels. The people were surrounded by thick darkness and blindness and made do with superstitious worship. Most of the shepherds erred, the sheep were scattered, the heads of state permitted themselves to be governed by the so-called clergy, and the blind were leading each other until both fell into a ditch. Once in a while a light was seen to break through in some places in the world, but the darkness could not endure this light, and it was extinguished by the enemies of the truth. . . .
>
> But then it pleased merciful God to permit various lights to rise again, which brought the Holy Scripture into the common language, to be read by many God-seeking people for worship and pleasure. . . . Among these was not least of all, Dr. Martin Luther, who spared no effort in the cause of the Reformation and in the translation of the Holy Scripture; Huldrych Zwingli, Conrad

Grebel, Michael Sattler, Philip Melanchthon, John Calvin, Oecolampadius, . . . and others in High-Germany; as well as Menno Simons and Dietrich Philips and the like in the Netherlands. And whether or not these were all of one accord in placing the light on the candlestick to save the world from darkness, there nevertheless were varying opinions and discernments regarding some passages of the Holy Scripture, not only in some commonly held points of faith, but above all in the proper administration or use of holy baptism. . . . Some have come to understand that child baptism is not founded on the Scripture. . . .

The Amish of Allen County regard themselves as descendants of "those rotting in dungeons, burnt to powder," martyr Christians, who in their day placed the light on the candlestick by standing for believers baptism. No longer in dungeons, they now are first and foremost farmers, the original occupation of all mankind (after hunting and gathering food). While not being the most productive by worldly measurements, they are beyond doubt the best farmers of America. They farm according to the command of the Lord, who on the sixth day of creation provided human beings "with all manner of plants which will multiply unto you food" and made all animals subservient to humans (Gen. 1-2).

The migration of the Amish to the New World brought no break in style of life for these people as it did for the vast majority of emigrants. As in the days in Old Europe, only a hard and full day's work could fill the earth and subdue it (Gen. 1:28). When night falls on Allen County and the soil is no longer being tilled, the plants keep on growing. Anyone who fills mornings, middays, and evenings with pigs' bellies, cows' udders, and horsepower has every reason to be tired at 9:00 p.m. on any clock. Thus the amiable get-togethers in the Grabill neighborhood end relatively early. For one thing, all their farmhouses remind one of wartime blackouts since they have no electric lights to disturb the calm peace in which they, as citizens of heaven, await the endtime sight which God will bring upon the earth (Rev. 1:7).

Culture, in these parts, is not equated with the achievements of modern times and with things external, formal, or technological. Instead, true culture is something value related, spiritual, and invariably bound directly to religious faith. Others place the progress of the human mind above the power of nature or the great wonder of God's creation. They will suffer the consequences. That is in God's hands.

With Protestant diligence, the sixteen-hour working day of these Anabaptists begins at an early hour with milking and *"Schtall mache* (doing the chores)." For this, every hand is welcome, even if it has all thumbs, as in the case of their worldly visitor who has taken temporary lodging in their midst. They tried to train me: "If nothing stands in the way, reach for the udder, then grab it, then press it, then pull, and then press it again. . . ." Work becomes a community experience, with the family choring together. How early was I to press and pull? About 5:00 a.m. by Amish time, God's "sun time," between Eastern standard and daylight time year-round and thus half an hour different from the clock of the world. The Amish seem to leave no stone unturned to be different from those out there and thus even call for their own time zone.

The little ones recited their prayer before turning in. Their age-old prayer went like this:

> Gone is another day. I fold my hands to pray
> to you our Lord of peace:
> Protect us from disgrace, direct your kindly face,
> and on us, please, your grace release. Amen.

Then all together they prayed the Lord's Prayer in German, as done wherever Amish bend a knee, in step with local Amish time and yet beyond earthbound time zones. Finally one more matter: my kind hosts expressed thoughtful concern over whether I needed a chamber pot for my bedroom, "in case you have to empty your bladder at night."

Just when the modern world tunes in to TV news, the evening on Elam's farmyard became perfectly still as the quiet of night descended, and all became pitch black. Aside from a wall clock with Westminster beat and chimes, the world around appeared to be many miles away. Strange as it may seem, everything now invited the stillness of peace: no telephone which might explode into shrill call, no dripping water faucets, no hum of motors, no drone of air-conditioning which might have reduced the temperature of the house to seventy-seven or even eighty-five degrees and diffused the smell of kerosene and lamp fumes. Only once in a while was there the sharp staccato trot of horses as they transported some late Amish homecomers along the lonely night road. Even the dogs sneaking around the house at night had shut off all their aggressive tendencies. I suddenly thought, If the weather conditions were just right, one could hear the very grass grow.

Elam probably lay beside Rachel in the marital bed and reflected on the world in his own way. Without really intending to do so, I had sent something along with him for the night. I had told him that my room was as hot as a sauna. He had wanted to know what a sauna was all about, and then why people sat there in towels just to perspire. Elam smiled with pity at the poor example of what we call our world.

Early in the morning when the sun called the little world around Grabill into action, just like on the first day of creation, some serious yodeling commenced. "The cows give more milk," Tobi Graber claimed. "The Lord in heaven be praised and thanked" for a piece of tradition handed down over time, going back to their forebears in the Swiss Emmental. The Amish yodel while milking as others play a skat card game to rock music. Milking is done by hand since the Old Order Amish of Allen County have no place for milking machines. The family shares the chores and chats and sings while they work.

What about this whole matter of yodeling, sounding forth to the cows at milking time? Tobi's cow seemed to agree with him and in turn with countless generations of Anabaptists. All this in spite of the sultry weather when Amish cows are stressed by the heat and give considerably less milk than in colder seasons. Some of their energy goes to swishing their tails to swat insects!

The Amish tend the fields with simple horse-drawn implements and reject tractors and much modern machinery. "Machines produce no manure," they explained to me, and manure is recyclable, fertilizer for the soil. Land ought to be treated and developed so that parents can face future generations without shame for what they have done to the earth. Thus they have a sense of working in partnership with God, subduing the earth, with accountability to God and their own community—past, present, and future.

2

The Rebellion of the Saints

The deeper they dig, the more connections they find. The Amish of Allen County are the children of many parents, among them the first Christians of Jerusalem and later evangelistic movements and revivals up to the epoch-making Reformation. They are the heirs of ancient church tradition, the early Anabaptism of Switzerland, and the Bible, newly opened in the German language. Therefore, they are part of the Germanization of Christianity.

On one side, believers see a picture of Erasmus, Martin Luther, Huldrych Zwingli, Conrad Grebel, Menno Simons, and the zealous young Jakob Ammann, with their Christian conduct of life. On another side, they see the followers of Rome, the abuses by the Renaissance papal system, the paralysis of the Catholic church, on account of which the old piety splintered. In the eyes of many sectarians, the theologians of the Magisterial Reformation brought a halfhearted renewal. Believing Christians now attempted to reform the old church and also its reformers. Their aim was to transform the people through religious guidance for the service of God, somewhat like the orders of the old church. Their model was the earliest Christian church.

The birth of the "old evangelical Anabaptist church" (as Swiss Mennonites called themselves) has to be seen from the perspective of the witnesses of that time. The decline of economic and social conditions in the sixteenth century had hit the rural population in the German-speaking areas particularly hard. Widespread uncertainty was caused by devaluation of currency, higher taxes, a rise in population, arbitrary rule by governments of the day, fragmentation of estates, confessional feudings connected to the dissolution of the old church order, and the introduction of various new customs and rules. People were now capable of plotting the movements of stars by applying mathematics to the universe. Gutenberg invented the printing press around 1450, and it had a dramatic effect in spreading knowledge and making the Scriptures available. These developments were changing age-old concepts of the world.

In 1516 the Dutch humanist Erasmus of Rotterdam published his edition of the Greek New Testament with his own Latin translation and a plea that the Scriptures be translated into every language. He wanted every person to be able to read the Bible and receive benefit. This stimulated others to translate the Bible, and many began to pore over it intensely in Bible study groups.

At Zurich, Zwingli as head pastor at the Great Cathedral from 1519 was using the Greek New Testament of Erasmus for expository preaching from Matthew and other books. Around him gathered a circle of students and followers. They hoped that through recovery of the Scriptures, all of Catholicism could be renewed. But Rome would not budge, so Zwingli took steps toward Reformation. By 1523 some of his younger associates became uneasy over his concessions to the city council in slowing church reform. From these dissenters, Anabaptism was born in January 1525.

Meanwhile, Basel in about 1523 was regarded as a safe haven for people searching out the theological interpretations of their day. Erasmus supposedly discovered a group of "opponents to child baptism" in these parts in 1524. The Basel Reformer Oecolampadius was in dialogue with several baptism-minded persons and conducted theological conversations with Anabaptists at his home in August 1525.

However, the clearest track behind the Amish of Allen County can be traced through those hectic times to Zurich and three Protestants, Conrad Grebel, Felix Manz, and Georg Blaurock. They were students of Zwingli, attempting an appeal to the historical Jesus, and bent on contradicting certain teachings of Rome by demonstrating the true faith and life of original Christianity.

Yet the tourist today may wonder what is still meaningful

about the original kernel and birth of Anabaptism in the city of Zurich. Little reminds one that the genuine spirit of Anabaptism crackled and sparked in the alleys near the Limmat River. Hardly anything informs the visitor to that historical site about what happened here in those days of religious upheaval and renewal. At the Neumarkt 5 is a commemorative tablet on the house of the patrician Conrad Grebel. On an excursion to Zollikon, one may chance upon the Gstadtstrasse 23-25, recently also marked by a plaque identifying it as the meeting place of the first Anabaptist congregation. At Zurich's Bahnhofstrasse 3 in January 1525, early "rebaptisms" were carried out. One may also note the Fischmarkt (fish market) of Zurich, where the sentence was read upon one of the first Anabaptists to be executed in Switzerland by Protestants. Then there is also the old Schipfe, opposite the place where Felix Manz was drowned in the Limmat in 1527.

Manz was attempting to "found a special church." The early Anabaptists of Zurich quickly pushed against church and state in order to expose any deviations from "true practices of faith." In a trustworthy manner, they condemned heresy and sin. They were at odds with a large institution since every sixth person was directly or indirectly in the employ of the church. The state church tolerated no other confessions and tried to stamp them out.

One might look outside Zurich for traces of Anabaptism in the country, close to the little castle in Grüningen, a former Grebel residence where Conrad grew up. Or one could climb up to the Anabaptist cave in the vicinity of Bäretswil, where the persecuted occasionally met. An Anabaptist bridge is located a little farther down the way, and an Anabaptist ditch, Anabaptist alleys, the Anabaptist pit at Sumiswald, the colony of refuge, the *Geiss* (goat) church in the Bernese Jura, and the dark dungeon in the castle of Trachselwald. One might look up old records and files on the Anabaptists. After all, there are still some letters to be found in St. Gallen, which Grebel wrote to the "loyal and dear fellow believer in Christ" Thomas Müntzer, but which the latter never received. Even Zurich itself shows few traces of Anabaptism. The water keeps flowing down the Limmat just as it would if no Anabaptists had been drowned in it for their confession of faith. In all of Switzerland, hardly anything is left as a visual reminder of the former importance of the movement. Even the massive Zwingli doors of

Zurich's Great Cathedral, displaying other scenes from the Reformation on its panels, have simply forgotten the Anabaptists.

This very cathedral dominated and still dominates the locale where Anabaptism began in Switzerland. There Huldrych Zwingli was the head pastor (from 1519) and the spiritual teacher of rebels of the faith. On January 21, 1525—the birth date of the Swiss Brethren—they used a soup ladle to administer their first adult baptism upon the testimony of faith. This took place in the apartment of Felix Manz, the son of the lord of the manor, in the Neustadtgasse of Zurich, behind the Great Cathedral. However, this reformer, Zwingli, became the most decisive opponent of the Anabaptists, whose leaders were earlier his students.

Zwingli had chanced upon the road to the Reformation during the hard times of the plague. He was more influenced by Erasmus of Rotterdam than by Luther, and Erasmus was regarded as "almost" Anabaptist. Zwingli had inwardly divorced himself from Rome in order to preach the moral renewal of many institutions of life, as well as a new church order. With this goal he spoke from the basis of a close relationship to the humanist tradition of Erasmus. As the religious disputes developed, Zwingli moved beyond the more-tolerant Christian humanism of Erasmus (who remained a Catholic) to a Protestantism in which he was actually instituting reforms.

In contrast to Luther, Zwingli was a politician and a social planner. He promised that a new faith would renew the Swiss Confederacy politically as well as socially and that justice and peace would forthwith prevail. "This Zwingli," so the early Anabaptist literature approvingly commented, "has started to storm the papacy and to teach and write against the ravages and the abominations of Babylon, the terrible whore [the Catholic church]." He was also successful in "smashing the chalice from the pope's hand." Yet in the opinion of the Anabaptists, Zwingli did not throw the shards and the sediment far enough from himself.

Grebel, Manz, and Blaurock instituted the first free church on German-speaking soil. Their circle saw Zwingli as letting the Reformation cause be too closely obligated to worldly authorities, who were expected to carry through church reforms. They warned against constructing a theocracy, a government by God's authority, an unholy union in which the church, to which everyone should belong by birth and child baptism, would be tied to the state. In January 1523 the Council of the city of Zurich heard Zwingli's 67 theses for reform and continued to back this preacher who had just renounced Rome. From that hour, the Reformation in Switzerland had finally become a highly political issue for the rebels. This reformer had granted to the worldly authorities power over the teachings and the deeds of Christ, to regulate the pace of reform in the church. With this decision, the Swiss Reformation had pitted itself against its own radical student group with which it had earlier formed a common front of Zurich and Basel humanistic circles aiming to shatter the Roman walls.

Like Luther in his monk's cell, Grebel and his group had posed the question of a merciful God. Now they were concerned that Zwingli's actions represented an unacceptable compromise which had nothing in common with the radical interpretation of the Reformation. If Christianity was incapable of bringing the Spirit into the world, then the world (the government) should not be allowed to bring itself into the church.

The Anabaptists took the position that the Reformation "should not confuse the divine word with the worldly word." They consequently intended to break with the medieval unity of church and state. Both Zwingli and Luther regarded them as even more dangerous than Rome. From the first day, Anabaptists expected martyrdom as part of the birth pangs of a new church. They believed that the walk to their places of execution expressed the very freedom of the Christian which had been basic to Luther's position.

On January 21, 1525, Georg Blaurock (blue coat, a nickname), who had formerly been a vicar in Trins in the diocese of Chur, asked to be baptized by Conrad Grebel. Blaurock was also called the "married white coat from the house of Jakob." Thus he became the first Anabaptist, bearing believers baptism as another sign of separation between the students and their teacher Zwingli. In fact, as the unity of the Western church broke apart, four parties were left: the Lutherans, the Zwinglians, the Anabaptists, and those who remained Roman Catholic. The Anabaptists held that the Bible ordered one first to believe and only then to be baptized.

From then on, the rejection of child baptism by the Grebel group was regarded as the most obvious outcome of the religious dispute. However, believers baptism was only part of what was even more important: a new understanding of the Bible leading to a purified worship and a holy lifestyle. Yet the public impression resulted in the sect being called *Taufgesinnte* (Baptism-inclined or Baptism-minded). They were also disparagingly called *Wiedertäufer* (Rebaptizers), because in their group, whether or not one had been baptized as a child, each had to be baptized on confession of faith.

The system of justice of the time found the term Rebaptizers quite handy because they had ready access to a thousand-year-old law from the time of Emperor Justinian. According to it, the unlawful repetition of baptism was to be punished "with a severe death." The Speyer parliament of 1529 used this decree as a basis for passing an imperial law that rebaptisms were to be punished by death. Previously the church rebels had been prosecuted by the church, but now the state itself assumed this role.

This leads one to conclude that the Anabaptists were feared not so much as heretics, but more generally on account of their attitude toward the secular governments and society in general. Luther also regarded these new believers more as "sinners against the state" than as "sinners against religion." They threatened the collection of tithes and taxes, especially when they were to support the state church. Those who were pacifist were not available to serve in the armies to fight the enemy. They regularly refused to hold public office or to swear oaths of allegiance. The Anabaptists thus were a rip in the social fabric of church and state interwoven.

It was of little consequence that the Anabaptists, who were accused of religious crimes as well as civil misdemeanors, objected to the common general accusations: "Because we do not baptize children, but only believing adults upon their statement of faith in accordance with the Lord's commandments, we have to bear the name of Rebaptizers (Anabaptists); meanwhile the Zwinglians have retained infant baptism and other customs of the papacy, and they keep the name of Reformed. At this point we request an impartial judgment, as to which of us is closest to the truth, who is more thoroughly reformed, and whom the name Reformed describes more aptly and accurately."

In spite of their challenge to Zwingli, the Swiss Anabaptists remained Zwinglians in many ways and for a while regarded themselves as part of the Reformation movement. They supported a return to the gospel as the way to resist the old Catholic church. The Anabaptists adopted Zwingli's demand for church discipline and his early criticism of infant baptism: "One ought not to baptize little children." (Yet later Zwingli defended the practice by equating it with Old Testament circumcision.) Anabaptists also followed Zwingli's symbolic doctrine of the Eucharist as well as his emphasis on discipleship, following Christ in suffering, even to the cross.

In addition, the Anabaptists copied Zwingli's concept of the renewal of the church on the basis of the New Testament, his criticism of medieval church customs, his defense of freeing citizens from the financial burden of the papacy, and his style of repentance. In general, they agreed with the traditional central theological doctrines of historic Christianity. This even Zwingli confirmed when he saw in them "a departure only in a few points." Yet the Reformer still called the new believers "devils disguised as angels of light" with the "barking of a three-throated hound of hell and a bestial disposition, while claiming to be Christian."

The rebels of faith stated that they were uncompromising with regard to true Christian baptism and that such baptism had to transpire both inwardly and outwardly: inwardly with Holy Spirit, and outwardly with water in the manner of John the Baptist. They knew that Christ commanded his disciples, "Go therefore and teach all nations, baptizing them in the name of the Father, and of the Son, and of the Holy Spirit . . ." (Matt. 28:19-20). From this biblical word, they arrived at the conclusion that teaching and faith had to come *before* baptism, even if it represented a contradiction to the Catholic and Lutheran understanding of the basic sin of mankind and their stress on Jesus' saying, "Let the children come unto me . . ." (Matt. 19:14).

To the Anabaptists, a child represented creation perfected. Children knew nothing about God or the devil and therefore could not be sinful and could not choose any kind of faith. A good example of this was Jesus, who received holy baptism at age thirty. Luther, however, had retained the Catholic ceremony of infant baptism with salt, saliva, and oil, based on the example of Jewish circumcision. After all, was not the Son of God a Jew?

The Anabaptists also rejected swearing the oath, since an up-right Christian should be able to make do with a "simplistic and simple 'Yes, Yes' and 'No, No' " (Matt. 5:37). If an oath was demanded to show allegiance to the government, the Anabaptists refused to cooperate. They strictly reserved their highest pledge of loyalty for Christ. They denied the physical presence of the body and blood of Christ in the Lord's Supper, which alongside baptism is central to church ritual. After all, the Lord had ascended to heaven and could not be eaten in the bread. The Anabaptists opposed professionalizing church leadership positions. Though at first there was some difference of opinion, they did reject military service, accepting Jesus' call to love the enemy (Matt. 5:44), even the Turks rattling the gates of Europe. Thus rulers recruiting soldiers to defend their states saw these peacemakers as a threat to their own survival and the social fabric. Anabaptists also refused to canonize dead saints, since they believed that only the living were capable of being holy.

During the time of fasting, a few Anabaptists provoked the church and civil authorities by eating sausage while translating the Bible in Froschauer's print shop. Others disrupted sermons by shouting opinions such as "The pastor is lying," in order to demonstrate that "the new priests still regard the old ones much too highly." Grebel's outspoken charges in the Zurich city hall are on record. Their words were usually more warlike than their actions. According to the Anabaptist Simon Stumpf, the Reformation could only be successful if a religious prairie fire were set and "all priests were to be bludgeoned to death."

One Johannes Brötli combined his missionary activities with the uprising of the Hallau peasants under the protection of armed men. Yet those of totally peaceful intent believed that Christians of any persuasion should conduct themselves as sheep among wolves and should always be prepared to be led to the slaughter. On May 29, 1525, Bolt Eberli was burned at the stake in his hometown of Schwyz, the first Anabaptist martyr in a Catholic canton. He became a model to the Anabaptists. A few months later, the council of Lucerne charged Johannes Krüsi with disturbing the confessional peace by causing "uprisings," and the council condemned him to die at the stake.

The Zurich authorities quickly tried to stamp out the Anabaptist movement. First they ordered unbaptized children to be baptized (Jan. 18, 1525) and forbade infant baptism in private homes (Feb. 1, 1525). They forbade baptism on confession of faith on penalty of fine and exile (Mar. 1, 1525) or even death (March 1, 1526). Before long the authorities put the leaders Grebel, Manz, and Blaurock in prison in Zurich. There they stayed from October 1525 until they escaped in March 1526. That summer Grebel died of the plague in Maienfeld. In the fall his father was beheaded upon orders from Zwingli. In Bern, Anabaptists taken to the Nüwen tower "were thrown on straw and given only water and bread, to let them die there."

On November 19, 1526, the Zurich City Council prohibited not only baptism but also Anabaptist assemblies on pain of death by drowning. In the Appenzell area, the authorities tended to be a little more lenient. They first decreed by law in 1530 that Anabaptists who did not deny their faith in those parts were to be drowned, stating literally that they were to be punished by a "third baptism." The judiciary no longer had to wait for God's judgments but was allowed to increase torture to extract confessions.

In June of 1526 the Basel government passed its first Anabaptist act, banning followers of the new teaching from Basel. In 1528, Basel decreed financial punishments against rebaptism. As of 1529, they were tortured for this offense and threatened with death. In January of 1530, the Anabaptist Hans Ludi of Bubendorf was put to death on the execution site of Basel. Upon threat of death, others had to leave the city "for all time." Thus barriers were staked out between Basel and the new teaching. The courts of the established churches had erected the gallows for executions.

In defense of the Anabaptists, the Hutterian chronicler Kaspar Braitmichel states, "Erasmus of Rotterdam is a jewel in the German nation. He exposed the abuses of the pope in courteous and polite manner in his Latin books. Also Luther, who pulled up the little robe to expose the Roman whore both fore and aft." But Luther had only broken down a dilapidated house and had erected nothing in its place. Zwingli, while doing battle with the papacy, had fallen out with Luther regarding the Lord's Supper. The result, according to Braitmichel: "From their ranks, two rough people emerged, but no good has come of it. All they have is bloated and swollen knowledge; they eat meat, they take wives, they scold monks and priests, and such is their ultimate service to God. But one fails to notice in either of them a change of life and a newly born person based on the Word."

There are also the scandal-ridden original reports on the Anabaptists which obviously emanated from the opposing camp. Among them was Heinrich Bullinger's book, published by Froschauer in Zurich in 1531, entitled *Regarding the Shameless and Outrageously Misleading and False Teachings of These Self-appointed Anabaptists.* In it the author implies that a devil in the form of an angel of light dwells even in the most peaceful Anabaptists. In Augsburg, Urban Rhegius wrote *Against the New Baptismal Order: Necessary Warning to All Believing Christians by a Servant of the Gospel*, while Melanchthon issued his *Instructions Against the Teachings of the Anabaptists.*

Whenever the Catholic or Protestant teachers of the day dealt with the topic of "Anabaptist heretics," both felt obligated to go all out in condemning the "damnable and hellish sect," as did Albertinus, court secretary of Munich. Rebaptism was regarded as a great mistake, more injurious than fleshly evils, greed, or pride of spirit, according to the Lutheran theologian Rhegius. Dipping their quills in gall, the critics attempted to equate the blameless walk of life of these brothers and sisters with being charlatans and hypocrites.

The Anabaptists were in an unfavorable position to handle such attacks since the media were opposed to them and they were mainly on the run. In 1528, even one who defended Anabaptist doctrine was placed under the penalty of death. The first relatively favorable report by an outsider regarding the movement came in 1668 from the pen of the German poet Grimmelshausen, who admiringly described life among Anabaptists, Hutterite colonies in Slovakia. Although he believed that they clung to a false teaching, he regarded their life as superior to that in the monasteries.

In spite of their publications being banned, some printing presses assisted Anabaptists in the distribution of their tracts. *Umbträger* (messengers) passed them out in marketplaces and in front of city gates and took them from congregation to congregation. Through these tracts in the language of the common people, Anabaptists of Silesia, Alsace, Tirol, and Hesse addressed contemporary church and political problems. They distributed leaflets which took issue with arguments, programs, and instructions of the day. They interpreted Scripture and sometimes reported the Spirit's inner enlightenment through voices and visions.

The Anabaptists thus tried to influence readers for their causes in accord with the central significance of Christ and with the Bible, newly discovered and available in the common languages of the people. Real faith meant discipleship, following the Son of God, participation in his suffering, taking up the cross, and commitment to the resurrection. The New Testament, especially the Gospels and the book of Acts, were foundational for Anabaptist ideals and guided their further use of certain Old Testament patterns of faith.

Those of the new faith considered themselves able to separate the chosen from the lost as they sorted out the true disciples in their congregations. Frequently they imposed strict measures to be true to the Bible and have orderly conduct among church members, always wanting "the heart and mouth and deed to be of the finest accord" (Hans Denk).

Anabaptists soon declared that separation "from a world of murderers, whores, and idolaters" was absolutely mandatory. Based on their understanding of the Bible, child baptism was of the devil, and they wanted to have nothing to do with it. Yet they were not so far removed from the main thrust of Protestantism or Catholicism. One wonders how the state churches might have avoided the bloody scenes of the persecution which forced the Anabaptists into their underground Christian existence, as though living in the catacombs. It had started as a quarrel among relatives who after separation forgot what they had in common. Zwingli used the word of John to describe the sorry events: "They went out from us, but they were not of us" (1 John 2:19). The state churches forced the Swiss Anabaptists to be a martyr church for some three centuries.

Yet from a contemporary vantage point, the Anabaptists at that time represented a serious danger to customary social order. Peasants were on the point of revolt, and governments were not as firmly institutionalized as we might expect. The new faith spread most quickly in the country or the mountains, remote areas where subjects were difficult to contact and where the people were mostly left alone in religious matters. Many who were discouraged because of the bloody suppression of the peasants' revolt (1524-25) found new hope and faith in the spreading Anabaptist movement.

In the hiding places of the time, the Anabaptists preached a radical consistency. They handed the Bible over to common believers, who now were allowed to interpret the Word of God by and for themselves. Often their concepts were similar to the pre-Reformation Waldensians. In the minutes taken from the interrogations of that period, the Anabaptists demonstrated a surprising knowledge of the Bible. This was true even though the Catholic church had previously banned the Bible in the common languages to prevent quarrels about its contents and doctrine. It was known that the Waldensians had instructed children with the Scriptures. As a result, many observers concluded that those of the new faith had been influenced by Peter Waldo, a radical thinker of a previous century. In addition to Waldo, writers regularly suggested that the Englishman John Wycliffe and the Czech Reformer John Hus had a degree of influence upon the Anabaptists.

Oddly, the Anabaptist teachings were sometimes closer to the Catholic church than to Luther's. While opposing the veneration of saints and the cult of relics, these people nevertheless preached a separation from the world which ran parallel to patterns of cloister life in the old church. Yet the monastery remained the privilege of a small group. These radical Christians now believed that the brotherhood—"the society as the body of Christ"—the entire congregation, was called to follow Christ. For them, the character of a chosen people lay in realizing a church without spot or blemish, a life of *Gelassenheit* (being yielded to God), and opposition to the sinful world in spiritual and temporal matters.

The church was there wherever two or three, thirty or forty, or three hundred were gathered together in the name of Jesus (Matt. 18:18-20). The idea of a synod was acceptable to them, as shown by the meeting from which came the "Brotherly Union," the 1527 Anabaptist confession of Schleitheim. This foundational Anabaptist gathering, led by Michael Sattler, was on the Swiss-German border, at Schleitheim, in the canton of Schaffhausen, perhaps on the edge of Hermmental. Here the believers passed seven articles of faith, "which we want to adhere to in the Lord, if we want to be obedient children, sons and daughters of God." They dealt with baptism, church discipline, the Lord's Supper, separation (banning), preachers, the sword, and the oath.

These articles were to become the standard for the new movement in southern Germany, in Switzerland, and in Austria. They were part of a common code of faith which has remained binding for the traditionally conservative Anabaptist groups until today.

This new faith had already been sweeping through German-speaking areas, and soon it was known throughout the larger part of Christianity. The high numbers of early Anabaptist martyrs who gladly died for their faith impressed, above all, the simple people. To this was added a general uneasiness and quest for righteousness, together with increased anxiety about personal salvation.

The ministers of the *Landeskirche* (state church) reported at the Zofingen Disputation of 1532 in Switzerland that "the most pious were simply taking off" in all directions. Peasants and craftsmen, humanistically educated citizens and patricians, radical Protestant theologians and even Catholic priests joined the Anabaptists, even though this compromised their class standing. Among them was Michael Sattler, prior of the Benedictine Order of St. Peter in the Black Forest; Dr. Balthasar Hubmaier, cathedral priest in Regensburg; and Johannes Brötli, pastor in Quarten by the Walensee—none of whom survived 1529. They were among thousands of Anabaptist brothers and sisters who died the death of martyrs.

This religious protest movement managed to attract wide masses of people, mainly in southern German-speaking areas and from the lower urban and rural classes. In some country areas, Anabaptists were as successful as the Catholic and Protestant churches. Nuremberg, Augsburg, and Strassburg (now Strasbourg, France) became the main support centers for the Anabaptists. In the Hapsburg principalities, the Anabaptist teachings broke out with the force of a natural catastrophe, and stirred up the major opposition to Rome. One wonders how much the social model of the Anabaptists influenced the later French Revolution in its call for liberty, equality, and fraternity.

In the sixteenth century, German shoemaker-poet Hans Sachs and the artist Albrecht Dürer frequently established contacts with the Anabaptists. In the next century, the Dutch painter Rembrandt, although a member of the Reformed Church, maintained close contacts to Mennonites and some documents even count him as a member of their church.

Like Zwingli, Luther gradually came to regard the Anabaptist teachings as a greater danger than the papacy for their destructive effects on the church. Some enthusiasts advocated separation from the mainstream of the "reformed German nation" and withdrawal into a group of the "holy." Thus they endangered the Reformers' goal of forcing Rome to its knees. From around 1528 the Reformation was no longer fully determined by the great Reformers. Some of their chief followers began to pursue other aims. In practice, Luther and Zwingli recommended freedom of faith only for their own circles. Zwingli soon held that the death penalty by drowning was justified for the "false Anabaptist doctrine." Luther expressed the opinion that "one should attempt to defend oneself against them and resist them with the Bible and God's Word. Little will be achieved with fire" (*Regarding Anabaptism,* 1528).

The authorities in Switzerland, the ancestral home of the Grabers, Yoders, Kauffmans, or Zehrs of Allen County, initially treated the Anabaptist problem on a regional basis. On Thursday of August 2, 1527, the city council of Zurich invited the "dear confederates" from Bern, Schaffhausen, Basel, Chur, Appenzell, and St. Gallen for a strategy meeting. They had been unable to subdue those of the new faith in spite of heavy penalties. By January 25, 1525, the first Anabaptist meetingplace had been established at a farmhouse (now Gstadtstrasse 23-25) in the fishing village of Zollikon, a suburb of Zurich. In the city proper, many parents laid claim to the new faith, categorically rejecting baptism of their infants. After threats of punishments because child baptism was decreed by law, Conrad Grebel responded to his brother-in-law, Fabian of St. Gallen, with an accurate forecast: "I believe persecution will not be spared us. May God grant us mercy."

The Anabaptists now fled from Zurich to Schaffhausen, in spite of the quick announcement by the latter, "We too are of the opinion that young children ought to be baptized." At the time Schaffhausen was largely dependent on Zurich in religious matters and had laws against drinking, gambling, and rebaptisms. On November 13, 1527, it decreed the death sentence for Hans Rueger, an Anabaptist. Small Anabaptist congregations consolidated in the Catholic canton of Solothurn and its districts of Aar-wangen, Niederbipp, Wangen, and particularly also in Bucheggberg. The new teachings never quite managed to gain a big following in these parts. So the systematic campaign against the "non-Christian sect" was not undertaken here with the same ardor as in neighboring areas. Yet in 1530 the Solothurners also declared that the Anabaptists were to be "eradicated and extermi-nated."

In St. Gallen the soil was favorable for the propagation of Anabaptism. There citizens literally flocked to hear Dr. Balthasar Hubmaier, as they did to Conrad Grebel. On Palm Sunday in 1525, new converts gathered for a procession from the city to the river Sitter in order to be baptized while the bells of St. Leonhard were chiming. The nuns were dismayed by such rebaptisms. In only a few months' time, the Anabaptists were also forbidden here "in word and in deed." Transgressors were fined ten pounds in cash for men and five pounds for womenfolk.

Because they severed the bond of church and state, serious re-percussions developed for members of the new faith. The uprising of the German peasants in 1528 showed the danger which such a separation implied for the destruction of the political and social order. Even though the ways of the Anabaptists and the militant peasants had clearly parted earlier, their opponents still assumed they were the same, since both longed for the immediate realiza-tion of a new kingdom, a world of divine justice in tangible form.

In any case, Anabaptist leaders like Grebel, Hans Hut, Hans Denk, and Dr. Balthasar Hubmaier were quite ready to proclaim the Word of God in calling for social justice. Grebel made strong attacks against capital, interest, and church taxes (tithing): "In matters of tithing, the people of the world of Zurich act tyrannical-ly and insidiously." They opposed oppressive taxation. They also held that a general brotherhood should guarantee the equality of all people.

From the beginning Anabaptists put less value on the Old Tes-tament and strongly emphasized the Sermon on the Mount (Matt. 5-7). They regarded the tradition of the New Testament not only as an example of teaching and commands but also as a social cove-nant. In their view, the existing world order was incapable of im-plementing the needed economic change. Their criticism was directed against the old established church to which two thirds of German territory belonged. They met with strong support among the disenfranchised sons of peasants and the serfs who worked for wages.

It was only natural that the Anabaptists' social doctrines received much sympathy from the have-nots. To them, reformation and revolution were synonymous. A hundred years of social unrest in Germany had led to a bloody revolution in June 1524, mostly suppressed by May 1525—the Peasants' War. These underprivileged thought the time had come to introduce a new, classless society. They armed themselves with axes and torches to institute the freedom of Christian people. The peasants demanded, according to the Twelve Articles developed by Sebastian Lotzer and others, the abolishment of serfdom and a new order against forced labor. They also insisted on the right to appoint their own pastors "who would preach the gospel pure and clear without human content." For the times, these were daring demands indeed. Yet Thomas Müntzer predicted that this social movement would succeed in dominating governments like the stone cut out by God which grew into a mountain and filled the whole earth—representing the kingdom of God (Dan. 2:31-45).

While unrest quickly spread, Luther, who had initially read the riot act to counts and lords, was startled by all the bloodshed. He attacked the claim of the rioters that they had a "divine commission" for dealing with the world. Luther, the son of peasants, maintained throughout that the civil law had to be separated from the gospel and thus clearly forbade the peasants from rioting. He took the authority of the state as in the divine order of things, based on the mutual relationship of church and secular authority.

Many Protestants thought he was calling for a return to the old powers when they read his 1524 *Letter to the Counts of Saxony Regarding the Riotous Spirit:* "Wherever they do more than fight with the word, they also want to break and beat with fists, and such actions should be dealt with by his countly grace, whether it is they or us. . . . For we, who bring the Word of God, should not fight with fists. It is a spiritual quarrel, which is to take hearts and souls away from the devil." But as fast as Luther tried to squelch the uprisings, rioters by the thousands followed the new teachings.

Men like Thomas Müntzer, who appeared in Mühlhausen in

Thuringia on August 15, 1524, began preaching that existing social orders could be changed with the help of theological insight and by chopping at the roots of the present world. Spiritual as well as worldly opinions greatly diverged. This student of the Holy Scriptures, a former restless disciple of Martin Luther, now became not only the leader of his rebels but was also regarded as the father of the Anabaptists. Although he himself had not received baptism on confession of faith, he proclaimed in the manner of the Anabaptists that true Christians were able to receive the Spirit of God only through the experience of the cross and suffering. The oppressed, those living in spiritual and material poverty, the peasants and the poor, had experienced the cross and were thus already the Lord's chosen.

Müntzer was in contact with some who later became Anabaptist leaders, such as Hans Hut. The latter was like Müntzer in preaching apocalypticism, but he opposed the use of the sword. Conrad Grebel wrote a letter to Müntzer, responding to his tracts and reproaching him for emphasizing church liturgy and advocating the sword. There is no evidence that Müntzer received the letter. Most present-day Anabaptists prefer not to be associated with Müntzer. When he was decapitated on May 25, 1525, after the battle of Frankenhausen, a new signal was sent to the *Täuferjäger* (hunters of Anabaptists). In their minds, peasants and Anabaptists became interchangeable terms. They set out to squash any social and religious protest movement, whether peasants or Anabaptists. As a result, Anabaptists became a religious minority in flight from the world. The constant fear of persecution led to permanent readiness to flee and molded the thoughts and deeds of Anabaptists. From now on, such pressures from the world colored their understanding of Christian discipleship.

Some who became members of the new Anabaptist faith were or had been involved in the Peasants' War. But there is uncertainty about whether Anabaptists were part of the uprising of the rural people in the canton of Bern some hundred years later. It is obvious that the contemporary reports were from authors negatively inclined toward their teachings. The claim that the Anabaptists had "sucked their venom from Thomas Müntzer" is wrong. Nevertheless, the German philosopher and friend of Marx,

Friedrich Engels, later called the Anabaptists the "forerunners of the modern class struggles."

During the first decade or so of the Anabaptist movement, believers split between pacifists and militants. The Anabaptists in Münster, Westphalia, demonstrated a bloody and a brutal will to fashion the various groups into their ideal model. There an apparently spiritual introspectiveness and a communist experiment of sorts exploded into gruesome excesses of an apocalyptically insane rule. This terrible episode of German history led to disastrous results, a brutal religious intolerance toward other Anabaptists too.

In 1530, one year before Zwingli, the "blossom of Zurich," died in the battle of Kappel, the furrier Melchior Hofmann from Schwäbisch Hall became an Anabaptist at Strassburg. He eloquently called for renewal and gathered elements dissatisfied with the established church in northern Germany and the Netherlands. Preacher Hofmann was highly successful in his mission work and baptized some three hundred people in a few days in Emden. From there he went on to Amsterdam, where the first Anabaptists had just been beheaded and their corpses placed on stakes as a warning to the general public.

Melchior, a former Lutheran clergyman, now held rather untypical Lutheran views. He had strong faith in dreams and visions which served him as revelations. Hofmann believed also that a sinful Mary had not actually been capable of contributing to the essence of Jesus. The Son of God therefore was "in" but not "of" Mary. This opinion was shared for a long time by some Dutch and North German Anabaptists. Yet there were disagreements between Hofmann and the Swiss Brethren.

In 1533 Hofmann interpreted biblical prophecies to mean that a millennium of justice would begin in the immediate future, which would be "the last seven years of the world order." The "Anabaptist capital city of Strassburg" was to play an important role in the commencement of a new world order, and this was confirmed by certain prominent Anabaptist leaders. Strassburg was regarded as the coming Jerusalem which opposed Rome, the blasphemous Babylon. It was to be the city in "the last age of humanity," and there the godless were to be consumed and the kingdom of God erected. Hence in that city Hofmann voluntarily went to prison, which he considered a proper place from which to expect the arrival of the Lord. He had just written *Vom Schwert* (Regarding the sword), and now he spent time penning new ideas about old topics on bedsheets, since he had no writing paper.

Practically overnight Münster (in Westphalia, western Germany) replaced Strassburg as the crusade center for those following these prophecies. In the 1520s the powerful guilds of the city had afforded support for a developing reform movement. In 1532 Bernhard Rothmann had established Lutheranism in this bishop city of Münster. Hofmann's followers were also in the city, and its population began to increase dramatically, partly from new believers moving there and partly from mass baptisms. Suddenly Anabaptists enjoyed a majority in the city council. The archbishop had his back to the wall and soon undertook countermeasures.

The prophet Jan Matthijs from Haarlem, a baker by profession, led this attempt to introduce the final political order of salvation by revolutionary means. At his side was the tailor Jan Bockelson (Jan van Leiden), who had been baptized by Hofmann and felt called to be king of the Anabaptist kingdom. On February 9, 1534, these revolutionary Anabaptists took over city hall. Hofmann's disciples adopted a radical gospel and prepared for the new kingdom by murdering "the yeast of the godless," citizens who refused to be rebaptized. Münster became the refuge for the persecuted, the "New Jerusalem" of radical Anabaptism. Evangelists spread this good news.

More members of the new faith now streamed into the city. They introduced polygamy, following the example of Solomon and David, and this became a way for them to care for women who lost their husbands in battle. They also held all things in common while they were awaiting the end of the world. Then imperial Protestant and Catholic forces laid siege to the city and ended the "New Zion" on June 24, 1535, after one and a half years. The leaders of the Anabaptists were executed. This dark episode is symbolized by the cages still hanging from the tower of St. Lambert's church of Münster, the same cages that exhibited the bodies and bones of these religious revolutionaries who ran amok.

The pacifist Anabaptists objected to being grouped with these militant millennialists with both vigor and resignation. According to the chronicle of their *Martyrs Mirror*, they opposed this "eye for an eye, tooth for a tooth" ideology. They claimed they had the "innocence of doves, who fled from the claws of the hawk and the birds of prey to the clefts of the rocks and the hollows of trees, secretly and in hiding." But they could not rid themselves of the fallout from the excesses of this misadventure. Wherever they appeared, they were greeted in the name of the devil. The Münsterite kingdom, utterly in shambles, clung to them like leaden weights. Münster! This was to become the site and scene by which society, both Catholic and Protestant, capitalized on the tactics of the pseudo-Anabaptists. Thereby their enemies justified their own attacks upon even the pacifist Anabaptists.

One Menno Simons (Simonszoon, Simon's son), a Catholic priest from Friesland of the Netherlands, took a strong stand against the excesses of the Westphalian religious perverts and their orgies at Münster. This episode must be regarded as one of the strangest chapters of German history. While some historians claim Menno Simons was a partial accomplice in the debacle, objective records contradict this position. After the Münster catastrophe, Menno decided to renege on his priestly office and to join the pacifist Anabaptists. He soon came to be regarded as their most important leader in the Netherlands and the Low German area, in the north. Menno attempted to consolidate those of the new faith, cultivating an inner identity that would protect them from other political, spiritual, and theological forces. Although the old church still resisted reform, Menno thought the new church had not gone far enough in reform.

Menno Simons was born in Witmarsum (Friesland, Netherlands) around 1496, probably from peasant background, accounting for his rural sympathies with the Anabaptist lifestyle. He had been ordained as a Roman Catholic priest in Utrecht in 1524. Later he received a parsonage in Pingjum, close to the place of his birth. If one is to believe descriptions of his early life, Menno was disposed to card games and alcohol. Besieged by doubts regarding the Catholic church's interpretations, Menno began personal study of the Bible and soon discovered differences between the Scriptures and official church doctrine. In 1529 he was first suspected of being a follower of Luther.

Menno heard of Melchior Hofmann as well as the reports of

the early Anabaptists martyrs. He searched the Scriptures, the church fathers, and consulted with scholars. Finally he concluded that adult baptism was actually biblical, and infant baptism could not be justified on the basis of the New Testament. Like Grebel, he regarded infant baptism as superfluous, contrary to the Bible, invented by the pope, and similar to indulgences, the veneration of saints, and purgatory. Only a mature adult was capable of making a decision for Christ. Inner baptism saved the soul, for otherwise the kingdom of heaven would be bound to the element of water and the blood of Christ would have been spilled in vain. He was kept from converting only by the political militancy of some Anabaptists, such as the Melchiorites who in 1535 participated in the raid and later in the defense of the Oldeklooster (Old Cloister monastery) near Bolsward, Friesland.

In January 1536, in the midst of greatest danger to those confessing an Anabaptist faith, Menno, the educated doubter, secretly disappeared from his priestly charge and the community of the old church and was baptized, probably in Groningen. He was immediately on the run since a bounty was on his head—one hundred guilders, equal to a priest's annual salary. Menno now organized strictly pacifist Anabaptists in Oldenburgian East Friesland and in the area of today's Holland. In his teaching, he was theologically oriented to the Swiss Brethren and the Hutterites. Menno preached to the churches that those who sought God with all their heart and did not want to be cheated should not depend on man or on human teachings, no matter how old, holy, or significant they might be: "One theologian was against the other in the old world, and that has not changed in the new. Build only on Christ and his word, on the secure teachings of the holy apostles."

The priest had been transformed into a prophet, with what was later called *The Anabaptist Vision* (H. S. Bender). Menno taught that the community of believers constituted a brotherhood, and the essence of Christianity lay in discipleship. The ethic of love had to govern all human relationships. Anabaptists had to experience a transformation, which in turn found expression in a life of holiness and of love. They were to show love by distancing themselves from quarrels and atrocities. True Christians must have nothing to do with the sword of the world. "Spears and swords we leave to such who make no difference between the human blood and swine's blood."

Menno's vision projected a church of peace, certainly revolutionary in its time but probably the only way to overcome the debacle of Münster. He was convinced that a violent radical Reformation would lead to disaster. In 1554 while in Holstein, Menno wrote in his *Reply to Gellius Faber* that "our weapons are not weapons to devastate cities and states, to break walls and portals, and to spill human blood like water, but weapons by which to destroy the kingdom of the devil, the godlessness in the conscience of man, and to crush hearts, stone-hard, which have never been sprinkled by the heavenly dew of the Holy Word. We have and know no other weapons, God knows, even if we were to be blown to a thousand bits and though many false witnesses rise up against us, their numbers being like grass on the fields and sand by the sea."

Yet this strict moralist was sufficiently realistic not to deny the state the use of the sword to check evil persons and protect believers from the outer enemy. The church would deal with threats from within. This was in accord with the Articles of Schleitheim, 1527. All, including Christians, were subject to the state, and rulers were not to misuse their God-given authority. However, Menno strictly separated loyalty to the church from the state's power to maintain order. He charged his Anabaptists, in the old Waldensian tradition, not to take on any state office so they would not thereby come into violent conflict.

In spite of Menno's plea for peace, some strong differences soon became apparent among his followers. These Anabaptists did not always live up to the example and goal of the original Christian church to be "of one heart and one soul" (Acts 4:32). From the start, varying doctrines developed among those inclined to be enthusiasts or fanatics, seeking a social utopia. Serious differences of opinion surfaced because those of the new faith came from all levels of society and were variously influenced by the Christian humanism of Erasmus. So it was only natural that splits and revelations of divine orders would occur.

Trauma soon came to them from the institution of banning, that dreaded weapon of papal hands which the Anabaptists had retained. On the basis of Matthew 18, Menno demanded that believers admonish backslidden members three times and then, if they do not repent, avoid their company. He supported immediate expulsion of coarse offenders and defended avoidance of the banned one by the spouse, asking that Christian kindness be used in applying the latter rule. Some Dutch leaders were even more strict, demanding unconditional avoidance in marriage and application of the ban without prior warning. The Swiss Brethren held a milder use of the ban than Menno. Eventually contention over the ban led to a division among Swiss Anabaptists which produced the Amish—but that came 150 years later.

While no Luther or Zwingli, Menno Simons was a rediscoverer and preserver of the Christian faith and a towering father figure to the Anabaptists. In responding to his appeal for brotherly love, this much-persecuted movement was able to renew itself thoroughly in spite of all its inner quarrels. As a result Menno's followers were soon labeled *Menist, Mennisten,* or Mennonites. In 1545 the term first appears in a mandate of Countess Anna of East Friesland. Yet rather than be named after a man, the Dutch themselves preferred to be called *Doopsgezinde* (Baptism-minded; used by 1578 as the Dutch version of *Taufgesinnte*). The road was long and hard. Menno started with the existing Anabaptist church of the time and applied the goal of living the faith in freedom. In the view of historians, Menno gave "wise and vigorous leadership."

In the New World, the free-church idea of the Anabaptists, including the complete separation of church and state, was accepted in the political order some 150 years after the Confession of Schleitheim. However, in Europe at the time, there was but slow progress toward that same freedom of belief and conscience, preached by Grebel, Manz, and Menno. The Peace of Westphalia of 1648 made some feeble efforts to that end although it deliberately ignored the Anabaptist cause.

In Switzerland, as a result of the French Revolution (1789-1815), "every kind of worship" was eventually allowed. "In view of the fact that God and only God has the authority to judge the thoughts and ideas of humanity," the government destroyed all existing monuments to religious persecution. In the canton of Bern, the original home of the Amish of Allen County, the Anabaptists enjoyed a certain degree of religious freedom in the first half of the nineteenth century, after the decline of the old confederacy. However, it was to take until the latter half of the nineteenth century before the ostracized and barely tolerated Anabaptists were to receive citizen rights in their own home country. Not until

1874, when the Swiss federal constitution provided for religious freedom, were the Anabaptists able to lawfully assemble for worship.

In Germany, the Anabaptists had stood in glaring contrast to the individual states and their institutions. The unsettling events of the Thirty Years' War (1618-48) resulted in them still being rejected. In the eighteenth century, this gave way to quiet tolerance, then to recognition, and finally to equal status of citizenry.

As a benefit to the world, the original Anabaptist call for separation of church and state is now accepted doctrine in many countries of the world. Only in this way did the Anabaptist congregations manage to triumph over the counts' and lords' varying opinions on doctrines. Their faith followed the beliefs of their forebears and remained relatively intact. Among them are the Amish, who split off from the mainstream of the new believers toward the end of the seventeenth century. In time they emigrated to America, settled in groups, and maintained their faith and obedience to Christ.

The value of the Amish today does not lie simply in the way their ancestors were crying in the wilderness of sin, announcing the kingdom of God. Nor is their importance so much in their retention of old traditions and outer attire as it is in the way they daily pose the question, "What must I do to inherit eternal life?" (Mark 10:17). Their longing for a brighter future has remained, as has their fear of the pope. Morally, they still regard the world with a dual view: the land of the Amish belongs to the kingdom of light, and around them is the kingdom of darkness. In the long run, they believe that God's kingdom of light will prevail. Today, however, their greatest concern is maintaining their faithfulness.

3

Secrets of a Simple Life

During their working years, the Amish swarm out in the morning like bees in spring. They scurry between chicken and pig sties, milkhouse and barn, and individually or in chorus, call the cattle from the meadow, enticing the bovines to their stanchions with fodder. All the world seems to be up and moving between five and six in the mornings. Only the slightly more colorful attire of the women stand out in the grayness of early light. Their "*Kumm, Bas, kumm, Bas, kumm* (come)," the call for Basie, Cindy, or Susie (cows), is part of the break of day on every farm and comes with the same beat as the call of the come-and-get-it bell in the house. It is the same at Tobi and Naomi's, Ruth and Joseph's, David and Barbara's, as with all the Amish on Cuba Road, which opens onto sideroads and lanes. They react to the first light of day, whether in joy or in sorrow, as part of nature and togetherness. There seems to be nothing more enjoyable for the Amish than to get up at five o'clock and milk cows.

Elam's farm, proof of parental love and private capital, lies a short distance beyond the outskirts of Grabill village. It is sufficient distance from town to isolate itself and yet near enough to be accessible for anyone buggying along Cuba Road to turn off and then pass the little side garden with simple flower beds and a mowed lawn. Here are many flowers which no one on the farm can identify by name. They do not worry about this, since what matters is that whatever grows and flourishes is to the honor of God and his creation and to the great joy and delight of Rachel. It is surprising that the Grabers grow roses when many other Amish think they are a bit showy.

Farms such as these certainly have the charm of cultivation, of being well-tended, even though they basically lack the artistic, rustic touch common to European farm dwellings. Living quarters and the buildings—barn, stable, buggy and wagon sheds—are separated by well-manicured lawns carefully laid out. Some slightly rusted machinery sits around, and a few windswept trees survive here or there on the periphery of the farmyard. From the perspective of the house, one's view is caught either by the flapping laundry on the washline or by the odd clump of willows, and behind and around them, stretches of open space. In a westerly direction one sees hay loaders, side-delivery rakes, disks, and mowers, and then the landscape extends all the way to the world, namely Grabill.

The immediate neighbors are all Amish. All around, the eye is greeted by domesticated vegetation, checkerboard-plot style, while in between are a few strips of plowed soil, turned over by competent Anabaptists to lie low, awaiting further tillage. The soil is good with a light sheen to it, what the farmer in Indiana calls "blackjack." House and barn, outhouse and sheds, interior walls as well as ceilings—everything is painted white, a reflection of the humility of the owners. Generally speaking, all Amish farmyards in Allen County, with the exception of a few brick structures, are painted white. This is different from the farms of the Amish in Pennsylvania, who frequently paint their farm buildings red. But the Grabill populace totally rejects the use of red since it represents the "rose-colored and precious blood" (Ammann's words) which Jesus shed for sinful humanity.

The Amish home is the refuge of the family for a totally pious life. It is a haven of security, certainly much more so than is the case for the worldly. They make do without Picasso's paintings, Tchaikovsky's *Fifth Symphony,* a detective movie on TV in the evening, or a shower in the morning, to say nothing of radios or telephones. In addition, they do without *Blitzstangen* (lightning rods), prohibited in these Amish parts. Their dwellings are meant purely for practical purposes, without decorations. As far as architecture is concerned, all it is expected to do is to remain erect and upright and live up to the rule, "One shall not have ostentatious houses and especially not houses painted with various colors or filled with beautiful furnishings."

An Amish house has to be of sufficient size so that, when Elam and Rachel's turn comes, they can accommodate the church service with a simple concluding *Liebesmahl* (love meal), not a feast. The Amish are quite capable of giving their dwellings a unique little touch. Outsiders who come to visit certainly do not gain the impression that the Amish, for all their sober ways, sit around living from day to day on only a temporary basis. The Graber's furnishings are much advanced from the time in Europe or that earlier stage when everything undertaken was done with an apocalyptic view toward a near end. Their house contains rocking chairs and commodes, tables, beds, floor clocks, two mighty ovens, a refrigerator functioning with blocks of ice, kerosene lamps, sewing machines, sofas, and even a few receiving pots, juice targets for Elam's chewing tobacco. Around and between is a liberal offering of childrens' toys and the well-ordered confusion that reflects the influence of the New World.

Rachel is a collector of painted plates, Elam gathers time in the form of pocket watches, and everyone collects postcards, which may be hung on the wall and give the living quarters a hint of color. The center of the house is the huge kitchen in which most indoor activity transpires, particularly in winter when much of life is played out in its cozy warmth. A small addition to the house serves as a summer kitchen.

In the warm seasons, a day on Elam's eighty-acre farm starts immediately after the first crow of the morning cock. At five in the morning, the world in Allen County is still in order, with the exception perhaps of a sow needing help with its offspring, or a raccoon having munched on the drumsticks of a pair of hens. Everyone of Amish persuasion is now at work while the world out there is still asleep. Elam starts the permitted diesel engine to pump water for the animals. Dogs have come into fashion on Amish farms of late and introduce the new day with a good deal of yelping.

The young Grabers tap around with bare feet even before the

dew of the morning has evaporated. They head straight for the *Kackhisli* (outhouse), the natural air-conditioned outdoor toilet. Elam has fashioned a series of various-sized oval holes in the board of the toilet so that everyone, according to size and shape, can enjoy a safe seat. Luxury is far afield, I am told. Little tykes respect their personal places in the order of things or risk falling through a large hole. The *Kackhisli*, for all its simple logic, presents some potential for pitfalls and danger. Recently an Amish painter and his unsuspecting son learned a painful object lesson. The father cleaned his paintbrush with gasoline, then poured the flammable substance into the toilet. Minutes later, his son smoked a *verbotene* (forbidden) cigarette in privacy. When he flicked the burning match into the realm below, there was a greater-than-expected explosion. Toilet and occupant collapsed into the miry ditch, but not before injury was inflicted on the seat of the sorry sinner.

It is one thing to speak about the Bible; it is another to live its message. The very institution of the outdoor toilet is for the worldly a total departure from the world, a departure, as it were, from an element of self. "Do not cling to things of this world," exhorts Paul in the book of Romans (12:2). If one intends to follow this passage as thoroughly as the Amish do, it means to begin thus in the early morning. For Elam and Rachel, anything else is part of the terrible indulgences of the world. Installing a modern toilet in the house would mean to "live like a king." Since their style of life tolerates nothing of a higher worldly order, water closets have no place in the daily battle between the civilization of today and the culture of yesterday.

The routine of the morning moves from the outhouse back to the house and straight to the hand-operated water pump. The ritual demands some manual dexterity to pump with one hand and wash with the other. In the Graber household, this is the practice of everyday life. No problem here. Always and ever the same routine and the same rhythm. Let the world around them go its way, with all its marches on, marches off, marches for, marches through, fall of dollar, fall of the Berlin wall, Chernobyl fallout, algae-death, acid rain. . . . None of the above does much to disturb the Amish, and nothing pleases the farmer in them more than to observe *"wie's Gwächs hüt schteht* (how the crop looks today)," growing toward the first alfalfa cut in June, grain harvest in July, hauling of straw in August, or corn and potato harvest in September.

For my host family, the undisputed master of the house, as I quickly came to recognize, is the dry-humored and intelligent Elam J. Graber. He is thirty-seven years of age and therefore young enough for the twenty-first century. Elam reminds one of the first-born son of Shem (Gen. 10:22), while the J. stands for Jacob, the name of his father. It is common for the Amish to insert the initial from the father's or mother's name into one's own name. For one thing, such definition makes things handier for the mail carrier. On this part of Cuba Road, almost everyone is called Graber, and these Amish even have no great reservoir of names at their disposal for the first or Christian name.

Elam owns, in addition to forty horses, so many cows in the pasture—"the Lord in heaven be praised and honored for such blessings"—that he could have worn, as an extension to his broad-fall pants, boots in the style of a real cowboy. In economic terms, he is part of the American middle class. But torn between creation and profit, the Amish as "modest folk" do not think highly of such class divisions. When it comes to finances, what is important is this: "Everything has to be in order" (1 Cor. 14:40).

Rachel, the robust woman of the house, moves self-confidently alongside Elam in the traditional role of her gender. She is up to any job or chore, whether in the kitchen or in the stable, and is an expert at wielding a flyswatter. Over and above these duties, she manages a little shoe store in the farmhouse basement. Chris (Christian), the oldest son of the family, got his name for having been born on December 24. He is at work on some bridles in his own bridle shop, opposite the barn. Ben and Barbara Ann are still at school. Sister Rachel is just short of school age.

The Grabers' real assets romp in the old grayish stalls of the barn or in the meadows. A short look around reveals a milk cow producing 3,075 gallons a year, 160-day-old pigs ready for market, calves, young steers, poultry, and also, of course, horses. These are light, handy trotters, setting a speedy pace. They are the engines for the "automobiles" of these people. The mares are worth approximately $1,300, and a gelding fetches $800. The heavy draft horses serve as four-legged tractors in the fields and vary greatly in value. Elam's greatest joy in his entire collection is a gigantic registered Belgian named Constable, with a beautiful head and well proportioned. He tips the scales at 2,000 pounds, which is no exception, and is worth some $20,000 in cash. Elam has even managed to sell one of Constable's daughters, an "All American Show Filly," for $11,000.

The horses of Allen County have increased in cash value for the simple reason that the inhabitants of Quebec in Canada like to eat horse meat. Slaughterhouses compete with the Amish when it comes to a trotter or pacer ready to be pensioned off. Such an animal will either land in a stew kettle or will pull a lowly hay rake during his last year or two. However, there is no guarantee that Nancy or Elsie or Champ or Christa, or whatever other names the horses answer to, will not be shipped off to Quebec for human consumption some day. If a retired horse is too tough for gastronomical purposes, it may well end up as dog food or as fertilizer. At fifteen, sometimes seventeen, or even twenty years of age, the most willing Amish horse will one day walk its last slow mile to the slaughterhouse. When a horse has done its share or when it devours more than it earns, its time has come to go and to be transformed into cash. When it comes to a buck, the Amish are careful calculators.

Back to the business of feeding. Elam's horses were doing poorly compared to his cows in terms of eating and production. An average cow produces approximately a hundred pounds of milk daily but consumes only half as much fodder as a horse. Moreover, a draft horse had to be fed in the slack time from October till April. A trotter or pacer is generally at work year-round, but a draft horse just stands around, eating and producing only manure while waiting for the work of spring. The Amish keep careful records on the productivity of every animal on the farm. If an animal produces only red figures, it is written off. In such cases, the Grabers apply the motto "A lame horse is better dead."

The same holds true of a fence-jumper, a horse which chronically jumps fences and is reluctant to be domesticated. After all, it was the Lord himself who instructed the Anabaptists to hold dominion over the animal world (Gen. 1:28). Total dominion! Thus one rarely if ever finds a spoiled or stubborn horse pulling an Amish buggy, or one that kicks or bites, or is in need of the whip. Before others have a chance to criticize such behavior, the owner has already noticed and retrained the animal or disposed of it.

The soil around the Graber house has been biblically fertilized by the sweat of the brow as the Amish earn their bread (Gen. 3:19). That is reason enough for such farms never to serve as a refuge for someone who bails out from the mainstream of life. There is no room for loafers of any description. Anyone reluctant to produce a lot of sweat is not welcome in these parts. Elam, Rachel, Chris, and Ben had achieved more by nine in the morning than most worldly people do in a whole day. They labored with brawn and brain in fine accord, as shown in the milkhouse or the barns, in the stalls or the shops. Here human potential is valued and realized; "out there," technology has for long blocked such fulfillment.

Elam divided up the farmwork to its last detail. Everyone had a part, and toil and sweat united the members of each family. Amish life is family life, with healthy discipline. A family that works together, stays together: that is the unshakable premise of the Amish. It is good for the daughter to milk with her mother; it is good for the son to plow with his father. "Standing water easily rots things" is an argument against laziness. Such adages give them persuasive and practical reasons not to lighten heavy and monotonous work. This bond of labor helps to make the family a dependable unit and to tie together the extended family. It is so strong that Amish who work outside their community miss that cooperative support.

The youngest, Barbara Ann, and the little ball of fire Rachel Mae, for example, feed the chickens and then go hunting for eggs on quick little feet, trained early for every job. Barbara Ann assists in stable work and also helps Rachel with domestic chores. The boys share the responsibility of practically all duties and chores in the stable and in the field since the multitalented Elam temporarily works as a carpenter "in the world." In earlier times this would have led to shunning, but today such employment outside represents the reserve bank of the family, funding larger expenditures. In any case, the family considers this job to be temporary. Every true Amish knows what Jesus meant when he said that "the field is the world," with a mixture of weeds and grain (Matt. 13:38).

The farm, the harness shop, and Rachel's shoe store together realize a substantial income with which, according to the head of the house, a six-member family can readily make do. However, Amish parents ought not to think first about themselves but about their children. One day they will need their own land to raise their own families in a Christian way, and for that the greenbacks realized from an eighty-acre farm were simply insufficient.

As others meander through an art gallery, Elam and his boys and I walk through the barn and then the stable by the light of early morning. Slowly we progress, orienting ourselves to new objects which obviously need to be explained to me. Then and there I receive the first lesson of a farmer's workday. A horse must have "style" shown by its form, posture, and gait. You can be sure that the horse with highest style is hitched up by the master of the house. Horses scratching their tails suffer from worms, which are regularly treated with Dichlorvos Horse Wormer or Wonder Wormer. A registered Belgian has to have its tail cropped. Mares generally give birth to colts between four and six in the morning. The birth of a colt may take a minute or so, but can take longer. If complications of birthing arise, Elam administers a relaxing "sleeping shot" to the mare.

The dung of a horse should preferably be dry, golden yellow or resembling olive-green. It has to be of a pleasant smell or there is something seriously wrong with the horse. Then I receive lessons regarding croup, the gutters, weaning, whip training, and breeding stallions. I am informed about artificial insemination, standard practice on worldly farms, but rejected by the Amish of Allen County although they realize its advantages full well. The refrigerated sperm of a breeding stallion can be used to fertilize numerous mares; it is easily transportable and keeps for long periods of time. The "outside" has an edge over the Amish in this respect, but artificial insemination would mean standing on an equal footing with the world and doing things contrary to God's intentions.

A horse has no soul, I am told. It will not enter into the kingdom of heaven. Hence a horse does not really care whether it is alive or dead. Intelligence? Yes, it has intelligence. Elam, cleanly shaved but for the beard, talks to each of his animals with "ho whoa hoooo, hoo, ho, whoa ho," which is clearly understood. You simply have to talk with horses, cows, and even sows this way. If you don't talk to animals, you're afraid of them. Well, and come to think of it, with a horse as with a cow, the rear quarters need to be strong and healthy. "You have horses like these in Germany?"

The Grabers have problems with one of their trotters, which suffers from psychic disturbances. It had been mistreated by the previous owner, a worldly man. It bucked, reared, and blew dust out of its nostrils. A horse owner from a city would have given up on it. Chris, however, even in his youth has capable training skill and treats the horse with great patience. He enters into its personality, a horseman who knows the horses of man. It would take a few weeks to successfully treat the animal and make it fit for the Amish buggy.

Now to the *Morgeesse* or *Esse zmorge* (breakfast). One cannot help but follow the pronounced aroma right into the summer kitchen. Rachel, Barbara Ann, Ben, and Rachel Mae all wear pale blue dresses. Elam's pants are only a shade darker. Those of feminine gender wear their hair under artfully folded, snow-white caps, even in early mornings. Amish women wear their hair-covering caps much like conservative Jewish women wear wigs. All of the Amish men of conservative leanings think alike in such matters, and they agree with the rules of tradition. They base concealing of women's hair on a biblical passage (1 Cor. 11:1-16) about "covering a woman's glory," referring to attractive feminine features. Nothing at all is to be openly displayed since it is decreed that a man is the glory of God, the woman is the glory of the man, and in turn hair is the glory of the woman.

Yet these folks also do not overlook the sexual attraction of hair. It is that which shall not be compared or rendered comparable by man. Only a husband is allowed to see his wife without her cap, and this ordinance lasts throughout life. For all others, it is ordained that the cap cut from organdy is to be stiffly set in place on the hair of the woman. And to remain in place. If the material gets flimsy, it has to be replaced in good time. Caps and bonnets, the honor of a man and of these women, are characteristics of which the worldly take little note to this day. "To this day . . . ," according to Preacher Joseph. But the good Lord, whose plans are of longer duration, punishes the world with the poisonous rays of the sun through the ozone hole. Sooner or later the *Englischers* (non-Amish) out there will have to compromise and wear protective caps and bonnets just like in Allen County where hair coverings are as institutionalized as long skirts or dresses.

Before us is a spread of culinary offerings, an eater's delight, cholesterol blockbusters. Peppered meat balls in warm milk particularly appeal to my eyes, then to my belly. There is sweet onioned salad also in milk, pancakes, homemade bread, salt biscuits, jam preserves, summer sausage, cracklings, eggs, and much fresh well water or thin coffee. Of course, there is pie, à la Amish, an improved variation of the American recipe. There are apple, cherry, rhubarb, vanilla, or raisin pies. Rachel makes a science of the art of pie baking and invests many hours in it.

This breakfast, at which a strict seating order is observed, is certainly more than a solid meal with a wide offering of dainties, treats, and tidbits. The Amish are no culinary chauvinists and have never been. Anyone equipped with a solid German stomach like Elam's, can pretty well digest anything. All the while the woman of the house, highly interested, asks all sorts of questions as to whether in Germany they have meat balls in milk or this kind of jam or that kind of food or the other. The *Englischers*—small wonder—know nothing of such things. And the Germans? She had heard that they change their menus from time to time.

"*Wann der Disch vull isch, woll mer bäte* (when the table is full, we'll say grace)." The children pray in chronological order to the accompaniment of the buzzing flies, the distant background snorting and spitting of the diesel engine, and the faint thud-thud-thud rhythm of a passing trotter on Cuba Road. First comes Chris, who at age fifteen is the oldest, "All eyes appeal to Thee, oh Lord." Then it's Benjamin's turn, barely fourteen, who recites the Lord's Prayer in German, by far the most common prayer spoken in an Amish house. Since this prayer comes directly from the Lord, they regard it as particularly suitable to remove the lust of the world from the faithful and their children. Finally it's the turn of the two little ones, six and nine years old, and as always, in comely dress: "Give food, O God, give drink, O God, for children small, on earth, to all. Amen."

The Amish are surprisingly sensitive when the situation warrants it. Rachel, for instance, spreads her slice of bread with copious amounts of butter and even more jam before dunking the whole goody deeply into a cup of coffee. While doing so, she asks me once, then once again, if her little culinary ritual does not offend me. Her attitude, I came to believe, was typical. Dunking jam in coffee is her right, yet a guest is a guest even if from the outside world. Rachel shows her good manners in other things as well: "Eat garlic. You haven't got a bed partner around here anyway!"

During breakfast lively conversations ensue. First they try to communicate, as usual, with their *Schwizerschwätze* (Swiss chatter) and then switch to Bible German to accommodate me. If the conversation gradually grinds to a stop, they opt for a bit of English. There are some terms for which the Amish simply have no equivalent in their dialect, and even Luther was as ignorant of them as were the Amish forebears. They all speak in an uncomplicated fashion and exchange familial-confidential comments generally at the expense of niceties or courtesies, similar to the peasants of Old Europe. "Thank you" or "please" are rarely heard here. . . . They simply expect that one or the other will do this or that or whatever is commonly expected of them. For that, you neither thank anyone, nor are you expected to request it.

In their conversations, the Amish pursue a different course from the worldly. They talk about fruit but not about toxins. Rain is discussed without acids and the side-effects known from chemistry. A tree is not a tree in the midst of a dying forest in an abused environment. However, when the conversation turns to the fall of the Berlin wall, they immediately draw parallels to the walls of Jericho. Elam's world champion cow, which has produced a whole pailful of milk, is next on the agenda. A sick calf has to wait its conversational turn, or a rat which Chris shot with his air rifle. Finally talk turns to a trotter which took off in heavy traffic, made its way home without reins, was ripped in the escapade, and arrived without the driver, who had jumped from the buckboard, clear of impending danger. At opportune moments Elam throws in a "thus says the Lord."

Once in a while the master of the house heads for the window when a particularly fine horse is passing by, or one he is not acquainted with. They also ask whether the Germans use mares' urine to cure colds or cow manure to heal a wounded leg. It's the same old thing: anything that tastes or smells bad is healthy. Also, they want to know whether the Germans believe in witches and if I believe they exist or not.

As an outsider from the world, and also in my capacity as

"doctor of writing," they regarded me as an authority in all kinds of things and also in matters a shade risky for them. Rachel's talk, a little muffled from her generous intake of salad, repeatedly assured me that no one around Grabill believed in witches anymore. Well, almost no one. However, there were still things happening for which the Amish simply had no adequate explanation. A bewitched horse remains a bewitched horse, whether you believed it or not. Therefore, some folks tried to provide security by fastening knives or brooms to the house doors to scare away witches. Miracles and wonders happen practically everyday in the world of the Amish of Allen County.

On this matter the brothers and sisters before me and around me remembered well the Swiss Emmental (Emme valley) of their forebears, which was full of spooks and legends, be they beeches planted by the devil's hand or the dastardly effects of the black spider. However, the Lord above saw to it that all evil here was kept in check. On this subject, I was told about Eli Lengacher from the "Amish Kraft Co." just around the corner, who recently had intended to dismantle the old workshop on his farm property and construct a new one. Exactly five days after the family circle had reached a decision to do that, the workshop burned down. "The good Lord heard it" was the general opinion going around. Again God had demonstrated his competency in all matters far and wide, big and small.

Elam had another particular interest. He wanted a precise answer as to which of the Israelite tribes was the original ancestor of people like him or Germans in general. Noah, Shem, the physical seed of Abraham, Isaac, Jacob—all are now on the agenda of discussion. Elam wanted me to locate a definitive biological source and home for the Germans and thus for the Amish.

Another little matter called for possible clarification. For three days now, a wonderfully beautiful bird had constantly been knocking on the kitchen window of Rachel's sister Barbara (Nolt). Surely there was some significance to this, or, come to think of it, possibly not.

There was one topic which they rarely picked up. They were not to speak badly about others and certainly not in a slanderous way. That, according to Matthew 5:21-22, could make the speaker, even a holy person, a "murderer of people." Not in vain did the apostle James warn against the fire of the tongue (James 3). Elam and Rachel knew that one day they would be held accountable for every unnecessary word they said. Anyone who speaks negatively about a brother or a sister assumes a judgmental stance and places oneself on the throne of God. Such positions are definitely off-limits to all Amish. A neighbor who regularly hitches a much-too-small horse before a much-too-big wagon has a "bug in his bean." That's all the commentary necessary. A worldly outsider might say, "That guy's crazy."

*****

Protective crupper under the tail, collars around the neck, breast straps between the forelegs: at an age when an average urchin is up to this or that, but generally up to no good, an Amish boy works twelve to fourteen hours on the farm for the family. Chris is no exception as he sprays Champ with mosquito repellent in the barn. Then he slips the freshly oiled harness over the horse and fastens the reins to the bridle. Race horses on the track come equipped with check reins to prevent them from lowering their heads but are not approved here. Champ is a former competitive trotter retired early, as often the case with race horses. He was no longer fit for the speedy sulky since he injured a leg while rounding a curve. His race training made him ideally suited for the buggy. Elam, a cunning farmer all the way and a man who knows his horses, could not easily be bettered in any deal, particularly at auctions.

Then we wind our way out to Cuba Road in an open-to-the-sun buggy, black as night, all four of us, cozily Amish, two in front and a couple in the back and as close together as if we were guarding a secret. Chris, in front on the right, is the horseman, and the two girls with pleated black bonnets above their white caps and I enjoy the exhilaration of a buggy ride. We are not about to be bothered by some young rascals who attempt to disturb the rhythm of our trotter by loudly honking the horn of their lead-gray Chevy at the crossroad to Grabill. "Yankees!" Chris mutters disparagingly: Yankees, who don't know what they're doing. When the Amish hitch up to take a buggy trip through the world, outside rovers are as difficult to keep away as the morning from a rooster.

At a traveling speed of some eight to ten miles an hour, we pass the lead-gray Chevy and travel on through buggy country par excellence. Around Grabill there are no hills to serve as topographic hindrances, just a few knolls. They pose no problem for a trotter, those tough fellows that stand in the barns of the Grabers, Zehrs, Lengachers, or Schmuckers, next to the Swiss alpine cattle. There is nothing to prevent this trotter from easily mastering a good twenty miles without a stop. In Allen County, so says Chris with a subdued grin, you have "fast horses and beautiful women," in contrast to Lancaster County of Pennsylvania, where he claims that the opposite holds true. Or in contrast to the Amish country of Ohio, where a horse has to be a mountain climber to survive.

As for the women, everyone has to arrive at his own opinion, Chris allows. It is a fact, nonetheless, that if one searches far and wide throughout the world, one encounters the most beautiful smiles on Amish farms. There was good reason for Joseph's warnings that the *Englischers* were after the Amish girls like the devil after a poor soul.

As far as the horses are concerned, these racers had absolutely nothing in common with *Hüjaho*, the old white horse of my boyhood memories. These horses reputedly are the fastest of the fast Amish trotters in North America, as long as you don't discuss the matter with the brothers of Lancaster County. There was no obvious single proof as to which of the Anabaptist stables house the fastest or the most durable trotters. If you challenge him, Elam's King will easily lay back nine miles in thirty minutes flat. The Grabers are capable of making the sixty-five miles to visit a cousin in the LaGrange area in about four and one half hours, a feat of which they have every reason to be proud—if only the Amish were allowed to be proud.

In addition, the brothers and sisters hold horsemanship in high regard. They seldom correct their horses with a whip, and some churches forbid the presence of an erect whip on a buggy, resembling the antenna of an automobile. Amish train their horses in the privacy of their homesteads, not on a public road. A whip serves the purpose of reminding the horse that there is an authority behind him and that this party makes decisions in case of doubt. The Amish allow a horse to reveal its natural temperament. Therefore, the Amish trotter or pacer is much more a partner to his master or mistress than a slave. A poor horseman is recognized by the wear on the grip of his whip.

The fast trotter of the Grabers was matched by a fast buggy. The roller bearings for a fleeter buggy, strikingly similar to those used in the automobile industry, were developed by Elam's father, Jacob, a man for all seasons, like his son. This is an invention the Amish did not oppose. Buggies mounted on Graber's roller-bearing wheels are used everywhere in Amish counties, and indeed, all around the world. Jacob was the legal inventor of the roller-bearing buggy wheel, but the worldly—so Elam claimed—simply stole the idea from his father. Since for religious reasons the Amish do not engage in litigation, no lawsuit was ever filed.

A person seated in an Amish buggy behind one-horse power is a traffic participant taken seriously on the roads of Indiana. This comes by way of a license which Elam purchases once a year for sixteen dollars. Anyone who ignores or disobeys the prevailing traffic laws is subject to tickets issued by the police. However, the preachers of the congregations are still not quite clear as to whether the stop sign at the Grabill railway track applies to Amish drivers or not. According to their logic, traffic signs exist for the ungodly car and do not apply to horses. If all the world would make do with one or two horsepower, one could easily get along without these signs. Some Amish buggy operators have run afoul of the law and have made international headlines with their tactics. However, the Amish of Allen County do not at all enter into disputes with worldly authorities.

The license fee does not mean the Amish are insured in case of theft or accident. To them, accepting insurance is like taking one's own life or the life of the family, thus one's own future, out of God's hands and entrusting it to a human being, a worldly institution. Joseph, a servant of the Word (preacher) and one who should know, states it like this: "Anyone who has insurance believes that something bad can happen to him. And that is equivalent to mistrusting God's power." Whenever an Amish party is involved in a traffic accident and found guilty, the entire congregation invariably assists and helps pay the fine or settlement. This principle is also in effect in other matters. If a building, likewise uninsured, burns down on the yard, the Amish Assistance Committee, a central committee of church districts, guarantees 80 percent of the value of the replacement building. In practical terms this means that each family of a particular geographic area will donate about forty dollars to help a family that has lost a building.

In general, the state shows greater concern for its Amish citizens than the Amish do for the state. If you accept nothing from the state, you also owe it nothing. Where the Amish live, one can often see road warnings about horse-drawn transportation. These signs with a horse and carriage painted on them alert other drivers to exercise caution. In all U.S. states where Amish live, the law requires their road vehicles to be clearly marked for visibility. This has led to serious problems for some of the Amish who prefer to remain invisible, even in street traffic.

Formerly in Indiana, these brothers and sisters were required to display a red flag attached to a stick whenever they traveled on public roads. Today they must affix a red and white reflective warning triangle to the back of the buggy. This innovation was reason enough for a number of conservative Anabaptists to go to prison since they regarded this triangle sign as too worldly and ostentatious. There are still some farmers in Allen County who fasten this slow-moving-vehicle sign to the back of their buggy only when they leave their farmyard and enter worldly territory, enemy territory. On their own farm, the gaudy sign is strictly rejected. Generally speaking, the state has already caught up and even passed the Amish and their vehicles in some parts of the country. For example, in some Amish-inhabited areas, there are separate parking lots for buggies and cars as well as parking meters for horse-drawn vehicles, which the bearded men have to feed when they go shopping.

The Amish would be no real Amish if they had not developed certain rules for certain churches regarding their means of transport. Like the beard, the buggy is one of those time-honored institutions without which they would be unable to provoke the world. The one-horse carriage is an exact indicator by which one can clearly determine how religiously conservative a group is today, to which immigration period it belongs, and in which area they live. Especially because the rules for the one-horse carriage cannot be biblically proved, disputes about them often led to schisms for families and entire church districts.

Back in the days when a buggy in America was an item of luxury, some well-off ordinary people made the transition from a horse or a donkey to a buckboard. But the Amish preferred to walk or to sit in a saddle. Around 1800 when one Amishman by the name of Christian Zimmerman simply became too heavy to ride a horse, he was allowed to purchase a one-horse carriage. The beginning of the Amish buggy was therefore an act of compassion toward one of God's creatures. Even today, considering all the divisions among them, many Amish believe it would have been better if that Christian had reduced his waistline or walked on foot, rather than putting existing custom to such a severe test.

The outer rim of the buggy wheels has remained a particularly heated item of contention among the Amish. Whether to have steel or rubber lining the hickory wood was a question leading to long and heated debate in many churches. There are Amish church districts which, in the course of time, have come to prefer rubber to steel. This seems incomprehensible to those of Allen County. "Rubber destroys the peace," so Joseph describes the problem in his own words. In worldly terms, he means that in a church one finds conservative members who believe the rubber-rimmed buggy wheels of the ruthlessly modern Amish are simply not pleasing to God, while steel on wood is pleasing in his sight. Progress at great risk!

The "moderns" prefer rubber for a softer ride; for others, this represents a departure from a tried-and-proved way of life. Both factions know that rubber is superior, that it is easier on the buggy wheel and the passengers. Yet, in this area, *improvement* is not sufficient reason for change. If no mutually acceptable compromise can be reached in the matter, the issue is officially presented to the entire congregation. When some members announce that rubber is grounds for a schism, the congregation agrees to retain the old ways, with steel rims. Peace within their community is the highest order of these radical Anabaptists.

Humans, according to a standard rule, are not to play Creator. This implies that they ought not to introduce new creations. Peace has been retained, and the "old" has demonstrated that it will not permit change without struggle. It is important to the Amish that they not continue their quarrel regarding the issue of rubber. If they cannot make peace with each other now, they might not make it into heaven when their time on earth expires. The earmark that continues to distinguish the true Amish community is its effort further to apply a relevant word of Christ, to "have love for one another" (John 13:35). The Amish are on their earthly sojourn for one reason only, to live for God and be ready for heaven.

All this does not mean that the discussion regarding the buggy has ended after the decision favoring steel rims. There is still much time and space to argue such other matters as buggy springs, backrests for the driver and passengers, fenders, hydraulic brakes, gas or oil lamps, high- and low-beam battery-powered lighting, or a generator for the rear wheels to charge the battery. May the chassis have a box, a window in the box or even two, and if so, what size window? May the buggy have a roof, and if so, what color? Should the corners be rounded off or not...?

As a result of all such deliberations, one sees pitch-black carriages in Holmes County, Ohio, brown-yellow ones around New Wilmington, Pennsylvania, and yellow ones just a few miles distant. Also there are brown carriages with white tops around Belleville, Pennsylvania. They are used by the so-called Nebraska Amish, who can be recognized by their cocoa-colored pants and white shirts instead of the darker attire of other Amish.

Immediately after folding buggy tops were introduced around 1870, they became the object of considerable internal arguments with opposing views based on theological considerations. The concern was not so much about folding tops as against things modern. Amish like the Grabill people did not come to America until the nineteenth century, after their churches had time to develop other traditions while still in Europe. Such Amish to this day have retained open one-horse carriages, the so-called *Schwyzer* (Swiss) buggies. Elam's church makes only one exception to the rule, for the period right after a baby is born. During this time, parents may temporarily use the "baby buggy," which has a roofed backseat for mother and small children. However, they strictly adhere to the rule that the driver and other adult companions have to sit on the front seat, open to the sky.

The Amish have taken many measures to oppose what they understand to be luxury. As a result, today there are some one hundred various styles of Amish carriages. Each of the different church groups holds to their version as a good and congregationally processed application of their faith. Most of the buggies in their basic form resemble the one-horse American carriage of the nineteenth century. The "Cadillacs" of the Amish buggies are probably the carriages of Lancaster County (Pa.). They are mainly of pearl-gray construction, feature a carlike dashboard, and come with a foot brake. Their battery-operated flashing lights at night on the streets of Intercourse or New Holland remind one of police cars in action.

Why do the Amish still prefer to use the disputed carriage instead of the disputed automobile? The folks of Allen County do not at all believe that automobiles are completely of the devil. As far as they are concerned, the car is simply not good for them. There are convincing reasons to bolster the case against the automobile. Joseph is persuaded that cars are from the world of luxury governed by technology. They dissolve family bonds and make it easy for drinkers to get to watering holes. The car shortens the road from home to the temptations of the city. The real Amish do not belong in the city but on their own farms.

Cars also introduce problems for the church district. Amish live in close proximity to each other, thereby enabling them to conduct their church services in their own homes or in a barn during the summer. Thus they find it quite manageable to attend the place of worship by horse-drawn carriages. If they introduced cars, they then would tend to live farther apart and would have to cover longer distances. Their togetherness would suffer since "pieces of flaming wood when separated tend to cease burning sooner." Togetherness is everything to them. If you separate Amish farms too much from each other, the families would have serious feelings of isolation and loneliness. Furthermore, cars and telephones make committing adultery easier. In America, so many marriages break apart because of the ease of phoning and driving, getting out of the sight of brothers and sisters who encourage faithfulness.

Based on all of these considerations, the old preacher arrives at his conclusion: problems become bigger in direct proportion to the pace of life, which is increased with a car, a speedy means of transport. In addition, a car symbolizes the pride of its owner. It gives him might and power behind the wheel, in public, at the very place where the sign of humility ought to be displayed. Not least of all, the car sharply increases one's contradiction to the living Jesus, who in the Gospel stories only rode once and that on a donkey. If he were to return, he would reject the technical-industrial fatalism of this world. Granted, the Amish make use of the worldly, modern streets, but did not Paul, too, walk on the heathen Roman roads without incurring sin?

This does not mean that all Amish think or thought like Joseph. Among them are groups such as the Beachy Amish, who have been using the automobile since 1927, although they may paint chrome parts black, which in turn is termed humility. Furthermore, some in the USA have pondered a proposal to build a car especially for the Amish, a vehicle devoid of any luxury. However, this project has never been discussed through to a conclusion; its time has not yet come.

The rejection of cars by the Amish has never gone so far that they themselves would not use public means of transportation under any circumstances. For instance, it is thoroughly acceptable for them to travel by bus, possibly "because it cannot fly." There no doubt are other reasons, too. In any case, the Amish regard the airplane as a temptation from the devil, a human handiwork of extravagance and pride, soaring all too close to God's great heaven. They may take a ride or a trip in the car of an acquaintance as long as they leave the driving to others. However, according to Joseph, there is one thing that has to be observed: "To ride in a car every day, that doesn't go." And so it doesn't go.

But once an Amishman sits in a car, his trust in God suddenly collides with another typical characteristic: while being driven, he is afraid, often dreadfully afraid. This starts as soon as he leaves the yard. Danger looms from the right, and he sounds a warning: a buggy with a "crazy nag." Danger now threatens from the left: a bush obstructs the view. Danger from the front: a slumbering Amish driver, lulled to sleep by the beat of the horse's hooves. Mortal danger when driving too fast: "Be careful" of the hill up ahead and at every crossing. An Amish passenger would issue instructions even to the most experienced driver on how he is to conduct himself in traffic, warning him ahead of time as to where danger lurks, what can happen if. . . , and all the reasons he yearns for his trusted horse and buggy.

Amish carriages, built in 120 hours of oak, hickory, or poplar and sometimes even of fiberglass, command a high dollar as collector's items, something which the brothers find inconceivable. They themselves are certainly no museum pieces. So why should their carriages be considered museum items? Collectors who gather for the great auctions every Tuesday in New Holland, close to Intercourse, Pennsylvania, see things differently. It was right there in Intercourse where the German immigrants had once been disappointed, deeply disappointed. When they gave this place a name, they wanted an English term for street crossings, such as *Intersection* or *Crossroad*. But their command of English at the time was so limited that they chose a similar name but with a double meaning, and it became Intercourse. This is a fine name except that *Intercourse* happens also to mean sexual cohabitation. Hence, this village sign in Pennsylvania's Anabaptist country has become one of the most photographed in all of North America.

But rubber, steel, or Intercourse—all that is of no interest to us whatsoever on board Elam's black buggy, our perch being a tad higher than Champ's lightly perspiring back. Rachel Mae is busy wielding a flyswatter on Champ's rear end, ridding him of pesky flies, while Chris has important matters to narrate. I share his opinion unequivocally that he will one day find a good Amish woman and that he will be just as good a husband to her. After all, he is only fifteen and has already demonstrated considerable talent in the manufacture of harness. Horses, wagons, and bridles are of great importance, not only for Chris but for all Amish boys.

"*D'Mädli achte druff* (the girls, they pay attention to such things)," he states. But when Chris talks about "the girls," he refers only to the ones who matter, the Amish. His people depend on themselves and God as far as their biological reproduction is concerned. When God placed the sons of the Grabers in this plot of his creation, he did so with the daughters of the Schmuckers, Lengachers, or Brandenbergers living just opposite. In spite of his young years, Chris strikes his audience as someone who knows what he is talking about.

In this setting, the discussion occasionally turns to the car. Chris's thinking on the matter is not quite as clear as one already baptized. The latter would claim that he would rather walk into the water and find its deepest spot with a millstone around his neck than sit, drunk by technology, behind a steering wheel. But

Chris is interested in everything associated with cars as he drives through the open country of little faith around Grabill, confidently directing Champ with a "Whoa, ho hooo, hoho" and rather satisfied that he can make do with his one-horse power.

*****

When driving to Grabill from an easterly direction as part of a weary line in a traffic jam, one chances upon a rather interesting sight at the entrance to the town. Two worlds converge in apparent harmony. Right here stand two telephone booths in use practically all the time. Long waiting lines are the order of the day here and in the town itself, for that matter, even though Grabill boasts more public telephones per capita than does New York City. The Amish are prohibited from having their own telephones, either in their homes or on their property. They consider it better for the members of their church family to visit each other face to face than to communicate via worldly technology. But what do members of the perfect church do when they simply *have* to use the phone? If the parties needing a phone cannot bypass the "wireless" decree by some handy trick, then they simply have to make their way to one of the worldly neighbors or to a public pay phone.

Among the Amish of Allen County are a considerable number of successful businessmen with a large worldly clientele, and they seize the economic opportunities. The public telephone booths belong to Grabill and its surroundings like the poles for high power lines, which have signs affixed that horses are not to be tied to them. Otherwise the Amish might suffer too many sparks for their own good. The brothers and sisters obey this command more often than the prohibition of telephones for their own homes.

Elsewhere, many Amish church districts allow a telephone booth to be installed on road property near a farmhouse. When a call comes through, an alarm sounds or signal lights break into bright action similar to the alarm system of a fire truck. Then the family heads for the receiver. No, they do not possess a private telephone. The one on the street of life will do. Sometimes one can observe that the most modern technology manages to find its way into the Amish realm. Mobile telephones, advertised "without a wire to the world," are easy to hide and might be loaned to the

102

business by an *englisch* employee during the day.

The semiprivate phone booth arrangement by the street introduces worldly problems to the Amish, and some are not of their own making. The fees are collected via an honor system by depositing coins in a handy box that serves as a kitty to pay the bill. In the phone booth diagonally across from David Kline's farm in Holmes County, an anonymous caller dialed a certain number long distance for weeks on end—without paying! Finally it was established that the dialed number was a pornographic agency, and a lock was promptly installed on the booth. Sometimes the decree prohibiting telephones has disastrous consequences for the brotherhood. In the year of the Lord 1989, when Chris Graber's wood factory was on fire, the Grabill fire department took thirty-five minutes to arrive at the catastrophe because the telephone connection did not work.

Aside from the Amish and Mennonites and the invariable nostalgia-hunting tourists who leave their temporary stamp on everything, this town of Grabill has come to represent a standardized architectural style that could be found anywhere west of New York and east of Los Angeles. During the day the town is always busy. In the evenings the road leading out of Grabill attracts those who want to explore. The route exudes the farm aromas of an average town that cultivates the customs of various countries. Yet it is small enough—one lengthy straightaway into which several smaller roads merge, as well as streets named First, Second, and Third.

Here everyone knows everyone else, including one Clifford Grabill from the pioneering family who gave this place its name. However the Grabills have long since disappeared from the church records of the Amish of Allen County. In this corner of the world, they had come to love the world too much for them to maintain the religious traditions of their forebears. They are by far not the only Swiss Brethren who, for weal or woe, dropped the "Brethren" and then the "*Schweizer*" (Swiss), became worldly, and simply drifted into the anonymity of America.

Other divisions came because of different religious emphases. Already in the mid 1860s in nearby Adams County, only a few years after the Amish arrived there, bishop Henry Egli stressed Bible study, regeneration, and assurance of salvation. When some members objected, he organized his followers into a separate congregation of the so-called Egly Amish, later called the Defenseless Mennonite Church, then the Evangelical Mennonite Church. Other Mennonites in Allen and Adams counties also share an Anabaptist spiritual heritage with the Amish but have adopted more modern conveniences. In various evangelical churches surrounding Amish and Mennonite communities are some with Anabaptist ancestors who have almost forgotten that connection. But to this day the Amish can still smell the smoke of believers burned at the stake in Old Europe, and this helps to set the atmosphere among them.

Yet Grabill continued to be spelled Grabill and remained symbolic for Swiss Anabaptists from the church cluster of Grosshöchstetten in the canton of Bern. In addition to the Swiss branch of the name, numerous progeny of this family also lived and flourished in Germany. Over the course of time, this name experienced some twenty variations in spelling. Some of these names are Graybills, Grebiels, Krabills, Krahenbühls. . . . Early Grabills are entered in church and legal historical records in the canton of Bern: one Hans Krahenbühl around 1538, Anna Krayenbühl in 1621, Barbara in 1645, Peter in 1655, and Margredt in 1678. One Peter Krehbiel fled in 1682 to the Palatinate and founded the Weierhof, which has remained a Mennonite model settlement to this day. It is located between Kaiserslautern and Kirchheimbolanden.

One Eva Grabiel married Christian Wenger in Lancaster County (Pa.) around 1728. In 1770 one branch of the family which had remained behind in Europe moved to Galicia and fifteen years later on to Russia, always in search of the kind of religious freedom without which Anabaptism could not realize its vision. In the 1800s, one Joseph Grabill farmed in Allen County, north of Fort Wayne. Then in 1860 the Wabash Railroad built a line from Detroit to Saint Louis, bisecting the old hunting grounds of the Miami Indians and also Grabill's farm. This Anabaptist, whose ancestors hailed from the canton of Bern, contributed his name for the railway station and thus for the surrounding area.

Grabill makes every effort to attract tourists by advertising a spring festival in June, an agricultural exhibition after Labor Day, and their own traditional Amish all year-round. The worldly

Grabillers stand in polarity to the area Amish, who particularly regard cameras of the photo robbers as a beam in their eye. That was why Rachel implored me, repeatedly, "If you absolutely insist on taking pictures, please be so kind as to go to neighboring Amish settlements where they know neither you nor me." Among these Anabaptists, the commandment "Thou shalt not make unto thee any graven image" still has binding force (Exod. 20:4). To these Amish, photos, pictures, and likenesses are all covered by the generic term "graven images." Owning such things borders on the practice of veneration of saints in the Catholic church.

In the Amish view, whoever possesses a likeness of oneself, a photo, has a likeness of God, since human beings are created in God's image. Such a person is proud of oneself and inwardly intends to replace God. Moreover, pictures lead the weak to the lust of the eye, a vice to be hated. Yet tourists who take pictures of Amish in this beloved-by-God countryside also spend money there. Allen County folks see no significance in the gentle irony played on them by history when Grabill came into being. Nearby are two towns called Waterloo and Napoleon. None of these folks ever gives it more than a passing thought that the forebears of the Amish of Allen County left Europe precisely because they would otherwise have been involved in preparations for the wars of Napoleon, who went down to defeat at Waterloo. Conscientious objectors of the Amish persuasion would not have served one single day in that kind of army, not to speak of seven years.

On the square in front of Grabill's shopping center is the dusty gathering place of all of this particular world with its permanent smell of horsepower. One can witness quite a bit of action during waking hours. Some place or another the Amish invariably meet, and one hears the laughter of both big and small members of the Amish clans, or the rhythm of a passing trotter.

Whenever these folks meet, there is more than merely small talk. They go beyond a word of greeting and references to the weather. If they are longtime friends, the conversational well is almost unfathomable. But if their acquaintanceship is superficial, then the following village gossip becomes typical: "So, you're the daughter of David Graber?" "No, I'm Chris Graber's wife, but Eli Graber's oldest. Rebecca Graber is the one who is married to my man's youngest brother, Sam Graber. And David Graber's grandfather is the brother to my grandfather, Peter Graber, who married Ruth Schwartz, and their second oldest daughter was the James Schwartz who in turn married a Graber. . . ." These would be stellar hours for genealogists, who generally are not around when the vein of their lode is struck.

For the young set, the trip to Grabill is a real experience, in spite of or because of the many dangers lurking on the way. Day in and day out one sees them around many corners in town. This is also the world for people which are in it but not of it: sweets for the children, which they devour by the fistful; and culinary items for the older set, who occasionally do not mind a carriage ride of eight to ten miles in order to arrive at the table of the worldly. For a while now, such a breach with old traditions is being tolerated in Allen County. These Amish are free to visit a restaurant. They avail themselves of this freedom with due modesty. Elam's family, for instance, goes to a public eatery only once each year, when the master of the house celebrates his birthday.

In the town of Grabill, a daring Amish youth might project some music from a tape recorder secluded in the buggy or from a little transistor radio, otherwise hidden under the big hat. Here young lads cannot avoid seeing tight sweaters and brief shorts, the ready-to-wear stylish clothes in sharp contrast to well-known biblical scenes and injunctions. Such actions are not typical Amish behavior, but they nevertheless play a part in the life of the individual and the community. The Amish know when the heart of one of their own youth is not yet with all of the rules, and the knowledgeable worldly detect this too. Their character is quickly determined by how they act beyond the parental home, when they feel unobserved and show who they really are at that stage of life.

Normal buggies are parked in front of the businesses of Grabill, but now and then a couple of luxury models are on exhibit. These belong to unbaptized boys seeking a good time. Some of their rigs are plain and simple, but others sport an array of technical baits and lures like battery-operated multitoned horns, digital speedometers, flashing lights, or reflectors—in short, all the equipment necessary to impress the ladies fair of Amish persuasion. If the horseman gets baptized, then buggy and dress must reflect the new person. The young man knows which direction his yearning must take. All things frivolous will then disappear from the public square from one day to the next. Such a transition could even happen sooner if a strict Amish father took offense at it.

As for the old ones themselves? It's not that the Amish shy away from contact with the world of Grabill. Such visits provide food for reflection and conversation. Take the long-haired boys who have come to town from Leo. Certainly they have never heard of Ezekiel, that great priest and prophet: "Neither shall they shave their heads, nor suffer their locks to grow long; they shall only trim their hair" (Ezek. 44:20). To the Amish, this means that the hair is to be cut where the back of the head meets the neck.

Or consider a clean-shaven man, the likes of which there are more than enough in town. A worldly Grabiller, like any average American, spends all told more than a whole month of his life shaving himself. But how is one to reconcile all this with the books of Moses? "God created man in his own image, in the image of God he created him" (Gen. 1:27). If God wears a beard, why should man not do likewise? What kind of a world is it in which a man shaves himself to look like a woman, and a woman wears pants to look like a man? Is the lustful eye of a woman not as much attracted by a clean-shaven face as the lustful eye of the man by a woman's uncovered hair, possibly even falsely colored?

For the Amish, this blurring of genders is all part of the devil's plan ever since he took Eve aside and tried to make her have dominion over man. For after all, has it not already gone so far that women preach in some other churches? Is not all that in spite of the biblical injunction that "women are to hold their peace" in church (1 Cor. 14:34)? And in matters of sex, isn't the devil's plan also that "men do what women are meant to do, and women do what is the work of men" (Rom. 1:26-27)? The immoral and the pedophiles, according to the Amish of Allen County, would be just as unlikely to inherit the kingdom of God as would idolaters or robbers (1 Cor. 6:9-11). For this reason God created *Eve* to be at Adam's side rather than some random John.

A further point of verbal excursion is worldly dress: bare, scanty, hooligans' attire. Modest attire is becoming, to cover nakedness. The Amish are different from the world not in what they experience but in the way they react to it. Why did the townspeople of Grabill not wear the beggar's robe of Jesus, like the devout descendants of Adam or Noah? Why did they always try to please each other by wearing designer clothes instead of being bent on pleasing the heavenly Father? Only those not ashamed of God's image in which they were created, could hope that one day the Lord would not be ashamed of them (Luke 9:26).

"How run-down the world has become," complains even Chris Graber as he shoulders a bottle of Coke like a gun. "It's better that we go home." There is no doubt in his mind about one thing: for people like these in Grabill, Jesus Christ would not have had to bear the cross, because they ignore his sacrifice.

On the way home, where Grabill turns into countryside, we are in for it. Suddenly dark thunderclouds mount, and we are hit by a cloudburst. It rains as if the end of the world has come. Within seconds the two girls resemble wet ghosts, and yet they engage in a little fun. They spit into the wind, and the wind returns the favor. Chris forces his wide-brimmed hat deeper over his face. From the buggy box, I grab the black umbrella with the clear-plastic peephole. It is of little protection for Chris, the girls, or me. Alongside us, cars jockey for advantage, and trucks squish up great fountains. Giant waves of water sweep over us by the barrelful. They flood the buggy, spilling mud and dirt over the horseman and his human freight.

Water, water everywhere! This would have been Noah's redletter day. Yet in the midst of that deluge, I could not help but think that Noah would have had a roof mounted on his buggy. Whatever else he was, Noah was certainly not old-fashioned. Come to think of it, Noah would have boarded up the entire carriage as he did with the ark in his day. Yet the Amish of Allen County are still prohibited from following his example.

That same evening, Rachel's sister Barbara heard that one of her nieces had died of cancer. A few days later, a "Yankee" ran into the buggy of an uncle in front of Barbara's house and killed his thousand-dollar horse. Soon thereafter Barbara's husband, David, was breaking in one of the largest horses that had ever been seen in this part of the country when the buggy capsized and buried David underneath it. For weeks it was uncertain whether he had sustained permanent harm from the accident.

The Grabers had rather expected accidents of this kind ever since that bird alighted at Barbara's kitchen window and knocked at the window pane for three days on end.

Bicycle shopping at Shipshewana, Indiana

Renno Amish of Belleville, Pennsylvania

A hot day in Berne, Indiana

A patriarch of Arthur, Illinois

At a Haiti relief sale, Mt. Hope, Holmes County, Ohio

Minnesota road wagon   *Holmes County road wagon*

Double horsepower in Shipshewana

*The Elam Graber family
at Grabill, Indiana*

A Shipshewana surrey

Weekday transportation in Guthrie County, Kentucky, for those who call themselves Amish but might be called New Amish. On Sunday they use a buggy.

Oilcloth sides on buggy of Fort Plain, New York, in a New Wilmington, Pennsylvania, style

Unmarried and beardless,
on a scooter, Lancaster County

Road warning signs:
Arthur, Illinois; Grabill, Indiana

Plywood buggy,
New Wilmington, Pennsylvania

Geauga County, Ohio

*Setting hand to
plow in Holmes County*

*Buggy trailer at
Canton, Minnesota*

*Training cart
at Shipshewana*

*Training cart in
Holmes County*

An Amish "truck" at Shipshewana

Rolling softly at Shipshewana

Holmes County Swartzentruber Amish buggy, with flaps ready for sun or rain

A bond develops between
a man and his horse

A weekday wagon-cart,
Goshen, Indiana

Amish rig of Aylmer, Ontario—ready for rain or snow

Goats to be sold.
Wayne - Holmes counties

Amish woman's cap.
Elkhart - LaGrange counties

Surrey for sale at Arthur, Illinois

Shipshewana fishing boat

*Parking lot, Elkhart -
LaGrange counties, Indiana*

*Nappanee, Indiana, buggy with
windows and windshield wiper*

Shipshewana, with rearview mirror, lights, slow-moving-vehicle (SMV) sign, reflective tape, and "NON MOTOR VEHICLE" license

Swartzentruber Amish buggy of Harmony, Minnesota, with legally approved reflective tape instead of SMV triangle

Off to market with livestock, at Farmerstown, Holmes County, Ohio

Patiently waiting, at Nappanee, Indiana

4

Old Faith in a New World

Matrjoschka! Why did this word suddenly occur to me in the middle of a worship service? Matrjoschka is the doll in a doll in a doll, a wooden, brightly colored symbol of Russian folk art. Every doll is like the other, like the one in which it fits or the one which it hides, and so the smallest is a miniature of the largest one. Matrjoschka could also well fit as a symbol of the Amish in their respective congregations. Brothers, sisters, the old, the young, each one seems inwardly and outwardly just like the next, the other one.

Although the Amish of Allen County live relatively close together, they have retained one tradition from the days of their persecution, even if the custom has undergone slight change. In Old Europe, the Anabaptists often lived so far apart that they managed to get together only once every four weeks for the so-called "gathering" in a private dwelling, a barn, or even a secluded grove. Today they meet every fortnight but not in church buildings, since "God dwells not in temples made with hands" (Acts 17:24). Wherever they gather to bend their knees in worship, they do so in the strictest contrast to the monumental architecture of Catholicism.

In addition, the Grabill group knows from history that all Amish congregations who built their own house of prayer departed from the true way, sooner or later. Church buildings are a sign of arrogance similar to buttons on Sunday jerkins or zippers on men's trousers. God, however, resists the proud (1 Pet. 5:5). The Savior preached in temples, in Jewish schools and synagogues, on the mountain, and wherever else he had the opportunity to do so. But that example does not change their decision against church buildings. On this matter they have adhered to the old ways even if conducting services in private houses within their community sometimes leads to problems. For instance, one family or the other might fall into the clutches of vanity and polish up their rooms too much, or spruce up an abused lawn at the last moment, or plant a few extra flowers in order to adorn the yard, all undertaken to please the brothers and sisters on the appointed Sunday.

This church service—also called *Tschöörtsch*—is held at all Amish farms in rotating order. Younger couples usually take their turn to host the services in summertime since they tend to live in smaller houses. In the warmer season of the year, their roomier barns can be used for worshiping. Sometimes they may be granted a chronological dispensation, with their turn skipped until later. An *Almanac* published by Ben J. Raber of Baltic, Ohio, designates the weekends of a year, suggests Scriptures and hymns for every second Sunday, and provides spaces to write in the family hosting the services. The districts or congregations are listed in the back of Raber's *Almanac*, each with a letter *A* or *B*. All labeled *A* meet on the same Sunday, and those with *B* meet the next. Thus everyone knows the time and place of worship. When one congregation has an in-between Sunday, with no service, members may attend a church meeting in another district.

On this *Gmeesundig* (church Sunday) an unusual, quite un-Amish kind of excitement pervades Elam's house. The Amish, all Amish, prepare for the worship service as the worldly do for a ball. Everything unwinds in a brisk "now, right now" tempo which means instantly and faster than possible. First and foremost, this means to put on "the good clothes." Every family member was scrubbed the day before. Part of the reason they set this hectic pace is to arrive in time to find a seat on a backless bench by the wall, to lean against it in the coming three hours and avoid a backache. Yet their anticipation seems to stem chiefly from a genuine desire to worship God and enjoy Christian fellowship.

All Saturday evening Rachel was working overtime at washing and ironing. Now she appears to do everything a second time. She invests special patience in preparing the white, artistically folded prayer caps with which Amish women keep their hair covered, beginning in childhood. They wear out three each year. Always before worship, the latest and newest cap is pulled over the hair, parted in the center and combed back. Nevertheless, this cap is ironed once more before they leave the house. This means that Rachel is nonstop commuting with an iron between stove and ironing board. She still uses old-time sadirons for the job, and each has to be placed on the cookstove for reheating while she is using another.

Meanwhile the *Hausfrau* (housewife) places eight pots of water at the ready for washing up after chores. At the same time she is supervising the frying of meat pies, the boiling of milk, and the expected baking of fruit pies. Barbara Ann smacks the hamburgers into shape for breakfast while Rachel Mae sets the table. Elam puffs the dust off his hat, which has a rim measuring exactly the prescribed three and a half inches: the wider the rim, the more conservative the Amish wearer and district.

Now the time has come for Rachel to fancy herself up to the extent allowed by the strict ordinances. She employs a few needles for the purpose—exactly seven pins secure the female dress. If a non-Amish woman were to fuss about with this secretive pinning-up, she might sustain injury, but an Amish lady knows what pins and needles are for. Younger girls up to about age ten have their dresses done up in the back with safety pins. "As soon as they can make do," they wear garments secured with pins only at chest level.

Rachel wears a white batiste pinafore (women her age wear black only at funerals and for communion) and ties on a white neckerchief, which has been part of her churchgoing dress since her twelfth birthday. For the daily dress of married women and to signify their gender, a so-called *Lapplein* (small flap, bustle), a double strip of material, is affixed at waist level on the back of female garments. One has to be able to tell with one glance who is man and who is woman (Deut. 22:5).

Originally this item was a considerably wider strip of material, a kind of backside loincloth, providing additional coverage around prominent parts which attracted the eyes of men even as early as the sixteenth and seventeenth centuries. However, in the course of time, this piece of material became smaller and smaller. By now the width, down to some two centimeters, has only symbolic character to keep upright men from crooked thoughts. This *Lapplein* is no longer a part of the apparel as such. It covers nothing and even escapes the notice of a fleeting observer. Yet the Amish do not want to give it up altogether, although in Lancaster County some attempts have been made in that direction. A similar function is served by a half-pinafore, worn by order. It does not provide protection from soiling but is meant only to *"den Bauch verdecken* (hide the belly)."

It goes without saying that Amish women never wear mini, midi, micro, or single-piece knitted dresses, but instead wear a well-tailored maxi or *Oma* look (grandma look). Our heavenly Father demands modesty as a bond between teaching and life. The hem of the skirt is to be nine inches from the ground; unseemly taboo zones are thereby hidden. Pants, trousers, or other invasions into the realm of men's haberdashery are totally *verboten* (forbidden). An exception noted among some Amish of Ohio is that, when a girl goes horseback riding, she is allowed to wear trousers under her dress to appear proper in the saddle. An Allen County Amish girl would not even ride horseback in public. Yet it would be completely false to assume that Amish attire is unattractive, even if the outside world frequently ridicules it as the dress of fools. Just recently a Toronto group attempted to enter the stylish market with a so-called Babel Collection, with simple and solid Anabaptist dress. Price range? Between one hundred and three hundred dollars!

When Rachel has completed her work in the kitchen, I again become conscious of the practical application of the Bible in the daily life of the Amish. According to their view, human beings are required to don clothing because of the Fall (Gen. 3:21). In the garden of Eden before the Fall, humans could have romped around in natural attire, stark naked. But then they suddenly found themselves enmeshed in sin. "It's on account of sin that we have to wear clothes," Rachel's mother Rosanna had instructed her daughter at an early age. First she explained the origin of the dress code to Rachel, who passed it on to Barbara Ann, Rachel

Mae, Chris, and Ben. The jerkin, trousers, *Lapplein*, and the lowly socks are all part of the memory of Eve's foolish desire for the forbidden apple, Adam and Eve's partaking of it, and their subsequent expulsion from paradise.

Since God creates all things perfectly, he has also fashioned modern humans in such a way that they simply cannot survive in the nude in the winters of Indiana. In the daily routine of getting dressed and undressed, the Amish are meant to reflect on the fact that something went very wrong with our original parents. With this in mind, one may deduce why Rachel today uses common pins to secure her dress and not buttons or zippers and why she entertains no desire for trendy fashions or for experimental forms and colors. Clothes have been given to humankind for humility and to cover shame, and this is to be remembered daily along with the expulsion from paradise. Every foolish ornamentation on shirts, dresses, or pants could be interpreted as pride. To regard Adam and Eve's mistake as anything but shameful would give out disastrous signals.

Amish women sew most of the dresses for everyday wear themselves, using old patterns for the purpose. However, clothes for Sundays are generally fashioned by Amish tailors. The decree regarding pins for women's dresses applies only to waking hours. The laws of night are much more tolerant: womens' nighties have buttons!

The outward appearance of the Amish also reveals a thing or two about their idea regarding the ideal human society. Clothes cover human nakedness, but that is not their sole purpose. They are worn to emphasize Amish self-understanding and are a challenge to the worldly as well as a silent advertisement for Christ. The Amish wear their distinctive clothing as a sign of solidarity with fellow believers. Their style of dress, although persistently subdued, is meant as a challenge: it is a countermeasure against the stylish trends and fashions which the world would inflict upon them.

In the sixteenth century, the South German Anabaptists promptly adopted the Strassburg Discipline of 1568 requiring Anabaptist tailors and seamstresses to keep to the plain and simple "custom of the land." In the seventeenth century, while the religious forebears of Jakob Ammann were struggling along, various Swiss and South German cities issued clothing ordinances for male and female members of the peasant class, to keep them from spending too much money. All things fashionable and luxurious were forbidden, and quality and cost of material was sometimes specified. Melvin Gingerich quotes such regulations in *Mennonite Attire Through Four Centuries*.

In the 1690s Ammann gave his followers strict rules on clothing. These were protested by a North German Mennonite elder, Gerhard Roosen, who however agreed that Christians should "abstain from luxuries, pride, and carnal worldly lusts" (1 John 2:16-17). The Amish retained old peasant clothing customs for simplicity, to maintain their distinctiveness, and to counteract pride. Such a pattern is understandable when one realizes that because of persecution, these European Anabaptists had shrunk into a peasant subculture. The world soon forgot all about those government-imposed clothing rules, but the Amish remembered the old ways.

To the Amish, being different means standing still and accepting or adopting nothing new. Hats and pants, pinafores and bonnets, all emphasize this choice of separation from the world of changing fashions. They correspond to the peculiar social form of this Anabaptist group and show their submission to God and to each other. Since each congregation agrees upon their own *Ordnung* (order, discipline, rules), there are minor variations in clothing customs from one Amish community to another.

Beards grow and flow and are God-given and approved. An Amishman carries his beard with natural dignity, like a bear his coat. The hair of women grows uncut a whole life long, while that on the man's head flourishes in accord with God's endowment. Amishmen wear their hair relatively long and remind one of the days in German districts when only serfs had their hair cut. Short hair is regarded as "Roman [Catholic]," and the Amish wanted nothing to do with Rome and will have nothing to do with it.

Whoever doesn't want to be conspicuous in a forest, must be a tree. I laid aside my wristwatch since only simple pocket watches are tolerated here. Then I pulled on a pair of broadfall pants without buttons and with a practical front flap instead of the usual zipper. The Amish call this flap a barn door, and it functions just like one. In contrast with many other Amish churches, a shirt in Allen

County may have a collar. Rachel's sister Barbara tailored for me a so-called *Mutze*, a sawed-off jerkin or vest made from a dark, coarse material. An earlier use of the word *Mutz* was for an animal with a cropped tail. Instead of buttons and buttonholes, this coat has hooks and eyes. It comes collarless and reminds me of a shroud. This style of jacket was favored by peasant farmers of the Emmental well into the twentieth century. Amishmen wear this *Mutze* for worship, and no one makes an exception, for to do so would mean that he is *upteyup*, a fashion guru. The *Mutze* for a baptized man has a slit tail, thus showing his full obedience to the church and to his baptismal vows.

Elam's family seemed thoroughly satisfied with my somber black-and-white exterior. Yet there was one further, minor matter. Elam suggested that I might want to shave off my mustache since the church objected to it. After all, like the buttons on a coat, it was a symbol of the military of Old Europe. But after due consideration, I considered this matter stretching my Christian ideals a little far. As it was, I already came close to fitting the model of an Amishman—but only externally. Aside from a snow-white shirt, I was dressed entirely in black. Today I was of serious demeanor and yet as excited as the rest of the family. But there was still this little matter of my mustache and short haircut.

In preparation for this Sunday, Elam had given me careful instructions on how to behave, almost as if I were a guest from a distant planet. He started by telling me to go to the family outhouse prior to the three-hour-long service so I would not disturb the meeting. Finally he warned me, the *Doktor der Schrift* (doctor of writing), not to take any notes on the sermon. Otherwise they might take me to be a "spy" of the world, a traitor, as during the religious feuds and suffering for the faith back in the Switzerland or Germany of their forebears. The Amish world is deeply colored by this suspicion anchored in their collective history. It is almost a sixth sense for them, helping them survive when the other five do not suffice. They know they are often regarded as "peculiar" (1 Pet. 2:9) by the "lip Christians" from the outside—those who say "Lord, Lord," but do not do the will of the heavenly Father (Matt. 7:21-23). So the Amish have used that image of themselves to erect a barrier against that world, to protect their island of blessing from the threat of errors and confusions.

Elam sternly warned me not *"in Schlof zfalle* (to fall asleep)" during the long sermon. Anyone who falls asleep during the proclamation of God's Word does so from lack of moral strength to stay awake. It would be egotistical and disrespectful toward God and his guidance, and it would also disturb faithful Christians on the bench beside me. Then toward the end of the service, if and when one of the servants (ministers) had something to say which was meant only for Amish ears, I was to leave the meeting room quickly and without comment and slip into the anteroom with the youth, the unbaptized.

The Grabers were still not clear as to how the rest of the congregation would react to me. After all, I was one from whom they had to distance themselves. With regard to the church service, their general understanding is that "those who are not redeemed to the obedience of faith and have not united themselves with God . . . are an abomination before the Lord [Deut. 25:16], . . . so one can not and may not expect anything from them except things abominable." Seekers may listen and learn but not give counsel.

Today, John the teacher's place—and a sedate spread it is—becomes the scene of worship and of fellowship. John's farmhouse appears equal to the task of accommodating them all. Every piece of furniture has been removed from the living room and kitchen. The beds in which the babies will be stashed under the careful scrutiny of baby-sitters are made and ready and look their Sunday best. Also, the simple *Liebesmahl* (love meal) has been prepared. Supplying this food may cost the hosting family up to several hundred dollars, plus much baking of bread and use of apple butter and garden stores from their own basement. This is a further reason why newly married couples are usually granted dispensation from having to make such an outlay in the first year or two of marriage.

A church service casts a mighty shadow long before the actual event transpires at an Amish farm. It comes as little surprise that a hosting family would respond as did the Elam J. Graber family recently. They quickly reshingled a part of the roof, tore out half the flooring, put in a new one for holy feet, and cleaned up the barn. All the while they scrubbed, scrubbed, and scrubbed some more. They obviously cared a great deal about what the congregation thought of them. In my opinion, there are three kinds of Amish in Allen County, although no one here would be prepared to admit it. The absolute majority constantly scrub, polish, and clean. Others scrub regularly. Then a small third set scrub only when necessary. Some Amish almost take pride in their cleanliness, which could lead to inner conflict because pride is not of the Lord.

More than fifty families are expected at John's place today, and that's a few too many for one household. Elam's congregation will soon have to divide peacefully. Not all who are expected come, as shown by some unoccupied bench seats. The sick are excused, and so are members of this congregation whose brothers, sisters, or parents of a different district are having the service in their homes today. In such instances, tradition dictates first loyalty to family rather than the congregation. In principle in Allen County, anyone who fails to attend church service three times in succession without sound reason runs the danger of being disciplined.

Today Barbara Ann enjoys the privilege of driving the family and me, "the vain abomination," to the church service in a highly polished carriage, under the glassy haze of the morning. She is deserving of this honor. During the last few days, she has learned to harness a horse just as quickly as her brothers, and that's no mean feat.

There is much action on Cuba Road and its tributaries, and yet they are all mindful of their ways, with one following the other. No Amish driver would ever dare to pass another on the way to a church service. The worshipers arrive in family lots on John's yard. Horses are unhitched and led to hay cribs where they will busy themselves for the next few hours. Then the family enters the house. The head of the house invariably walks ahead of his wife. Each take a long drink from a huge container of drinking water. Dignified discipline marks every action, including the intake of water.

Today John's house is devoid of any decoration. Not a single symbol hangs on the walls reminding one of the Crucified. The rooms do not smell of church or town. The breath of farmyard and the austerity of hard toil pervades all. The air is heavy, warm, and dry. The women sit on long rows of church-owned benches in the kitchen, facing a wide opening into the living room, where the men have taken places. Each one wordlessly surveys the others. Little girls and boys sit by mothers or fathers and practice their patience, for it is another hour until the worship service begins. One follows another, no audible word of greeting, everything on course, all routine, rehearsed a thousand times, and proved a thousandfold. When all the hooks on the walls are used up, the men simpy sail their wide-rimmed hats behind the stove, where soon a hundred of them are piled.

Most of the brothers, with head supported on the palm of a hand, are deeply reflective and seem sad, reminding one, somehow, of victims. They are not nearly as full of life as I know them on weekdays, with rolled-up sleeves and suspendered trousers. Instead, they appear to bear the full weight of the world on their own shoulders. It is their way of preparing for things to come. From my vantage point, I can see only a few of the sisters. How did their contemporary of four hundred years ago describe these Swiss Anabaptists? "Expensive clothes they disdain, they refrain from expensive food and drink, they dress in coarse material and cover their heads with wide-rimmed felt hats; their walk and way is marked by modesty. They carry no weapons, neither sword nor dagger, only a short bread knife. All other things are the clothes of wolves, which should not be worn by sheep. They swear not at all and do not pay their governments the oath of citizens. If anyone trespasses therein, they ban him from their midst; this they do daily." Has anything really changed among them, or with them?

Once in a while, one or the other neighbor asks, "Are you a *Dütscher?*" and adds, "Nice to meet you." This is a superlative of the Amish form of courtesy. No further word. I am no "sensation," just an outsider, a sinner among the faithful. They know that but they do not let me feel it.

It is exactly 9:15 when four dignified men's men enter. The servants of the congregation and a guest preacher walk into the room and greet each man with a handshake and the traditional brotherly kiss. This happens quickly and is strangely mechanical, yet most cordial. A firm shake of the hand, a kiss on the lips with the language of eye encounter. I sit next to Elam and ask myself how the deacon will handle me, the worldly one. Already approaching us is the first one of the threesome, bishop, preacher, and deacon. He is Bishop Victor (Graber), who knows me, extends a hand, and smilingly moves on. Then the guest minister Elmer (Graber) approaches, and things are different. While shaking hands, this minister puckers his mouth for a kiss and bends toward me. At the last instant he observes from my mustache that I am not one of the "holy nation" (1 Pet. 2:9) by Amish standards and that my hair is not of Amish cut. With a hint of dismay, he moves on.

Now a longer break ensues. One brother coughs his lungs empty during the severe solemnity, while a few potent *Bäuerl* (burps) issue forth in the manner of a grateful belly giving expression through the mouth of a farmer: God blesses only things genuine and their origins. Together with a *Gluxi* (hiccup) of a child, nothing much disturbs the total silence. About 220 persons have filled John's house, sitting closely together, then crowding closer, and now even finding seats in the bedroom since living room and kitchen are simply filled up. At exactly 9:30 the bishop asks for the singing to commence.

Now there is considerable conferring back and forth. Everyone knows that singing will shortly commence, but it has yet to be determined which song and which singer will start the worship. A bit of whispering commences within the cousin clan: "Sam, you sing." "Eli, *kumm sing.*" "Joe, start singing." "Go on, John, *tu singe* (do sing)." Perhaps they all want to sing, but nobody wants to be first. Probably the whole exchange merely illustrates Amish humility and democracy. Whatever, the members of the home congregation always offer visitors from other church districts the position of *Vorsänger* (precentor, song leader). Courtesy dictates such invitation.

Suddenly Ben Graber, who up to now has not been part of any discussion, calls out in a powerful bass voice, "Eighty-eight." All around me the brethren reach for a black-bound bulky volume with the yard-long title, *Ausbund* . . . (Paragon, which means some beautiful songs as they were composed back and forth in the prison of Passau in the castle by the Swiss Brethren and by other truebelieving Christians. Impartial and very suitable for all and every Christian of whatever religion they might be). They call it "the thick book." This *Ausbund* with its uneven verses and its didactic and moralizing tone is the oldest Protestant hymnary still used for singing. Its songs might be called the poetics of the Anabaptists. The hymns of the *Ausbund* memorialize these Anabaptist brothers and sisters of Old Europe as they were awaiting their hour of execution. The first known edition by the Anabaptists is dated 1564, and in America it was published by Christopher Saur's Germantown (Pa.) press in 1742.

In the house of Teacher John out there by Cuba Road, it was not the best setting for me to entertain thoughts on the origins of the tunes. Yet I could not help but notice that the Amish were singing martyr hymns to the strangest of melodies, such as "A maiden fair went with her jug" or "A flower on the heath." Headings for each hymn indicate the tunes, mostly drawn from popular folk music of the sixteenth century, but notes are not given. The *Ausbund* has songs, indeed ballads, which Anabaptist martyrs composed while imprisoned in Passau Castle during 1535-40. This prison of Passau somehow motivated early Anabaptists to sing, much like the Schubert linden tree in the Viennese forest invited Franz Schubert to compose a timeless refrain. Among the lyricists were even Anabaptist prisoners from Durlach, today part of my home city of Karlsruhe, or from Bruchsal, not far from there. Could the early Anabaptists ever have imagined that their songs would one day conquer the very ocean and be retained far into the twentieth century?

One of my neighbors opens the mammoth hymnary to song number 88, which begins on page 460. When I whisper to him that I can not sing it because I do not know the song, he responds rather gruffly, "But you can read, can't you?" He is right; I can read. We are already into the song, *"Kommt her zu mir, spricht Gottes Sohn* (Come unto me, speaks God's Son)." The precentor begins with the syllable and draws it out on several pitches with a nasal bass voice, *"Füü—üüüüü—üüüüüüü—ü—üüüü—üüür* (for)." Then the others also join in unison, following him on the same tune trail.

Song follows upon song. After all, we have a whole hour's time until the *Anfang* (beginning), the first sermon. But what does an hour mean around here? During the next sixty-seven minutes, we manage only the first two verses of five songs. This has little to do with the fact that every time we finish a song and are waiting for the next, the same whispering goes on as they in honor prefer one another (Rom. 12:10): "Sam, *sing du.*" "*Na*, David, *du musch singe.*" "Ben, you start a little song." The major reason for needing extra

133

time is because the Amish sing all their songs in church by "*langsam Weis* (slow tune)," a kind of rigid, monopolized form which reminds one of the tunes of medieval Catholicism, such as the Gregorian chant. But in this traditional Amish group singing, memorized melodies are dragged out with added embellishments. Thus the worshipers take exactly five minutes and thirty-two seconds to master a four-line verse, as for instance of song number 13 of the *Ausbund*, "A beautiful story about a maiden fair," sung "very consolingly."

> A maiden fair with members slight,
>   Lovely, nice, with features bright,
> Elisabeth she was by name,
>   Through Holy Writ she gained her fame.

The Amish sing this mournful song as others sing of a broken heart, but they reduce every word to little syllables with up to nine tones per syllable. The more conservative the church, the slower they sing. This means that the precentor or melodic starter (an office which dates back to Swiss traditions) or whoever decides to lead a song, announces a number from the *Ausbund*. He begins by singing the first syllable solo while the group gradually joins in with the remainder of the line. Every letter is emphasized and every word is stretched and sung to its finality, but according to a melody.

The *Ausbund* names twenty-one various tunes for its songs, but in order to perfect the art of singing them, one has to learn them like one's mother tongue from an early age. Up and down goes the song, without any melodic sense I can detect, and only explainable with that breath of timelessness which surrounds us in John's house. All this takes place without any musical accompaniment since the Amish believe God has many good reasons for giving them beautiful voices, and no musical instruments should be allowed to drown them out. Just why these folks retain their slow-paced manner of singing is unknown. Those scoffers are surely wrong who believe that they only do it so that no one would be tempted to dance to it.

> At Lewarden right in that town,
>   The maiden there did settle down,

And when they counted fifteen hundred years,
And nine and forty without fears.

From only two verses, I cannot determine what actually happened to this maiden fair. The story is told in the rest of the hymn and an age-old report in *Martyrs Mirror*. The celebrated maiden fair, Elisabeth Dirks, was caught "in the month of January" in a widow friend's house with a Latin New Testament. "She was asked to swear to query, if she with no man had made merry." Her captors assumed that she was married to Menno Simons, with whom she had been seen. Likely she was a teacher, perhaps a deaconess. As can be expected of a real Anabaptist and as further incentive for the Amish of today, she declined to swear. She only told the simple truth, that she had no husband.

There is a constant back and forth between the questioner and the questioned from verse four to thirty-six. Elisabeth knew the Scriptures well and gave a moving defense of her faith. Verse 37 arrives at the conclusion that

She shall be shortly drowned today.
Grace is shut, no use to pray.
The goodness of the wolf, a mother,
For every lamb she'll care and bother.

Finally in verse thirty-eight, one discovers why the Amish of Allen County seize upon this very song some four hundred years after the actual train of events:

Let us remember when we part,
The Elisabethan noble heart,
How filled she was with pain and sore,
To God for grace she did implore. Amen.

The Amish church can hardly do without memorializing its martyrs for the faith and rehearsing such history, long past. The songs usually include critical remarks about the life of the priests, the hypocrisy of the monks, and the false teachings of the pope. The Amish of today deliberately turn to religious revolution and conflict of yesteryear, to verses and rhymes which sprang up from the community of faith as members were tortured in dark dungeons of death and stuffy holes of fear. Their forebears gave their lives for their confession, as did the models of faith in Hebrews 11. In their songs the Amish remember this blessed "cloud of witnesses" with acoustic thunder, aligning themselves with those who died in the Lord, faithful unto death (Rev. 14:13). Thus they remind their radical Christian community where they come from so that they will not stray from the way.

Now during the singing of the second selection, the *Loblied* (Praise song; *Ausbund*, no. 131), the ministering servants withdraw for an *Abrot* (counseling session), an intimate holy conference, which is a three-hundred-year-old practice. While the congregation on the first floor of the house continues singing, these leaders gather in a room on the upper floor and discuss who will be delivering the first sermon and the main sermon of the day.

These sermons have to be delivered without a draft, without notes or a Bible (except as present in memory), and must be solely from inspiration. The Amish want to make sure that the servant will say only what God inspires him to say right then, while preaching. An exception to this rule is made only for the deacon, who briefly reads from the Bible and interprets the text. Also, it is permitted to "read a prayer or two, no more." Since their earliest days, the church services of the Anabaptists went much beyond the usual Catholic sacramental ceremonies, conducted in Latin. Instead, their preachers aimed to impart teachings independent of difficult-to-understand rites, in a language which everyone understood, even the peasants.

As the final opening hymn, number 65 from the *Ausbund*, coasts to a slow stop, the ministers return from the upper story and take seats along the broad side of the living room. A short pause is used to pacify the unrest among the small set with potato chips. Considering everything and even the standards of the world around us, the behavior of the little Amish tykes is exemplary. The grown-ups also fill hands, then jowls, with chips and munch rather heartily. A boy who sits next to the big bucket is kept busy filling glasses with water. The ministers, however, go without chips, for they say, "You cannot preach well on a full stomach." The Amish of Allen County have no Sunday schools, so their young set attend church services together with their elders from cradle days on.

Where the church is, there is the Spirit of God; where the Spirit of God is, there is the church. . . . This theme is initiated by a short sermon, the responsibility of Henry Zehr, who extends a cordial greeting to us in the name of the Lord. "First I wish you the grace of God." Then he revs up with the power of the Word and settles accounts with the old (Catholic) church and its human teachings. For seventeen minutes he preaches as the Spirit inspires him, in a certain singsong above the heads of 220 people. When he lowers his voice he speaks almost softly, but then as the content demands, his voice mounts and rises and his exhortations roll through the rooms like thunder.

"My dear brothers and sisters," so says Henry, "let us seriously reflect on what we have promised before God and the church, that we renounce the devil and the world . . . as well as our own flesh and blood. Let us flee all vices, whether they be pride or stately dress. Such vices produce sorrow and offense, and strengthen disobedience. . . ." But Henry does not want to make his admonishments too long in order not to take too much time from the brother of "*die schwere Deel* (the heavy part)," meaning the main sermon.

In place of the deacon, who has taken ill, Bishop Victor reads from an old edition of Luther's German Bible, in which married couples still become "one flesh" and "the Word becomes flesh." Victor explains "as far as this Scripture reading extends." Following him, the guest preacher, Elmer Graber, brings the main sermon, which takes until 12:30. Before and after that part, we kneel for prayer in response to his call, "Let us fall down before the Lord who has created us."

The Amish confession of faith is relatively simple: Jesus is the leader, they are the followers. They confess that Jesus Christ is the Son of God, conceived and born of the virgin Mary. He was sent by God for their righteousness, wisdom, sanctification, and salvation. Christ is the peace, the resurrection, and the judge. No one comes to the Father but by him. The Amish believe in God as a Trinity, Father, Son, and Holy Spirit. For them the Bible is the unique, concrete history of God which reached its summit in Jesus Christ and is in no need of new interpretations. The Bible is the guide for the modern world.

Elmer, who is about to speak on these things, is called "Spot" by the Amish, who show great liking for nicknames. Spot was also the nickname of his father and grandfather, who had once hitched a spotted horse to his buggy. This name was passed down from generation to generation. In addition to Spot, there is in this very room one called "Pacer," and another rangy fellow who answers to "Pencil." In the vicinity, one fellow is named "Commander David," while another one is known as Hank "Checky."

Elmer now winds up mightily to preach the Word. He is an heir of Jakob Ammann, a laborer for Christ, and a predictor of God's judgment, all in one person. Obviously the soul of the Amish preacher needs to be expressed through various pitches of voice lest he become lukewarm and tired when burdened with a heavy message. First he speaks in a conciliatory voice to all the brothers and sisters, all subject to God's scourge as shown by sober biblical teachings. Spot suggests that all the loved ones should seriously examine their lives to determine whether they are equal to scriptural demands.

Then he raises his voice and tells them straight to their face, "I don't believe that Jesus is satisfied with us. I really don't believe it." Those thus addressed bend their heavy backs and bow their heads in fear and trembling. Actually, a few brothers have already hidden their heavy heads in mighty palms for a while now and might be fighting sleep. The transition from the cool of an Indiana morning on an open buggy to an overly warm farmhouse is a little much for some. Not far from me, I witness a drowsy brother slip a lozenge into his mouth.

Elmer reminds us of his own "bodily mother" (to distinguish her from the church as spiritual mother) who had lived a life pleasing to God. But what would she say if she were to look down today on this congregation? "Maybe she can do it, who knows?" His reflections circle around dark words; he believes he is being understood. His mother would not be satisfied, but the servant does not enter into the details of all the things being done wrong in Allen County. He hints that the good mother would have rejected all things modern, that she would have entirely disapproved of the empty world of progress, and that the children now owed it to God "to be worthy of her," meaning that they ought not to dabble in things technical, matters modern.

What Spot is obviously getting to is that in his opinion the old generation lived a much more God-pleasing life than the young ones of today. He reminds them of Noah's day, when people walked in fleshly shortcomings and "did not allow themselves to be rebuked by God's spirit." The time has come for the servants to "wake up in teaching and in warning." Then he enters into the subject of "the last things," the day when Christ will take home his bride, the church. In order to become a member of this church, it is necessary for everyone to "have a blessed death to sin and self." Elmer regards such spiritual death to the old nature as his greatest desire for this life, matched by his gentle longing for a life after death. Eventually Spot launches into the story of Daniel and Nebuchadnezzar, particularly Daniel, prophet from the house of Judah, and Nebuchadnezzar, before whom, according to the preacher, "everyone trembled with fear."

Elmer is a speaker of God's grace, who time and again comes up with astounding biblical formulations which would likely checkmate many a studied theologian. Moreover, his preacher-German is of a high order. Elmer communicates eternal truths of biblical Christianity in the language of Luther, thereby reminding everyone that the religion and ethnicity of the Amish in America depend strictly on their own resourcefulness and God's grace. It is only the gospel and the historically significant events of Anabaptist history which here provide the key to a persisting German culture.

This gospel and Anabaptist history recorded in the German language were passed on in German, not least of all because the theology of Rome once made do without the German language for hundreds of years. Hence it became a responsibility for the brothers and sisters to retain their Germanness as well as possible. This facet of the Amish character was never threatened; it is only of late that it is becoming a problem. Yet this rather antiquated language of a foreign country helped to isolate them in modern America; it is a bulwark against things *Englisch* (non-Amish).

The air becomes ever closer and heads sink lower. Children are shuffling with their feet and asking for fresh supplies from chip bags. Small children enter from the kitchen where the women are assembled and look for their fathers in the living room, while others walk in the opposite direction. More and more frequently individual brothers head for the stable or sisters to the outhouse. But Elmer plows straight ahead, looks and dreams in the distance, and then while retreating into his own spirit with apparently final words, he again sallies forth with a mighty vocalic barrage on things eternal and things transitory, whatever he thinks needs to be handled. His sermon now becomes a charge against the lust of the eyes, the lust of the flesh, and an arrogant life (1 John 2:16), well-known "abominations before God," so that the judgment of the great flood to punish evildoers shall not be lost on us here in these rooms (Gen. 6).

The gentle yet raging proclaimer of the gospel throws his full head of silver-gray mushroom hair back into his neck. This is the usual hair style of the picture-book Amish. Yet Elmer does not lose himself or his congregation for even one second. He makes only one mistake in it all, a mistake against which Amish preachers are constantly warned. Time and again he says he does not want to make the sermon too long. This makes it especially hard for the children, who are longing for the service to conclude. They might believe that the end of the message is at hand, but if the preacher starts again, then yet again, they may—according to reflective Amish minds—think the minister is tricking them.

Finally, as if to draw a breath of fresh air—but where would it come from?—Elmer declares, "I can't tell you everything. You have to read it on your own." In the Bible one can find everything, just as he says, but in the meantime, the hour of noon has struck, and he soon has to conclude. This allows those trembling from the mighty message, especially the sensitive women of the cooking crew, to compose themselves somewhat by furtively drying their tears with their handkerchiefs.

After the sermon, Elmer sits down on his bench and asks rather submissively of Bishop Victor whether he agrees with what he has said, whether everything was according to the Scriptures. Victor rather woodenly responds, "*Jo*, I believe you have spoken well unto us. . . ." This "questioning of the witness" goes on a bit longer since the sermon is subject to testing by "the mouth of two or three witnesses," so that doubt and faith will be disclosed (2 Cor. 13:1). Further "witness-givers" weigh what has been said and agree that they also "have heard the teaching and nothing but" (1 Cor. 14:29). Elmer "has done his solemn duty." One states, "I understood nothing but what is God's, and I can testify that what the brother has said is true," while another says, "*Jo*, such has also been said in the Gospel by Mark."

Elmer feels "grateful that the teaching has been recognized as God's Word," and he tells the congregation as much. It can happen that after a *Donnerwetter* (scolding, thundering) sermon in which a preacher gets somewhat carried away and expresses himself with excessive liberty, one of the faithful gets up and declares frankly and freely that this or that did not please him since it did not agree with the Holy Word. If he is right and the majority of those present agree with him, then the minister has to retract the offending words.

The Amish view of what "is God's" is what all Christian churches believe in principle. These people cling to the Protestant concept of biblical interpretation. The great difference lies chiefly in how they apply the interpretation and weave it into their daily life. The New Testament, the teachings of Jesus, and particularly the Sermon on the Mount (Matt. 5-7) constitute the center of their beliefs. They emphasize that foremost to them is discipleship, to be followers of Christ like their forebears back in the reforming days of Switzerland. Anyone interested in understanding the Amish in one quick session should read 2 Corinthians 6-7. There believers are told to go through life "unknown yet known," as "sad but yet always rejoicing," with great patience, in tribulations, in fears, in beatings, in prisons, in hard times, in purity. They seek to live as the poor, who make many rich, who touch nothing impure, who cleanse themselves of the impurities of the flesh in order to stand out as lights in the surrounding darkness.

For a good conclusion, Karl Schwartz calls for the singing of the "Song of Parting," number 136, one of four farewell songs in the *Ausbund*, and he serves as the *Vorsänger* (precentor). For the last time a song sweeps through the house like a whirlwind, then a final prayer, and after "Jesus Christ. Amen," both brothers and sisters curtsy. Then all the unbaptized leave the room after the bishop remarks, "There are matters brought to the attention of the church; all nonmembers shall now leave and make room for members."

I also must leave, but I have heard of the type of thing that may be discussed at such members' meetings. For example, a young Amish couple not yet formally married might shyly and fearfully admit that they have committed some "sexual indecency," meaning that the woman is pregnant and the matter is "pressing." It is favorable to their case to confess their sin and state, "We would like to make this matter right." Of course, they are prepared to marry with due haste if the church will allow them to do so.

The older generation would rock their heads reflectively, complain in the early Bernese dialect of crumbling morals among the youth, and lament about parents who do not take proper care to prevent "unmarried cohabitation." The congregation would deliberate, as a warning, on whether they should "allow Satan to have them" (1 Cor. 5:5). But then they would quickly and generally agree that the wedding might be held after three worship meetings, in six weeks' time, but without a huge feast since such would reward the bed of sin.

After a few announcements of a general nature, which include the next place of meeting, the brothers and sisters arise and take their places at one of the mighty tables for a substantial *Brotzeit* (bread time), the meal of love, which the women of the house and their relatives have spent days preparing. Who prays much, now eats much, but not all that much and not too much of good things, in order not to win the reputation that one attends the church service on account of a good meal. Whatever, these folks know what good food is for and what it's all about—"the Lord in heaven be honored and praised for it."

They heap their plates in the best Amish tradition and discuss the latest news, including some matter in one of the churches in Berne (Ind.), practically within buggy range of Grabill. Then one of them launches into English and is immediately reprimanded, for the God of the Old Amish still speaks German, just as in the Luther Bible, "Adam, Adam, *wo bist du* (where are you)?" High German is for them like "Latin" was for the early Anabaptists, and some of them at this round table are not fluent in it. Already there are signs that German one day might even become a foreign language to them. For instance, in Tennessee a Preacher Stoll, a conservative no less, recently started up a church in which only English is spoken. It is not that Stoll wanted to give up his traditional ties to the forebears of old. However, he is of the opinion that the Amish gain no membership from the surrounding world because outsiders are simply incapable of understanding them.

The conversation turns to Berne. The Amish are now permitted to adopt children. This is in contrast to former times when the state government simply regarded them as too old-fashioned to do so. Many in Berne are already busily adopting children. A few years ago a family adopted a girl who grew up, married recently, and had a baby. But—and what a terrible shock to the Amish—the baby was black. So the church at Berne began proceedings to shun this woman for infidelity and to throw her out of church, since both father and mother obviously were white. It took some detective work to establish that the adopted girl had a dark-skinned ancestor. That genetic color factor had been transmitted through her even though it didn't show in her own skin. This baby is probably the first black Amish person in North America, and the world of the Berne church is again in order.

As appropriate for a Sunday church gathering, the Amish have no intentions of neglecting or not coming to terms with their past. Now they dish up a few biblical themes and Anabaptist stories. Anyone who knows about the early Anabaptists is in demand. In such conversations, the martyrs assume gigantic proportions. There are stories about all the things they had to suffer and endure (generally true), all the things they managed with God's help (only partly verified), and all the miracles which happened in the fires at the stakes (about which I managed to find nothing in the archives of Europe).

Even though these detectives on the trail of their ancestors' faith have no recent witnesses to this history, they are skillful at making the suffering of their Anabaptist forebears become the suffering of their listeners. There will never be any danger of their history being forgotten, nor will they ever act as if they have forgotten it. They have sustained deep psychological hurt, and now they accept or even welcome suffering as a role in life because it shows that they are in the line of the prophets (Matt. 5:11-12). While they seek no revenge, they insist on remembering everything. The discipleship of the spiritually immortal martyrs, showing what it means to follow Christ in the daily walk of life, provides joy and makes them free.

They certainly do not regard these stories of victims and persecutors simply as entertaining drama. The Amish use their martyrs for the forging of their identity similar to Israel's use of the deliverance from Egypt or the Holocaust (Deut. 26:1-11). This centuries-old history of suffering is their own history even today.

And isn't it true, after all, that God is setting things right? Formerly the martyrs were dead while the tormentors lived. Today the tormentors are gone, but those once judged by them are spiritually alive and well and presented in the song about the virtuous girl sung in the house of John Zehr on Cuba Road.

Thus the Amish have no need for an updated or revised understanding of the world or history, which in their view has just celebrated its six thousandth birthday since the creation of the world. To all this, no revision is called for or necessary. When I ask what they think God was doing prior to creating heaven and earth six thousand years ago, Elmer's answer is typical of the Amish and in accord with the psalmist, who says, "Before the mountains were brought forth, or ever you had formed the earth and the world, even from everlasting to everlasting, you are God" (Ps. 90:2). God is God, and that's enough to know. It isn't edifying to ask what he was doing before creation. That's Elmer for you: his faith permits absolutely no doubt, no doubt at all.

The fellowship meal served after the church service is much more than a copy of rigid custom. It reminds one of the solidarity among the Anabaptists during the hard times of previous centuries even though the Amish of Allen County have included a little more variety than the traditional menu. The time is not long past when, after church, groups ate bean soup from the same pot, first the men and then the women, without washing dishes in between. The Amish regard this as a sign of brotherly and sisterly solidarity and love of neighbor. Today kitchen knives are sharpened, and everyone gets one's own plate and cup, but frequently they still do not wash dishes between eating shifts.

The word for this regular love meal, *Liebesmahl,* was also known to other Anabaptists and to the Herrnhuter, the Moravians. Ironically, this very word, *Liebesmahl,* found its way into the vocabulary of the German military. It was used for the convivial or social occasions of the officers' corps.

Around 2:00 p.m. the first families, often only the husbands, leave for their farms in order to look things over. For the rest of the day, there is a constant coming and going in John's farmhouse. In the evening after the chores are done, a huge dinner is served for close relatives of the family, followed by a Ping-Pong tournament for the teenagers. A feature attraction of a church Sunday is the evening communal singing, which in Allen County no longer happens with the former regularity.

In contrast to the Amish around Grabill, the New Amish of Ohio have introduced the Sunday school, held every second Sunday, on the in-between Sunday of the fourteen-day cycle when a worship service is not held. On this occasion, faster songs are sung, and after a prayer, the congregation is divided into four classes by age groups. The New Amish also permit women to instruct the youngest set, explaining that the institution of Sunday school is not necessarily biblical, so nothing prevents a woman from assuming this role.

******

On a wet misty morning, Rachel is baking pies, her son Chris is manning the harness shop, Barbara Ann and Ben are still in the stable, and Rachel Mae is playing with two deer fawns which have wandered into the yard and simply stayed. Elam and I drive to visit Victor Graber, the broad-bearded bishop of Elam's *Gemee* (church), which is entered in Raber's *Almanac* as the West Spencerville congregation or district. If one is to trust old caricatures, this Victor looks like a parody of Moses, the traditional *Mensch* (human being). There is a noble streak to the man, the completely unshakable totality of a human being.

In addition to a flourishing farm, Victor builds plastic buggies, which the chief shepherd sells among the brotherhood for $1500. One can deduce that he is no poor Lazarus, yet he is not a wealthy man, either. As I expected, Victor immediately puts all the usual questions to me, the German from the *aalt Land* (old country). First he asks about the top speed limit on German autobahns, although not only he, but all the other Amish from far and wide know by now that there are no speed limits on the autobahn. Nothing around here surprises them more than to hear that when Germans drive a car, they *drive* a car.

Then Elam introduces what he had actually planned to say all along. Amish are not allowed to argue, and certainly not with their bishop. Elam circles around in the conversation, hoping that this tactic will bring Victor to the point he has been trying to make all along. As we admire the carriages on display, Elam casually remarks that one he bought recently from the venerable man has something wrong with the paint job. He, Elam, does not want to lodge a complaint, of course, but the carriage is not as pitch black as it ought to be. Not quite. Naturally, he, Elam, has not come in order to mention this, but other carriages . . . well, they are somewhat blacker than his. As mentioned, he has no intention of complaining, but. . . .

Elam only intends to beat the bush of the buggy builder gently and determine his opinion on what is black on a buggy and what is not quite so black. Not a word falls which could in any way disturb the peace between Elam and Victor and lead to disturbing the peace in the congregation. Yet Elam chews his tobacco more vigorously than usual, and he squirts the brown juice farther than one is used to him doing, all of which leads me to conclude that the matter is embarrassing to him. Then Victor answers him kindly, much like an old village pastor would, and offers to make it right.

An Amish church district is a geographic area within which a congregation lives and meets for worship. In Allen County, judging by the numbers of people, the worldly and not the Amish strike one as the exotic party. Here a district is between one and two square miles in size, in which live a set of relatives or *unsre Sort Lüt* (our kind of people). Today there are twelve church districts, each with thirty families, about two hundred people. In a district with too many people to meet in one house, the church members will discuss the matter of a peaceful division. A district may then be divided by a street, an aqueduct, or, ironically, once by an electric power line. Any Amish living in the identified geographic area have to belong to the same church.

The members live so close together that the distance to their neighbors of like faith can be calculated in trotter minutes. This proximity of community reduces the feeling of estrangement in a world radically different from their own. The Amish also make sure never to live so far from their parents that they can't easily reach them by buggy. "The world" especially profits from the living arrangement of the Amish. Wherever they live, the neighborhood land becomes a hot, competitive, overly appreciated, speculative commodity. The Amish are simply forced to purchase more land and often have to pay up to $3,000 per acre in Allen County, whether they want to or not. The alternative is to pack up and move on, which means a rift not only in the family but in the entire religious neighborhood.

This situation has assumed drastic proportions in the Lancaster (Pa.) area, where land has been inflated to $10,000 per acre and the Amish have been offered up to a million dollars for a farm. Wherever the Amish live in such a concentrated fashion as around Intercourse or New Holland, they attract tourists. These in turn attract hotel chains and restaurants, souvenir vendors, and so forth. Land becomes scarcer and scarcer. The Amish author Gideon L. Fisher states, "For thirty years the tourists came in order to see us. Now they come to buy our land. As to what the future will bring? This is totally uncertain." Likewise, the area around Grabill is filling up with more and more people, although it is not yet approaching a state of emergency.

In every congregation one finds names which predominate on account of fellowshiping in close geographic circles or through numerous marriages among cousins. Some of the names are Americanized. In Allen County one notes the Grabers and Schmuckers; in LaGrange (Ind.), the Bontragers, Millers, Hochstetlers; at Nappanee, the Slabaughs, Chupps, Yoders; in Holmes County (Ohio), the Masts, Troyers, Millers, Hershbergers, Swartzentrubers, Weavers, Rabers; in Lancaster County (Pa.), the Lapps, Stoltzfuses, Kings, Fishers, Zooks; and on and on.

The Amish keep in close contact with each other by visiting back and forth and through reading *The Budget*, of which a special edition is published for these plain folks. One of the most unusual publications in the world, it is printed in Sugarcreek, Ohio, in an area where some 22,000 Amish live. This weekly paper has a staff of five hundred reporters and a Lutheran editor and boasts more "journalists" than does any other American paper. It is published in English, which the Amish understand, and features no photos. The newspaper offers a unique thematic profile. It carries nothing about politics since the Amish do not vote, nothing about crime because they do not want it, and little about "science falsely so called" (1 Tim. 6:20) such as evolution, except to refute it, because they wish to protect God's act of creation from scientific snoopiness.

The Budget, aside from the paper *Die Botschaft* (The message, news) published in Lancaster (Pa.), is the only more-than-regional weekly paper of the group. It has a writer in practically every congregation who regularly reports on births, weddings, deaths, visitors, weather, crops, and sicknesses, or when the first robin has been seen in Kishacoquillas Valley, Mifflin County (Pa.), and what was butchered most recently in Coshocton County (Ohio), and whether the intestines ripped or not while being stuffed with sausage meat. Every copy features some three hundred news items of this kind from various church districts.

Amish life plays itself out in the security of the church: birth, growing up, baptism, wedding, and death, with a wide spectrum of psychological, pedagogical, biological, and social mutual assistance. In all this, the congregations make do with a sensible and intricate system of wheels and gears of life. Most Amish of a district have the same education, the same upbringing, the same models, and they come from the same families and consequently are of the same thought pattern. One knows about the other's personal makeup, talents, and weaknesses.

Spiritual support comes from the older generation, who explain the inevitability of death or the second coming of Christ. The church serves as the rope to the mountain climber, and only in the framework of the church are these strict believers able to divorce themselves from the world, from evil, and from the bad which the devil is busily and constantly planting. In the refuge and safety net of the church, the Amish anticipate the apocalyptic return of Jesus, in whom they see their salvation. The church demonstrates to the Amish how they can gain the future without giving up the past. In all that, Amish life rarely rotates around the "I" but almost invariably around a seriously meant "We."

In a religious sense, the congregation is the church of Jesus, anointed by the Son of God with the Holy Spirit at Pentecost (Acts 2). It was expanded to include peoples of all nations, united with each other through faith and baptism, in one body of Christ, with Christ as Lord (1 Cor. 12:27). However, the Amish of Allen County do not send out missionaries. For them, Christ is the head of the body (Eph. 4:15), meaning the community in the breaking of bread and in prayer, and thus the church district. Few of the people of all nations are being gathered here, since the Amish do not actively search for those searching for God. They believe that their obedient life and love for God and for each other in their congregation can attract seekers better than words alone or one or two itinerant messengers of gospel peace.

These saints in Christ do not turn away anyone who wants to join their small flock. But they do not make efforts to seek out such a one at all costs. Here and there are examples of persons who came into the Amish church from the outside, usually through adoption or marriage, and made an acceptable confession of faith and keep the *Ordnung* (order, discipline). Yet the church as the great societal stabilizer can get along quite well with those born into Amish homes. They fear that new wine might cause old skins to break, that weeds could mingle among the wheat. Their prime task is to pass the gospel on to their children. This is their first mission field. One raised Amish is only an Amish believer by personal choice, but yet even that depends upon whether the brothers and sisters accept such a person as one of theirs. Thus they have retained much of the early-church strictness about boundaries and faithfulness.

The Amish desire no assimilation with the world, only a peaceful coexistence. They no longer make any attempt to convince the surrounding larger cultures about themselves. With few exceptions, they do not engage in any such public relations. Yet when asked, they will give an account of their faith. They are satisfied with the fact that they are among God's chosen people. There are few outsiders who, after trials and errors, stumble into the lap of their church. Yet one third of all Amish family names stem from "Converts from the Outside, Made in USA." That may seem to be a rather small number for the 260 years since the first Amish pioneers immigrated to the New World, but it is significant.

Recently the Graber church has accepted a family from the outside "on a trial basis" since God even offered a way to the heathen, which led to a turnaround. Yet the Amish find it difficult to recognize the work of the Holy Spirit among such seekers. Even old Joseph has not made up his mind on this point. He merely rocks his ice-gray hairy head in thought. The way of the Amish is narrow and difficult, and they may even tell a visitor, "You could not live this way." First, the worldly would have to learn *Dütsch*, and then they would have to make do without many modern conveniences of their previous lifestyle. This transition is about as extreme as changing a cannibal into a vegetarian. Then, only then, would one give the matter a second thought. Today the worldly who want to join the Amish church are mainly those who have worked on Amish farms and fallen in love with one of their fair maidens.

The inner structure of the church has its roots in the New Testament and in the monastic orders of the Catholic church. However, the Catholic orders removed themselves from the world in order to live a pure teaching in cloisters, while the Anabaptists walked among the people, started their own families, and led a normal life of work. They regarded it more important to serve than to be served, to give rather than to receive.

On the basis of their traditional and biological ties and mutual care for each other, the Amish of today have become a distinctive ethnic group. This is shown by their customs, usages, mannerisms, tenets of faith, skills, language, and tools. They retain this ethnic identity as long as they do not blend into the general population, as long as they do not give up their unique way of life. For centuries these people have adapted to current conditions but not sold out to the surrounding culture. The net effect is that they have barely changed. *Heimat* (homeland) to them is their community of faith, something lasting, whose piety is determined by Scripture, even though the world around them be an ever so dynamic and variable American fatherland or German motherland. The brothers and sisters still cut their own track. This is a bold social and religious strategy which belies their reputation for being quietistic.

The highest moral leadership in the church belongs to a bishop or "full servant" like Victor, but only with the cooperation of his fellow members. In important decisions (almost anything can be important) he consults with the other ministers and deacons, to whom anyone can bring any matter, as long as it is biblically based. The leaders counsel together in their *Abrot*, a session at the beginning of the Sunday service. They plan who will preach and what matters (if any) they would bring for deliberation and decision to a members-only meeting at the end of the Sunday service, a *Nachgemee*. In case of an emergency or something major arising between the biweekly worship services, the leaders may call a *Dienerversammlung*, an extra meeting for the servants (bishop, ministers, and deacon). Within the framework of the church district, the trickiest questions are resolved.

I am told that trendy worldly issues like homosexuality, drug addiction, emancipation of women, or abortions have no place on their agenda, since they already agree in disapproving such. They contend with other problems like the length of skirt hems, whether they are allowed diesel motors to operate a pump or a welder (as in a neighboring congregation), how matters stand on acceptability of horse-drawn balers and side-delivery rakes, whether milk may be cooled and if so, whether with electricity from the outside or that generated by one's own diesel motor. There may be questions about clothes washers operated by compressed air, or battery-operated coffee mills, or who has what against the introduction of short pants for field work.

Some Amish districts have used some machine or other on the edge of the field or outside of the house but not on their own fields or in their own houses. Something permitted on one side of the road may still be strictly prohibited on the other side, which lies in a different church district of the same larger Amish community.

With regard to congregational decision making and its authority to excommunicate, the art of the Amish has been perfected. The issues invariably are about how to be interwoven with the world and yet to keep this very world at a safe distance. The church is invariably the gardener who lovingly tends healthy young shoots and props or even removes unhealthy ones from the main stem. The purpose is to retain the difficult synthesis between the original Amish steps toward paradise and the Amish life here and now. Their authority is of Christ and therefore God-willed. Their jurisdiction involves not only spiritual matters, things of the inner world such as pride or repentance, but also those of the temporal world, members' lifestyle.

The use of lightning rods is an example of such deliberation, according to reports I have gathered from Ohio. Some families have secretly installed them on their barn roofs. This leads to disagreements. A members' meeting is called to resolve religious disparities, "as in the times of our forebears, the holy martyrs." First they sing, then listen to an admonition to love. This is followed by a prayer and again by an admonition to peace, love, and accord. Then the "purpose for the gathering is introduced." After a spokesman and an assistant are elected, the two confirm that the meeting is to transpire completely according to God's Word. If "a charge" is brought against a member, that one is not allowed to sit in on the counsel meeting. Now the spokesman states that they should best proceed with the business at hand.

Next one member (lets call him Moses) advances a proposition. Moses speaks long and loudly with displeasure that some of the members use lightning rods. Jesus Christ made do with less. He, Moses, cannot associate with persons who approve of such things. (Instead of lightning rods, they might be dealing with "marriages of close relatives or cousins," or "worldly enjoyments such as ornaments, braids, gold, pearls or expensive garments," or playing cards or musical instruments, or engaging in other "ostentatious practices.")

As far as Moses is concerned, "It would hardly be comfortable to bear with a brother who has a lightning rod on his house." Then he states that he would "hold no grievance" against those who would remove the rods from their houses and barns, but then everyone would have to "come under the *alte Ordnung* (old order, as in *Old Order Amish)* so that no rifts would be caused." This would satisfy him. The Savior promised his followers nothing but the cross and tribulations. Lightning rods represent a parting from the Lord, who says, "Without the will of your Father, not a hair will fall from your heads" (Matt. 10:29-31). Why then attempt to make do with such "useless things"? One ought to take action in time so that later "no bad feelings with name-calling and insults" would arise.

Again one of them admonishes the congregation to come to "accord," and another would appeal for them to "keep the peace." One should leave old matters rest and rather reflect on how love could generally be reinstated. Fuller discussion continues. Again the appeal is made "to let love prevail in order to heal the wounds." Everyone agrees to "briskly pursue peace if healing is to be found therein."

If one of the members has understood nothing for a long time and now, suddenly, understands everything, then he has "received some light in this matter." If one is still unsure, he says no, which can, however, later change into a yes. If an issue is to be decided, members vote "by rising." On this point, differences exist as to whether the counsel of the congregation merely decides on something for now or whether the members "formulate a law . . . which a hundred years after us will be used as an example by our grandchildren."

If someone is contrary minded on an issue but does not wish to engage in a quarrel with the majority, then he does not vote for it but "wants to stand here in patience." If one of them does not understand the entire issue, then such is "a strange matter" to him which he intends to investigate "before he decides on it." Questions arise: "Could this or that be tolerated without offense?" Is it not true that in the Gospels one cannot find a single passage which expressly forbids lightning rods? If things get really difficult, a leader seeks a word from the *Martyrs Mirror* "as to what the opinion of the old fathers was regarding the matter." However, there is no reference to lightning rods in that book.

This can go on for hours. If the congregation arrives at a decision, the meeting is concluded with song, admonition, and prayer. "Through and by the grace of God, various difficulties have been removed and a considerable part of the divisions have been brought to the point that healing can be hoped for. We are much in debt to the Giver of all good things, we return thanks for his rich blessings and his undeserved grace, and we fervently beseech him through the merits of our Savior for his constant help and presence so that we can walk according to the counsel of the apostles. . . ." If no accord is reached, a further meeting is necessary. If no one speaks to a proposal and total silence ensues, then that likely means an absolute no.

The Amish place great value on the group decision-making process of their congregation since it alone holds the spiritual power of authority, delegated to it by Jesus Christ (Matt. 18:18). This process, when properly pursued, guards against the possibility of a religious dictatorship. There are strict Amish and flexible Amish, and opinions occasionally diverge between the districts. However, they are agreed that there is no genuine road in the middle, and that such a way cannot exist between the world and the true church. Not everything the church concludes is in the Bible, and some passages of Scripture are more important to the Amish than others. Sometimes pettiness takes precedence over understanding of human weaknesses. Nevertheless, the Amish believe that, in order to prevent a religious dam from breaking, their church can and must establish rules as long as such rules are not expressly contradicted by the biblical word.

Victor humbly calls himself a "servant of God." In his bishop's duties, hearing "two or three witnesses" is necessary to resolve a matter. While preaching, he enumerates sins against the *Ordnung* to prevent any kind of budding defection from the teachings of the church. He—and only he—presides over the breaking of bread or the Lord's Supper, and he presides over marriages and baptisms. With the agreement of the congregation, he excommunicates, and he accepts the banned back into the bosom of the church after penitence.

Alongside the bishop, a church district generally has two or three preachers (*Prediger*) or servants of the Word. Like the full servant or bishop, they are chosen by lot from laymen without formal training. Their main duty is preaching in turn at Sunday services. It is acceptable for any men who are members to exhort the others by bearing witness to the sermon. After the worship service, in the members-only meeting, any member may give counsel, including the women, although they usually say less than the men. However, for delivering the sermons, the Amish deviate from the example of the early church, where every member still had the right, according to one's gifts, to serve as a preacher or a teacher (1 Cor. 14:26). The Amish permit only those to preach who have been called by God through the drawing of the lot, and who (like the twelve apostles) are of masculine gender.

What about female bishops, female pastors, or educated theologians? In principle the Amish of Allen County are opposed to "women as servants," ministers. To support this they cite Paul (1 Tim. 2:12-14), who seems to say that their faculties for judging between good and evil are in doubt since Eve's disastrous desire for the forbidden fruit. In addition, in good *old* Anabaptist tradition, they reject people who have engaged in harmful and unnecessary formal studies of theology. God never had his messengers educated in anything in particular. According to these brothers, in order to proclaim the Word, one needed no erudition or worldly wisdom, but only to seek the right word on the right passage of Scripture. Thus we read in one of the oldest Anabaptist confessions of faith, dated 1617: "The people of God shall not turn to leaders who have been educated in the high schools of human knowledge and who talk and dispute and who then attempt to sell this purchased gift for timely profit" (Twisck; see Braght, *Martyrs Mirror,* 395).

For this position of preacher, the Amish look for a brother who is holy and without guile, who "has consumed the entire Bible" and thus is ready to proclaim a message from God for today (as in Ezek. 3; Rev. 10). He is one who keeps his body under control and feels the Holy Spirit working in and through him. Anything else would be a grievous error, with the congregation being "led by fools." At his baptism a brother accepts the possibility that, if selected by recommendations and the lot, he may assume the position of a servant (minister), with divinely given competency. A servant flourishes whenever God and the church place him into office.

In addition to the preachers and bishop, there is the *Armendiener* (the servant of the poor, deacon), the Mother Teresa of the Amish, who most fittingly symbolizes the Amish sense of being a good Samaritan to the neighbor. This is the most difficult responsibility among the servants. His function might seem to show that the Amish are anchored in the Protestant "social gospel" tradition. But the Amish have kept up such mutual helping from their Anabaptist heritage of the sixteenth century, long before Rauschenbusch of the early 1900s, of whom they have not heard.

The Amish express their caring by not letting anyone in the church go without having basic needs met if the members are in any position to assist. They base their help for needy fellow believers upon the obligations of brotherly love, already a distinguishing tenet of the early Anabaptists and thus older and more powerful than their sense of mission or their ordinances. The Anabaptists of the time of the Reformation were trailblazers in caring for the poor. In accord with the apostolic example (Acts 2—6), they collected voluntary contributions for the common purse in order to relieve need wherever it existed. To this day, every member of an Amish congregation can rely on being surrounded by a caring body of the church, which makes the outer and inner isolation from the world much easier to bear.

Each individual helps to guarantee the general welfare by

taking social initiative and a duty to assume an active role in neighborliness. Although the church depends exclusively on freewill offerings, such moneys are never used to accumulate church assets. Tobi Graber's congregation has opened a "Poverty Elimination Account" for this purpose, from which they can draw funds at short notice. They take great care that the bank does not pay them any interest on this money since worldly profits for such purposes are regarded as un-Christian (Ps. 15:5).

The *Armendiener*, the deacon of Acts 6, has various roles. He assists in the church service and also is the courier of the church. One of his duties is to be the first to know when or what somebody is up to. He is the first to know what is going on, who dates whom. In many congregations he is the person who, as the *Schteklimann* (go-between), asks the father of the bride for her hand in the name of the groom. He referees minor quarrels within the church, and if a church member has transgressed or trespassed, the preachers and bishop hear from him in the *Abrot*. However, his most prominent responsibility has remained to collect money for brothers and sisters who have fallen on hard times.

In performing this task, he is the true-to-the-Word servant of the poor who sees to it that no one of their circle ever remains an outsider, that everyone is always part of a greater family, part of the community. This church grants its members and families security from the womb to the tomb within the framework of the Anabaptist order of life and faith. One brother bears the burden of another (Gal. 6:2), and the most famous example of this Amish principle is their quick assistance after a fire. The Amish community (not just one district) rallies for a barn raising or to erect a new shed. After the foundation is ready, hundreds of men band together like a colony of ants to raise a barn after a fire, and all that in a single day (Prov. 6:6). Simultaneously, hundreds of women get together to cook and fry and provide food for their men, husbands and sons. Though chiefly farmers and not carpenters, they are handy with tools and able to work together smoothly under the direction of the master carpenter. As an overflow of their mutual aid, Amish and Old Order Mennonites may even help *Englischers* in their neighborhood or beyond who suffered loss in a fire, flood, or other catastrophe.

All these servants fill the leadership offices without financial

156

recompense. After all, the disciples of Jesus were not allowed to make their ministry into a profession. Jesus told them, "Provide neither gold, nor silver, nor brass in your purses" (Matt. 10:9). They are chosen from the ranks of church membership. One of the conditions is to be of strong personality since neither God nor humans are well served by a weak brother. To quote a bit of peasant logic, "Tools made of soft wood are no good for work." Also, the servant leader is required to present a "good testimony," showing his ability to master challenges in teaching and admonition, punishment or excommunication, and yet have the necessary *Demut* (humility) not to consider himself superior on the basis of his office. A candidate for this position has to be married, living "like a shepherd according to the order of Paul" as God commanded (1 Tim. 3), and always in a position to stop the mouths of scoffers.

All members, women and men, take part in the selection of preachers and deacons. During the process, an atmosphere of great sadness pervades the congregation since they already pity the party who will be blessed by God with such a heavy responsibility. Although the Amish themselves would not admit it, choosing spiritual leaders invariably stirs up great personal problems and inner soul searching. If a brother desires a position, then he is regarded as totally unsuitable for it from the outset because of such ambition. If he does not want it because he regards himself even with God's help as incapable of doing justice to the position, then he is not deemed to be the proper candidate. In principle, one can assume that most brothers do not desire such a calling. Before every selection they pray, as once did Jesus in the Garden of Gethsemane, that this cup might pass them by (Mark 14:36).

The choosing of a servant leader has to be announced in the church service. The congregation now has "time for reflection" in order to decide which candidate they want. They spend days and nights in prayer about the matter. During the ordination service itself, as when they "make a preacher," they first have a "serious prayer in the manner of the apostles." Then members saunter past a slightly opened door and whisper the name of their candidate into the ear of a brother, who records it in writing.

Selection practices differ among various Amish churches, but they all stem from traditions of the first generations of Anabaptist history. In Allen County the two candidates with the most votes come into the lot (*Lote* or *Los*). The use of the lot follows the example of the apostles in calling a successor to Judas (Acts 1:23-26). Those in charge produce two hymnals, one containing a scrap of paper bearing a Bible verse (such as Prov. 16:33 or Acts 1:24). The books have been shuffled so no one knows which is which. Now each candidate chooses a hymnal, and the one who finds the scrap of paper is then ordained for the office.

The charge is given to the new servant with the words, "In the name of the Lord and the church, the service to the Book is conferred upon you, to preach the gospel and proclaim it, to pray with the church, and to speak through the fathers of old. . . ." The Lord, who knows the hearts of all, has participated in the selection through responding to their prayers, guiding the discernment of the members, and determining the outcome of the lot.

Democratic elections in Old Europe were an act of protest toward the great churches in which the hierarchy routinely appointed clerics for spiritual positions. The Amish believe that if the Lord has "a purpose" with a man, and the Holy Spirit marks that person, then it is up to God to advance that chosen party by means of the lot. This office is for life unless a bearer of the office commits some serious misdemeanor, whereupon he is "brought to a stop in office" with a public rebuke (1 Tim. 5:19-20).

The Amish do not have a grand bishop or archbishop, no shepherd who stands above the entire group of Anabaptists and represents them collectively in their internal relations or to those outside. In case a district has problems with its full servant, they call as mediator a bishop from a neighboring congregation with whom they are in fellowship. However, every church is autonomous. There are and have been great gatherings of Amish servants of the Word, constituting the highest leadership of many congregations. On occasion bishops, preachers, and deacons have assembled to decide collectively how the Bible is to be interpreted in one matter or another and how such interpretations are to be applied to the practical life of the Amish. Some of these decisions lasted for centuries, while others were ignored by some congregations or changed during another meeting. A standard Amish voice has never existed.

Certain factions among the Amish have stemmed from the

typically Anabaptist group character of local decision making. Some became even more conservative than the conservatives. An entire world may well lie between being Beachy Amish, with a car instead of a horse in the barn, or Nebraska Amish. The Nebraska Amish are part of a group founded in 1881 in Pennsylvania. Their men have their hair about shoulder length as in the seventeenth century, and their wives wear the flat strawhat of the Swiss peasant women from the time of the Reformation. In addition to these, there are the New Amish, the Old Order Amish, the Amish Mennonites; the Egli, Hostetler, Miller, Yoder, and Weaver Amish; Stuckey Mennonites; Swartzentruber Amish, Burkholder Amish, Reno Amish, the Stoltzfus Church. . . . One group is called the "Beansoup" (or Byler) Amish and got that name from eating a pot of bean soup out of a common dish after the church service. They can also be recognized by their yellow-topped carriages.

Today the diversity in the spectrum of Anabaptists of German background is most convincingly reflected in the great weekly markets around Lancaster, as at New Holland. On Monday horses are sold, buggies and quilts on Tuesdays, and cattle on Wednesdays. In the surrounding area there are by now some 100 Amish districts with around 20,000 people, estimating thirty-five families per district and six members to a family. Intermingled are Old Order and conservative Mennonites of every shade and color.

A few years ago, the so-called New Order Amish were established in the Lancaster area and recognizable there by their cropped beards. Ohio New Order Amish have full or only slightly trimmed beards. Formerly of Old Order Amish persuasion, they allow telephones in the home and farming with tractors, but not the car. Also, these contrary-minded New Amish have forbidden smoking. Occasionally, at the market of New Holland, one can witness an Amish of the Old Order smoking spectacular cigars or fat-bellied pipes which so much provoke the New Amish that the latter deliberately turn away and get on with the business of shunning the smoker. After a mass exodus from the Old Amish to the New Amish, this shunning today cuts right through families.

The old horse dentist Smucker can sing many a lament about this. He lives in the Smucker valley east of New Holland, roughly in the area in which the first Amish settled in North America. The tooth doctor looks out from his practice, resting his elbows by the window on bleached horse skulls and countless horse teeth. From there he can see the house of a son, one of five children who have left the church during the last while. Only one son, Jacob, returned after he had witnessed California, hell on earth by Amish standards. All that so much worried the old man that he fell seriously ill. However, he recuperated with God's will. For a few weeks, various horses in the vicinity were much the worse for dreadful toothaches, since no one wanted to replace the venerable old horse dentist.

Yet again and still again, new trouble is brewing. In the Smucker Church, some members have changed the German *Schmücker* and become Schmuckers, Smuckers, or even Smokers. Some districts have departed from their fellows technologically by introducing water toilets and allowing telephone booths at the road with their alarming rings. Other congregations do not tolerate such innovations. Will there be yet another parting of the ways on account of this?

It is interesting to observe the New Amish near Berlin, Ohio. Because of the World Wars, even the Amish pronounce the name of the city as *Börrlinn* because anything else was regarded as the language of the enemy. The New Amish think of themselves as more conservative on many points than the Old Order Amish. Today there are ten different variations of Amish groups around Berlin, among them the Swartzentrubers, called various nicknames because of wearing longer hair and keeping old customs more strictly. That there are so many groups here clearly shows that it is not usually the worldly who cause serious crises in Amish country. Whenever a religious upheaval is recorded these days, it is invariably a self-made dissolution. The threat from within, from their own religious temperament, is the greatest danger for the lifestyle of the Amish. Their history amply shows that this community cannot be destroyed from without, by the world alone.

As members of their church, the Amish never believe that they have already been saved, but they carefully tend something akin to a living hope in paradise. One who leaves their church seeking more spiritual excitement is no longer one of them and breaks with everything. At most, the church may provide such a renegade with a "crate of hens" for his journey into the world so he will not immediately starve to death. Aside from that, no help is to be expected from brothers or sisters, family or friends. American inheritance laws do not create any problems in such a situation. An apostate, one who has dropped out of the Amish church, receives one dollar from an inheritance fund without regard for how much money such a fund contains. The Amish pay this dollar voluntarily. Whenever one of the baptized members leaves the Amish, the church in counsel discusses the case with much agonizing.

Yet the church districts lose some of their members and many potential members. For those raised in Amish homes, the records show more disembarkers than embarkers on the Amish ship. The quicksand cannot be contained. In some areas, parents may produce ten children and only have two or three remain faithful to the old faith. Not everyone who leaves does so with longing for the world or from being immune to the Christian message. Sometimes young and old are searching for a new and different religious understanding. Once, after some disunity in Allen County, twenty-three families left at the same time, only to establish an Old Amish community in the state of Michigan.

Hard by the edge of the Grabill church district, members of the King congregation have settled. They have gone beyond horse and bicycle (rejected by Allen County Amish) to arrive at owning cars and using them on a daily basis (not just hiring a driver and car or van occasionally, as the Amish do). Since the Kings thus set themselves against the Amish mainstream, they were banned for being so daring. Although many persons from Amish families are attracted to non-Amish churches or to the non-Christian world, the total number of the Amish has doubled in the last twenty years, mainly on account of their large number of children. This is further proof that the Lord looks after his church even though it suffers from religious ailments now and then.

The faithful Amish assume that people suffer the same fate as animals do in the wild. If one leaves the herd, it disappears. For ex-Amish, this means disappearing in the religious sense and not necessarily in the physical sense, since descendants of the Amish are to be found practically everywhere in North America. They are soldiers and professors, poets and politicians, educators and athletes, vagabonds and gourmets, pious and impious.

5

Reformers Without Luther

"For other foundation can no one lay than that is laid, which is Jesus Christ" (1 Cor. 3:11). A tenth of a mile from Courtébert, in a narrow clearing of the Jura Mountains beyond Bern, heavily wooded on either side, this verse from Corinthians appears more cynical than consoling. The trip up here in a small vehicle appears rather pointless. A narrow ice-covered path, threatening falling rocks, snow even in May, and then a forked road with a small note by the tourist office: Pont des Anabaptistes (Bridge of the Anabaptists). There are other places in Switzerland which remind one of the *Täufer* (Anabaptists), but the Bridge of the Anabaptists is the only historical place in the country which today officially bears the name of the group so fiercely persecuted. Consequently, *Anabaptist* has come to be a synonym for one of the most devastating periods of Swiss church history.

The original bridge here in the mountains has been long gone. By the cracks inflicted by age in a dark and dreamy hiking part of the forest, it reminds one of the twilight zone of forgetfulness. To the world, it is only barely noteworthy, and down in the valley hardly anyone ever speaks about it. There is one exception: the small Anabaptist congregation of Courgenay which owns a chapel at the exit from the village. Today it is no longer a disgrace in the Swiss Alsgau to be a religious outsider. In former times the Anabaptists from the vicinity of Courgenay or Courtébert had to undertake a two-hour ascent of the mountain to reach their secret point of meeting. There in a wild chasm covered by a bridge, they were safe from those hunting down the Anabaptists. In any case, they were safe enough so that the persecuted could even afford to etch their names and dates into the rock. A younger generation of Anabaptists, successors in the faith, have affixed a memory plaque here, but only a serious searcher manages to locate it.

The old folks of Allen County never tire of telling the young about the early persecution of members of their faith, to open the eyes of generations of listeners. Nobody here has ever seen the Bridge of the Anabaptists, to say nothing of Switzerland or Europe, for that matter. However, they find references to all this in their histories. They have a general feeling that they are the victims of history and transmit that imprint like a genetic mole. Yet there is no record in Europe of a single genuine Amish witness dying explicitly because of Jakob Ammann's faith. This religious group was founded after the persecution of the Anabaptists was much less radical. However, the forebears of their own forebears still serve the purpose of reminding them of Anabaptist heroes who suffered horrible deaths in their common allegiance to the faith shared with Hutterites and mainstream Mennonites.

The Amish of Allen County see themselves as successors to a long series of martyrs, commencing with Christ, the "head of all martyrs." He is followed by John the Baptist. These models serve to reinforce their history, which starts not with them as rootless offspring of the Reformation, but rather in the first Christian century with highly visible Christian characters. The deeper they dig, the more certainty they receive. Great is the number of the holy who died for the true faith, commencing soon after the birth of Jesus in the manger of Bethlehem, "approximately 3,970 years after the creation of the world." Among them are such as Stephen and James (Acts 7 and 12), Peter and the evangelist Mark, Dionysius of Athens and Hermogenes, Antipas the faithful witness of Jesus (Rev. 2:13), Philip and Paul, and shortly after Paul's death some of his brothers and fellow prisoners.

All this is according to *The Bloody Theater or Martyrs Mirror of the Defenseless Christians Who Baptized Only upon Confession of*

Faith, and Who Suffered and Died for the Testimony of Jesus, Their Saviour, from the Time of Christ to the Year A.D. 1660. In German, this is a 1,129-page jumbo volume for every Amish household (1,156 pages in English, with engravings by Jan van Luyken). Here are Christians of Nero's Rome, the Berengarians (Deacon Bérenger de Tours voted against child baptism around 1060), the Albigenses from the vicinity of Albi (in northern Italy), and the Waldensians (in southern France and elsewhere)—all of whom faithfully followed this tradition. People died by the thousands, simply because they professed the Christian faith and lived out nonviolent love.

Among these accounts of martyrs are those who did nothing unusual but deny child baptism, an inheritance from a few strands of pre-Anabaptist Christianity. The chronicler Thieleman Janz van Braght first published this voluminous document in Dutch in 1660. He discovered as early as the second century some who "practiced no other custom of baptism except in flowing water and . . . were capable of knowing and understanding what benefits were gained through baptism." These he calls upright witnesses and criers in the wilderness, in accord with the convictions of Anabaptists.

The great Reformation time of the Baptism-minded martyrs, who had rid themselves of the "papal leaven," was initiated by Felix Manz from the group around Conrad Grebel. In January 1527 Manz "with great zeal practiced, taught, and preached the recognized truth of the Gospel. . . ." Then he was charged by his opponents and incarcerated in the Wellenberg Tower of Zurich below the later Quai-bridge, after which he was tied up and muzzled and drowned in the Limmat River opposite the Schipfe.

With this measure, the city council attempted a scare tactic: fearless Anabaptist orators, misleaders, and teachers were to be drowned without mercy. Manz, an illegitimate son of a noncelibate clergyman from the Great Cathedral of Zurich, was thrown bound into the water by his Protestant executioners after two priests tried in vain to persuade him to recant. This notable Anabaptist leader, one of the first disciples of Zwingli, chose death by torture instead of giving up his stand for believers baptism and nonresistant love. To him, a martyr's death meant both agony and ecstasy. After he was sentenced to death, the Anabaptists turned to their theology of withdrawal.

Manz was only a precursor; thousands of Anabaptists followed him to their deaths—death as the high point of a life faithful to the Father's will, as Christ himself first led the way. Among them in 1527, the year of the first great wave of persecution, was one George Wagner from Emmerich, denying certain doctrines of his former faith. He did not believe that child baptism was necessary for salvation or that priests were capable of forgiving the sins of penitents. The executioner bound him to a ladder, tied a little bag of gunpowder to his neck, and thrust him into the fire.

There was Michael Sattler, who had initiated the Schleitheim Articles of Faith and now became the victim of a judgmental decree at Rotenburg on the Neckar:

> In the case of the Governor of his Imperial Majesty versus Michael Sattler, judgment is passed, that Michael Sattler shall be delivered to the executioner, who shall lead him to the place of execution, and cut out his tongue; then throw him upon a wagon, and there tear his body twice with red hot tongs; and after he has been brought outside the gate, he shall be pinched five times in the same manner.

This sentence was then carried out, and a few days later his wife was drowned. Both had consoled their friends with the statement that God chastises those he loves.

Leonhard Kaiser, formerly a learned priest of the mass, was arrested in Schärding, Bavaria. On the Friday before St. Lawrence Day 1527, he was bound crosswise to a ladder and pushed into a fire. When his intact corpse was pulled out of the ashes, the executioners cut him to pieces. Although older accounts took him to be an Anabaptist, he was a Lutheran. The judge in the case was so disturbed that he resigned. His assistant, who apparently thought Kaiser was an Anabaptist, soon became one himself, joining the Hutterian Brethren. Known Anabaptists were later martyred in Schärding: Vigilg Plattner in 1529 and Wolf Binder in 1571.

In the Hague, Netherlands, after long interrogations, the widow Weynken Claes of Monickendam was strangled for her faith on November 20, 1527. She held Sacramentist views, rejecting some of the same Catholic doctrines refused by Anabaptists, who appeared in Holland three years later. Remarkably, her steadfast faith is celebrated in Lutheran, Reformed, and Anabaptist martyr books. Two months after Weynken's death, Leonhard Schiemer was beheaded and burned at Rattenberg in the Tirol. In the next few years, seventy-two persons from the same congregation bore witness with their blood. The former Roman priest Hans Schlaffer maintained his Anabaptist testimony even through torture and was executed with the sword in 1528 at Schwaz, Tirol. One Hans Leopold Schneider (a tailor) met his end in Augsburg on April 25, 1528. At the stake in Salzburg, eighteen believers with apocalyptic hope were burned to death on a single day, "awaiting everlasting joy."

The former priest Georg Blaurock, called the "Second Paul" because of his courageous preaching, was executed close to Klausen, South Tirol, on September 6, 1529. Blaurock, the first to receive adult baptism in 1525, had practiced missionary work in Zurich, Appenzell, Bern, Basel, Bünden, and St. Gallen. He was regarded as one of the foremost figures of the Swiss Anabaptists. These as well as many others of the time and persuasion considered dying in faithfulness to be more attractive than a compromised life, and they counted martyrdom as the highest form of death. Possibly this is why history books of today report on them only in footnotes, if at all.

The affirmation of the cross as providing salvation and the high numbers of Anabaptist blood sacrifices started weakening some congregations, particularly in Switzerland. In certain areas, small Anabaptist groups managed to survive only because they met for their services somewhere in the anonymity of the *Hölzli* (woods), deep in the forests, in hiding places like the Anabaptist cave above Wappenswil near Bäretswil, or under the Anabaptist Bridge in the Jura Mountains.

Anabaptists were stigmatized, ostracized, and quarantined as they followed the "Christian duty of the defenseless and non-vengeful Christianity." But the Lord "shone into their hearts and brightly lighted them . . . so that they awakened, opened their eyes, rose up from sleep, and were taken to the way of peace; and eternal salvation was brought, in and through them." Luther's friend, Justus Menius, however, was of a different opinion about them. Whoever did not stand on the side of the Wittenberger (Luther), he considered to be a blasphemer. He held the Anabaptists to be "treacherous, superficial thieves of God and murderers of the soul." Yet the blood of the martyrs and the "drifting ashes" from burning saints became seed for the church (Tertullian). At Antwerp, Belgium, a tongue screw was used to prevent Anabaptists from witnessing to their faith while being executed and thereby winning converts (1573). In the Dutch province of Friesland, beating a drum served the same purpose (1531). Sometimes they were strangled before being burned or gunpowder was ignited in their faces. Such reactions show the power of the Anabaptist testimony and how it frightened the established powers.

Many cruel notches adorn the executioners' swords of both the Protestants and the Catholics, although the Anabaptists continued to regard "the Catholics" as the bigger culprits. Even though all lands affected by the Reformation were anti-Anabaptist, their counts and lords reacted variously to the challenge of this "diabolical sect." The legal basis for their prosecution was first the violation of civil law, then heresy and rebellion, and finally the imperial law of the Speyer parliamentary decree of death for all who persisted as Anabaptists. This mandate of April 23, 1529, was repeated in 1544, renewed at the diet of Augsburg in 1551, and used as late as 1694 to justify expulsion of Mennonites from Rheydt in Prussia. Lutherans, Zwinglians, and Catholics busily competed in their application of cruel medieval punishments. Crowned heads battled against Anabaptists as against national revolutions.

Many stage managers wrote the script. Even as clever a man as Melanchthon, who held deep loyalties to Luther, demanded the death penalty for the heretics, not on account of their faith but because "the government has a duty to punish rebels." Melanchthon personally accompanied "pitiful erring sinners" to the scaffold. Nuremberg lawyers recommended that the ears of the Anabaptists should be cut off, "in order to warn the people and to cause the heretics to become red as scarlet." However, in Augsburg it was possible for a while to save one's life by leaving the city upon giving an oath. In Aachen (Aix-la-Chapelle, western Germany) midwives were required to report all parents who did not have their children baptized.

Bavaria passed a stern law that all Anabaptists were to receive the death penalty. Count Wilhelm there pronounced a strict decree without regard for age or gender: "Anyone who recants will be beheaded; anyone who does not recant will be burned." Numerous cities in southern Germany followed this example. During that period, there were no compromises made between Anabaptists, governments, and the established churches, except for occasional respites due to fatigue.

The Protestant city of Zurich took particularly severe measures against those termed heretics. In 1525, parents who did not have their children baptized were able to get away with a money fine of five pounds, but anyone who rebaptized adult believers had to pay between fifteen and twenty pounds. After Manz's drowning in 1527, the authorities took other Anabaptists one by one to the Limmat River and drowned them: Heini Reimann, Jakob Falk, Georg Karpfis, and Hans Herzog.

By 1530 in some of the Zurich suburbs, the Anabaptists or their sympathizers had already gained the upper hand. In response, the governing city council issued a ruling:

> We strictly order all inhabitants of our country as well as all likeminded, namely the superior and lower officials, noncommissioned officers, city clerks, judges, church bishops, and church officials, that when they encounter Anabaptists, they require them to declare an oath of loyalty to us. Do not tolerate them anywhere or allow them to propagate, but have them imprisoned and turned over to us. We shall punish Anabaptists and all those who support or follow them with death in accord with our laws. This action also applies to those who have aided them or have not turned them in, expelled them, or handed them over to us as captives. Such persons shall be punished by our laws and without mercy, according to their actions, for they have transgressed against their loyalties and oaths sworn before the government.

Anabaptists were mercilessly chased through alleys and streets of Zurich and driven out of the city with whips and cudgels or drowned as heretics. Georg Blaurock was chased and beaten all the way from the Fish Market to the portals of Niederdorf. These policies were in force for a long time. The last execution of an Anabaptist in Zurich, Hans Landis from Wädenswil, took place as late as September of 1614, after he as pastor returned to minister to his flock.

In the political bastion of Bern, the citizens had early been attracted *vom klar Luther Wort* (by the clear word of Luther). Officials attempted to convert its inhabitants to the evangelical-reformed faith, by force, if need be. In the process, however, the Anabaptists stood in the way of the mighty. Traces of the radical believers there go back to 1525. They were described as an "erring and miserable lot. . . . In time their numbers and their danger increased, causing many desertions and dissensions, misery, bloodshed, and unrest." Even Zwingli's brother-in-law, the master tailor Lienhard Tremp, supposedly joined those of the new faith in the Bern area. In May of 1527, the Anabaptists and the Catholic rulers held a religious discussion in the city hall on the river Aare. Then in August of the same year, the Roman Catholic offices issued a strict order against those of the new faith.

In 1528 a great public disputation took place in Bern when Anabaptist teachers met with Zwingli, among others. This discussion regarding faith turned out to be a futile effort to refute Anabaptism through late-medieval theological arguments. As a consequence, officials decreed banishment and the threat of the death sentence for the instigators. The next year these were put into effect when, "in order to uproot such weeds," they executed Hans Hansmann, sackmaker from Basel; Hans Treyer (Troyer); and Heini Seiler, hatmaker from Aarau. The believers were probably drowned in the harbor in view of many spectators on the nearby Platform.

Later Anabaptists from Bern were preferably executed on market day, to expose them to more ridicule and to warn the populace. Such punishments took place where today the *Kram- und Gerechtigkeitsgasse* (Shopping and Justice Alley) merge with the—of all terms!—Alley of the Cross. Here was located the *Schandpfahl* (shame post, pillory), to which those of the new faith were publicly chained for citizens to mock them and pelt them with rocks. Then they were led off to be burned or beheaded. Among them were Mortiz from Losenegg, Anken Peter, Oberlen Christian, the tanner Waldi, and one Konrad Eichacher (Eicher, Eichner) from Steffisberg. Eichers are to be found in Amish congregations around Grabill to this day.

Heated discussions frequently broke out in the respective Swiss cantons as to how the dead Anabaptists were to be buried. In some German-speaking areas, the government did not allow "non-Christian dead" such as executed Anabaptists to be buried in the general cemetery. Instead, they were to be interred close to the public place of execution. Other martyrs received the so-called donkey funeral, meaning that their corpses were transported to the grave by donkey cart.

In 1541 the council of the city of Bern heard a query on whether people who separated themselves from the official church while alive were to be permitted to share common property with "Christians" in death. The council decided, "We do not wish to prejudge God's sentence regarding the salvation of the Anabaptists.... We do not wish to separate their corpses from others of the faith because the corpses of other impure persons from paupers' houses have also been buried here." When some "honest people" took issue with this practice, it was decided that Anabaptists were to be buried "without accompaniment and bell-ringing." As of 1695, "excommunicated Anabaptists were no longer permitted to be buried in any churchyard or other public cemetery."

By 1528 Bern had consolidated itself with Zurich in matters of persecuting heretics. The officers commissioned for that bloody task now became serious about dealing with the *"teüfferische Geschäft* (Anabaptist business)." They held "meetings to discuss the eradication of this un-Christian, damned sect" and whether they should immediately deliver "men to the sword and women to the water." Meanwhile, in Bern and elsewhere, new mandates were constantly being issued to either diminish the sentences or increase their severity, as shown by Hege's long list of "Mandates" in *The Mennonite Encyclopedia.* For several centuries, governments in German and Dutch territories of the Holy Roman Empire ruthlessly waged war "with secular means against spiritual forces" (Hege). Between Grimselpass and Boncourt, Sustenpass and Gummfluh, the *Täuferjäger* (Anabaptist hunters) tried to "tie up these saints in ropes, threaten them, and punish them in body, life, and property."

"The gracious gentlemen of Bern" regarded Anabaptist marriages as nonconsummated, meaning that they were not legally married but were "whoremongers and scoundrels and despisers of Christian orders." Their children were regarded as illegitimate and consequently not entitled to the law of succession. The chattels of the fleeing Anabaptists were seized and became property of the state treasury. The Bernese went so far as to compel worshipers to bear arms in church so as to single out and expose the pacifist Anabaptists. Furthermore, no longer could anyone obtain employment without a certificate issued by the local pastor of "right persuasion." Between 1528 and 1571, forty Anabaptists died a martyr's death on the *Felssporn* (cleft of rock) above the Aare River. According to the old stories, the latest known victim in the canton of Bern was the Anabaptist teacher, Hans Haslibacher of Haslenbach, a missionary in the Emmental, the ancestral home of the Grabers of Allen County.

In Amish circles, this Hans has remained one of the great faithful dead. He is among the martyrs of whom they sing most often. According to the legend, the old Haslibacher was "treated mighty roughly" in the Bernese prison, but he remained true to his faith. Such courage was no exception among the Anabaptists. However, when Hans later defended his faith to a few preachers, they warned him that if he did not recant, "his head should be laid before his feet." Witnesses of the time "credibly narrate," according to *Martyrs Mirror* and the last song in the *Ausbund*, that in the night before he was to die, Hans dreamed he was being led forth to be beheaded. This woke him up, as well it might, and an angel let him read a book about three signs that would accompany his death. His own head would spring into his hat and laugh after the executioner swung his sword, the sun would turn blood-red in the Bernese sky, and blood instead of water would flow from the town well.

The next day it apparently happened just so, as documented in a "beautiful spiritual song concerning Haslibacher, when he was judged from life to death." The Amish of Allen County sing it according to the melody "Why do you grieve yourself, my heart." There are thirty-two verses in the *Ausbund*, song 140, and verses 28-29 say (adapted from *Martyrs Mirror*, 1129):

> Down comes the sword, when lo, the head
> Springs in his hat, as he had said;
>   And all the signs were seen—
> The sun was red and looked like blood,
> The town well shed a crimson flood.

Amazed, an aged sire said:
"The Anabaptist laughs, though dead."
   Then spoke another sire:
"If you had let this Baptist live,
Eternally you would not grieve."

The public city well of Bern was above the Aare River and at an angle below the city hall. From then on, it became the favorite spot in Switzerland for Anabaptists migrating to the United States to meet and for a last time to take a good drink of Haslibacher water. To this day Anabaptist tourists from all over the world are attracted to this well and to the Haslibacher farm at Haslenbach in the Emmental (Emme valley). This mighty farmyard under age-old linden trees would certainly be marked as a place of pilgrimage if Anabaptists believed in doing such things. The surrounding land is still being tilled by the Haslenbachers, and while their family tree dates back to the sixteenth century, it reports nothing about the old Hans. However, in the six-house hamlet of Haslenbach, one today finds a modest memorial plaque for "Hans Haslibacher, beheaded as an Anabaptist on October 20, 1571." Not a word less and not a word more.

Martyrs Mirror says he was "old," and he likely was between seventy and eighty years old when executed. After all, as early as 1532 he is mentioned as being a preacher, and he took part in the great Bern disputation of 1538. He was exiled, then arrested and executed after he returned to his former home in the Emmental, and his son (of the Reformed faith) was fined heavily for receiving him. It is no longer important that recent findings suggest Hans Haslibacher was likely executed at Trachselwald instead of the city of Bern. The story of the head in the hat of the Anabaptist and the well producing blood already made the rounds in Switzerland forty years before the execution of Hans and apparently was attached to the tale of this faithful martyr. The Haslibacher song remains popular and was generally sung in the wider environs around Bern as a folk song.

The Anabaptists being hunted down were frequently referred to as "garden brothers," because at night they secretly met in gardens. They were also called *Stundeler, Stundisten,* or *Stundenleute* (people of hours) since they attended services or Bible study groups beyond those offered by the official churches. The prisoners were regularly interrogated by a Reformed pastor, a state prosecutor, two town council members, and a representative of the government. If the accused parties were stubborn rebels in matters of faith, they were dragged into the *Marzili,* the place of torture by the Aare River. Often the person who refused to talk voluntarily was "stroked by a whip and had the ears burned by a glowing or hot iron."

In practical terms, the Bernese Anabaptists, once caught, faced the two possibilities. If they permitted themselves to be "converted," they could return to the established church. If they persisted in their faith, they were tortured and died at the hand of the executioner, or in some cases spent a lifetime behind bars, or were exiled from the canton for life. One punishment harmed heart and soul, the other the human body.

The interrogations were documented in the so-called tower books which have in part survived and can be found in the state archives of Bern. These records reveal that not all imprisoned Anabaptists were constant in their devotion and that some of them departed from their new faith due to torture, pain, and death threats. Whoever reported on one's own Anabaptist group was able to purchase release by a payment of a fine. These deserters informed the *Täuferjäger* as to who had attended a meeting in the *Hölzli Biglenmatt* (Biglenmatt Wood) or in the forest by Eggiwyl, or that the new teaching was widespread among the farmyards of the Kurzen (Short) Mountain and the Buchholter Mountain, or that a "*Fraueli by nächtlicher Zyt* (a young lady by night)" got married down the Aare by Kiesen.

In the face of such persecution, there remained on the battlegrounds of the Anabaptist front only those who were particularly strong in their hearts and in their faith. Bern, for example, was successful in delivering a death blow to Anabaptism in the city proper. As a result, the new teaching became the doctrine of artisans and peasants, particularly in the Bernese mountain and hill areas, south and east of the metropolis. A good number of Swiss Anabaptists fled to Moravia, where Nikolsburg, Austerlitz, or Neumühl for a while were noted centers of the old-evangelical movement. This is surprising because Moravia's rulers were Hapsburg and Catholic. The Anabaptist farms in Moravia were soon regarded as beehives of the land, well developed. This is where the Hutterian Brethren organized themselves in 1529.

From Moravia, Hutterian Anabaptists set out to fish for people (Mark 1:17). They engaged in such dangerous evangelistic activity that few of their missionaries survived. Some two hundred years later, the Anabaptists in Moravia and in the bordering Slovakia had either been absorbed into the Catholic church or had saved their skins by emigrating. Some of the Hutterites made their way via Romania to Russia and then to America, settling in South Dakota in the 1870s.

By the late 1530s (or earlier), Swiss Anabaptists began retreating to the solitude of the Jura Mountains, which were German up to the French Revolution. They acquired pieces of land in that area. At first they met in caves or concealed clefts, then later in private homes. In the Münster valley, a rural Catholic count did not persecute the "highly damned sect of the Holy Roman Empire" with the same vehemence as the Reformed Bernese. Others saved their lives by escaping to Alsace, Baden, and the Palatinate, where surviving descendants own farms to this day. Many descendents of these displaced Swiss Anabaptists eventually emigrated to North America. Among the persecuted in Switzerland were also some of the forebears of the Amish of Allen County, including the Grabers from the flower town of Huttwil, by the Langeten River and near Trachselwald, in the lower Emmental.

Seventy-one years after Grebel, Manz, and Blaurock baptized each other in Zurich, one Georg Graber came into conflict with the law of the "highly respected merciful lords" of the canton of Bern, since he belonged to a forbidden church of "Anabaptist disobedience." This Georg had been baptized by one of the numerous itinerant ministers. He was a simple peasant who walked through the countryside in the winter as a house weaver to pick up work here and there and also to proselytize for his newfound faith. When Graber was "fastened in irons," he insisted that the state-appointed clerics of the Emmental spent their time, above all, with "lying, deceiving, seducing, suppressing, and tearing like wolves, robbing, murdering, butchering, and oppressing," in order "to seduce people and subjects in body, effects, and soul." This was contrary to his understanding of the Bible.

After that, the tracks of the Anabaptist Grabers disappear from Huttwil. A mysterious lack of files in the city hall of Huttwil

174

renders further research futile. Over the centuries, the name was also written Gräber, Grayber, or Greber. The next record on these Grabers is from around the beginning of the eighteenth century. The canton of Bern had issued a recent mandate that all Anabaptists who did not give up their faith, men and women, were "actually and bodily" to be beaten with sticks in public, or strapped to the bench of punishment, pelted with refuse, and led beyond the borders. If they returned, a branding iron with the symbol of the bear, the coat of arms of the Bernese, was to be branded onto their foreheads. With that encouragement, the Grabers finally turned their backs on Huttwil. Their property was confiscated and turned over to the opposing church. In this way the Grabers of Huttwil involuntarily contributed to a new Reformed church building in their hometown, where Anabaptists were soon heavily attacked.

Emmental in the canton of Bern is famous worldwide for various high-quality cheeses, as well as stories written by the rural pastor Albert Bitzius (alias Jeremias Gotthelf) from Lützelflüh. It is regarded more or less as the original home of most South-German Anabaptist families and thus of many Anabaptists who migrated to America. Some 200,000 descendants of these Bernese Anabaptists are today in the USA and Canada, even if not living according to the religious tradition of their forebears or even as Amish. This Emme valley in its upper regions extends to the Alpine foreland and even in its lower areas demands that farmers work hard every day. For long, it was the home of Anabaptists who later moved to Alsace or territories in what is now southern Germany.

The Bernese files on persecutions and executions of Anabaptists lead again and again to this green heart of Switzerland and "to the possibly most appetizing farmhouses of the world" (Gotthelf). In this area, the villages of Sumiswald, Rüderswil, Lützelflüh, Tannental, Schüpbach, Hasli, Langnau, Röthenbach, and Signau were quite positively disposed toward Anabaptists. Yet in this romantic Alpine foreland, the police would escort children to the official church for compulsory baptism, as required by law up to the beginning of the 1800s. Not until 1846 did this canton incorporate religious equality into its constitution.

The Emmental Anabaptists received some support in their

Heimat (homeland) from numerous *Halbtäufer* (Half-Anabaptists) or *Treuherzige* (Truehearted), people sympathetic to them but still attending the state church. These people warned Anabaptists about *Täuferjäger* by "horns, cries, and similar signs" so that those of the new faith could escape and hide in their "Anabaptist holes." They took risks in helping Anabaptists, sometimes sheltering fugitives or giving material aid to those impoverished by fines. On occasion the infamous hunters were in for a "bloody beating," as happened in 1714 at the hands of about sixty irate citizens in Sumiswald. In that case, the local government was fined one hundred taler to recompense the hunters for their loss of the bounty price on the Anabaptists.

The German Emperor Karl V, son of Philipp the Handsome and Johanna the Mad, chief guardian of Catholicism, now decreed that various dissenting spirits who spread disrespect should be chastised and punished. This would serve as an example to others. The princely head, of course, gave particular attention to "that reprehensible sect" which had misled a great many men and women into shame and disrespect regarding the sacrament of holy baptism. "Whoever will be found having been soiled with the damned sect of Anabaptists or Rebaptizers, irrespective of what class or standing they may have or be, or whether they are leaders or followers or whatever part they may have in it, shall lose their lives and their effects and be punished most severely by fire, and that without any delay." Karl's 1529 law against the Anabaptists, renewed by the imperial parliament of Augsburg in 1551, was also supported by all German sovereigns, with the exception of Count Philipp of Hesse.

Child baptism was now the law of the state, and the refusal to obey it was regarded as a crime punishable by death. Capital punishment was the inner reaction to the outward loss of power by the *Volkskirche* (established church). The history of the Anabaptists, similar to the massacres of the Jews of the fourteenth century, now became the history of martyrs and was to remain so for the next 150 years.

The list is long: Bastian Glasmacher, executed by sword at Imst and then burned. Jakob Hutter, burned in Innsbruck. Hans Peitz and several others, died in prison. Twelve persons, men and women, burned and beheaded near Herzogenbusch. Christina

Michael Barents, drowned in Rotterdam. Anneken of Brussels, burned together with the cobbler Jakob after their tongues had been twisted by a mouth vice. Six brothers and two sisters, burned alive at the stake in Amsterdam. Others were sentenced as oarsmen on galley boats, a punishment meted out in Catholic France to the Huguenots (French Reformed). Yet others "were tortured some eleven times and still managed to escape, true to their convictions."

According to the Hutterite chronicler Braitmichel (died 1573), the Anabaptists had "more enemies than hair on the head." And yet, everywhere in German regions, these faithful Christians, with the stamp of death already upon them, went happily to the gallows, always in anticipation of their final vindication on God's day of judgment. God's coming triumph was regarded as an immortal Anabaptist truth, which "allowed them to be taken prisoner and crucified and to be resurrected again on the third day" (Preacher Balthasar Hubmaier).

"They dance and they jump into the fire, they see the gleaming sword with serene hearts, they speak and they preach to the people with a laughing mouth, they sing psalms and other songs until their soul is extinguished, they die joyfully as if being at a happy social occasion, they remain strong, consoled, and steadfast unto death" (Faber of Heilbronn). "Some of them were stretched and warped until the sun shone through them, others were so much pulled apart by torture that they died, others were burned to ashes and powder, roasted at the stake, torn apart with glowing pincers, locked in houses and burned, hanged on trees or cut up by the sword" (Braitmichel). Their virgins adorned themselves for the fire "as brides for their grooms," their men called upon the people to do penance, and their women died with a prayer on their lips. . . .

Luther had stood his ground against the malicious eye of the Roman church. Now in view of the impending Counter-Reformation, he could not risk a split in his ranks and exhibited a terrible determination. This reformer, sensitive to anything smelling of pope or Zwingli, seemed more bent on retaining followers than on their renewal. About the Anabaptists, he concluded, "One can not bring these monsters into line by sword or fire. They desert wife and children, house and yard, and everything they have." Thus far

Luther had failed to oppose the Catholic principle of the Middle Ages that the church interrogates while the state executes.

However, the God of the Anabaptists also did not spare his judgments. Anabaptist chronicles report how badly things went for some of the judges presiding over them. One executioner's nose fell off, a *Bürgermeister* (mayor) lost his voice, another one went mad, one judge died suddenly, the church of an opposing congregation burned down, while in Rome the river Tiber caused much devastation through flooding.

The Anabaptists also noticed their own weaknesses of the flesh in dealing with the world and its institutions. They sometimes responded with exaggerated religiosity, spiritual narrow-mindedness, intolerance, enthusiastic movements, authoritarian measures, and a fiercely rigid church discipline. Such anesthetics against pain became a pressing problem when the theologically educated leaders of the new faith were almost all killed off after "the first hour." "The seed of the holy gospel could no longer be broadcast among the darkened population in dignified fashion." This meant that the leadership of their congregations sometimes was passed on to incompetents who had been ravaged physically and spiritually. Some of them "sketched the devil on the wall," prophesying doom, and not all of them were genuine prophets. Certain leaders swerved from being in God's service to merely speaking in his name but actually promoting self.

The shortage of qualified leading personalities now led to fear of education and fleeing from the world. People with private visions and an apocalyptic bent now set about to realize an earthly Zion, while deceitful hordes cloaked themselves in Anabaptist apparel. New radicals, ecstatic groups, cohabiters, Adamites and sobbers, muted, barefooted, praying supplicators, priest murderers, or the purely holy—a wild crop shot up overnight from the fertile religious soil. In Teufen, for instance, just south of St. Gallen, worshipers now regularly fainted during their meetings, since they took Paul's words literally: "I die daily" (1 Cor. 15:31).

The persecutions also deeply affected the social life of the Anabaptists. Early believers came from all classes of society, from monks and priests (Balthasar Hubmaier), the nobility (Leonhard Liechtenstein), the trained artisan (Jakob Hutter) or *Bürger* (townsman, as Pilgram Marpeck, mining engineer), right on to the

Emmental farmers and Tirolean miners. However, after early gains, Anabaptists lost most of their supporters in the cities of southern Germany. With their arm-in-arm flight into remote rural settings, the persecuted were gradually forced predominantly into farming and related occupations.

Yet the martyrdom of one strengthened the hope of another, and this forced the typical Swiss believer ever deeper into a puritanical and pietistic separation. Some congregations were on the increase in spite of persecutions. "God the Father begets his children through the seed of the divine word with unspeakable joy" (Menno Simons). Such an atmosphere prepared the soil for one Anabaptist named Jakob Ammann, a young, restless, and zealous leader who was to become the collective spiritual father of today's Amish. Ammann, a servant of the Word or elder, was still in the process of finding his own way when he left Switzerland. As countless Anabaptists before him, including the predecessors of the Grabers of Allen County, this preacher was drawn to the Alsatian hinterland, where Anabaptists were tolerated, although they lacked official religious status. In this area during the 1600s appeared many names common among North American Amish today: Hostetlers, Yoders, Millers, Roths, Schmuckers, Kauffmans, Eichners/Eichers, and Freys.

Alsace was a traditionally tolerant country for immigrants. Here Reformation and Counter-Reformation combined to form a decisive turning point in the development of the church. This happened as a logical consequence of the humanism initiated in these parts by Wimpfeling, Brant, or Geiler von Kaysersberg, plus their followers of the liberal Erasmian persuasion. Luther's teachings soon took hold in Strassburg (now Strasbourg, France) because of church political quarrels and social, moral, and religious circumstances. The great cathedral fell to the only Protestant doctrine tolerated in the area. Shortly, the real danger for the Alsatian Reformers was not from the efforts of the Old Catholic Church but from the Anabaptist side. Once again this was an indication that Luther's most dangerous opponents were to be found among the freedom-seeking spirits he himself had summoned.

As early as 1561 the first protest against the Anabaptists was formulated in, of all places, Markirch, the later birthplace of the Amish. On that occasion, the mining confederate lodged a complaint to the presiding count, Egenolph III, to the effect that "Anabaptists without jobs crawl into houses and teach and preach and surround the poor people with their barbed arguments." One hundred years later, one finds large Alsatian Anabaptist congregations in Illkirch, Ohnenheim, Jebsheim, and Baldenheim.

The Alsace was frequently divided up territorially in the course of its history. It was a unique border country, sharing German and French influence, and a key travel area into which new teachings were allowed to travel relatively unimpeded. Most Anabaptist leaders like Hubmaier, Denk, and Hofmann appeared in Strassburg, which alongside Wittenberg and Zurich became the focal points of German Protestantism. As early as 1533 the city defended itself against radical Christians. Two years later it issued a penal schedule: (1) Anabaptists were to be banned. (2) Anyone who returned was to receive bread and water for four weeks and then again be banished. (3) Anyone returning thereafter was to be placed in neck irons, have one's fingers chopped off, and branded. (4) Any party captured yet again was to be sentenced to death by drowning. In spite of all of the above, the fleeing Swiss Brethren continued to find asylum in Alsace.

After the devastations caused by the Thirty Years' War (1618-48), Swiss rebels of faith favored migration to the Leber valley of Alsace and the electorate of the Palatinate (Germany), especially in the regions of Alzey, Heidelberg, Neustadt, and Kaiserslautern, as well as the principality of Zweibrücken. In the Leber valley they became prosperous in a relatively short time, attaining something like *Bürgertäufer* status (townspeople *and* Anabaptists). These believers were meeting for worship and fellowship in a tract of forest between Markirch (earlier Mariakirch, today Sainte-Marie-aux-Mines) and Schlettstadt, but some also attended services in the German Reformed church.

It was in Markirch, a small city in the rich mining area of the Vosges Mountains, that Ammann assumed public significance in 1692. This place was partly Protestant since 1530. In 1550 one magistrate, Lord von Rappoltstein, had permitted some Calvinist miners from France to found a Reformed congregation, and by 1658 a German Reformed parsonage was added. For a long while miners from Tirol and Saxony had been working in the mines of Rumpapump, Sainte Anna, or Eisenthür, and they had a positive inclination toward Anabaptism. Near the city, other Anabaptists were occupied as farmers, foresters, and millers. Initially they had found work with the Rappoltsteiners and then later with the Prince von Birkenfeld-Zweibrücken, after this county had been transferred to the duchy of the Palatinate through marriage. Thus the mining city of Markirch, divided by the Leber Brook into Protestant and Catholic divisions, was something like an Anabaptist center in Ammann's time.

Regarding Jakob Ammann's role in Markirch and the actual upheaval among the Anabaptists in the 1690s, we have various versions transmitted to us today. One of them reads: "God created the world, while Jakob fashioned a true Christianity; for wherever God permits a desert to flourish, he also is quick to place a Moses in it, but only now and then." The Amish historian, Eli Gingerich, near Shipshewana, Indiana, sketches this reformer of the reformers as a "concerned young bishop" who seriously set about to take the church of the Swiss Brethren to the letter-of-the-law faith. He followed the confession of faith accepted in 1632 at Dordrecht in Holland and adopted by a group of Alsatian ministers in 1660. Later it was adopted by other Mennonites in the Palatinate and North Germany. But most Mennonites in Switzerland had not accepted it, likely because it teaches shunning, although they did use it to defend themselves before the Bernese government.

Ammann appears to have had a thorn in his flesh, like the apostle Paul in his day, except that Jakob immediately knew what was going on. The believers in Alsace and Holland held foot washing after receiving the Lord's Supper as an expression of *Gemeinschaft* (community fellowship), after the model of Jesus washing the feet of his disciples (John 13). Apparently foot washing was not a common practice among Swiss congregations at the time, and Ammann wanted to introduce it there. To this day it is strictly practiced among the Amish of Allen County as a sign of humility. Further, the Anabaptists conducted the holy *Abendmahl* (Lord's Supper) only once a year, but Ammann wanted it twice. Because participation in communion was linked to church discipline, this was a call for stricter discipline.

What really disturbed Ammann was the fact that in the churches of the Swiss Brethren, the ban—that strict instrument of church discipline for erring members—was not enforced as rigorously as he believed the Mennonites in Holland meant it to be. The banned were not excluded "from physical and spiritual nourishment." Generally in South German and Swiss areas, the spiritually banned were excluded from communion with the congregation but allowed to retain social relationships and church membership. Among the Dutch Mennonites, anyone banned and shunned was not to share table or bed with the spouse, and this meant total exclusion from the *Gemeinschaft* while the church waited for signs of repentance. Ammann held that only by strict adherence to banning and shunning could the impure be separated from the pure. On this issue he differed appreciably from the Lutheran theologians, who believed "that all people were required to remain in the church, including those who sinned."

"Some matters caused Jakob to be concerned," says Gingerich today regarding Ammann's protest. "One was that there was a woman who had denied a matter, but when witnesses confronted her, she admitted to it and made restitution. Jakob felt that such a person should be banned and shunned until penance and a change of life was in evidence."

Jakob also believed that in matters of dress and hair cutting, a greater difference ought to exist between believers and the worldly (as in 1 Pet. 3:1-7). In his view, the hair of the men was too long and the beards too short (Lev. 19:27). He vehemently attacked the style of laces on shoes or buttons on clothes. It was also a serious matter, Ammann thought, if the church associated with the "True-hearted" people. These neighbors and relatives belonged to the state church but as "Half-Anabaptists" sympathized with the radical believers and offered them support during persecution. To Ammann, half an Anabaptist, a middle-of-the-road-walker, was no more and no less fit for paradise than any common heathen.

Before long the minister Ammann met opposition. His spiritual opponent was, above all, one Hans Reist from the Obertal by Zäzlwyl, in the Emmental. When Reist failed to appear at a meeting held in the Emmental where these matters were to be discussed, Ammann banned Reist. As a result, a general quarrel broke out among the Anabaptist leaders of Alsace, the Palatinate, and Switzerland. Ministers and members were now forced to decide whether they would follow Jakob or not. "They conducted many conversations about the matter, but no good fruit came thereof," Gingerich states today. Among the Anabaptists, arguments became heated on the proper interpretation of God's Word.

This chapter of Anabaptist history was partly attributable to human frailty and mistakes, in the compassionate view of later generations. Ammann traveled through the countryside with typical German impatience, sorting out things and people. He met Bishop Nicholas Moser in Friedersmatt near Bowill, was scheduled to meet Hans Reist in Eutingen, and met Peter Geiger in Reutennen and also a group of Palatinate Anabaptists in the mill at Ohnenheim. Whoever seriously opposed Ammann and "considered his teaching and faith as sectarian" was excommunicated. Such persons were hit by the ban, with which Ammann meant to free the church from "the leaven" (1 Cor. 5:6-8). For Ammann it had become a means of power. Yet without doubt his main consideration was a strict church order. Hence, he began every confrontation with the Swiss Brethren by asking the same question, how they resolved matters of "shying away from and shunning." Did they believe that the sinner should be separated from the marriage bed and from table fellowship?

In the spring of 1693, this back-to-roots Anabaptist leader invited all "persons, women and men, servants or disciples of the congregation," to a meeting of accountability. "Those not appearing," declared Ammann, "are of one kind with the already banned and shall, as sectarians, be excluded from the *Gemeinde* (church) of God and shall be shied away from and shunned until they have been converted in accord with God's Word." Believers, particularly from the Palatinate, requested patience and more love, but that availed them nothing.

Among the *Letters of the Amish Division* and other writings that survived time and circumstances, one today finds a letter by Jakob Gut disagreeing with Ammann: Gut believed that Paul (1 Cor. 5) meant a spiritual ban rather than a total shunning because the apostle says "not to company with fornicators" who call themselves church members; "with such you are not to eat" the "unleavened bread" of "Christ our Passover," meaning the Lord's Supper. Furthermore, Gut recommended that a brother who was a fornicator should first be admonished and not immediately placed under a strict ban, since a misuse thereof would cause much harm.

One Gerhard Roosen from Hamburg wrote to the brothers in Alsace in December 1697 about his difficulty in understanding that the conscience of the individual should be bound to the form of his hat, the clothes, shoes, stockings, or hairstyle. If the apostles would have desired this, they would have stated so in their writings. "From where then does friend Jakob Ammann get that which he adopts as the basis for giving commandments to those people and expelling from the fellowship those who do not want to obey him?" For if Jakob truly desired to live like a true servant of the gospel, then he "must not have two coats, nor money in his purse, nor shoes on his feet."

In March 1694 the preachers met again, but they were not able to reach accord in the questions which Ammann had raised. Then one group declared that they could no longer regard Jakob and his followers as brothers and sisters. Those who now followed Ammann had cut themselves off from the mainstream of Anabaptism. Among them were most of the Alsatian congregations, but also some from the Palatinate and Switzerland. Ammann's Swiss followers were located mainly in the *Oberland* (high country, hence sometimes called *Oberen Brüder*) of Bern, in the Simmental, in Frutigen, and in the area around Thun and Hilterfingen.

From this time on, Ammann's group was recognized by outward appearance, how they wore their hair, that "in winter as in summer one was dressed in linen cloth." Clothing styles became petrified to be like the peasant dress of the time. Initially Ammann's people became known as *Häftler* (those using hooks), in contrast to Mennonites, who wore buttons. They restricted themselves to hooks and eyes, as Elam still does on Cuba Road. Ammann's folks were also called foot washers, bearded men, Beard Mennonites, Amis, Amish Mennonites, or simply Amish, the name that stuck. Those who did not agree with Ammann were occasionally called *Reistleute* (Reist's people) or *underen Täuferen* (Anabaptists of the lower country of Bern), but those names did not last.

According to Eli Gingerich from Indiana, matters took on a turn in which "no one wanted to give in or give up. Everyone stood by his opinion, and no one wanted to concede personal failings or errors. And so matters took their course. A split was the result." Without this schism, the Amish of Allen County would probably not exist today. In any case, they permit no doubt that "Jakob at the time had the right faith and the basic biblical principles. After all, a group of some twenty bishops and ministers stood behind him, by him, and with him."

However, the fiery preacher Jakob was possibly not all that perfect, nor are any of us. Even today the bishop of an Amish congregation, although invested with great authority, has to seek out church counsel in serious decisions. It is certain that the Lord made a sharp sword out of Ammann's mouth (Isa. 49:2). And yet, we find a letter of 1700 to the Swiss Anabaptists, cosigned by Ammann, in which he expresses his "heartfelt grief" regarding his own mistakes and simultaneously places the ban on himself. He asked for "forbearance" and expressed a desire to be "reconciled with God and man as much as possible." However, the rift was deep enough to last and to have long and bitter consequences. In 1711, for example, the followers of Ammann and those of Reist did not want to board the same ship for migration from the canton of Bern, as facilitated by the *Doopsgezinde* (Dutch Mennonites).

In ensuing centuries many attempts were undertaken to draw the Amish (Mennonites) into the bosom of the larger group of Mennonites. In 1860 discussions on the theme "Whoever does not gather, disperses" were held in Sembach, in 1867 in Offenthal by St. Goarshausen, in 1871 in Kaiserslautern, in 1873 and 1904 at the Weierhof in the Palatinate. By this time the Amish had mostly migrated to the New World and had no influence on their last remaining congregations in Europe, who now united as one flock behind one shepherd and joined Mennonite churches not in the Ammann camp.

Jakob Ammann, as a gatherer of the just and a judge of the world, was more disputatious than exceptional or heroic, in the opinion of critical historians. He had the great rage of a prophet, but he did not die in the smoke of the pyre or fall victim to the sword, like Jakob Hutter or Michael Sattler. Even if he was watching for a martyr's exit, he did not manage to find it. His *Ordnung* (order, discipline) can be seen much more as a watershed than as a genuine revolution.

At the same time, one should remember that the Ammann biographers were chiefly Mennonites who were not Amish and thus not all that favorably disposed to Jakob. Even among the Amish themselves, this preacher is not secure against the erosion of neglect. Most know little about him, many nothing at all beyond his name. There are no Ammanns left in their congregations. As with *Christian, Hutterite,* and *Mennonite,* so also *Amish* is a leader-label given by outsiders, not always appreciated by insiders. The Amish do not directly identify with the one for whom they are named, thus preserving their strict monotheism. In fact, their forebears for a long time objected to the term *Amish.* However, they walk through life as if they had vowed faithfulness to Jakob on his deathbed.

Little has been left to posterity about Ammann. His private life exists mainly in the gray zone between history and legend. Ammann himself never created a personal archive about himself. As a figure of speech, Jakob's time as a draft horse was longer than his performance as a derby winner; in any case, both were relatively short. No one ever established beyond a doubt where Ammann was born, whether he had Anabaptist parents, or if he was in the first generation of his family to be converted to the radical faith. Research is made difficult by the fact that the name Ammann is relatively common in Switzerland. An *Ammann* in the language of southwestern Germany was a chairman of the municipal council; however, his authority could vary from place to place.

It is assumed that this preacher came from Erlenbach in the Simmental (Simme valley) and that he was born prior to 1650. The Amish make things a little too simple by claiming in old documents that he was the "Jakob Amen, *Bürger* from the Swiss Amenthal." In the county church baptismal registry of Erlenbach, one Jakob Ammann is named as born on February 12 in 1644. If this is the one, his father would have been Michael Ammann (whose death certificate is extant), while the mother's maiden name was Anna Rupp. We surmise that Jakob lived for a while in Erlenbach, southwest of Spiez on the Thuner See (Lake of Thun), and he can be traced as of 1692 to Alsace in Kleinleberau (La petite Lièpvre) at the exit of Eckirch (Eckery), which today belongs to the administrative center of Markirch.

John A. Hostetler, author of the classic *Amish Society,* suggests an alternate theory, that Jakob was born February 19, 1656, to Jacob and Katharina Leuenberger Ammann in the Madiswil area of the canton of Bern. He was baptized as an infant and may have been a convert from the Reformed church to Anabaptism. Perhaps his Reformed background contributed to his high regard for the office of elder and his authoritarian approach to church discipline. Hostetler points out that his frequent use of "I, Jakob Ammann" in his 1693 letter to Palatinate ministers is "out of character" for Anabaptists, who attached more weight to the counsel of the membership than did the Reformed. Ammann's great commitment to traditional forms might have come from the extra zeal of a convert. This birth date of 1656 would fit better with Hans Reist calling Ammann a "young fellow" at the time of the Amish division in 1693.

The preacher disappears in the fog of historical doubt in 1712. His congregation did not record the year of his death or where he died. Most places he went, he failed to leave tracks in official records. One of the last signs of Ammann is a document found in Colmar. According to this, three people owed Jakob 600 livres from a commercial transaction. Anabaptists kept no written contracts, so we know the debtors were not Anabaptists. Perhaps in 1718 Ammann had died outside the canton of Bern, and certainly by November of 1730. The archives at Bern show this in the baptismal record of one of his daughters, who joined the Reformed church in Wimmis near Erlenbach in the Simmental, canton of Bern, in 1730. The document says her father was an Anabaptist teacher who had died outside his native country, Switzerland. There is nothing else new regarding his posterity except that, within the larger framework of Anabaptism and the Mennonites, his Amish and their ascetic culture have survived to this day, held together by the steel bond of the Word.

Letters on the Amish division do refer to Ammann, but otherwise he seems to have remained rather anonymous because he probably had not developed his writing skills. Today there are some fifty documents in Alsace signed by Ammann, or Ami, Amme, or Amen, or simply with a childlike scrawl, "J. A.," affixed to them. Ammann used a different signature every year. It is interesting to note that whenever he wrote to his Brethren, such as those in Switzerland, he used his full name. Yet one can easily see that these letters were signed by someone else for him. Two letters of 1693 came from Jakob Ammann together with ministers and elders, and his confession letter of 1700 was written with ten other ministers. Even though Ammann and his companions were dictating these letters, likely someone other than Ammann served as the secretary to write them, in the honorable tradition of the apostle Paul (2 Thess. 3:17).

However, when it came to official letters or documents, Ammann really had no recourse but to sign them himself, and then he used only his initials or "mark." One example of this is a document drafted after the hard-of-hearing husband of one Verena Zimmermann, while mowing, was killed by a tree felled by another Anabaptist. The Amish resolved the matter in a fairly uncomplicated manner: they buried the dead person without reporting his death. When the police intervened, they sent for Ammann as a witness, and he was required to sign his testimony. He sketched the "J. A." but did so in the large and rough script of a child, whereupon the French notary confirmed that he could not write.

Even though Ammann's writing was undeveloped, he may still have been able to read. However, in 1697 he asked Peter Lehman and Rudolf Hauser to read aloud to him letters being sent to Switzerland which put Ammann in a bad light. This might have been Ammann's way of bringing the matters up for discussion, or perhaps he found it easier to listen than to read. Ammann was not happy with what he heard, and the meeting degenerated into mutual name-calling. Ammann's reading skills likely improved over time. So the evidence is not conclusive. Anyhow, in those days many Anabaptists and peasants did not have much opportunity to learn reading and writing, especially while undergoing harassment and persecution. Furthermore, literacy is no measure of competence, integrity, and discipleship.

The Amish of the Lebertal (Leber valley) were vehemently attacked at the royal court of Versailles several times due to their neighbors' protests. For one thing, they were quite prosperous, and second, they appeared as a group to be arrogant. For example, when they greeted each other, they did so with the kiss of the Lord, while they offered non-Amish a greeting borrowed from earlier Christians, "May the Lord come to your assistance." Such expressions did little to endear the Amish to those outside their faith. The wrath of the people was also ignited by the religiously inflexible Amish, who rejected the oath and military service and attempted to buy their release from public offices such as being custodians of public property. In the eyes of the world, they were irritating outsiders pursuing peace and holiness at the expense of others while throwing around themselves a cloak of perfection.

In 1712 the superintendent of Alsace, under orders from Louis XIV, issued a proclamation that all Anabaptists were to be banished from the country. Old documents report on the migration from areas around Markirch, where probably the largest number of Anabaptists in Europe ever lived. The next year many houses were sold by Anabaptists, among which were five buildings officially belonging to the church. At the time, the Anabaptists in the Lebertal had assets of 45,000 livres, one third of the total holdings of the population in the area, although they composed only one quarter of the population. The tax officers greeted this directive of banishment with horror since one third of the taxes would be missing in coming years. This decree regarding Anabaptists led to the coining of the common expression "black October."

Some of the banished Anabaptists remained in Alsace or returned soon afterward but had to limit their numbers by sending most of their grown children out of the country. Others moved west to Salm in the Vosges Mountains or on into Lorraine. Some fled to Montbéliard (Mömpelgard), to regions of the Palatinate such as Leiningen, to Hesse-Darmstadt, the margravate of Baden, and a number of smaller domains under spiritual and aristocratic rulers. Many settled on rundown or deserted farmyards. Already in 1699 in the duchy of Zweibrücken, two Anabaptists from Markirch had competed for the renting of the estate of Dusenbrücken. Now this Palatinate duchy in 1713 permitted "some Anabaptists dispersed from the duchy of Rappoltstein" to settle in a forest area of the "upper and lower Frankenweide." Here in the vicinity of Zweibrücken, the Amish were to survive longest in Europe.

In 1988 only one Mennonite family still existed in the Markirch area which still maintained direct family relationships with the Amish of North America. Today numerous typical family names of Swiss Brethren still appear there, but most of them belong to the Reformed Church. In general terms, one can conclude that the Amish from the Lebertal either migrated or that by 1840 they joined the mainstream Mennonites or other churches. In gray-with-age alleys, the Anabaptist meeting rooms of Markirch have in the course of time become private living quarters, while the Mennonite prayer hall has become a *Gasthaus* (restaurant).

Older Markirchers, however, remember quite well the times when Mennonite congregations were active in these parts. Up to World War II, Mennonite church services were held in Kestarholz (the Châtenois of today). When the film *Witness* was shown in Schlettstadt in 1986, the people in the Lebertal again became conscious of the Amish. In the archives of Markirch, interested parties can find documents relating to these Anabaptist "chief milk deliverers of the valley."

Even today some large formerly Amish farmyards exist between the Sugar Bread Mountain and the Small Bull Mountain in La Haute Broque on the periphery of Markirch, where the streets turn to alleys. In these yards are cellars in which once the Amish Münster cheese was produced. They are still of granite and typically Anabaptist. Farmyards, such as the one belonging to Ives and Monique Jeanroy, lie a stone's throw from the bunkered Maginot Line, on an old boundary between Germany and France. Various wars have blasted the buildings right down to their brick foundations. But all that only happened after the pacifist Amish no longer lived there. . . .

One Peter Graber from Huttwil in the canton of Bern never felt totally at home in Alsace. He was a weaver by occupation and spent several years in Jebsheim. In 1708 he left Alsace again and settled on a farm in Frédéric Fontaine near Mömpelgard, which belonged to Württemberg at that time. In all the time since the

Reformation, no Anabaptists had been executed there. Mömpelgard changed to Montbéliard in the period between 1793, when France occupied it, and 1801, when it officially became part of France as part of the Peace of Lunéville. This happened after the French Revolution, which began in 1789, influenced by the American Revolution. Although Catholic France had a policy of severity toward Anabaptists and had no native Anabaptist movement within its own borders, Montbéliard remained a real home and refuge for displaced Swiss Anabaptists.

Already in this time period, a famous author in the area spoke on behalf of the Anabaptists. In his 1758 novel *Candide*, the philosopher Voltaire tells how the youth Candide in many adventures found such misfortune that he could no longer believe that this was "the best of all possible worlds." Then Candide met an "Anabaptist" named Jakob and called him "the best man in the world," one opposed to every form of force—who thus remained true to the Anabaptist tradition. In this book Voltaire promoted the idea that the secret of happiness is "to cultivate one's garden"—something the Amish surely knew how to do and still know how to do.

6

Idyllic World Before the Fall

The Amish paper *Family Life* offers tips for good neighborliness, thoughts on the impending return of the Lord, and even pieces of advice for safe driving: "Keep to the right as far as possible, and do not tailgate, so passing cars find space between you and the next vehicle if traffic forces them to do so. Remember that the road does not belong to you even though you pay taxes. However, most of the taxes come from the sale of gasoline, and horses use no gasoline. Always remember that it is the duty of Christians to drive carefully."

I am dressed in casual zipper-equipped pants, an old jacket, appropriately called a *Sack*, and a hat made for the outdoors, an *Arschkorb*, so-called because it indeed has the basket form of the human posterior. Thus camouflaged, I surely looked like one of the plain folks to every horse and every sinner. However, I wasn't going to fool any of the experts, who would think that I came from someplace disguised as an Amish home. There dressed-like-Amish Yankees do a lot of yakking at gullible tourists, telling them about the Anabaptist heaven as if Jakob Ammann had just left their farmyard. Surely I would fit well in the Dutch Essenhaus in Shipshewana or in its *Bock Kich*, where nowadays one can down an American Coke and eat an Amish *Wurst* (sausage) and thus fortified, travel through the Amish countryside.

In the twilight nooks of the barn stalls, I run my hand over a four-legger, which the Amish claim is "child-safe," meaning too old to manifest spirited wherewithal. In spite of all the time I've spent among the Amish, my dealings with horses are tinged with a good deal of respect, particularly for Constable, the giant Belgium with his sparkling eyes. What had Elam said on this topic? A horse which has been standing in the barn for a lengthy period of time is particularly ticklish around the belly. If a horse is angry, it pulls back its ears, etc. But not this older model. Blinkers against sideview, buckles strapped against rearing, bridle, reins—all means of power to allow even city people to manage horses. I look deeply into the fox-brown face of the horse and talk to her consolingly. She demonstrates a little cooperation herself, snorts, and is ready for a bit of action.

For my little ride, Chris has readied a photogenic buggy, rendered crooked by age. It is a rickety, one-horse affair long since unsuited for Sunday rides to church. One of those stable-warm, slightly moth-eaten blankets on the seat, a last look back, and now we are three: the horse, the carriage, and I.

An Amish horse will put its shoulders to the traces if you blow it a kiss, loudly and audibly enough for it to hear. Beyond that, they are trilingual, understanding English, Bernese German, and that primordial lingo which only the horses of the Amish and their teachers understand. My horse is willing to gitty-up, slowly past the barn and from the shade into the sun, then in the shade down the farm lane to the paved road. Once there, she sets out at a brisk pace. Sitting on the buckboard behind a horse's back and falling prey to the rhythm of the trot with one foot now braced against the splashboard instead of the accelerator, one is immediately transformed into a new and total man's man. The buggy frees one like the Rütli oath in its day, seven hundred years ago when the Swiss Confederation was formed by three cantons asserting their freedom from Hapsburg rule (1291)—at least until. . . .

Where road X joins way Y, some repugnantly indifferent fellow applies the spurs to a few hundred horsepower. Sixty-five feet long, eight feet wide, permissible gross weight some forty tons. The rascal double clutches, revving the engine and putting it into another gear. In my mind I can even see into the cab of the growling monster: the tachometer needle is swinging and vibrating at the red line, registering the speed of the engine's revolutions. David versus Goliath, semitrailer versus buggy! How did John explain the matter to the schoolchildren on Cuba Road? While horses smell better than cars, a passing car roaring by can still make your perky trotter rather nervous.

The buggy rocks onward ten, twelve, or even fifteen miles per hour. Past the disheveled front gardens, fields of heavy yield, and always along the path at the edge of the highway, where the Amish buggies of Allen County daily travel. The ecstasy of felt speed, a seat as in a sulky. Whenever I meet another Amish vehicle, I exchange a short greeting from here to there. I barely look up and pay no particular attention to whom I wave. The genuine Amish, the ones close to each other in theological and biological terms, recognize each other by the trot of their horses long before they raise their hand in greeting. Each horse has an individual gait.

Here and there my four-legged steed tries for the shortest way home. This age-old struggle between chauffeur and horse, and horse and wagon! This contest between man and nature! My mare with its suspiciously long shoulders and mighty rear end seems a little too eager in her reactions, too highly trained, too aggressive, too sensitive . . . whatever. The days of rest probably did that to her. I remembered her as something quite different while she was under Amish care and guidance.

What does it matter if a car driver reaches the destination sooner? The man in the buggy, in the midst of the modern and artifical world of flight and acceleration, observes more on the road to "there" even if he knows the way from Grabill like his own pockets—if only he were allowed to have pockets. The eyes feast on a tender blue sky, a corn-green field, a wheat-blonde schoolchild, a weather-beaten house, and the entire landscape as a bonus. The air tastes of earth, horse, and street traffic. The relaxation comes from the rhythmic trotting sounds and pulls. One feels the wind even though one never knows from which direction it is blowing. Does any reinless car driver still have a feel for distances, for short stretches of road shriveling behind the steering wheel? A drive in a buggy again sharpens this consciousness—and gives much more.

194

A mouth full of dust, one's rear end already a bit sore, small black bluebottle flies on the one looking like an Amish hero or farmer. Uninsured and without brakes and horn, since anyone believing in insurance has no confidence in divine Providence. How long are two or three miles? High-speed passenger cars flit past me, alongside me—or even under me? God forbid! These cars could be Rome's revenge upon the Anabaptists. What would the Amish be on the buckboard without their serene "Blessed are the peacemakers, for they shall be called the children of God" (Matt. 5:9)? Desperately I attempt to stay the course, but the Amish runner and I are not remotely the perfect team which one could imagine on this stretch of road.

I know I have it made when I reach the stop sign at the entrance to Grabill, just behind the railroad tracks, at the triangle formed by Souder's Antiques, the general store, the cabinet company, and the hardware store. From here on, I drive with other Amish buggies as in a convoy, free of fear as well in accord with Joseph's logic that when two buggies crash, there are no fatal accidents. However, I encounter something foreign, a fellow in tight Bermuda shorts who has come into these parts to capture on celluloid his experiences with real bearded men. Antiques of 1988 and other old objects are obviously enjoying a brisk trade. How happy he is to meet an alternative-life expert with horse and buggy, one with 400-year-old social customs, with a 400-year-old schooling in the patience of Anabaptists. And in addition, he can catch the railroad tracks, the general store, the hardware store, and the ribbon of Grabill Road in the background of his photos.

While stared at in this situation, I know what I am supposed to call out: "*Mir welles nüt* (we don't want it)," no less and certainly not a word more. The rascal zoomed in on me without the least respect for the second commandment, "Thou shalt not make unto you any graven image, or any likeness of anything that is in heaven above, or that is in the earth beneath, or that is in the water under the earth" (Exod. 20:4). He had no real feeling for one about to guide his buggy down Grabill Road. I turn head and hat in order to meet the crafty outrage head on. This obviously excites the photographer still more. He jumps from one side of the street to the other, cutting a comical figure, trying to bring a little closer in his lens this exotic growth in its home environment. The photographer shows no consideration for Amish sensitivities. However, this churl is but a single drummer announcing the following overture. A tourist bus has set its sights on Grabill, though it has long since ceased to be a secret bestseller.

Even Amish inclined to be thoroughly "progressive" take serious exception against this *Bildle mache* (picture taking) or *Leiknes mache* (making a likeness). Amish generally display little humor when it comes to matters important to their faith and practice. This *Bilderverbot* (prohibition of pictures) reminds one of the logic of the rabbis, great Jewish teachers of the past who opposed every kind of picture, particularly depictions of people and animals, to make sure no one gave them the reverence belonging only to God. If an Amish person were to pose for a picture, a church punishment would be more than likely. If one sat dressed like an Anabaptist in a buggy in Grabill, one had better heed the fact that cooperation with the camera could have serious consequences among the picture-abhoring Amish. Word culture versus image culture—that was simply the way it was.

Pictures and images have become one of the insurmountable contradictions between the Amish and the world. When "taking a likeness," a camera-happy tourist could encounter an objection from an Amish person who feels deeply insulted: "*Du hasch mi gschtohle* (you have stolen me)." Occasionally, but only rarely, a rugged and thick-skinned brother might even utter something more than that in a language rich in imagery, for which he later would ask for pardon from the Father in heaven. Some Amish think the effect of this invasion is like the crumbling Acropolis at Athens: several years of tourists have inflicted more damage than prior centuries. A few Amish teenagers rather like photos to be taken of them. Once in a while I was asked to take a picture of this horse or the other. Then one or the other teenager would quickly slip into focus with the steed. The photo was put in a strictly secret archive, for which every farm had a hiding place.

This animosity toward pictures prevents many Amish from traveling abroad. They may have no personal objection against their own passport photo. However, they fear that brothers and sisters might ask whether they have a picture in their passports and how they came by it. Now and then Amish receive special permission to have passports with only a thumbprint where the photo is meant to be. Yet the Amish do not object to looking at photos—particularly of themselves. If it cannot be avoided anyway, and they have not posed for it, the reason for objecting to it is also lacking. Do they, when so confronted, love themselves just as they have been created? They simply do not speak about it. With men, the crown of creation (Ps. 8:5), one may assume that they accept themselves as they are. As for the Amish woman, all superficial beauty aids are strictly taboo, such as makeup, the bronze tan, the hairstyle of the "town girls." They know how to make the best of whatever they happen to have.

The snap-shooter photographers frequently zero in on the Amish like a big-game hunter on his quarry. They are a plague, with cameras here, telephoto lenses there. Gideon Fisher from Intercourse (Pa.) insists that the Amish have to be courteous in relationships toward their fellowmen, and so he wriggles like a worm on a fishhook whenever he is confronted by a *Bildlemacher* (photographer). One clever Amishman wonders whether, when Christ returns to this earth, the destruction of cameras and TVs will happen simultaneously. On this matter, Amish businessmen of Lancaster County (Pa.) have erected signs in front of their places flatly prohibiting all taking of photos and trespassing by tourists. This ban applies to would-be photographers as well as to souvenir-hunters, who on occasion have in seconds managed to clear out entire Amish smithies, down to the last horseshoe.

In spite of these measures, today there are pictures of Amish as well as symbols wherever tourists intrude among these folks. For a half century, commercial ventures have attempted to capture Amish on peppershakers, money kitties, towels, sides of bacon, posters, and coffee pots, usually "Made in Taiwan." In the Lancaster area, Yankees on scenic flights, from their lofty perch in an airplane, are able to take pictures of the Amish, who resist being photographed from the streets of earth. In Elkhart County (Ind.), on the highway of the "Great Army," ex-Amish in their neon-lit watering holes sell Amish dolls in the garb of Swiss peasants.

Amish also appear on postcards. These regularly waft down into my house. Senders are the Grabers from Indiana or the Hostetlers from Pennsylvania, who add "Christian greetings from . . . to you in Canada." Yet they demonstrate good style. Rachel in Indiana sends me only pictures of the Amish of Iowa, the Hostetlers in Pennsylvania sent cards showing brothers and sisters of Indiana, etc. Thereby they do not disturb the peace of the church back home. Photos of Amish are not infrequently awarded high international honors and prizes, simply because it is so difficult to take excellent shots of them.

Full speed ahead, I pass Grabill's Country Shop, the mission church, the car wash, and at C & C Super Valu, I turn right. Now I don't trust my eyes. The one with camera and Bermuda shorts has managed to precede me and runs toward me from the Chevrolet dealership of Max Hofman, that paradox to the Amish style of life. With a wide smile he says, "You know, *Ich bin Deutscher*, you know, *deutsch*, Germany, Allemania, *so wie du* (I am a German . . . like you)."

His tongue is South German, possibly Bavarian bent, his shorts of American cut. Right through my black Amish jerkin, I can feel his excitement and also his photographic enthusiasm. He stands before me as he a few weeks ago had probably stood before the *Hofbräuhaus* of Munich (the most famous restaurant in Germany), and the day before yesterday visited Disneyland or the Chicago zoo. Who has not seen a picture of cringing and squirming Amish which reveals more about the spiritual state of the photographer than the state of the people he captures on film? Playing with religion as an adventure trip! After all, I had myself exercised this art for a while now and had even purchased a lens from the Far East which pointed toward the north while unobtrusively taking a picture to the southeast. I at least confessed my weaknesses in good Lutheran fashion and did not ask Amish church members to violate their convictions by posing for photos.

Now I simply did not want to explain myself to this photo thief, that I was not one of the Amish, not a sorry spectacle with a sheep's patience, but merely a sinner from the world of luxury. One of those stinkingly normal beings of fleshly disposition rather than spiritual, capable of understanding the comically blunt *Bärndütsch* (Bernese German) but still unable to speak it well. The Anabaptists reflect eternity, but I merely reflect the zeitgeist and the temporal. The genuine Amish, people stemming from an old German tree, in this world but not of it, are the Grabers, the Schmuckers, the Zehrs, or the Yoders. What do you want with me?

There I sit, smiled at, astonished at, made strange, photographed by tourists as if they want to encapsulate the event of the century. An exotic specimen worthy of four or five pictures for every Amish connoisseur, or even a whole roll of film for others, similar to a rare bird, the abnormal from the animal world, or a newly discovered star. Collectors of pictures—but are collectors not people who collect rare things in the hope that they will become rarer still? "*Mir welles nüt!* (We do not want it!)" For a brief second I remember the ABC of genuine Christianity: Suffering, hope in God, and patience. However, all I can mutter are words of disgust not fit to print.

Then a tourist woman addresses me. She is carefree, likewise from South Germany, and dressed in terrifying gaudy-as-a-parrot Bermudas. It sounds as if she is asking whether we have already planted potatoes. *Potatoes, Grummbiere,* in May! They have been stuck in the ground since April, just like the barley, wheat, and oats. This is not a particularly intelligent query, but she has probably been told beforehand that in Amish country, knowledge puffs up people (1 Cor. 8:1), and that she ought to ask questions as stupidly as possible. The Amish certainly do not want *their* women to be so bold. When in public, their *Weiber* (wives) adhere strictly to Paul's word, "If they will learn anything, let them ask their husbands at home" (1 Cor. 14:35). "Women in pants" is an especially despicable Amish appraisal of modernity, rivaled by men without beards. If the Amish ever assumed that *Gott ein Dütscher ist* (God is a German), then it is surely occurring to them now that God most certainly has stopped being one.

When one of them offers me a five-dollar bill, I do not even need to recite the Lord's Prayer, "Lead us not into temptation." I turn my hat once again, relieve myself of an earthy age-old *bärndütscher* (Bernese German) sound, and then we execute a circle in the wind and take off in the direction of Cuba Road. Homeward bound, I come to fully appreciate the fox-brown mare with her long shoulders, mighty rear quarters, and energy stored up from long days of rest.

Tourists scatter to all sides. No longer is this Amish country to the time-travelers but rather the wild West, and closer to their skins than they wished. Surely from now on, whenever an expert guide—usually from the Mennonites, typical know-it-alls who like to skim off cream wherever the Amish produce butter—tells them about the peace-loving, tranquil Amish, they might raise a bit of an eyebrow or interject a groan. Yet they likely retain their image of quaint people wearing permanent *Kostümfest* (as for a fancy-dress ball) in proper Grabill, people whose uprightness and German character represent a rejection of the American decay of morals. Thereby they contribute an item for the nostalgia catalog of tourism.

Quickly the Bermuda shorts shrink to the size of a TV screen, and my mare sweats away her last bit of stable dirt. In the evening when I am again in religious barracks, after munching thickened apple sauce, I practice with Ben the prefixes *Bei-*, *Für-*, *Neben-*, and *Vor-*, and the *Verbindungswörter* (conjunctions) for his German lessons. Then we read in the thin, diffused gleam of a lightly sooted lamp a few German sentences from a simple moralizing devotional book, "newly reproduced": *Geistliches Lustgärtlein . . .* (Spiritual happy little garden of pious souls, that is, wholesome instructions and longing for a godly life as well as beautiful prayers and songs). This 1984 printing, including "spiritual incense," was published by the Amish churches at Lancaster. I probably should have read it in the morning to be ready for the day's trials. However, when it comes to "taking a likeness," the tourists met the wrong party in me.

About thickened applesauce: the apple is the most important fruit among the Amish of Allen County, as it ought to be for people in general, dispersed as they are from paradise.

******

The Amish understand horses, and the horses appear to understand them. The family allocates special roles to their horses, but now and then one of them in the farmyard takes things a little too far, perhaps thinking it is more intelligent than human beings.

During this fragrant night, the action centers around the mares of the Graber stable. Constable, the gray-legged tribal boss of the Belgians and polygamously inclined, stood all day in his mating stall as though encased in iron, peacefully taking his rest. By outward appearances, this highly bred power package is in charge around the farmyard. He weighs a good ton and is equipped with a mighty chest and short legs, standing six feet tall, a heavily boned draft horse with a coarse mane. In short, he is a good-natured, and muscled heavyweight, the kind that pulls beer wagons at the *Oktoberfest* in Germany.

King, on the other hand, is a trotter who takes people to see people, a Haflinger with the temperament of the cold-blooded mountain breed, even though this might seem to be a bit of a contradiction. All day long he has busied himself being a lawn mower, with the exception of one visit to Grabill. Possibly during this excursion he already caught a whiff of a mare in heat. Whatever, that evening King and Constable were lustfully aroused and competing, two highly explosive mixtures whose readiness for mating is not restricted to any specific season of the year. Both were in their stalls in solitary confinement until sometime at night, when they somehow manage to break out.

Now they stand facing each other between the barn and the house on Rachel's lawn, which soon becomes trampled and ripped up. Constable, a ton of savage meat on the hoof, and King, like a carnivorous animal on the prowl, his head close to the ground. They rear up, grunting and squealing and thrashing about with their forelegs, trying to inflict a deadly bite on the other's throat. Then some prancing spins, some mighty kicks, and always again a lunge to get a nasty nibble at the sex organs of the opponent.

Elam, Ben, and Chris rush out of the house, arm themselves with baseball bats, and go for the stallions with trust in God and much male courage, as if they intend to break each of the two hundred and fifty-two horse bones piece by piece. Around them the dogs are so excited that they rip at the last pieces of laundry on the wash line. In the stable the lady horses are eagerly applauding their favorite champion, displaying their equine solidarity. Such a three-way fight between man, animal, and animal leaves scars on all parties. One night like this can cost an Amish farm a horse fortune, and if it really gets bad, it can even bring down the family, the chief breadwinner, or his son.

There is a positive side, according to Elam: such a fight proves the Creator has done everything, absolutely everything, just right and perfect. Part of that creation is the neck of a stallion, twice as strong as that of a mare. It is right there at the necks that the two stallions are locked in with their teeth.

The next morning, everything again is in order, and peace prevails. But after the chores and breakfast, the family conducts its regular morning devotions with extra earnestness. As they kneel for prayer, their eyes are sincerely directed toward Jesus Christ, who has promised to come again and to collect his flock so that they can be where he is (John 14:3). Whoever follows Christ as a disciple leads a different life and also has a stronger sense of sin. This challenges one to a more intensive prayer communion with God . . . even if the sins of the night were of an animal nature. Sin presses in from eternity to eternity, but God is over all. Amen.

With a ragged voice, Elam reads a passage from *Die ernsthafte Christenpflicht*, the favorite prayer book of the Swiss Brethren, a fountain of family faith. The Amish often pray the prayers of others before them: "All the godless archenemies, O God, who have not chosen to convert, according to your eternal decree, you have cast away to eternal damnation; from such grant us merciful protection. Prevent and protect, break and destroy all their evil intentions, and put to shame all their evil counsel and attacks. . . ." And then the head of the house adds, "Where is the source, Lord, we entreat, that all the world's full of deceit?" Quickly follows the children's prayer, "O Lord Jesus, make me pure, fit for heaven, peace assure."

A morning prayer, the early communion of the devout with God, frequently lasts up to ten minutes, long enough to put any non-Amish knees to severe test. The Amish know that the kingdom of God is not the kingdom of this world. They do not vote or hold worldly office, so in a political sense, they seem to be spectators in the bleachers of life. Yet every morning their prayers include petitions for the presiding government of the USA—"not for the president personally," but for the government in general, as helper of the church and the "sword" of God's wrath, appointed to protect those who are good and punish the bad (Rom. 13:4).

Those who are good? Such are the Amish. The bad? Well, the top of that list is occupied by the godless Communists, about whom even those in Allen County daily hear worldly news. Elam and others conclude that they, like the early martyrs, would die a traditional Anabaptist's death if "*die böse Buwe vun Übersee* (the bad boys from across the sea)" were to come to the Grabill country. He assumes that Communists are anti-Anabaptist. The brief death pain from the stroke of a sword is nothing compared to eternal torment in hell, so the Bible tells him (Matt. 10:28).

The Amish also pray during the day. Barbara Nolt's natural reflex is to pray spontaneously when she sees dark threatening rain clouds drifting over her wash as it hangs on the line under God's sky.

It is surprising how quickly the paradoxical life of the Amish can still the longing for an otherworldly reality, like the *verboten* (forbidden) telephone, radio, and television. How quickly the present can repeat the past. Somewhere Elam is singing, "The Bible, oh, how sweet a book, from it flows honey pure; revives and gladdens every nook, its sweetness will endure. . . ." Somewhere a horse trots, for trotting is constant and everywhere, a part of the Amish farm music like cats' meows, pigs' grunts, the chirping of birds, or the childlike calls of foals. From the house rattles a sewing machine as an Amish woman tailors a garment for herself. No acoustic pollution. Unequivocal joy of life everywhere, with man the pinnacle of creation.

Mares are led to the stallion. Children show a feel for animals as they train the *Hutschela,* a young horse. Others are getting calves used to the bottle. Chris hitches up an octet of horses, "*e Mutter un irre vier Döchter* (a mother and her four daughters)," along with three Belgian mares from another family. Barbara Ann hops like a Ping-Pong ball on a trampoline, love-crazed pigeons hang onto the silo roof, a staring steer kicks up some cow manure, and a wandering sow seeks out the freshly repaired barn door for a good side scratching. The farm dogs sun themselves on Rachel's clump of modest flowers, of all places. Woe to any businessman who might want to discuss a little mercantile proposition with Elam. Then the dogs make for the stranger. They wouldn't bite him, but they know their job is to announce the intruder and bark a few threats to keep him in line.

Such is the world of the Amish. But is it really all that serene? On this day, the 22nd of July 1988, in the year of our Lord, one Gideon Hershberger makes (Anabaptist) history in the Fillmore County Jail of Minnesota. Sheriff Don Gudmundson has given in to the sixty-two-year-old Amish. Hershberger—victim more than culprit—does not wear the orange-colored prison garb of the other prisoners. He squats in his cell wearing blue work pants plus a blue shirt and marine-blue suspenders. The Bible in the German of Luther and his wide-rimmed hat lie by his side. Gideon shares this cell with two drug dealers, a second-degree murderer, and an arsonist.

What has brought Gideon Hershberger to jail? First, it should be mentioned that this graybeard comes from a family of "rebels," but which of the Amish doesn't? Hershberger's father had gone to jail some fifty years ago in Ohio because of a chronic conflict between the Anabaptists and the school board. Hershberger senior stated at the time that going to prison is the least he can do for the real faith of the Amish. Likewise Hershberger junior, a bold and steadfast window maker, father of thirteen children, has explained to the district judge, Margaret Shaw Johnson, that going to prison is the least he can do for the real faith of the Amish. The judge chose not to contradict him. She was of the opinion, however, that the Anabaptist faith should not be allowed to wipe the state law of Minnesota from the books all that easily.

Gideon Hershberger brought himself into conflict with the state authorities when he declined to fasten a fluorescent orange-colored danger sign to his buggy. Here they call it an SMV, a *slow moving vehicle* sign which warns car drivers, particularly at night, of a traffic obstacle. Twenty-five other Amish joined this old believer in refusing to allow the reins of the state to pull them in, and they were soon to appear in court. Gideon received a sentence of seven days in Fillmore County Jail. This signaled an end to the special status of the Amish. But what does a prison sentence mean when compared to what Christ once suffered on the cross for him, Gideon? And who is to say that one can't serve the Lord in prison?

The Amish of Fillmore County have patiently and resolutely argued their case with worldly authorities ever since 1973, when they moved from Ohio to Minnesota. Always the bone of contention was the color of the warning triangle on the horse-drawn carriages. The result was discussions, a bonus of sympathy for them, compromises by the state, and splits among the Amish. The younger Amish tended to accept orange, and others attached a triangular black sign with a white wreath to the buggy. However, the steadfast like Hershberger rejected every sign and made do with a simple white reflecting strip.

These Amish of Minnesota modeled their reactions after some

Amish of Michigan, and those of Michigan after some Amish of Ohio. There, also, these plain folks would rather go to prison than attach traffic signs to their carriages. They did not regard this as strategic civil disobedience to make a point but simply as keeping a proper Amish tradition of obeying God more than any human authority (Acts 5:29). The God of the Minnesota Amish rejects traffic signs and worldly symbols, especially those with a garishly provocative orange color. Hershberger's predecessors in the faith had no triangle on the buggy, so why should he?

In Michigan, the Amish maintained their right. There an amendment to the law was passed permitting them to put on the buggy a white reflective warning tape rather than an orange warning triangle. In Minnesota, things were not yet that far advanced. Two years later when I met Gideon near Canton, he told me he still managed to make do without an SMV sign.

No doubt Gideon before a court of law was unable to quote a scriptural passage according to which the color orange was forbidden or was of the devil. However, he did refer to Romans 12, which calls one to be separate from the world. Anyone who uses a triangle in order to warn others about oneself, places more confidence in the sign than in God. Moreover, blazing orange is in contradiction to the humility of a proper Anabaptist. Orange screams to be noticed, but Amish are not meant to be noticed.

A lawyer, Philip Villaume, offered his services free of charge to help the Amish in this spiritual and legal contest. In 1989 the Minnesota Supreme Court decided the case of the State of Minnesota versus Hershberger in favor of the Amish. The state appealed the verdict to the U.S. Supreme Court, which referred it back to the state court. The 1990 precedent-setting outcome was that the Amish do not need to display that gaudy SMV sign. Instead, they are to have modest strips of white reflective tape outlining the back of the buggy and a lighted red lantern at night.

The Amish have always had to suffer seriously because of rejecting the world. For an example, take Tobi Graber, a herculean fellow with hair on his chest and a sweetness to his voice. Tobi's baby daughter was maltreated by a physician, and since then she has suffered from an irreparable hearing defect. The doctor and the nurses remarked, "Thank God, an Amish child!" since it is well known in Grabill country that Amish never take matters to a worldly court of law. The servant of the poor (deacon) now had to collect $17,000 for extra treatment—with every family donating whatever they were capable of giving.

A further incident arose on Cuba Road. Collisions always happen in these parts. Recently a vehicle without lights ran into a buggy at night and so severely injured an Amishman that he suffered from the effects of the accident all his life. The police report names the worldly driver as the guilty party, but the injured will never collect a single cent. So the Amish community has to bear the expenses, which they gladly do. They either donate in cash or sometimes collect a few hundred chickens to auction off at a charity occasion. In any of these cases, to call the worldly authorities means not to entrust people to the judgment and providence of God. To go to court might also mean that an Anabaptist would be asked to swear an oath, but Christ forbade swearing (Matt. 5:36). When compelled to go to court, the faithful ask for the legal option of affirming instead of swearing.

Yet the law—as in the case of Hershberger—always deals with the Amish, deciding either for or against them. In 1972, a court exempted them from the regulation of wearing protective helmets, as required by law for various kinds of employment. In 1981, the Supreme Court of the USA recognized that Amish businessmen did not have to pay social security tax for Amish employees as did other businesses. In their community, one loved the other and they looked after their own, making insurance superfluous. However, as late as 1972, a judge in Ohio refused to allow children to be adopted by Amish families.

Recently in Ontario a member of the Amish church was sentenced to a fine of $10,000. On the road with his horse and buggy, he had cut off a car driver. The worldly car driver was injured and went to court. The Amishman was in trouble since the insurance of the worldly has a legal claim even if the guilty party is not insured. Nevertheless, it turned out that for the claim to stick, the uninsured party has to be motorized, meaning he has to have more than one-horse power to move his carriage.

The world inflicts suffering in various ways upon these meek disciples of Christ. In Pennsylvania, irony of ironies: the nuclear plant accident at Three Mile Island threatened, of all people, a group of Amish living near that demonic technological monstrosity. Other attacks of a general nature are leveled at these Anabaptists. Aside from the sporadic stink bombs of the press, crude mixtures of fact and fancy, the Amish have more enemies than friends. Stones are thrown when the brothers and sisters gather here or there. In Pennsylvania, throwing stones at the Amish was at one time practically a sport for worldly kids. In other places, firecrackers are ignited to scare the horses. At times, shots have even been fired at the Amish. Halloween nights at the end of October are particularly dangerous. Then the Yankees disguise themselves in the Anglo-Saxon tradition of the Celtic New Year in order to create mischief for the plain folks. A girl at St. Joseph River north of Grabill was startled by an erotically charged streaker. In Adams County to the south, an Amish baby was killed when some young worldly fellows threw a brick from a truck into a buggy. In March 1992, an arsonist destroyed seven Amish barns at Belleville, Pennsylvania; 139 cows and 38 horses perished in the fire (on this, see chapter 10).

Government representatives sometimes appear and seize cows and horses owned by Amish. In Lancaster County they have even confiscated a few manure piles in order to achieve this or that—matters the Amish do not always understand. Sometimes the authorities mean well with them, as in cases where they tried to force the Amish to pay social security tax. However, the Amish gratefully declined since in the Amish community, one is committed to look after the needs of the other. In Ohio, there was even talk of sending in the National Guard when obstinate Amish refused to have their children attend public schools.

In Allen County, a thunderstorm looms since the large city of Fort Wayne, once a good nine miles from Grabill, encroaches ever nearer upon the country one-horse town—well, it actually has many horses on some days. Already the first urbanites are getting miffed at the stench which blows toward them from Amish farms on the north wind. Soon borders between city and country will be totally erased in this area. But through God's acts and man's facts, pressures emerge which have to be resolved.

The Amish are firm in their faith that without the Lord's will not a hair will fall from a head (Luke 21:18). They take everything serenely in stride and never waver in their principle of non-resistance. After all, they believe that the peaceful are blessed and will one day be called the children of God (Matt. 5:9, 39). Thus their life remains strict and without complaint, purposeful and disciplined. Recently a gang of Yankees ignored posted signs for NO HUNTING and trespassed upon an Amish farm near Grabill. Yet the family did not phone the police. Instead, they fetched axes and saws from the shed and started chopping and sawing firewood in the woodlot where the hunters were shooting at animals. Such action fulfilled their purpose without involving the authorities.

For the Amish, the opposite of love can never be hate. After a birthday party on May 13, 1993, five young Amish were killed near Fredericksburg in Ohio's Wayne County by an automobile that went out of control. Another five children were injured. For the Amish bishop who officiated at one of the funerals, it was obvious that "God could have protected the children. It must have been his will that it happened that way. But . . . there is a prophet in the Bible who says our lives are hanging by a thread, and when the thread is cut, our lives are finished." Most Amish at the time were not angry at the troubled young man who drove the car that caused the accident. They expressed some hope that the tragedy would help him to lead a better life later on.

If the situation requires it, the Amish simply retreat into places where worldly ones are less likely to follow them. Yet in Pennsylvania, a thousand plain folks gathered in a quiet protest to prevent the $100,000,000 project of putting a four-lane highway through their district. This had sensational effects. Later, however, they bent their knees to God, realizing that they had made a mistake by demonstrating publicly. New problems are arising, particularly in Lancaster County where people cannot fall asleep if they fail to hear horses trotting. Manure, produced by numerous Amish cattle, is penetrating the groundwater level, thereby endangering drinking water. Rain carries it into ditches and streams, then into rivers, causing fish to die right down to the Chesapeake Bay, which itself is affected. Environmentalists are becoming concerned, and the government wants to restrict the Amish to only one farm animal for every two acres of land.

Ammonia gases, nitrates, carbon dioxide: all this is confusing to the Amish sphere of thought. The world speaks to them in a language which leaves them speechless. Their reputation is one of building up the land and practicing agriculture sustainable over the centuries. Why should they, of all people, be held responsible for environmental sins in general and especially for global destruction of the environment? The Amish indeed reject the pharmaceutical arming of farm industries, the pressure on farm animals to be superachievers by using hormones and biotechnology, chemically doped fields, and above all, the automobile.

Each day new complaints pour in, ones which may become problems for farmers everywhere. Not long ago environmentalists argued whether the plain folks were the last of an old order or, possibly, the first of a new world. Now suddenly their cattle have become cholesterol sinners, responsible for heart attacks. Certain famous scientists have joined a crusade against the old form of agriculture in their recent call for a boycott. With their own form of illogic, they warn about cattle in general.

According to hot-off-the-press reports, an average cow, a four-legged beast like the Amish Basie or Susy, belches stomach gas and expels intestinal gas that threatens to bring the world to oblivion. And all this comes from the world of the Amish! Intestinal and belly winds daily relieve the chock-full stomach of a single cow by some 162 quarts of combustible methane gas while that bovine serenely chews its cud! Two-thirds of this is burped out through the nose of the cow, and the remainder makes for the rear exit. The scientists calculate that the entire bovine world population emits 129 billion quarts of methane gas that powerfully and constantly nibble away at the ozone layer. As if to prove the point, Amish children occasionally have a little fun by flicking a lighter at one end of the cow and trying to convert this gas of the ruminants into a flamethrower.

If the Amish sometimes do not understand the world, the world often also fails to understand the Amish. An Amish group in Maryland recently had a falling out with their neighbors. The reason was not the buggies, the Bible, or the school curriculum. At fault was the *Hisli*, the outdoor toilet. The world over there had dared to instruct the Amish to get rid of their outhouses since in the heavily populated area, bacteria had entered the groundwater. The plain folks were to avail themselves of the local sewage system or install septic fields when constructing new houses.

"No way," said the Amish. Their church simply stopped building new houses and planned a mass migration from the state of Maryland. Their spokesman informed *The Washington Post* that the Bible instructed Christians charged in one city to move to another (Matt. 10:14). Future-fearing Amish pessimists invariably see a danger that if they accept civilization in general—exemplified in a modern *Hisli* (indoor bathroom)—they might lose their values and their very identity. A water closet would displace the culture of yesterday with the civilization of today. The more they think in traditional categories, the harder they hit the brakes to prevent life from growing beyond the world of the Amish.

******

The Amish have perfected the art of visiting. Guests cause a constant restlessness and excitement, activating something like an age-old flock instinct. Visits, like attending church services held in homes, demonstrate an Amish group tradition. On a farm like Joseph and Rosanna's on Cuba Road, the Graber children are shaking hands of welcome or farewell all day long while the Graber grandchildren frolic in the shadows of Chinese elms and maples. Other relatives appear again and again. Like Mennonites using Low German, the Amish speak of first and second cousins and uncles and aunts as *Freundschaft* (*Freindschaft* in Pennsylvania German), the kinfolk or extended family, a meaning the German dictionary calls "obsolete." This Swiss term *Fründschaft* was formerly a legal term for relatives who had to pay fines for wrongs committed by Anabaptist family members.

The visitors come and go by buggy, for the Amish seem to avoid walking unless there is no other way. Moreover, they can hitch up a horse as fast as a worldly person can drive a car out of the garage. Every day the stately stretch of renovated yard, home to the preacher family, is converted into a great buggy parking lot and a *Platz* (place) for *Klatsche und Schmatze* (talking and eating). They invite people to "stay a while."

Three Graber generations live in Joseph's farmhouse, an ideal Amish structure. The grandparents have their own apartment since all of them could not sit around a common table. Parents are meant to be together with their growing children and to rear them until they are adults. Once the children are grown, those of the

210

older generation—while highly respected—do not directively involve themselves in their children's matters as long as they live a God-fearing life. The honored old folks appear back on the family scene in a guiding way only if and when it is absolutely essential, and then quite deliberately. In general they simply provide an example through life and living, a link to familial ties, tradition, historical consciousness, the norm, and Amish understanding. All of this preserves the string of total development so that it will not be severed nor allow the zeitgeist from outside to cross their threshold.

The relationship of father-son and mother-daughter is congenial throughout life because the later generation learns in time to identify with their parents. The aging Amish live out many beautiful days in the fall of life, when knees groan and muscles pinch. This is in contrast to the modern age, rich in information but poor in conversation. The old men are always doing something by way of giving responsibility to the young set, even though they may no longer be part of the regular routine. They regard it as advisable never to take so much work from the young that they will have idle hands and too much spare time. Free time may turn into boredom—a further reason for the Amish appetite for work. To every informed veteran of life, boredom makes room for evil. However, the old are always there when needed. On an Amish farm, there is something useful for everyone to do, no matter how young or old.

On some of the Amish farms, one finds small retirement houses attached to giant farm homes, similar to the retirement abodes alongside the main houses in the Bernese heartland of Switzerland. In America, however, these are called *Grossdawdy* (granddaddy) houses.

The farm work of the preacher is done mainly by Tobi, his wife, Naomi, and Joseph's deer-eyed daughter Ruth. Since they are the youngest children of the family, they are also heirs, although they will have to pay their siblings fair shares of the holdings. This arrangement has a long tradition. The Alemanns were the only German tribe that always had the youngest son, or the youngest daughter, the "yard angel," take over the estate of the parents. In his capacity as a successful businessman, Joseph has been able to feather the financial nest of each of his children. His sons are mainly businessmen as well, and his daughters are married to such. The Grabers are knitted according to this pattern. With every passing day, the young become more like the old set, as they take over the spirit these have received in turn from their forebears.

Whenever possible, I avail myself of the opportunity to walk the farm on Cuba Road with Joseph. During such walks, the old preacher talks about practically everything, giving me sufficient time to reflect on it while he enjoys the landscape and farm animals like works of art. He knows the ax of time is nearing his own roots—an apocalyptic Amish symbol for the impending end of the world (Matt. 3:10). Joseph calls his Herefords and Holsteins and strokes a Black Angus's shiny coat while assessing the weight, which presently brings a dollar a pound on the hoof. He enjoys musing on just how good the baby beef will taste in Rosanna's skillet, either as hocks, filet, or brisket. Dealing with their animals helps the old remain young, while the young are old in experience of relating to animals.

Now and then a hearty burp from Joseph shows appreciation for a quick lunch. The Amish do not worry about being themselves and thus present themselves in public more naturally than most others. They are thoroughly honest spiritual fighters, who live and die, work and eat in their own way. In such things, they see humanity as made by God. With *Gelassenheit* (yieldedness) they accept and enjoy their span of life, recognizing their human limitations and expecting thereafter to meet the Lord God Almighty.

The preacher has just come from a neighbor's farm where he has looked for water *mit einem Steckli* (with a divining rod). He is regarded as the expert in this field. Wand in hand, he walked across the ground. When the rod became excited, he knew the direction of water underground. In fact, the divining rod whipped up and down in such fashion that Joseph was able to tell his customer exactly how many feet down the water vein was located.

Joseph, this steadfast servant of God, is a man whom one could immediately pick out among a hundred thousand. He does not carry his faith hidden within himself but rather freely displays it in his walk of life and in the way he relates to people and animals and to the soil which he cultivates. Joseph knows the secrets of the Amish way of life. He has produced enough children, fifteen in all, and has reared them all to adulthood with the exception of his son Daniel, who one day was found dead under a heavy Belgian horse. Joseph himself profited from the work of the family. He taught the Graber boys and girls how to work in a practical apprenticeship superior to any worldly institution of training. Now he lives with the hope that his children and his fifty-three grandchildren and four great-grandchildren—and counting—will one day do things exactly as he has done.

Joseph knows that one cannot bring heaven to earth, but he trusts God for the blessings of the kingdom of heaven (Matt. 5:3, 10). An Amish life has fulfilled itself, a *Heiliger* (saint) can die peacefully, if he knows that children and childrens' children have been reared in the right faith, have married *unsre Sort Lüt* (among our own kind), and have lived a farm life. In Amish land, one can often determine only from the behavior and the ways of grandchildren and great-grandchildren if one's own children have been reared properly in their day. Joseph's children have all remained Amish. They have withstood the temptation to take the church out of the provincial setting into an industrialized world.

Up to this day the venerable old man suffers heavily from Daniel's early death. Yet was it not true that God sometimes spoke by allowing fate to trip a human being? Possibly the Lord had reason to scold them and had waited to show them mercy until the family or the congregation had reflected once again on how their lives measured up to God's instructions. It had been this way in the past, and the Amish future is the Amish past. Danny had known horses well. An Amish person knows horses by their gait and by their rear quarters. The one he hears, the other he sees constantly. There was no other convincing reason why he died out there in the field.

However, farm accidents are the second greatest killer in the USA, and they show no favoritism: they don't spare the Amish. But of all people, why Danny? Two days before his death, Danny had seen a powerful and mysterious beam of light in the barn. From that hour on, he had a shine on his face which he repeatedly but unsuccessfully tried to wash off. Danny had been marked. The day after he had been found in the field, two mares suffered miscarriages. The grief of the family was shared by the horses.

The evangelically pious Joseph is one of the most open-minded conversational partners of Allen County. He is a *guter Mensch* (good human being) and totally removed from sorting people into camps of friends or enemies. Joseph knows no one with whom he would change places in life. Like many of the older Amish, he has an uncomplicated nature. Everything, but everything, is recognizable in contrasting categories. Light without shadow is unthinkable for him. Joseph has the wisdom of age. He is relaxed, enlightened, and surprisingly well-read, whether in old writings of the Anabaptists or the book by Hitler's architect Albert Speer. What Joseph speaks about, he knows a lot about. Whatever he is required to remember, he commits to paper in old Gothic script. He is a man who could have become something other than an Amish farmer, had he only wanted to do so.

Joseph is satisfied with me and my fascination for the Amish. My sprouting beard . . . yes, with a beard I would look like a real Amishman. Happy in his memories, he strokes his long ice-gray hair and asks why all the worldly don't wear a beard. Jesus had a beard. In Joseph's dreams, he had seen Daniel, Jonah, John the Baptist, and the disciples all sporting the ultimate male adornment, sans Gillette, sans Remington. Isn't this, after all, the feature which distinguishes man from woman, boy from man? God created man with a beard like a lion, and the woman with a mane like a horse, and the world has no right to interfere with his handiwork. Naturally the New Testament does not explicitly dictate the wearing of a beard, but it also does not forbid the drinking of alcohol, the smoking of drugs, and yet everyone knows full well that such is sin.

Not that long ago America had been a land of beard-wearers, but then somewhere, somehow, the evil one had whispered to mankind that men looked better clean-shaven. That's how crazy the world of today is: Whoever wears a beard is regarded as a tramp out there, as an outsider, as someone who doesn't count. For centuries, the state of things had been exactly the opposite: the shaved face was a sign of the antichrist.

First God had created Adam according to his own image, which means with a beard. Yes, the beard was already there before Eve existed. Then God created the woman without a beard, so that she should know who her "head" was. In the wilderness, the Lord commanded the children of Israel to wear beards to be different from the natives (Lev. 19:27). Even prophecies of the Servant Messiah give him a beard (Isa. 50:6). In old Rome, the heathens shaved themselves, but God's early martyrs went into the arenas with bearded faith. Throughout all times Christian revolutionaries have worn beards. Since the early days of the Anabaptist rebellion, the beard has been the symbol of the true Christian, and it stood for the solidarity in which they lived. Luther and Zwingli had shaven faces, while Menno Simons had worn a beard. Meetings of the Swiss Brethren in Strassburg (1568), in Steinselz (1752), and in Essingen (1759) had decided to ban the trimming of the beard and certainly the shaving of it.

No doubt there have always been such in history or even today who are bearded and yet are no Anabaptists but are explicitly anti-Christians. However, from early times the Lord already warned the church about wolves in sheep's clothing; the true sheep should not be startled by this (Matt. 7:15). Yes, indeed, if all people were to live according to the Bible, one could meet a thousand or even ten thousand persons at one time, and all the men would be of common persuasion, wearing beards. But as matters stand, the Bible strengthens only the Amish, who in principle think the same thoughts and do the same things. . . .

That was Preacher Joseph for you, a man who believed what he said and said what he believed. One who wanted first to be a Christian and only then a *Mensch*. A man who, because of his beard, had already been asked by the children in the shopping center of Grabill, "Are you Jesus? You look just like him."

I spent many hours with Joseph at the pristine pond behind his farmhouse, in the stable, in the field, or in the large living room with the wall motto: "Sharing means a great deal, friendship is the highest gift." From the well-rooted preacher and his belief in the future, I know how the Amish handle their book of memories and their opinions. Joseph, whether he paged around in the archives of his early youth or addressed himself to the contemporary scene, never claimed to be saved. He was not even totally certain where Jesus would first visit if he were to return today: the enclosed community of the Amish, or possibly the slums of New York or Chicago. However, he did believe that one day in the life hereafter, he would receive a hundredfold reward for his suffering in the name of the Lord while on earth (Matt. 19:29). This hope should not make anyone self-righteous, but it could encourage and help preserve all those searching for the true road to paradise.

Joseph was well acquainted with the weaknesses of his community. His ascetic enthusiasm was not a matter of course. He struggled for it daily. Allen County, too, had its hypocrites, who at thirty below zero had the cross of Christ not on the open buckboard but in their own automobile—a car hidden away, going to great lengths not to get caught. And others paid into old-age pensions in order to draw cash out of such strange accounts in twilight years. Yet such were exceptions, practices of people who did not fear the laughter of the world observing inconsistency.

Time and again, this old patriarch returned to the point that if all the world were like the genuine Anabaptists, there would be no wars or injustices. Beyond a shadow of doubt, he was right, but . . . where would the world be if in fact all people were to commit themselves to Jakob Ammann? Joseph was always compassionate, always understanding, but as far as the world was concerned, he never showed any regret at all about the great fire of God's judgment that would engulf them all one day (2 Pet. 3). After all, neither the Protestants nor the Catholics had, up to this day, ever asked pardon of the martyrs' descendants for the excesses inflicted upon them in Old Europe. To him, the worldly were those who preached water (for infant baptism) and drank wine. Cuba Road, Grabill, Fort Wayne, the USA—all would lie there as on this day, and suddenly all would cease to exist, like Sodom and Gomorrah (Gen. 19).

In every serious discussion between a worldling and an Amish, the theme of Sodom and Gomorrah invariably surfaces. More than anyone else, the Amish reflect on this theme. To live beyond the confines of Sodom and Gomorrah gives them the same feeling of security that the Hutterites have while rocking on the worldly seas of sin in the safety of Noah's ark. Living with the prospect of God's impending judgment on the world, they maintain a sense of proportion regarding the future, ready if necessary to be the only human group in the world. As a result, the Amish are actually more optimistically inclined than the average American. Amish have no fear of the future, for whatever comes is of God and therefore totally in order. What comes from God is good.

It would never occur to Joseph to single out any worldly or religious groups and to call them by name or condemn them. One exception, however, is the alleged Catholic underground forces, since the Amish fear of fifty-three million U.S. Catholics and the pope is a prominent object of *Angst*. It has not evaporated over the centuries. To isolate such enemies by name would not be in keeping with Amish thought, and it would be impolite toward the visitor from outside. Joseph speaks quite generally about "the world" in which, for him, Christ is not central. At one time the Reformers had understood certain features of Catholicism to represent the world—vain talk, false church services, veneration of saints, misuse of the Lord's Supper, godlessness in general. From these things, evangelical Christians ought to distance themselves, according to the Word: "Wherefore come out from among them and be separate" (2 Cor. 6:17).

The kingdom of Christ was "not of this [Catholic] world" (John 18:36), and consequently the strict Anabaptists can also be not of this world. Early Anabaptists quickly gathered their impressions of the evangelical Reformers. "The new clerics had inherited and taken over far too much from the old ones of the trade," the Catholics. Thus the other Reformers remained far too worldly for the Anabaptists and therefore not acceptable. It has remained like this until today. Vain things stem from the Catholics, and that is what Joseph and the close-knit Allen County Christian community of Amish understand to be their favorite enemy, the world, whether they say so or not.

Joseph assesses matters rather passively when he talks about the Mennonites, whom he describes as *gute Lüt* (good people). But "we would say about them, that they are rather willful" and thus different from the Amish. Likewise, he also considers the Hutterites to be good people but *komische Lüt* (peculiar people), since their understanding of the Bible differs from that of the Amish. They wear their hair shorter and prefer narrower brims on their hats, which the Amish regard as proud.

What about the *Dütschen* (Germans) in general? Well, Joseph, sitting on a stretch of forest green behind his house, somewhat confuses the exemplary cross-bearers Grebel, Blaurock, and Simons with all Germans. On this matter, the Amish in general wrongly interpret the signaling knocks that still echo from the coffins of their martyred forebears. In principle, Joseph holds a steady opinion about people, German or others, who see themselves merely as the spiritually successful relatives of the apes. Although God did fashion them in his image, they are not really Bible Christians anymore. I can read in the old man's features that this truly distresses him.

In addition to Joseph's abilities with the divining rod, he is reported to have the gift of healing as well, a gift attributed to some Amish of the *alte Heimat* (old homeland) as well. A predecessor of this servant of the Word, one Peter Graber, was famous as a healer in the area of Montbéliard (Mömpelgard). In general, the Amish gift of healing was as successful as mysterious in Europe in those days. Anabaptist nature-doctors—as for instance, one Hans Moser in Champoz of the Bernese Jura—were widely famous, particularly after the Anabaptists no longer had to keep in hiding and therefore could become well known. Visitors claimed that Joseph once even healed a worldly person; he simply analyzed the malady on sight. He appeared to be particularly accurate when it came to identifying a lack of vitamins.

Take my case, which had been no case at all until I arrived at the farm of the preacher. In the living room of his house, the venerable healer put his hand on my shirtsleeve, then lifted my arm until it was at a right angle to my body, with the palm facing upward. Joseph then took from his pocket nail clippers, fastened to a thin chain. These he always carried around with him. For the diagnosis, he held the clippers completely still above the middle of my hand. He moved not at all, and you have that in writing. But just look: the clippers suddenly did exactly the opposite, suddenly starting to swing quite forcefully in circles. That was sufficient for Joseph to determine that I was lacking vitamin C. I was to correct this deficiency forthwith.

As if to prove his point, Joseph took me along the next day to the vicinity of Berne, where the most successful naturopath of the Amish in Indiana, one Solomon J. Wickey, hangs out his shingle. This Solomon possesses credible attestations to his art. All manner of patients hang out there, mainly ones of worldly persuasion, and from numerous states of the USA. Among them are women with pregnancies under their aprons, babies at the breast, handicapped cases, the very sick, the chronically ill. There are also numerous Amish who suffer above all from muscular dystrophy, a typical hereditary condition among the Amish of Berne.

Solomon likes to make what the worldly also like to make: money. A few years ago he was still a simple carpenter in the area of Berne, a region which the Grabillers claim is even more backward than their own. One day this Anabaptist realized his talent of being able to determine illnesses by looking into the eyes of farm animals. He became something like a lay medical practitioner for animals, curing foal lameness, intestinal staggers, and dourine. Soon he also opened his practice for people, initially for Amish brothers and sisters, who established a relationship with him as do Indians with their medicine man. Then he received those of the world.

There is hardly an Amish person in these parts who has not been helped by Wickey. Eventually some problems descended upon this good-natured Solomon when he simply became too wealthy. His consultation fees were not exorbitant, for he charges none. However, the pills he prescribes for his many patients are the source of his real income. Solomon was prescribing a certain natural health product so frequently that the pharmaceutical company presented him with, of all things, a Cadillac (which he did not keep). This kind of success became highly suspect in the eyes of his church. Success is not at all un-Anabaptist, but Solomon was up to things that raised questions.

There I, the *Doktor der Schrift* (doctor of writing) stood before the famous Amish doctor in his narrow treatment room, arms stretched out like the crucified one. Initially, Solomon looked long and hard into my eyes and even managed to discover "German fibers" in them. Then he started to do battle with my right arm but was unable to pull it down in spite of vigorous exertions. Now he took a series of natural health remedies—for instance, some rosehip pills, high in vitamin C—and made me hold them with my left hand while he again made for my right arm, which he now managed to pull down with ease.

The Amish of Allen County reputedly are the best masseurs in all of Indiana. The brothers secretly own many private recipes and natural healing substances which they bring to the light of day when sicknesses strike, as done in former centuries by the little herbal woman. Yet nowhere does the Bible forbid them to visit a hospital when necessary. Before that happens, however, they have specific plants, trees, and weeds which can heal afflictions of mankind. The recipes are age-old—the older, the better—but if they no longer help, then a man like Joseph has to "use God's name." That helps for burns, hemorrhaging, and pains in general if the preacher prays for healing "*im Namen Jesu*." While doing this, the servant of God bows and places his hand on the afflicted.

In Allen County, one can find numerous patients who are convinced of Joseph's healing abilities. Also, they are sure that it is thoroughly biblical to use the name of God or of Jesus Christ when healing. Amos Zehr, for instance, well remembers how as a child he fell sick with measles. An old servant of the Word (minister) had come up to him and asked, "You're not feeling well, are you?" Then he had taken Amos's hands as if he were going to wash them, and he had done this three times in succession. Amos immediately felt much better. It was not as if the servant had completely healed him. Chris Graber reported that once when a member of their church was very sick in the hospital, the doctors told them he would die for sure. The bishop gathered the church for a special praying session. Afterward, the man recovered and lived for another ten years.

For such things, these devout people "*gewet Gott d'Ehr, nüt de Mensche* (give God the honor, not people)." In Amish country, God's miracles are daily visible. One only has to believe in God with all one's heart, the God "who alone does great wonders" (Ps. 136:4). If they are praying for rain, the Amish take along an umbrella when they walk to fields cracked by drought. One brother in Ohio gave unusual expression to his faith by building the chair on which Jesus would sit when he returns. In any case, the chair is there and ready.

The Amish have no undisputed disciple of Hippocrates and also no state-approved veterinarian for their animals, since they reject higher education. They are dependent on the *Englischers* (non-Amish) if their old home remedies and Joseph's *elektrische Hände* (electric hands) fail them. It is not easy for them to find the right medical person because they are suspicious of anyone who looks too educated or speaks to them in learned lingo. In the Amish church districts of eastern USA, some four hundred cases of rubella or measles were registered during 1991. The state health departments blamed the outbreak on Amish resisting vaccination.

The most certain remedy for every ailment, therefore, is the right kind of faith in God. For example, anyone who carries a copy of Psalm 91 during serious operations, has a good chance of surviving. The preacher knows a number of Amish whose life was saved in this manner. If the Psalm did not help, then he was the right party to administer consolation to the dying. Joseph was firmly convinced of this. After a heart attack, he always carried a copy of the Psalm 91 in a pocket of his trousers.

There are still Amish families around Grabill whose old customs are mixed with a generous dash of superstition. Many Amish women will not take a sewing needle into their hands between Christmas and New Year's Day, or all year long they may take great care in not allowing a horse to look through a window into their house. To this day, some of the folks drench three blades of straw in the urine of mares and draw them through their mouths for throat aches. Skunk fat is used for rheumatism and arthritis. A person with a high fever may supposedly be cured if one carries around the bed a shovel with hot coals. These are remedies much like a concerned mother's infinitely repeated "*Geh weg Weh, geh weg Weh* (go away pain, go away woe)."

Such superstition appears to be dying out in Allen County. Today the average Amish people are simply better educated and informed than their predecessors of a few years ago, who attended school for only a few years and barely learned to read and write. However, they all still believe in miracles, and obviously they must be doing something right. According to the most recent findings of the Harvard School of Medicine, the Amish have a lower rate of heart disease than the average American. One family, Yost T. Hostetlers from Fredericksburg, Ohio, measured the lowest cholesterol values in the world, even though witnesses say that they don't refrain from eating meat from chickens, cattle, and pigs. On the other hand, the American Human Genome Project is studying and analyzing factors behind hereditary diseases which tend to crop up in genetically isolated groups such as the Amish. Of course, the researchers are of the worldly sort, but Amish families with suffering children are thankful for the help.

The Amish emphasize their sense of community by donating

blood more frequently than any other comparable ethnic group in the area. In any case, they donate much more than they receive. If it were not for the Amish blood donors, according to information from a hospital in Fort Wayne, there would on occasion be serious shortages of blood.

******

The Amish are quite good at celebrating when the occasion arises. Such festivities help to balance out physical and psychic heaviness of everyday life. These events are not meant for those chronically short of time. At social gatherings, the wind might blow little ammonia clouds from the stable in their direction, but such clouds do not call them to blow the trumpet of the gospel (1 Thess. 4:16-18). Religious powder is generally kept dry on these occasions.

Today they meet on the yard of David and Barbara Nolt, who live along Cuba Road, surrounded by growing things, like the first couple in the garden of Eden. There an assembly of eight women have engaged in a great deal of cooking for the event. The octet works together like a balanced perpetual mobile. The invited guests are the entire Graber-Nolt families and their relatives, along with a few of Joseph's worldly business friends. The latter in turn bring along some of their own business friends, who in the space of a few hours' time intend to get acquainted with a dusty genre of Bible Christians and with a narrow world in which one supposedly makes do without any form of luxury.

Men in pin stripes, people of success with expense accounts, all are soon using pointed fingers to feel up the warm hind quarters of young steers or to trace out muscles on horses. Children are straightening curls on funny pigtails. Wavy-haired society women with farm-stained high heels strut about, determined to party, slurping water out of whiskey glasses, although gin-inclined. In order to keep faith and the modern world reconciled, alcohol remains taboo. The Amish believe that one who grasps the bottle also drowns in it. The worldly and the plain, after initial hesitation, gradually warm up to each other. Once a year Americans love to attend such a party, like a summer operetta under open skies. And when it is all over, such fetes later provide conversational fuel for fireside chats.

David, bearlike, yet a reflective and compassionate shepherd, was not born into the Amish fold but stems from Pennsylvania Old Order Mennonite stock. He had made his confession in the Amish church in order to marry Joseph's daughter, a widow whose first husband was a Miller. David serves as an example to those of Allen County that anyone with the right desire can be converted to the Amish faith. In order to stay Amish, David had to move here, among the Amish. Now he lives by the same Cuba Road as Elam and Joseph, works in the family-owned wood factory, and is regarded, together with Teacher John, as the best man when it comes to castrating farm animals. He also trains horses, teaching them good manners in fifteen days, and using thirty days to suit them for the buggy and get them to be calm in traffic.

David has become an integral part of the community and is no different from any of the others, except, perhaps, that in Mississippi he recently purchased a saddle horse by the name of Max for the steep price of $1,200. David believes this stallion is the most beautiful horse in the area, but he would never say this since such a statement might be interpreted as pride. Max lifts his tail as only a saddle horse does—a peacock among equines—and runs and runs and runs. The other horses of the area, including the pacers and trotters, appear to hobble by comparison, secretly think the Nolts. Of course, none of the other brothers and sisters, horse-lovers all, would necessarily agree with him. Max, elegant and of fine form, may run well, but for all that, he is scared of the train and is not beyond playing a trick or two on his master to demonstrate his resentment of the iron horse on tracks.

One of the items of current *Neuigkeita* (novelties) is the film *Witness*, which became such a hit, not only in America but also abroad. The Amish criticize the film since it represents an intrusion into their philosophy of life. Some of them supposedly even attempted to sabotage the shooting of it. This Hollywood thriller shows a young Amish boy who witnesses a murder from a *Hisli,* a railroad station toilet, while on a trip and a long way from home. The action deals with drugs and corrupt policemen, but little Samuel understands nothing about all this. Of course, in real life neither he nor the other actors are Amish.

Briefly, Samuel is taken back home by his beautiful—and now famous—mother Rachel, a widow. Since he is a witness of the murder, the killers intrude into the peaceful Amish community, intending to shoot Samuel to cover up their drug racket. And then it happens. Detective John Book sees danger reaching out for the boy, wants to protect him, then falls in love with Rachel. The film features a night scene with Rachel baring her breasts while she is bathing in the kitchen and John walks by. All this may be everyday fare to moviegoers and people of the world, but if John and Rachel were to try this out in the real world of the Amish, they would be shunned and banned into obscurity. There is no typical happy end to the film, with the worldly marrying the Amish, disregarding the barriers. Instead, Amish life goes on.

Whatever, the Amish of Allen County are not pleased with the whole state of things. They are opposed to taking any kind of likeness and particularly the "running likeness," the film, and the use of Amish stage effects. They are against every form of publicity which only causes new and fresh streams of tourists to invade Amish country. There is one point, however, on which they agree: The "filmer" did not do everything wrong. One could see that the main actress combed her hair strictly toward the back and fastening it tightly, unlike the Amish women of Allen County but like those in Pennsylvania, whose hair as a result often simply starts falling out by the age of thirty-five.

The worldly in this circle are polite and do not ask how the Amish know this film well enough to discuss and evaluate it in detail. After all, they are not allowed to go to the movies, and certainly the film had not rolled all the way onto their farms. One wonders if they have been tasting worldliness for a couple hours.

Now a more swinish story is told, causing a good deal of laughter. On a yard, close to somewhere, one Yolande entered a farmhouse when Pa and Ma weren't around and ate all the *Schmutz* (pork lard). The sow knocked over whole batteries of lard and then wallowed in the fat of her relatives. In short order, kitchen and living room were converted into a slide. When the farmers returned, what a slippery mess! This causes the merry circle of Allen County to double over with laughter. Then it is Elam's turn. One day he set out on a visit and forgot to tie up his King properly. Hence, the horse made off with the buggy in directions unknown. It took all of two days to find the runaway King and carriage hung up at the edge of a field.

Now comes the food, a feast of nourishment. Only the sick or the sickly fail to gorge themselves on such occasions. No one can equal the Amish as hosts when they run the risk of giving devotion to the *Bauchgott* (belly-god), about which their ancestors sternly warned (Phil. 3:19). When it comes to eating, the Amish show little of the Anabaptist's permanent flight from the world, in contrast to the Hutterites, who wolf food against the clock so that eating will not turn to enjoyment. Amish are people who do not worry much about adding pounds. After all, their lives are full of physical activity, and they can work it off.

Here the cooks offer chicken tolerably well-done, mashed potatoes, noodles with brown sauce, and short egg-noodles which resemble dumplings—"Do they eat these in Germany? *Die Englische kennes nüt* (those not Amish know nothing about them)." The spread includes head cheese, a sweet salad, gulash, white and yellow carrots, bread with jam, and much fresh water. Plates are filled, bones fly on the table, and the culinary satisfaction of it all is attested by a few powerful burps or other release of gas, a recipe for healthy living, according to Luther and these folks.

Then a few jokes are mined from the vein of Amish humor. Every society has its own joker to lighten life's serious load, and the Amish are no exception. This convivial circle particularly enjoys Tobi's tale. A person from the Grabill area hitchhiked his way through the countryside. He was soon surprised to find that his host driver tried to run over every black man on the road. Again they saw a black man by the road, and although the driver went out of his way to get him, he failed. "I didn't manage to hit that one," muttered the driver dejectedly. "But I did, with the door," returned the hitchhiker, smiling. Amish humor à la Grabill—but a hint of something more. The plain people in these parts do not enjoy a good rapport with blacks. This is probably due to a black policeman in the area who rather enjoys issuing traffic tickets for errant buggies and drivers without giving them much benefit of the doubt.

The Amish of Allen County appear to be of more jovial disposition than other North American conservative Anabaptists, even though their occasions for humor and laughter are sometimes not fully appreciated by an outsider. Their sense of the world is more secure than that of the Old Colony Mennonites, and they are more confident than the Hutterites, possibly because an Amish fellow like Joseph is really quite wealthy and only has to think poor. The poverty of some other Anabaptists is real.

There are times when especially the conservative older brothers take issue with the wit of the newer generation. Thus Elam admits that much of what is part of today's life and living would earlier have been banned and swept away as leaven. They have become more grandiose. Oh yes, indeed, in earlier times "when people were slaughtered by the thousands in many ways for our spiritual freedom," then no one ate too much and instead feasted on the Word of God. Those faithful souls rejected every vain style of life and gossip. However, the relatively prosperous times of today have made poorer Christians out of the Amish of Allen County, in Elam's opinion.

The party goes on, and now the agenda for the children calls for a sunflower seed spitting contest and pony rides over the pale-green grass. The adults are treated to a ride in a carriage down Cuba Road—a museum-like demonstration for the visitors, memories of the "good old days." Then the girls sing "*Gott ist die Liebe* (God is love)," "*Jesu, Joy of Man's Desiring,*" and "*Mei Voder isch en Appizäller* (my father is from [the Swiss canton of] Appenzell)." Finally Rosanna and her team sing their yodel song, while I, by now half-Swiss myself, at least for the day, become involved in the fun and sing the song of "the brightly colored cow."

Occasionally one of the boys steals away in order to smoke a cigarette in some quiet corner. The Amish here are not categorically against smoking as long as it is done secretly. After all, doesn't the Bible say that what defiles a person is not what enters the mouth but rather what sometimes comes out of it (Matt. 15:11)? Whole Amish districts in Lancaster County earn their money today with tobacco plantations, a cash crop, thus producing something which by U.S. law has to carry specific warnings about its deadly danger. In this lies a certain contradiction. But then some Amish also collect the urine of mares, used for the manufacture of cosmetics, which are off-limits to them. Amish boys in Berne practice karate, which they certainly are unlikely to put to the test in real life.

In some church districts, pipes and cigarettes are tolerated, and many an *Oma* (grandma) smokes with a smile of pleasure. In doing so, she depends on age-old rules about nicotine. As early as 1607 at the Anabaptist assembly at Strassburg, a little back door was left open to smokers. That decision reads, "With regard to the use of tobacco, it is known that public smoking of tobacco can be annoying and therefore should not be tolerated. However, if it has to be used as a remedy, then such party should do it in secret." Elam's comment is that "people with some class do not smoke at all." He claims that it tastes *englisch*. And then he spits a squirt of chewing tobacco off to the side. Some Amish chew in public and smoke in secret.

As a grand finale the Amish place their last card on the table for a *lustige Zeit* (merry time). They play "the thing with the flight passenger." One of them sits on a seesaw opposite a visitor and then after a few ups and downs, suddenly dismounts, and an unsuspecting worldling becomes a birdling, in for a rough landing. This is followed by an earthquake game, the O-HI-O, and then, to aid digestion, they play *Moschballe* (mushball, cornerball), in which throwers stand at four corner of a square and try to hit someone in the center with a sponge ball. Next comes a little "family fly," in which the tender hand of a girl lands you a few resounding ear cuffs. This is followed by the appearance of *Grossmutter* Schlabach, a comedy of disguise which constitutes the absolute climax.

In the midst of all this, I briefly ask myself what the old Jakob Schlabach from the region of Signau might have said to this game. That old Jakob appeared before the lord commissioners of the canton of Bern and was known to be a particularly "malicious original Anabaptist" during the bloody times of persecution. A great nephew of this selfsame Jakob was later to become a respected member of the Prussian house of parliament. Schlabachs today live in twelve U.S. states and also play the grandmother in numerous Amish festivities.

After the rest of the worldly have left, the women clean up by the tired light of the kerosene lamps. This is followed by a few *schnelle Liedle* (quick songs) out of the *dinne Büchli* (thin book), which sound out in glaring contrast to the *langsame Liedle* (slow songs) from the *dicke Büchli* (thick book), the *Ausbund*. But the songs of quick-tempo also have religious content. There is nothing in them about the typical German subjects of wine, women,

227

and *Wald* (forest). They claim that these songs from the thin book can be sung by "the simple farmer behind the plow, the diligent reaper cutting the grain, and the gardener—followed by a powerful hallelujah!" Even the old can now serenely close their weary eyes and dream of paradise. The godless song is an abomination unto the Lord, but those faithful whose heart and mouth are full of praise, gratitude, and prayer—such are pleasing unto the Lord.

Then they put every energy into gear in the stillness of the late evening hour. Remaining are only the young, the horses, the buggies, innumerable fireflies, and the frosty cackle of coyotes. Hooves beat with the intensity at which others may cycle, surf, or skydive. Now is Western time in Amish country, buggy races in the style of the Anabaptists, in a night where not a star goes missing in the great sky. To sleep would be a waste of time.

A few riders and buggies now juggle for position in the emptiness of night on Cuba Road for the Olympics of the Farmers. The lateness of the hour has dispersed the cars from the streets. Upon a start order, the quick-paced trotters take off, right toward the moon, low on the horizon. The buggies often come within split inches of each other, all without light, and even during day the rigs are pitch black. Tobi yodels for joy like a Swiss Alpiner, and the female teenagers dispense much advice. The referees are two brothers riding bareback.

I sit beside James and behind Christa, the mare, who has just recently been broken in and now runs me dizzy in a few seconds. My main weight is concentrated on the lower part of my anatomy, like a skier. As a child I wanted nothing more than to be a cowboy, a rodeo rider, or some such thing. A real man in the style of a Marlboro advertisement. But somehow, now that I could use it, that cowboy feeling has deserted me. By now I have walked many miles in Amish boots, and I have learned to ask forgiveness of God and in the Lord's Prayer to request that his kingdom come. Generally, I manage to speak believably about belief. "My buggy" and I can outrun the best-trained hobby cyclist from the worldly area around. In the dark dress of Amish disguise, I resemble an Amish. But in my heart of hearts, right now, behind Christa, I am a scared man of the world. This has nothing to do with the Amish.

These Amish, however, urge on the horse instead of reining her in. They know their buggies and their horses. Here is James, with one hand managing the reins and the other on a worn whip handle, claiming it as his gearshift lever. With Christian optimism, he imitates a sports-car driver, accelerating with one foot, double-clutching with the other, shifting gears with the whip, and flooring the throttle. Time and again he asks me, "You still alive?" as if convinced that before the evening is over, one of us will end up in heaven (he) and one of us will land in hell (his partner on the buggy seat). Christa runs as fast as she can, as though horse and driver have decided to put an end to it all. Providence protects us both. That Providence comes in the form of a guardian angel, in whose existence I choose to believe.

A rodeo in Amish style is quite the circus, even though the clowns are not all that funny. It doesn't matter who the winner is. Later, I am the one who feels the victor while sweating in David's barn. Possibly the reason for it all is that Christa's real name was "Holy Ghost" before she was disqualified as a race horse and the plain folks purchased her. That name really didn't stand a chance on an Amish farm of Allen County.

From now on, my admiration belongs equally to James and Christa. After all, she is the one who this very evening trampled underfoot that old cliché anchored in my subconscious: "Anyone can become a coachman, but when it comes to driving, only those in Vienna can." What nonsense! Of course, James and the Viennese know nothing about each other. But when it comes to driving, there on Cuba Road of Allen County, some five thousand miles from Vienna, they sure know how to spin the wheels!

7

Peace as a Lifestyle

The Peace of Westphalia (1648) confirmed the religious status quo of the Peace of Augsburg (1555). It made concessions to the Reformed and allowed full evangelical freedom to the three great confessions. These treaties did not necessarily end the sometimes embittered persecutions among the groups—Catholics, Lutherans, and Reformed.

Freedom of conscience was granted only to those who pledged absolute loyalty to the prevailing faith of the region in which they lived. In matters of faith, reckless disregard of conscience prevailed, along with the fatefully rigid "*cuius regio, eius religio* (whose region, that religion)," meaning that one must accept the religion of the ruler and country to which one belonged. The inhabitants of the Palatinate suffered severely as a result. Already in the sixteenth century, much of the population had changed faith five times, in step with politics. They experienced all the ravages of the Protestant Reformation and the Catholic Counter-Reformation in their backyards, if not indeed upon their own bodies. However, around 1700 this region most susceptible to religious upheaval, the Palatinate, became a temporary home for many of the Swiss Brethren.

In 1648, the Swiss Confederation accomplished final independence from the Holy Roman Empire, which included principalities now composing Germany. In Zurich and Bern, a strict Calvinistic church regime was in power. The injustice of prison and torture chambers drove the Anabaptists out of the country. They had never totally managed to rid themselves of the shadow of Münster (see chapter 2). By the second half of the seventeenth century, Zurich was practically free of Anabaptists. While Bern never managed to disperse all of them, it did manage to infiltrate them first and then to suppress them with Swiss thoroughness to the point where they ceased to be much of a factor. From now on most of the Swiss Brethren lived in the diaspora, scattered. It was difficult for these Anabaptists to maintain contact with each other. Hence, they set out on somewhat independent spiritual roads, splitting brother and sister. This led to ever-widening schisms that persist to the present.

In Kraichgau of Baden, the knights depended on the Anabaptists to restore their estates ravaged by war. Swiss Brethren churches now were located in the land of Hesse, in the Eifel plateau, in Elsace, around Montbéliard (Mömpelgard), in the Jura Mountains, and concentrated in the areas around Zweibrücken, around the gathering places of Offweilertal, Kirschbach, Hirschberg, Ringsweilerhof, Bickenaschbach, Unterhof, Klosterberg, and after a split, also in Ixheim in 1844. The Amish of Zweibrücken appeared as an independent congregation during the great meetings at Essingen close to Landau in 1759 and 1779. However, after the Palatinate became French in 1797, some left and there was a division.

A new, partial exodus from the Palatinate in the direction of Bavaria took place starting in 1800. Local authorities were reluctant to see the Anabaptists leave, as had previously been the case in the Lebertal (Leber valley, Alsace). The intolerance of the world had stimulated their resourcefulness. Wherever they fled, they had to provide for their own sustenance as a tightly organized religious group of outsiders, settling in some desolate areas. They were not allowed to purchase larger estates. However, they had learned to prosper, using intensive farming on little strips of land and developing highly revolutionary economics. This is illustrated by a letter from the prefect of one Mosel area: "The emigration of these Anabaptist agriculturalists is unhealthy since they are

231

highly efficient; furthermore, they are completely law-abiding. Several families from the region of Zweibrücken have already been enticed away by the elector, their former county lord, to Bavaria. . . ."

In the Palatinate razed and depopulated by war, the elector Karl Ludwig in 1664 extended a general concession to these ascetic Protestants and promised religious tolerance. However, this tolerance was hardly free of self-interest, as can be understood from the annually imposed "Mennonite Recognition Fees" and other special levies. The Anabaptists, who lived here but did not feel at home, were instructed to "refrain from rebaptism . . . but to cultivate the land properly. Whatever was still covered by thorns, hedges, and brush, or otherwise growing wild, shall be totally eradicated and cleaned up and brought into good order."

On account of their simple old-evangelical proclamation of the teachings of Jesus, the Anabaptists were decried by members of the recognized confessions as heretics, repressed by censure, and treated as third-class citizens. Their standing was low, very low. The number of Anabaptists allowed to live on a little plot of land as temporary settlers or pensioners was arbitrarily increased or decreased, forcing them to either come or go.

Great bitterness came from the religious battles of the Catholics against the Protestants, Protestants against Catholics, and both together against the sectarians such as the Anabaptists. In addition, tax burdens mounted in general, and demands for percentages of products, tithing, and tribute were ruthlessly enforced. Compulsory labor for landlords was also exacted in the most severe terms. Small wonder, then, that many Anabaptists in the fateful Palatinate regarded their stay in those parts as temporary. In their state of homelessness, they were preparing themselves for emigration, "obedient to the faith like Abraham in his time." Some left for Prussia, where King Frederick William I offered them protection in the early eighteenth century, and settled near Lemberg in Galicia. From 1530 Prussia was already a home for Anabaptists from the Netherlands.

The greatest agricultural achievement of the Anabaptists in Prussia was in draining the swampy lowlands of the Vistula, although with substantial loss of life from swamp fever. Their descendants subsequently were to open up southern Russia and even

Siberia to modern methods of agriculture. Others, including most of the Amish, now took a distant look at the *engelländische Amerika* (at England's America). This *Wanderfieber* (wanderlust) always had the imminent apocalyptic end of the world in view. It was the result of their forced migrations due to the struggles of faith, the Reformation, Counter-Reformation, and a socially restricted life with daily reverses.

Even deeper than their desire for official tolerance ran their religious longing in general, leading to a spiritual frame of mind. The Anabaptists divorced themselves from their earthly homes and made themselves into pilgrims. In a hopeful and free new world, they wanted to seek "in good time a Noah's ark, a Zoar," a refuge (Gen. 19:22) in which to await the return of the Lord. They believed that in their migration they were continuing Christ's way of suffering, even though the transfiguration of the martyrs' death might no longer be repeated. The farewell to old Europe was not at all easy. On one hand loomed the possibility of leading a God-pleasing life beyond the ocean. On the other hand, the adage, "Remain in your country and prosper in it," was a major consideration (Jer. 29:4-7). Migration was because of hardship, but often hardship resulted from migration. There was also the uncertainty of the trip in general, beginning with a long sea voyage. On board ship, the Anabaptists were in cramped quarters and had to rub shoulders with the worldly.

The rulers also made the matter of migrating even more difficult for the Anabaptists. Authorities in the Palatinate rushed to impose fines on persons who "without explicit permission of their superiors intended to emigrate," since the "considerable number of such subjects represented a great source of wealth for the state." The princely councillor, one von Schmitz, tried to resolve the matter harmoniously through a memorandum with a distressing heading: "The punishment and confiscation of property from those intending to migrate to foreign lands or within the empire, without permission of local officials, be they free or serfs." When this failed to deter them, it was suggested that people like the Anabaptists, who were "needy or otherwise mediocre inhabitants," should immediately be moved to barren areas of the Palatinate, in order to curb their wanderlust for English plantations.

Meanwhile, so-called *Neuländers* became active in German

states then experiencing shortage of "food and sustenance." These immigration agents, often nothing but recruiting scouts for American colonies, misled interested parties to migrate to *Amerika* by making all kinds of exaggerated claims. The most attractive state of promise was *Insull Phanien* (misnomer: Island of Phania), Pennsylvania (Penn's Woodlands), probably the only place in the world of that day which took Luther's earliest concept of freedom of conscience seriously: "Here I stand; I can do no other. God help me. Amen."

William Penn's pamphlet in the German language, *Eine Nachricht wegen der Landwirtschaft Pennsylvania in Amerika* (News concerning agriculture of Pennsylvania in America [Amsterdam, 1681]), circulated among leading Anabaptists acquainted with the author from his travels abroad. Contemporaries called Penn the depopulator of Germany. He called his project a "Holy Experiment" and promised "to give people a chance to be good" in his land. That was exactly what the Anabaptists wanted to hear and read. Yet in Bern, the Palatinate, and other areas, all but negative news about America and from America was strictly forbidden lest too many taxpayers and workers leave.

It is small wonder that the Anabaptists, mainly Mennonites, and Quakers were among the first of the German groups to migrate to North America. They comprised the most homogeneous German special community of evangelical faith. In 1683 the *Concord,* a ship with three masts, arrived at the mouth of the Delaware River with a few Anabaptists. This was some sixty years after the Puritans had arrived at Plymouth Rock. Today this voyage is officially regarded as the beginning of the German *Völkerwanderung* (people's migration) to the New World. In the next three hundred years, members of many confessions arrived from the *Mutterland* (motherland). In the course of time, almost all of them changed themselves and their prayers (to English). Yet the Amish, the Old Order Mennonites, and the Hutterites were most thorough in resisting change. At the beginning of these westward migrations, the *Concord* was the German *Mayflower.* As an echo of its flapping sails, the 1990 census recently reported that every fourth American was of German extraction, some 58 million U.S. citizens.

Just when the Turks were besieging Vienna, German Anabaptists were founding Germanopolis, later named Germantown. It

234

was a two-hour walk through forest and brush from the gates of the one-year-old Quaker city of Philadelphia. At first this "German brothers' place" was nicknamed "Poor Town," since many of its inhabitants did not even have enough provisions "for a few weeks." In spite of this, in 1708 a house of God was erected, the first Mennonite house of prayer in the New World. Anabaptists, Christian outsiders with a transportable, transplantable religion, now were among the first Germans to clear America's virgin forests, giving their imprint to entire areas. In time they would be inscribed on the honor roll in the history of agriculture.

The dam finally broke in 1707, when the Kolb brothers Martin, Johannes, Jakob, and Heinrich, sons of Dielman Kolb (1648-1712), summoned enough courage to dare the jump from the Palatinate to overseas. They wanted to escape the permanent state of religious siege. Their youngest brother, Dielman Kolb (1691-1756), was later to become one of the most significant Anabaptist leaders in America. He was mainly responsible for the first German-language edition of *Martyrs Mirror: Der Blutige Schau-Platz oder Märtyrer-Spiegel der Taufgesinnten* (the 1748-49 edition at the Ephrata, Pa., cloister). Dielman also encouraged Christopher Dockk to write his book *Schulordnung* (School order or management [written in 1750, published in 1770]).

However, Dutch Anabaptists had arrived in the New World decades earlier. References to *Menists* in Manhattan (N.Y.) appear in 1644 and on Long Island in 1657. The first Mennonite immigrant named in the records, one Pieter Cornelisz Plockhoy, had landed at New Amsterdam (Manhattan) in 1663 together with twenty-five Anabaptist families. With forty-one persons, including Mennonites, Plockhoy attempted to found a communitarian settlement in "New Netherlands," at Horekill on the Delaware River. He wanted to have a classless society, without landless people, servants, and lords. A year later Plockhoy's project was destroyed to the last board by British troops when Holland was forced to surrender to Britain. Thirty years later Plockhoy finally surfaced as a blind beggar in Germantown. Already during this period, some Anabaptists from Zurich were planning to migrate to the New World but had not yet managed to do so.

Early Amish may have come to Pennsylvania in 1710. Some historians believe that a group from Pirmasens arrived, but not before 1728. However, in 1727, 1733, and 1736, passenger lists of ships arriving in Philadelphia list Amish-like names in clusters, a fairly sure sign that some were Amish, according to John A. Hostetler, author of *Amish Society*. Examples are Beydler (Beiler), Kurtz, Miller, Pitscha (Peachey), Stutzman, Swartz, Zug (Zook), Lap, Slabach, Hostedler, Rupp, Detweiler. The Amish author Gideon Fisher resolutely claims, on the basis of documents he has seen, that Amish were already in the country in 1714. Gideon, who bids farewell to the worldly from his farmhouse at Intercourse (Pa.) with *"Sei en braver Bu* (be a good boy)," has managed to trace his own family back seven generations on American soil. According to his words, the first Christian Fischer arrived in 1757 in Berks County and there laid the foundation for some eleven thousand successors. In fact, most Amish of Lancaster are somehow related to him.

The earliest original Amish pioneers who can be definitely traced are the Tschantz, Kurtz, and Gerber families. They managed to escape the middecks of the *Charming Nancy* in 1737, after a voyage of eighty-three days, and founded a church in Eastern Pennsylvania. On their heels were Müllers (Millers), Yoders, Oberholtzers, Nafzigers, Gingerichs, Brennemanns, Souders, Wengers, Stauffers, Kolbs, and others in the next 150 years. The Amish arrived in the New World in larger numbers between 1735 and 1755, and then also in united groups between 1815 and 1860. By 1800, there were twelve Amish settlements with around one thousand persons. By 1993, this was to grow to 918 districts with around 150,000 persons in USA and Canada, even after major numbers had transferred to the Mennonites or joined other churches.

The earliest Amish settlements were in Chester and Berks counties of Pennsylvania, eventually lapping into Lancaster County. From there, Amish moved elsewhere in Pennsylvania, into Somerset County by 1767 (many directly from Hesse), Mifflin County by 1791, and Union County by 1810. The southern Somerset County settlement (Springs, Pa.) spilled over into Garrett County, Maryland (Grantsville, Md.). A few families continued to go west (see maps, pages 13-16).

Mennonites and Amish who today live in Pennsylvania are mainly descendants of approximately fifty Anabaptist families.

The passenger lists of the times only record the names of the immigrants but not their place of origin. All German immigrants of the time were held to be from the Palatinate, although such was not necessarily the case. At Philadelphia beginning in 1727, they were asked to swear and sign an oath of allegiance to the British king. The Anabaptists were left out of this registration because they rejected the oath on religious principle. This accounts for the lack of written records about them in archives today. The local Quakers, who themselves rejected the oath, demonstrated compassionate understanding on this matter of conscience.

When Europe came to America, Penn's Holy Experiment became the perfect asylum for the Anabaptists. It was a place of anchor for the Flying Dutchman, far enough from Rome, as well as from Bern and Zurich. America promised and kept making more promises while the Anabaptists, based on their history and skillful trades, became tried-and-true *Kolonists*. This land, richly blessed by nature, was accessible by sea and offered a climate that agreed with Europeans. They established friendship treaties and commerce contracts with the Indians all the way to the Blue Mountains. As opposed to all the other American provinces, Pennsylvania was founded by Penn expressly as a refuge for the oppressed of Europe, for people out of the Anabaptist "Babel of Christianity."

Penn made one exception. He viewed Papists, or Catholics, with no joy, much as the French were regarded in the Palatinate. Penn, son of the famous father who had conquered Jamaica for the English, received a block of land by the Delaware River in lieu of a debt the British government owed him. He was friend to the cobbler George Fox, the founder of the Quakers, to whom the Mennonites were related by faith. Both groups stood out particularly in their rejection of military service. This privilege so much attracted German settlers that Governor Thomas soon saw his province as a refuge for persecuted Protestants of the Palatinate and other parts of Germany. He therefore truthfully stated that Pennsylvania owed its prosperity in large measure to the diligence of these people.

In Anabaptist places of worship, people who could not understand English and did not think or perceive in that language, prayed loudly to God: "Since it has pleased you, Lord, to make out of this state a blooming garden and out of the barren areas a verdant meadow, especially through the Germans, help us not to misjudge our nation but to remember to rear our dear youth in such fashion that they will not only maintain German churches and schools but further improve them into a prosperous condition." The Anabaptists of the time still believed that "the fences which God has erected between the peoples should not be crossed without punishment." This cannot be seen as exaggerated national pride since the Puritans likewise remained British in spite of suffering severe persecution.

The Anabaptists succeeded in creating a thoroughly German *Lebensraum* (living space) "in the final borders of America toward the West." Here they retained the German language, in this case *e kräftige und säftige Sproch* (a language powerful and juicy, strong and expressive), called Pennsylvania Dutch (*Deitsch, Deutsch,* German dialect originating in the Palatinate). To this day it is spoken in Amish churches of Pennsylvania, Ohio, and elsewhere and is the main language of their homes. Immigrants wrote back home, describing an America with farms so large that one had to hitch up early if intending to drive all around them in a single day.

This America was still not nearly full, although in the meantime many had arrived and each pioneer family needed at least three horses to do the work. In fact, so many people now immigrated that governments became fearful. Benjamin Franklin argued that as far as the German immigrants were concerned, they were nothing but "Palatinate country bumpkins, . . . the most stupid of the nation." He claimed that they imposed themselves upon English settlements, living together in packs, retaining language and customs at the expense of English, and Germanizing the country instead of Anglicizing themselves. Based on the concern that a Germany could rise up in America, the new immigrants were required to swear or affirm allegiance to the king of England before they were allowed to enter the country. When even this failed to achieve the desired effect, foreigners were required to pay a tax in the amount of forty shillings before being allowed to cross the coast to America.

A new chapter in the history of German immigration to Pennsylvania, almost totally Protestant at first, commenced with the settling of the fertile soil in a wide area around Lancaster by the old evangelical Brethren from Switzerland, Alsace, and the Palatinate, among whom were also Amish. The Bernese Ludwig Michel, a former officer, had traveled the area around the Pequea and Conestoga rivers a few years earlier and recognized its value for colonization. Back home, he joined with merchants Rudolf Ochs and George Ritter in submitting a petition to the government of Bern, requesting permission for the Swiss Anabaptists to emigrate.

For centuries Anabaptists were used to being exiled from one country to find refuge in another. Now in this period, Bern was seeing deportation to foreign lands as a way to settle its Anabaptist problem. From 1671 to 1717, the government sentenced a few Swiss Brethren to row boats as galley slaves in Italy. In 1699 it planned to relieve bulging prisons by shipping Anabaptists to an East Indian island, but the scheme failed. Dutch officials and Mennonites repeatedly protested such forced emigration in messages to Bern and Zurich. Any deportee coming down the Rhine who set foot on Dutch soil would be set free. Then in 1710 Bern was ready to pay George Ritter 45 taler for every Anabaptist actually delivered to "Carolina." When the Rhine ship arrived in Holland, fellow Anabaptists intervened and rendered the further voyage impossible. Those from the group who now chose to leave Holland, did so by their own choice. Most headed back to the Palatinate, Alsace, and Switzerland to search for their wives and children. In 1711 Bern issued an amnesty to allow Anabaptists to sell their property and freely emigrate as families to a country where they could enjoy religious liberty and not be required to bear arms or swear a civil oath of allegiance.

The colony of Pennsylvania was a democracy offering that longed-for religious freedom. While not perfect, it was nevertheless the most progressive in the world of that time, with English politics and German culture. The land around the Delaware River quickly became known as something of a paradise for German churches and for a whole spectrum of sectarians from German states. Among them were Dippliander, Gichtelianer, Schwenkfelder, Herrnhuter, Tunker, Siebentäger (Seventh-Day believers), Sinless, New Moon Order, Separatists, Inspired, Born-Againers, and Socinians, to name only a few.

Nothing harmed their cause more than the fact that they

lacked any kind of spiritual unity between groups. This was in contrast to the unifying force of Polish Catholicism, the Lutheranism of the Scandinavians, or the Calvinist Methodism of the British. There was an attempt to heal this wound, a unification of "German people who confessed that they were all liars, that their flesh is guilty, and that they ought to meet under the peaceful fig tree or the vine of love." But this Protestant-German Circle of Pennsylvania failed because each group persisted in its own beliefs and way of thinking, as had the Amish from the time of the Amish Division in the 1690s. The views of these groups were still formed by impressions of the Old World, and so the Lutherans now suddenly became more Lutheran, the Mennonites even more Mennonite, and the Amish more Amish than ever before.

Most of the Anabaptist immigrants were able to raise the funds necessary for the trip to America. Yet some among the Amish and others had to turn to the system of redemption. Originally this plan was devised to obtain advances financing the voyage of those not able to pay their own way. At first this worked perfectly well. However, unconscionable practitioners and the slave-market methods of shipowners and captains abused the system, making it into a veritable "German trade." Germany, a former world power (in the Holy Roman Empire) but reduced to a one-horse power by the Peace of Westphalia (1648), could not defend itself against such injustices.

Immigrants who arrived in the New World on credit now had to take positions close to serfdom, paying off their debts in servile conditions. Amish, also, were offered for hire in American papers like animals. "For sale, the servant time of a maid. . . . For sale, a boy who has five years and four months of service left. . . ." Families were torn apart, people auctioned off, and the buyers gained an advantage since these servants were cheaper than black slaves.

Today the Amish farms of Lancaster are sought by tourists. But in those days, no worlds separated the Amish farms of Pennsylvania from their neighbors of other faiths. Neither had discovered the age of technology. The German Anabaptists were rather rough-and-ready small farmers even if they also managed small craft and trade shops on the side. They were always eager to come immediately to each other's assistance, in accord with the example of the early church (Acts 2—5). However, the needs of the individual were also included in the corporate policy of other early settlements of the USA, to help everyone make a start. The Amish farm, and the German farmyard in general for that matter, differed in outward appearance from the English settlements. This difference was based on the varying economic ethics of the two groups. The English or Scotch worked their farm with a view to selling it one day for profit, but the Amish planned to stay on their farm all their lives and retain it for future family generations.

This meant that the Germans, after erecting sheds and barns, built huge farmhouses, a characteristic of eastern Pennsylvania. A farm had to be a profitable enterprise for the Amish family. To bear children was a religious duty for Amish parents. During their working days, they had to provide for these rich blessings of children. They needed more and more new land, to support a Christian farm life for their progeny. The Amish achieved this by reducing their personal needs to bare essentials. As a result of land purchases, the Amish, for all practical purposes, remained pioneers for centuries, immigrants for generations on end.

Onto the Amish farms, the prudent plain folks brought along the hard labor of women and children as well as a close relationship between humans and nature. Both of these features were foreign to the English. In this kind of philosophy, it was typical that the Amish owned only as much land as they could work with the help of their own families. The *Buwe* (boys) prepared themselves for work on a farm as once their fathers had done. At an early age, children learned how to milk and to do house and garden work, spinning, and sewing clothes. Child labor was and is most important. Frequently this is criticized by those observing the youth of the Anabaptists. But such weep without taking into account that the Amish not only teach their children to work but also impart to them a love of that work by laboring with them, joyfully cooperating with the Creator God.

Some five hundred Amish crossed the ocean to Pennsylvania in the eighteenth century. From their European home turf, they retained a reliable eye for fertile soil and the signs of heaven. When purchasing land, they preferred heavily timbered areas and heavy wood. Underneath it, after difficult clearing, lay the best of soils. They worked their farms with the acquired thrift of Old Europe, utilizing every inch of land. The Amish planted wheat, oats,

241

and also commercial plants such as flax and hemp. From abroad they had brought shoots for fruit and vegetable gardens: apples, peaches, and German herbs for kitchen use. In addition to their farms, they operated grain mills, saw mills, and hemp mills with power from streams in the countryside. Amish districts had their own smithies for shoeing horses and making nails and other needed items such as sickles and scythes. They had wagon makers, carpenters, and saddle makers. The land was not yet home, but the soil was soil, and they knew what to do with it.

In 1889 the *Philadelphiaer Zeitung* reports on the Amish:

> There are hardly any poor among them; never has an Amish person become the responsibility of a poorhouse. Their dwellings are true examples of cleanliness and orderliness, simply and comfortably furnished, and free of all fripperies of style. Their lifestyle is frugal. Their hospitality is proverbial. . . . In their fieldwork, they conscientiously follow the basic principles which they have learned from their ancestors, and they invariably do so successfully, as their bounteous crops prove. . . . In their interaction with others, they enjoy general respect. "An Amish word is as good as a bond" is a well-known expression among those who do business with them. They avoid all litigation, accept no public office, baptize only adults after such have professed their faith, swear no oath, not even as witnesses in court, and carry no weapons. They live their days in patriarchal family life, hard work, happy in their simple faith of praising God. This healthy, blossoming tribe contributes honor and blessing to the community and the state.

However, not nearly all of the observers were pleased with the sterile and isolated Amish way of life in their enclosed economic and social communities. The Amish were criticized for avoiding certain challenges of the time and resisting the rampage of the English to make all things English. This attitude stood in stark contrast to the planned American melting pot. Amish radical religion carried over to practical life. The alleged stinginess and wealth of the Amish soon became as proverbial as their strict isolation and estrangement from life outside their communities. They were marked by ascetic inflexibility, which set them apart from most cultural influences, worldly comforts, and perceptible joys of life.

On the other hand, this very isolation helped the Amish retain their German ways and language, in contrast with the average immigrant, whose inner and outer loss of identity was extreme. However, the Anabaptists kept that hybrid complex of running without discovering a finish line, the dilemma of leaving the old home and yet not being able to relax upon arrival in the new.

The Anabaptists were faithful to Jesus' words in Scripture: "My kingdom is not of this world: if my kingdom were of this world, then would my servants fight" (John 18:36). This was of greater importance to them than their own life. They tried to live in peace with everyone. During the French and Indian War, many Native Americans sided with the French against the English and sometimes attacked frontier settlers. One Jakob Hochstetler emigrated from Europe in 1736 and farmed north of Reading. When Indians came on the night of September 19, 1757, Jakob would not allow his family to fight. The Indians scalped a son, daughter, and his wife. They captured Jakob and two of his sons and kept them for several years. After this collision of cultures, some Amish were suspicious of American aboriginals. Yet in any case, the Anabaptists were always glancing back over their shoulder to see who was after them next.

Around 1812 the Amish congregations in the USA were largely secured, even though this meant passing some hard tests during the War of Independence, triggered by British economic policies. Heavy taxes were imposed on pacifists whose settlements lay right in the hotly embattled areas. The Amish, in contrast to the Quakers, paid a war tax while publicly opposing it. Since these Brethren totally rejected all use of force and declined to take up arms under any conditions, they quickly acquired the reputation of being enemies of the people. During the birth pangs of the new nation, some Amish were arrested as "traitors" and taken to prison at Reading (Pa.). Still others were treacherously assassinated, victims of marauding Indian bands who made common front with the English. All parties seemed incapable of recognizing the difference between a pacifist and a warrior.

Today a series of historians believe that in the space of time between the American War of Independence and the Civil War, a degree of ossification had set in among the Anabaptists of America. In fact, during that time a good many young Amish left their parental homes and joined other churches. One reason was the death of great leaders of the early Amish immigrants, role models of a high order with whom one could identify (as in Josh. 24:31). Ties to Europe were rapidly being loosened. Bibles, catechisms, confessions, prayer books, and hymnals were often lacking, and the Amish were too far from Germany to profit from its sustenance.

On the other hand, the Amish were not yet up to dealing with new currents in America. This resulted in phases during which stresses from inner contradictions caused old vessels to burst. These old forms were patched only because the pressures from outside were even greater than those from within. Some Mennonites and almost all Amish reacted to the changes in the country by isolating themselves even more and becoming even more suspicious toward things *englisch* (non-Amish or Mennonite). Outer forms like dress codes were reinforced. Essentials were now intermixed with nonessentials, and secondary matters now became of great importance.

Many conservative Anabaptists, for example, eventually rejected the public school system, funded by the government. An upright student was able to make do with a minimal education. Such an attitude quickly led to a deterioration of the educational level. With this typical suspicion toward education, Amish regarded with disfavor any servant of the Word (minister) who spoke in learned fashion. They assumed that he had studied his sermon beforehand instead of relying on the Holy Spirit to direct his sermon, as is still the unwritten rule among the Amish of Allen County.

New movements of awakening separated the progressive from the traditional and gained in importance. The River Brethren separated from the core of German Anabaptists. These River Brethren lived by the Susquehanna River and were bent on becoming even more pacifistic than the pacifists. After them came the Maple Grove Mennonites and the Allensville Mennonites, the Beth-El Mennonites and the Holdemans (also called the Church of God in Christ Mennonite, 1859). The latter follow John Holdeman, who once claimed to have the gift of prophecy and of interpreting dreams and visions.

The Amish certainly had to deal with quarrels from within and attacks from without. In the area around Lancaster, so reminiscent of the South German landscape, religious life was emphatically patterned after German examples. Anabaptists became "awakened or revived" and "enlightened" and joined the United Brethren in Christ, the Weinbrenners, or "Albrecht's People" (United Brethren, 1800). The German Christians of America, depending on the kind of Jesus they now followed, tore the holy garments again and again, taking the piece desired or regarded as best (1 Kings 11). Nowhere did Christian pluralism become more widespread and apparent than in this area of the New World.

Still, there were Amish who managed quite well by tracking the old path. Their religious consciousness, tempered by images of a utopia modeled after yesteryears, enabled them to cling to the teachings of Grebel, Simons, or Ammann firmly enough to remain a historical reality to this day. They did this in spite of the hot spice of a foreign environment and their modest interaction with strange peoples around them.

A large group of Anabaptists moved from Pennsylvania to Ohio beginning in 1809. That year Preacher Jacob Miller moved from Somerset County (Pa.) to Tuscarawas County and his nephew Jonas Stutzman built the first Amish cabin in nearby Holmes County. But the majority of the Amish stayed behind in the area around Lancaster. There, around Intercourse, Soudersburg, or Bird in Hand, the land holdings were tenaciously kept in the hands of the Anabaptist pioneering families. According to 1910 statistics, this became the richest agricultural area of the entire United States, in spite of or on account of the conservative views of these farmers. The Amish now lived on some of the dearest agricultural lands of North America. Yet the soil was well cared for and would remain attractive for following generations.

After 1814 the reverberations induced by the French Revolution, the Napoleonic Wars, and the economic difficulties, a second great wave of Anabaptist immigration commenced from Europe. Among them were 3,000 followers of Ammann's teachings. In addition to Pennsylvania, the states of Ohio, Illinois, Maryland, Iowa, New York, Indiana, and Missouri now received Anabaptists from Alsace, Lorraine, Hesse-Darmstadt, Waldeck, the Palatinate, Bavaria, Hesse, and France. Each group brought along its own understanding of church teachings.

Formerly the eighteenth-century voyage across the ocean was

buoyed by the apocalyptic expectations of the early pioneers. Now in the following century, those embarking for western shores had replaced such illusionary idealism with a disillusioned realism. America was not only the land of religious freedom but also of economic opportunity. The incoming Amish were somewhat critical of their brothers and sisters who had lived in the USA for a while and were even more conservative than the Europeans, who themselves were quite conservative by European standards. In spite of that, the Amish generally have maintained close contacts between church districts up to the present.

In Canada, Mennonites and Amish from the USA are counted among the pioneers of the province of Ontario after the government had set aside a section of land for the Anabaptist groups. Beginning in 1786 and at the invitation of a representative of the Crown, the Anabaptists trekked along the 400-mile so-called Conestoga Trail from Pennsylvania to Upper Canada. Some walked, others rode on horseback, while still others made the trip by the famous Conestoga wagon, which the Mennonites had originally built in the valley of the Conestoga in Pennsylvania in 1736. This was the wagon which conquered the Wild West.

Legends and stories transform these Anabaptist groups into heroic figures who forded the Susquehanna, crossed the Allegheny Mountains, and floated across the Niagara River. Whenever the going got too rough, the Anabaptists simply took their wagons apart, carried them piece by piece through forbidding terrain, and reassembled them again. These Anabaptists were especially grateful that they were excused from performing military service in Canada. In times of war, they had to pay five pounds, while in times of peace, twenty shillings. All men between sixteen and fifty years old (later sixty) paid this annually to gain their discharge, after the pattern in Pennsylvania and, prior to that, in Prussia. During the war of 1812 to 1814, which pitted the United States against Great Britain and France, Anabaptists engaged in "alternative service," supplying this side or the other with food.

Amish from Europe migrated to Canada after one Christian Nafziger, a farmer on a feudal estate in the Munich area, arrived in Waterloo County in 1822 as a scout. He hitchhiked from southern Germany to Amsterdam, and after borrowing fifty taler by providing proof of an allowance, he embarked for New Orleans.

Upon arriving there, he set out for Pennsylvania on foot. There he was given a horse for his trip northward. For his resettlement in Canada, Nafziger and his church waiting in Europe were offered a strip of land in Wilmot District, west of Waterloo. This was later divided into Upper, Middle, and Lower Streets and known as the German Block.

Then according to newspaper reports, Nafziger the scout set sail for London "with an innocent heart to tell King George IV about his lot." Thereupon His Majesty graciously confirmed the agreement that each family of Nafziger's *Landsleute* (compatriots) could buy 150 acres and receive an additional 50 acres as a gift. Christian Nafziger returned to Bavaria in January 1823. On his way back, he stopped by to share his experiences of the New World with his Brethren in the Palatinate, to stir up in them a mood for leaving. As of that day, the Amish laid plans for final re-settlement. Not much more than a century later, the only place where Amish were to be found would be in the New World. To them, the prophecies of Scripture had again been fulfilled: "Thou shalt be removed into all the kingdoms of the earth" (Deut. 28:25). "I will even gather you from the people, and assemble you out of the countries where you have been scattered" (Ezek. 11:17).

Between 1823 and 1824, the first European Amish arrived at the German Block of Ontario. From Hesse and the Palatinate came Schwartzentrubers, Brennemanns, Benders, Gingerichs, and Zehrs. From Bavaria came Oeschs, Nafzigers, Steinmanns, and Schrags. From Alsace-Lorraine came Lichtis (Lichtys), Zehrs, Roths, Nafzigers, Gingerichs, Gaschos, Erbs, Runys, Litwillers, Jutzies, Kropfs, Steinmanns, and Jantzies. Since all of these immigrants came from the Old Country and knew nothing about bush life, they initially were dependent on help from their neighbors. To a certain degree, this opened up their communities to the world. At present there is a whole spectrum of conservative Mennonite and Amish congregations, especially in the Kitchener-Waterloo area, around Elmira and Aylmer, and around towns bearing the names of memories like Baden, Manheim, Zurich, Strasburg, and New Hamburg. Even the chief city was named Berlin for some years, then in 1916, during World War I, it was renamed Kitchener.

In spite of the New World governments granting Anabaptists

official relief from such worldly activities as serving in the army, the first World War hit the Amish particularly hard. The very next day, the Frankfurter *Würstchen* had become a hot dog, and sauerkraut had turned into liberty cabbage. The Amish and the Mennonites reminded everyone that they had been called to Canada and the USA to fight and conquer the wilderness, not to shed human blood. Yet public opinion was against them. The English Goliath had found the Amish David. Anabaptists were accused of being friendly to the Germans, although the government knew that on the basis of their faith, the Amish would leave the war alone and live in peace.

The *Englischers* (non-Amish) certainly knew how to start an artificial war scene far from the bloody battles of war. On one occasion an incited mob attempted to tar and feather a bishop, one of the last drops from the bitter cup the faithful had to empty. Yet they patiently insisted on the principles of the early Swiss Brethren and on the example of the Lord, who had commanded Peter to stick his sword back into his sheath (Matt. 26:52). "*Raubt nüt, kriegt nüt, schlägt nüt zu Tod, sondern leidet eher alle Ding . . .* (rob not, war not, do not kill, but rather suffer all things)." They remembered this dowery from European Anabaptist teachers, who granted God the monopoly of vengeance (Rom. 12:19).

The sword, made for real heathens, was regarded by the Amish as an assignment from God to the rulers, who were to protect and shield the good and punish the bad (Rom. 13:3-6). To carry the sword was a matter for the worldly, since the worldly regiment is equipped for the flesh. Christians, however, are equipped for the Spirit. The worldly are armed with steel and iron, but Christians are protected by the spiritual armor of the Lord, the "gospel of peace" (Eph. 6:10-17).

In Allen County of Indiana from 1919 to 1923, school instruction in the language of the German enemy was forbidden. In the World War II, when the old in these parts were still young, the Amish were instructed to work their fields with tractors instead of horses in order to produce more in times of need. Furthermore, horses on the meadow simply ate too much of the meat producer's grass. However, the Amish regarded the tractor as too heavy for the ground conditions and said so. The young men were forced into alternative service, as also later during the Korean War. This service, done in homes for the mentally handicapped or in Civilian Public Service camps, had to be carried out at least seventy miles from one's own home church district. This caused great problems in the church. Often it was simpler for a young man to go to prison than to be somewhere far removed from his congregation and exposed to the temptations of the worldly.

To this day, Joseph of Allen County can remember how crazy the worldly women co-workers were for the Amish boys during their alternative service. According to the minister, the greatest reason was because the Amish were not wife beaters. This really aroused the holy man's ire. Love instead of beatings! An Amishman who did not beat his wife was faithful to the Anabaptist tradition. If, however, this advantage lead to making a match with a worldly woman, then the man so involved had to take his leave from the Amish faith (unless she joined the Amish). The protests of the faithful were heard in Washington. It was not long before their young men received permission to do their alternative service in an Amish church district far enough from his own home to satisfy the regulations.

Many Mennonites performed alternative service, but some were ready to bear arms. The conservative Amish, however, let no doubts come up regarding this matter. Anyone who went to war would be banned. The Amish of Allen County did promise to pray for their *Wahlheimat* (home of choice), which after all, in contrast to their lands of origin, had offered them a decent existence in exile. Anyone close to these brothers and sisters knew that they included petitions for the USA and its welfare in their daily morning services. However, in their prayers they also took note of humankind in general, including the Germany of their forebears.

The Amish were among the first who sent CARE (*C*ooperative for *A*merican *R*elief to *E*verywhere) packages to wounded Germany after the wars. Today they send similar packages to Romania. They have remained pacifists. This does not mean, however, that the Amish do not own any weapons. Some of the old fathers of the faith would become livid if they knew. Yet some churches tolerate boys and men taking up arms to go hunting. They chatter with cold in the frosty dawn at the beginning of December and wait at the edge of some remote highway of Holmes County for geese. One sees them more like Halloween pranksters in their hunting disguise than successors of Jakob Ammann. As darkly dressed as ever, the hunting brothers have to meet regulations and wear large bright-orange patches on their clothing! On this safety issue, the Amish and the world have signified a truce, a gray zone, a buffer to the world.

The Grabers of Allen County take up air rifles in their crusade against rats. They also shoot animals on butchering day. At mercy killings of animals, sometimes, but rarely, one of the Amish asks a neighbor to aid him by shooting a horse. Such was the case in the winter of 1988 when the lungs of a horse burst at twenty-six degrees below zero. The Amish have a close relationship to their buggy horses, so close that they would not have the heart to shoot their own steed. It is bad enough for them to imagine that a faithful trotter would one day, after slaughter and processing, again come face to face with them in the form of soap.

At the Klines of Holmes County, a little shooting goes on and off, now and then. It is part of the routine of the youngest one, Michael, that he shoots to warn the cows when they arrive for milking in the sparkling clean stable and raise their tails to dispose of finely chewed hay. The hamburgers-on-the-hoof are supposed to use the bigger toilets of the open field. The shock sounds of the air rifle inhibit such bovine instincts in the stable.

However, the Amish restrict weapons and use them only on animals in accord with the biblical role for human beings and their position within the divine mandate. Humans work the fields of the world by assuming, as well, some measure of control over the animal world. This means that people are authorized to breed and feed and shoot animals. The Amish believe that animals accept this order.

Love of animals on an Amish farm finds expression in respect toward animals rather than in exaggerated attachment. In some aspects, one could even set the animal up as an example for people. Thus their thinking goes: it takes no drugs, starts no forest fires, breaks no Amish taboos. . . . But then, it does not know how to preach the Word of God. In addition, animals fight among themselves for food, for a female, or to defend their territory. They desert their old and sick and sometimes even kill and eat their own kind. So it would be wrong to attribute human roles to animals.

8

The Past in Present Blossom

A Sunday morning in early spring. The weather keeps the grass short, last year's crop is all but gone, and the slatted silos of feed corn are empty. To live their way, the Amish must have a *Lieb zum Bode* (love of earth), and they do. Their land for wheat and oats has been turned by a two- or three-bottomed sulky plow, pulled by six to eight horses. Some still put their hand to a one-bottom plow, walking behind and looking forward, as fit for the kingdom of God (Luke 9:62). The alfalfa revives on the meadow. Everything points to the springtime of year. The sky is close, the world far away. A day in the present, above which hovers the gleam of past. A baptismal day.

The Amish basically observe two most-holy occasions: communion, and *Taufe* (or *Tunken*, baptism) of Christians of responsible age, who can make their own confession of faith (Rom. 10:9). Three other events are also of great significance: confession, transfer of leadership office, and marriage.

Baptisms are accorded special significance. After all, it was this ordinance which in the eyes of the world first stamped them as outsiders and anointed them with the stigma of their group. For those in Allen County, child baptism has remained a vice-drenched idolatry, since children, as known by common sense and according to Scripture, can have no sin. As in Catholicism or Protestantism, the Amish accept persons into the church by baptism. Amish church order insists that whoever takes membership in the church must never go back out into the world again. The early Anabaptists seriously contested state-church baptismal practices and maintained that those baptized as babies or merely due to custom could hardly be accountable throughout life for baptismal pledges others made in their behalf. The church could only require a mature, informed person to make the decision for or against reception in one church or the other, and to keep the baptismal covenant.

In Allen County, only those are baptized who understand what repentance means, accept the truth, and believe that Christ can forgive all sins. Baptism is for those who decide to walk with Christ in newness of life and want to be buried in death to sin in order to rise with him (Rom. 6:4). "With such people, all child baptisms are rendered impossible, that highest and first abomination of the pope."

The way baptisms were conducted often led to great differences within the Amish brotherhood since it played such a consequential role in the life of the devout. Since such differences invariably surfaced, they agreed that they would be unable to agree. Those of Allen County today are of the following persuasion in the matter: "With regard to baptism, we have retained exactly what was good enough for our forebears. This means that we baptize by sprinkling in houses or wherever convenient. In this regard we are totally in agreement with Paul, who says that he who plants and sprinkles is nothing, but that it is God alone who provides increase and growth (1 Cor. 3:7). Baptism is the bond between a good conscience and God (1 Pet. 3:21). When we, through the grace of God, are ready to receive the inner baptism of the Spirit, we hope we will not find it necessary to indulge in much discussion regarding the form of water baptism. In our opinion there exists nothing in writing and no explicit word stating that baptism is to take place in the water [of a stream or pool] or out of water."

A Sunday morning in Amish land. On the farmyard a few naturally bred mares return, much disheveled, from a night of serious horsing around. Cows in heat keep the herd moving. Dogs are on the lookout for their favorite wheeled target. Cats and chickens cross the heavily rutted way. Swallows fly low, hunting for fat moths. Cows lick their calves dry. Mosquitoes swarm over troughs. Everything which has a place on a farmyard is up and around. A day, so it would appear, like any other.

Then polished buggies arrive from the street, bobbling over the rough road like ships on high seas. There they are: a few earnest men in homemade jackets of heavy material, their faces halved by their Sunday hats; older women in collarless, dark dresses, skirts bulging into great circumferences by the blowing wind; young women, pushing pregnancies before them, and with them packs of ruffled children, who flutter about like big black birds. A cocktail of unreality, a picture distilled from centuries past.

At the barn, in the shade of elm trees, mighty roofs sag, planks creak, floors sink, crooked beams strain under the weight, and outside walls are covered with weathered paint. Inside, however, one observes nut-brown rows of benches on the finely raked floor, separated into men's and women's sections. Then there is one empty bench for the baptismal candidates to be received into the community of the faithful.

Slowly the rows fill up with swarming families. Yet in Amish country, anyone who wants to get ahead does so with careful deliberation and seemly action. Visitors arrive and sit down, among them preachers and bishops and deacons from neighboring church districts. Anyone who arrives late has to sit at the rear, where straw bales stab one in the back.

First the Amish observe their *Spiel mit der Stille* (a time of silence), serene peace in pale illumination, the joy of being sad. Meditation, rest, quiet, everyone together yet so much occupied with one's own spirit communing with God's Spirit that everything, absolutely everything around is forgotten, dispersed into oblivion. The faithful worshipers again place their heavy heads into the palms of their hands, a few of the very old rock in their seats, and in the women's section tears quietly course over concerned cheeks. Over everything hangs the smell of stable and hay bales, which only the uncomprehending would term as stench.

The scene has been perfected for the baptismal service, in which the instruction class, those ready "*die Gemee noch geh* (to follow the church)," go through an initiation ritual remotely resembling Lutheran confirmation. Amish are not only born of the mother; they are also born again through the word of God and baptism (1 Pet. 1:23; 3:21; John 3). The ordinance is simple but momentous. If a human being knows the difference between good and bad, baptismal age has been attained. Baptismal candidates are usually seventeen to nineteen years of age. Joseph's daughter, Ruth, for instance, entered the community of these devout when she was seventeen years, seven months, and five days old.

At about Pentecost (Whitsuntide), the bishop, baptizer of the Anabaptists, and the preachers had challenged those of age to be baptized, to deny the sinful world and affirm faith in Christ. The servants of the Word (ministers) also explained the boundaries between the height of heaven and the abyss, being a Christian or not, and that it would be better for them not to make this firm statement of faith than to break the vow in the future. Acceptance into the church is voluntary, although parents are not above exerting a considerable amount of psychological pressure to that end. Decisions to be baptized are more often a confession to accept the family faith tradition, a commitment to the family bond and the congregation, rather than directly subscribing to Jakob Ammann's teachings.

Much preparation leads toward the baptismal service. During the first meeting with the church leaders last fall, each candidate had to list reasons for the *Begarung* (desire) to be baptized. Where, please, is the road to paradise? One's request follows this pattern: "*Mi Begarung is dos ir mir eigedenkt seid in eirum Gebate, das ich Austritt machen kent aus die auriche base Welt, um ein Eintritt in die auriche Neue Testament, um mit Gott un seine Gemein ein ewige Gebund und Frieda mache durch Jesum Christum. Amen.* (I request that you remember me in your prayers, to enable me to leave the sinful world and enter the New Testament, in order to make an eternal bond with God and his church and peace through Jesus Christ. Amen.)" At this age most candidates still have a fraction of a light year to go before Martin Luther would be proud of their command of German.

Instructions for the young Amish in Allen County take eighteen church Sundays, amounting altogether to thirty-six weeks. The ministers meet with them separately while the congregation is singing. They instruct the class on the eighteen articles of the Dordrecht Confession of Faith (1632), biblical stories that show the right relationship with God and the church, and Jesus' life and work, especially the Sermon on the Mount (Matt. 5-7). Amish youths converting to a new life have to renounce everything they have done or made that was against the *Ordnung* (church order, rules). Before the baptismal service, the congregation is asked whether anyone has anything against the baptismal candidates.

The introduction to the baptismal worship is made, as always, by a precentor in a mighty archangel voice, "Join in, ye holy in the Lord, sing now a song with the heavenly choirs of upper and lower Jerusalem, yea, everyone who has an ode, praise the Lord." Today he starts with a baptismal hymn from the *Ausbund,* number 54, according to the tune, "Oh keep us, Lord, within your Word." The first vocal beats commence with the greatest musical extensions of the art and more powerfully than usual. Worshipers join in while the bishop, preachers, and servant of the poor (deacon) withdraw in order to speak with the candidates one more time.

> Attention pay, for this is dear,
>   And I'll confirm it plain and clear.
> The matter leads to much contention
>   By scholars of our generation.

> Start and end on Christ rest still,
>   Who makes known the Father's will.
> To sprinkle children, we request
>   Some Scripture proof that they're not blest. (Mark 10:16)

Everyone helps to sing this song as never before since it rehearses the basic Anabaptist reasons why child baptism is unbiblical. The twenty-third verse issues this challenge:

> Oh Christian, now arise and say
>   Which is the Holy Scripture's way.
> Give God the honor and proclaim
>   The truth in *Wiedertäufers* (Anabaptist's) name.

After the singing has concluded, bishops and baptismal candidates return to the barn. The fellows are gently tanned for the occasion from their spring work in the fields, and the girls are beautified by excitement. Most are newly attired for the occasion, since the day of baptism is the absolute zenith in the life of an Amish person. The girls wear black but have a white neckerchief; the dress is secured at the bosom with safety pins.

The baptismal candidates follow the worship service, deeply immersed in meditation. After the sermons and instructions, they are told that *"Ihr wisst die Sprüch* (you know the sayings), you have had sufficient instruction in accord with the Lord's command. If you still hope and believe that you are worthy and ready for baptism, you are now to kneel down, in the name of God." At this point, the bishop questions the faith of the candidates and their adherence to old values. Meanwhile, on the sisters' side of the congregation, tears flow even more copiously.

"Can you confess before God and the church, 'I believe that Jesus Christ is the Son of God'?" (Yes.) "Do you renounce the world, the devil, together with his assistants, as well as your own flesh and blood, and do you desire to live only for Jesus Christ, who has died for you on the cross and risen again?" (Yes.) "Do you promise before God and the congregation that you intend to keep this *Ordnung*, to give and receive counsel, to work in the church, and not to deviate from such intention, with God's help, even if it means life or death?" (Yes.)

Then a prayer follows from *Die ernsthafte Christenpflicht* (The serious Christian duty), a prayer book of the Swiss Anabaptists. The candidates are still kneeling while the congregation stands. Finally the bishop places his hands on the head of each in turn and declares, "On the faith which you have confessed before God and many witnesses, I baptize you in the name of the Father, the Son, and the Holy Spirit. Amen."

The servant of the poor (deacon) then pours some water into the cupped hands of the bishop, who slowly lets it run onto the head of the candidate in order to cleanse each one for birth from above. Now the young people have reached maturity in religious terms: they have become Amish. Upon baptism, they have surrendered their individuality to be one body with the church, just as many kernels of grain give themselves to be merged into one loaf of bread (1 Cor. 5:7 and the Didache, Teaching of the Apostles, second century). The bishop now extends his welcoming hand to each new brother or sister with the words, "In the name of the Lord and the church, I extend to you the hand of fellowship, so arise. May the Lord God complete the good work which he has

The Amish—the last of an old world or the first of a new world?

A breaking cart for training a young horse, Wayne County, Ohio. Pulled by one-horse power, the Amish are serious about their alternative transportation.

Left top: Swartzentruber Amish of Holmes County, Ohio, using their strawhats to shield their faces from the eye of the camera.

Bottom: The Swiss Amish of Allen County, Indiana, regard only an open buggy as pleasing to God.

Yellow-topped buggy, used by the Byler Amish of the Belleville area, Mifflin County, Pennsylvania

Left top: A roofed carriage (Dachwägeli) at Berlin, Ohio. By the style of the buggy, one can tell how conservative an Amish group is.

Bottom: Mary Mae Miller in the "baby buggy," partly covered to protect mother and newborn infant. Allen County claims to have fast horses and beautiful women.

A notorious place for the "dangerous-to-society" Anabaptists: the castle-prison of Trachselwald in the Emmental, Switzerland

Left top: The old Anabaptist house-barn of Hinter-Hütten in the Swiss Trubtal, with its hiding place for hunted Anabaptists

Bottom: A temporary home for religious refugees. The historic Graber farm at Couthenans, France

Cooperative milking. Family members chat and sing as they do chores together.

Left: The Amish teenager, in the world yet not part of it

*Close to God's creation. An idyllic setting for one class of a New
Amish school, Holmes County*

*Left top: Typical Amish school of Wayne and Holmes counties, Ohio.
The Amish educate their children for heaven and for life on the farm.*

*Bottom: Amish girls and boys playing ball during school recess at
Shipshewana, Indiana*

New Amish girl of Holmes County using milking machine run by power generated on the farm

Left top: Amish living room, simply furnished, and with children–the real treasure. Smucker valley, Lancaster County

Bottom: Horse providing rotary power for sawing wood. Adams County, Indiana

"Our kind of people" at a Grabill autumn auction.

Left top: The Smuckers of Pennsylvania's Smucker valley.

Bottom: Chris and Barbara Ann Graber, in his harness shop. The family that works together, stays together. Allen County

"Be not conformed to this world." Amish youths, always clothed simply but never sloppily, sitting on the edge of an Anabaptist water trough

Left top: The "Mennonite cow," bred and developed by Joseph Graber near Montbéliard, France–a great success by 1870

Bottom: The back buggy box is handy for cargo or for use as a "rumble seat," guarded by a slow-moving-vehicle sign. Lancaster County

Using God's clothes dryer–sun and wind

Elam Graber persuades one of his investments to step out of the barn

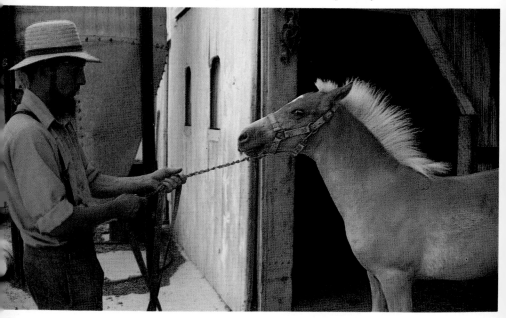

Working the field with plenty of power, in Allen County

Amish of Allen County do not relax old traditions.

Barn raising in Holmes County area. The Amish practice mutual aid by gathering to quickly replace a burned-out barn. (Photo courtesy of Atlee D. Miller)

Right top: New Amish maiden of Holmes County, skilled in riding a horse

Bottom: Baling hay in Allen County. The Lord has given all kinds of plants, which yield seed and produce for food.

White-topped Nebraska Amish buggy waits outside Amish school in the Mclure area, Snyder-Mifflin counties, Pennsylvania.

Left top: One Amish damsel manages eight mighty draft horses in the field.

Bottom: Rachel Mae Graber in homemade clothing, always dressed simply and neatly

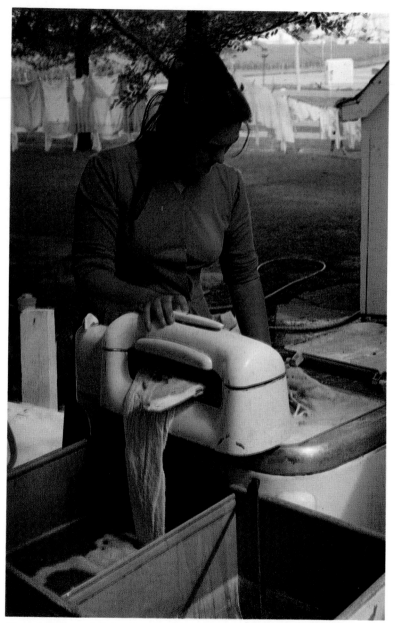

Naomi Miller of Cuba Road with gas-powered washer, fulfilling her place in God's world

The Graber maidens braving minus 32 degrees. To guard themselves against the icy wind, they hold an umbrella with a plastic window.

Adams County Amish girls enjoying Shipshewana for the day, protecting their eyes from the sun

Mixing it up, in the kitchen at Chris Graber's place, Allen County

Preacher Chris Graber's cabinet shop burns out—but is speedily rebuilt by the brotherhood. (Photo by Thurman Johnson)

A wagon ride, with one-person power, in Geauga County, Ohio

Food fresh from the garden, being processed by grandmother and granddaughter

Water handy, daily exercise–God's free gifts

Amish quilt of LaGrange County, Indiana

Beachy Amish quilting at Shipshewana, with Elsie Miller and daughters. Colorful traditional patterns today have worldwide appeal.

Fraktur in an Amish library in Holmes County: "This book belongs to me, Jonas M. Beiler, East Lampeter Township, Lancaster County, Pennsylvania. Written the second of January 1894."

Amish farm in Wisconsin. The farmhouse is large enough so that the church can hold services in it.

Typical visiting on the lawn, after the Sunday church service and before their turn to share in the simple love meal. Shipshewana

New Order Amish of Ohio use roadside telephone booth for urgent calls but do not want it to displace face-to-face relationships.

begun in you and strengthen and comfort you to a blessed end, through Jesus Christ. Amen." At the conclusion, this full servant kisses the young men while his wife kisses the young ladies, as the Amish have always greeted each other in their own wider family.

Now it is time for the bishops and preachers who have come as visitors from other congregations to speak up. They bear witness and confirm what they have seen and heard: "I cannot do otherwise than to confirm that what I have heard is the truth. . . . I have understood nothing but that which is of God. . . ."

After four hours of sitting, everyone is hungry. For the *Liebesmahl* (love meal), the congregation assembles, grouped according to gender and married or single state. The old converse and are carried away by talk of miracles, the baptized sit together and appear to dream of paradise as a worldly person dreams of winning a grand prize in a lottery. However, not everything is a dream. As starting capital, in a manner of speaking, baptized Amish can lay claim to a considerable amount of faith and grace. They know full well that family, church, and neighbors are with them and will help to sustain them. They need this assurance, for the new life ahead will be more, much more, than fun and games.

****

Chris, the son of Elam, shaves every morning until the day he gets married. Ever since his sixteenth birthday, he hitches up and is gone quite often in order *"nach de scheene Mädle zgucke* (to look for the beautiful girls)," as Rachel says. For this purpose he harnesses a muscular Standardbred, a trotter which can polish off a mile in mighty short order. Chris's sisters are both too young to be of much use as chaperones when Chris engages in *Rumschpringe* (running around). So the boy is left to his own devices, and he doesn't much seem to mind.

Starting at age sixteen, the offspring of the Amish look at the opposite gender with a changed focus. The boys are considerably more mobile than before, with their own rigs. The girls, with the most innocent sex appeal under God's heaven, are dressed up smartly with containing pins and propriety and start blooming like spring flowers. Now the first erotic sparks start flying during gatherings for youth singings, without the teenagers getting physical. It may happen occasionally that a son or a daughter spends the night away from home, beyond parental scrutiny, even if this is not really permitted. "Foolishness is bound in the heart," so spoke the wise old Solomon (Prov. 22:15).

Childhood and old age are the summits in being Amish, but the interlude between the sixteenth birthday and marriage is regarded as the happiest in Amish life. In fact, some youths, even in Allen County, postpone their baptisms a bit since the maxim holds and applies: no baptism, no wedding! However, marriage is synonymous with a more strictly regulated life. Babies born with predictable regularity are only one part of the catalog of responsibilities.

The custom of painting the door of a house blue if it holds marriageable daughters was not common everywhere among the Amish. Even Joseph knows it only from Pennsylvanian hearsay. However, there is a widely practiced tradition of Amish boys racing around and trying to impress the girls with the speed of a horse hitched to a spruced-up buggy. They do this especially on Sunday nights, far afield, perhaps even in a neighboring state. Who will hitch up the faster horse to impress a Pennsylvania-Deutsch *maydel* (maiden)? Will the stars be Yonnie and Lavina, or Henner and Katie?

In Amish country, the young people know each other. In addition, everyone knows with whom, where, and when they are planning to tie the nuptial bond. Joseph's daughter Ruth, so one hears, was a rather daring rider in her teenage days. Then the day came when she was concerned as to what the boys might think of this hobby, and from one day to the next, she dismounted. Because they are exclusive, the Amish girls of Allen County especially attract worldly fellows. They know full well how to play out their feminine charm within limits, without jeopardizing their faith. Pious and cheerful, they have both feet planted on Amish ground, and yet they retain a touch of that complete innocence native to their homemade (but faceless) dolls.

Amish girls are not boisterous or loud, neither do they invite noisy behavior. They do assert themselves on the milk stool in their battle with grudge-bearing cows, and they certainly cannot be taken for fools. Their strength is of the sensitive-tender variety. Girls who do open their mouths appear cheerful and patient. Yet, when one of them suddenly breaks into a yodel like a mountaineer, the audience is in for more than a little surprise.

The Grabers generally are dark haired with dark sparkling eyes, of Mediterranean temperament and Alemannic stature. The Brandenbergers are blond and of North-German aloofness. All know how to work like true Anabaptists. When an *Oma* (grandma) Graber, Brandenberger, Schmucker, or Zehr reviews her life from the vantage point of old age, she counts some 73,000 cows milked, eight or more children raised, 160,000 cattle fed, 182,000 hours spent at housework, a further 55,000 hours spent in the stable and garden, and several times 10,000 flies swatted—all with not one complaint uttered.

In their relationships between the sexes, Amish young people are much like others, but with standards laid down. Soon after reaching age sixteen, their *Buwe* and *Mädli* (boys and girls) start a period of courting and kissing. In these parts, people say they do "*miteinander rumschpringe* (running around with each other)." The God of the Amish is not prudish nor a spoilsport in sexual matters. The parents subscribe to the wisdom that it is better to marry than to be devoured by desire (1 Cor. 7:9).

In a few areas, but not in Allen County, teenagers fully clad lie down on the same bed for sessions of visiting. In some church districts, this practice of bundling has become rather systematic. It has its own rules, one of which says that bundling always has to take place in the house of the female partner. A further prescription states that bundling is not to become a sexual apprenticeship, since there is a firm standard for virginity before marriage. Everything else is regarded as sinful flesh.

Bundling is a custom dating back to a legendary Alpine custom of love called *Fensterln* (windowing). This old custom was practiced in the large, unheated homes of Europe and early American colonies. Bundling was imported to America with the Welsh, the English, the Dutch, the Germans, and even the Scotch. Not counting the Amish, it was still practiced in the 1950s in some mountain and rural areas (*Mennonite Encyclopedia*).

Youths did not always observe the prescribed rules, and problems developed, but the Amish never managed to abolish bundling. Instructive letters drafted in Old Europe warn time and again about premature intimacies: "Parents are to take particular care and keep good order in their homes, for all housefathers and housemothers are responsible to God for their children if through their fault and through lust something is forever lost. Parents should not go unpunished if through their carelessness young people lie together at night. If, however, it happens behind their backs, then the parents are exonerated."

Early Anabaptist teachers occasionally raised doubts about whether such unmarried desire in the bedrooms could still be brought into line with the commission of the early martyrs. What would the world think of those "who regard themselves as the chosen people of God" and yet have children forced into marriage? After all, the book of Hebrews stipulates that believers are to lay aside all sins which stick to them and hold them back (Heb. 12:1). Paul calls Christians to cleanse themselves of all filthiness of the flesh (2 Cor. 7:1). Again and again, the Amish have admitted that bundling amounts to such spots of the flesh, and most leaders have sharply condemned it.

A further letter states that much "excitement, care, and grief" has been caused by bundling since it became popular at the beginning of the nineteenth century. "Whether one wants to admit it or not, . . . what was once practiced by hundreds is today done by thousands," wrote Bishop David Troyer in 1870 from Ohio. For him, bundling was an abomination before God, "premarital cohabitation being Satan's greatest power in the matter." It was a serious matter. When their parents were young, Troyer claimed, courting youths took care to keep a rough board between the two. Now the board had disappeared and with it one or the other piece of clothing. However, not even David Troyer managed to "uproot this terrible lusting," although he tried. The evidence is in the number of children "born out of premarital cohabitation and as a result of the sinfulness of the parents, if one were to ask them. . . ." Ironically, in the nineteenth century, the Amish lived in some parts of the USA in which premarital cohabitation was prohibited by state law and yet sometimes practiced among Amish youth.

In certain districts bundling is still practiced "cleanly," while in other districts it opens the door to low morals and pregnancies before marriage. If opportunity leads to more than innocent frolic, cohabitation on a trial basis may occur, although everyone knows that God casts a disapproving eye on the practice. Few traditions have led to such frequent discussions among the Amish as the one of "going to bed." In Elam's church, bundling is forbidden, or more accurately stated, the young people are shamed into limits with the command to meet only in the light. Also, they are told to stay above the belt while clinching—that is, where the worldly wear their belts, since belts are forbidden to the Amish.

The Amish are convinced that bundling is an age-old German custom. After all, traditions do not arise out of nothing. In earlier times, particularly in the Bern Alpine foothills, it was the custom for young people to crawl platonically into bed together, fully clothed, since farmhouses could not be heated adequately. Moreover, the word *bundling* may be derived from the bands of material with which a young Emmentaler decorated a tree before the house of a youthful love.

Obviously the Amish are capable of putting a stop to anything, including old traditions. However, some are not that firmly opposed to the custom, either, because it lends atmosphere to relaxing evenings and reminds them of their home country. Parents as well as others in the church may prefer that two unmarried Amish youths lie together (properly clothed) than that one would begin courting a worldly person.

In practice, this custom of bundling takes the following form: a boy who is seriously running around with a girl steals to her house when the lights are down. He patiently waits for the parents to retire, and then he lets his flashlight do the talking by blinking at the window of the young woman. She opens the kitchen door and takes him up to her room. On Cuba Road, a girl's room is generally cozily furnished, possibly with some artificial roses, peacock feathers, or sometimes even a cowboy hat hanging on the wall. These are items with which an Amish certainly would not be allowed to go public. Also, the wafting fragrance is not meant for public noses since the favorite evening perfume, "Making Love," has a fairly potent scent.

The two young people visiting in such a setting do not necessarily jump into bed together. But if they do because of the cold, unheated room, the rule says that the boy has to remain clothed in his shirt and pants, while the girl is allowed to discard her dress but not her petticoat. It is taboo to engage in a little lust of the flesh, like ordinary sinners of the world.

The claim that bundling is still practiced in all Amish churches is just as false as the claim that all female spiders eat their male
partners after copulation. However, the fact that the custom does
indeed exist led Hutterites to publish a pamphlet for their young
people in 1988, mentioning bundling as a way not to court. Worldly mockers in general and the Hutterite warners in particular are
partly right and partly wrong. In the course of time, Amish bundling has become such an established human institution that the
church cannot easily do away with it. Holmes and surrounding
counties in Ohio have the highest concentration of Amish in the
USA. For the Amish, the area is something like the second ark of
Noah. Here they are a world to themselves, and bundling is practiced to some extent, but only after youths reach age sixteen. This
once was the hunting area of the Delawares, whose arrowheads
are still regularly exposed by plows, but now another kind of hunting goes on.

One evening in northern Holmes County, the cows are home,
and the thud of the diesel motor has long since ebbed into silence.
After a hot and full summer day, everyone in the farmhouse has
retired for the night. However, in the upstairs room someone has
forgotten to extinguish the pale gaslight. Suddenly the farmer is
awakened by the squeaking of a horse's harness. The family may
expect the visit of a lusty, lusting, possibly even strange Amish
boy. Attracted by the gaslight, he may attempt to gain entrance via
the door and head for the upstairs. The more mature Amish girls
repose in these quarters.

The head of the house would not be all that surprised. But certain measures of tranquillity, which distinguish all Amish, have
been unduly strained. In short, his patience has worn out. He rises
to the challenge now imposed on him. This episode throws salt on
the new wounds of the Amish, since the renegades have singled
out the wrong farmhouse. The Amish here have strictly distanced
themselves from the practice of bundling. The gap between love of
God and love of flesh has inflicted many psychological scars not
only on the young, but also on adults, and even on churches, causing splits. Those who permit bundling and are afraid to break with
tradition still call themselves Old Amish, perhaps "too old" to mo-
tivate themselves for things new. Without a doubt, they constitute
the majority. However, some groups broke away because of bun-

dling and are termed New Amish. They are all the more strongly opposed to the custom.

David Kline is a thoroughly approachable farmer and herdsman, like the biblical Abraham in his time. He has his electric typewriter attached to two car batteries, and he hunts and pecks his way on the keyboard, producing newspaper articles about farm life. Once he told me in his German drawl that bundling is really only from a pairing urge, from God-given health, and thus corresponds to Amish tradition. Young horses have to be exercised, but within restraints. Amish boys certainly do not try to demonstrate heroic deeds like macho men, although they may keep a fast horse and a sharp-looking buggy. But one cannot overlook "the man in the man," the devil who instructs him "to do this and that. . . ." Well, the very thought of this and his three beautiful daughters had caused David to cast his lot with the New Amish.

Such an evening brands the heart, particularly of Amish teenagers who desire to be different from those who guard their past. It may be true that anything worthwhile has to hurt, but it is no great consolation. The girls of the New Amish do not get to know their men during bundling, using home-team advantage, but rather at singings, mainly on Sunday nights. At such times the properly mannered youth sing in accord but according to old melodies. Their songs are addressed to God and good Christians, concentrating on the goal of their faith. The girls are the ones who set the stage and provide a good tone for an evening of the Spirit and the eye. After the singing is over, custom lets a boy offer to give a girl a ride to her home in the buggy. The girl is allowed to accept, and much visiting and courtship happens on the way.

The final word with regard to bundling and many other matters of Amish life will not be resolved before heaven. Abraham Troyer of Holmes County, father of twelve children, believes he has proof that Amish churches which allow bundling lose fewer young people to the world than those which prohibit the practice.

Amish are taught not to choose partners on the basis of lust of the flesh and external trappings. Original man and every person has been created in the image of God and therefore resembles God, no matter what the size of nose or slant of eye. Happiness does not depend on the flesh, for in the eyes of the Lord, everyone is an original. But it is as risky to assume that Amish boys are always guided by such adages as to believe that all Scotsmen are thrifty. What God has created is good. In this context, such a saying may sound a trifle theoretical, and that's exactly what it is. The boys and girls are perfectly well aware of what *schee isch vum Angesicht* (has a beauty of face and form) and is therefore pleasing.

As if to prove this, the boys often ask me what girls are like in Germany and whether they are beautiful. Even Joseph is of the opinion that the girls in his family look "*wie sie schöner einfach nicht gemacht werden können* (as though they could simply not be made with more beauty)." He is probably right. Marriages without a wedding license are unthinkable. Among some 300 Amish families in Allen County in 1990, there was not a single illegitimate child. This statistic is aided by the fact that if any Amish boy makes a girl pregnant, he also marries her, or he is no longer Amish.

Young girls generally know that boyfriends are thinking of marriage when they get something for a Christmas gift such as a grandfather clock. As taught by the Dordrecht Confession (art. 12), an Amish person may only marry another Amish since Paul says to marry "only in the Lord" (1 Cor. 7:39). After all, when it comes to marriage, the Lord even ordered each tribe of Israel to keep to itself so that the share of inheritance did not diminish (Num. 36). The Old Testament states that one is not to mix linen with sheep's wool, not to mix animals as in plowing with an ox and a donkey together (Deut. 22:10-11). The Amish are no longer quite as strict when it comes to mixing animals, as evidenced by the mules in Ohio and Pennsylvania. After all, a mule is the product of forced copulation—the jenny has to be blindfolded before she will accept the stallion. At least so claim the Amish of Allen County, who regard this crossbreed as displeasing the Lord.

Yet no matter what is possible in agriculture, the Amish show no mercy for a mixed marriage, based on their biblical principles. Up to the present they have been successful in following this rule only by reminding themselves "that foreign (meaning non-Amish) women with the help of Satan have not been able to lead their people away from the paths of God." Even marriage to a Mennonite of conscientious-objector status would regularly lead to excommunication from the church, unless the partner "from the *abfälligen* (straying) people" were to convert to the Amish faith, like David of Cuba Road. A union with one who is "not from the [Amish] house of the Lord" is regarded as a mixed marriage. The Swartzentruber Amish take the matter of marriage one step further: if one belongs to them, one is not even allowed to marry into a different Amish group.

Any Amish member who marries out of the church has no means of return (unless both parties make a confession and apply for membership). The Amish adhere to the principle that God himself instituted marriage "with two newly created people in paradise." After the Fall, two peoples or tribes emerged from this first union: the children of God and the children of man, light and darkness. When after a period of time, the children of God looked upon the children of man and took these as their wives, the Almighty regretted that he had made man (Gen. 6).

On this subject, the Amish of Allen County remember that the Almighty warned the children of Israel not to unite "with foreign women" so they would not be led astray (Deut. 7). This happened with Solomon. He was wise and beloved by God but, contrary to higher instruction, took foreign women. When he was old, his heart tended toward graven images. Because of this sin, his empire was divided (1 Kings 11). Israel, when misled by the Midianite women, was so severely punished that 24,000 died (Num. 25). If anyone, in spite of these warnings, still lusts after a partner from the world, he will have the words of Paul written on his sinful body: "Don't you know that he who is joined to an harlot is one body? For two, says he, shall be one flesh. But he that is joined unto the Lord is one spirit" (1 Cor. 6:16-17).

From the old days comes the rule stating how close the Amish may be allowed to marry their relatives. This had become necessary because the Amish often lived in isolated groups, shared the same line of ancestry, and had no regular contacts with other congregations. Such a rule is still needed. Elam's Rachel, for instance is a Graber by birth, and she married a Graber. Whichever way she looks, she is surrounded by Grabers. In fact, the approximately 33,000 Hutterites (fifteen family names) and the approximately 150,000 Amish (about a hundred family names) are some of the most intermarried groups in North America.

Some genetic problems are obviously a result of their geographic isolation and religiously based restrictions in the choice of a partner. Around Grabill, hereditary deaf-mutes are common, while in Berne a form of muscular dystrophy is prevalent. In an extreme case, eight children of one family are confined to wheelchairs. There is a high percentage of hemophiliacs, while some congregations have a greater-than-average number of dwarfs, persons with six fingers or small feet, whole families with short upper lips or certain ailments which can clearly be traced to the immigrating person and quite frequently beyond that to corresponding genetic factors also found in Switzerland.

Such difficulties can crop up anywhere, but the Amish have always known problems of this kind. Now and again they deliberately accept the increased danger of recessive "guilty genes" becoming dominant genes from marriages of relatives. The biblical command to multiply is held in higher regard than the risk of passing on certain forms of suffering and the accompanying grief. According to the rule, marriages are allowed "if the blood relationship" is no closer than second cousins, having a pair of great-grandparents in common.

Couples who intend to marry in a given church have to present a form of certificate of good conduct from the home church district. This is read to the brothers and sisters before they decide whether to accept such a party into the church. As a rule, the man leaves his parental home and moves in with the parents-in-law, even if temporarily, since it is written that he is to leave father and mother and cling to his wife (Gen. 2:24).

Marriages are concluded after both partners are baptized and accepted into church and generally not before the man and woman have known each other fairly well for three to four years. Most often the servant of the poor, the *Schteklimann* (deacon, mediator), gets involved in the matter as a go-between. When the time for marriage comes, the groom dispatches him to the parents of the bride to determine whether the relationship is welcome. The bride's father and mother have to agree to it. In many congregations, the *Schteklimann* also accepts a positive response from the bride. The deacon informs the bishop of the planned marriage, and the bishop announces it to the congregation.

Couples intending to marry may expect a fairly rough roasting from all angles. Thus a betrothed couple guards their secret as long as possible. However, when the garden of a farmhouse with marriageable candidates shows more celery planted than normal, when more than normal amounts of corn are dried, or when calves are fattened beyond season, most neighbors surmise that a marriage feast is being cooked up. Celery is swallowed by the fistful during wedding celebrations.

Preferred dates of weddings are generally prior to seeding time or after harvest. For one thing, the workday is not as full or heavy then. Also, Elam says, the boys in autumn simply don't wish to drive their ladies for late courting nights all winter long in an open buggy or cutter when temperatures are in the below-zero range. In the colder times of year, it is also simpler to prepare the gigantic mounds of food and to keep them fresh without modern cooling devices. A *Hochzüt* (wedding) turns out to be a great family festivity. The recent marriage of Tobi Graber and Naomi Brandenberger cost $2,500. When Martha Graber from Campbell Road married Wilmer Schmucker from South Whitley, a small congregation west of Fort Wayne, some 500 guests were invited to the feast.

During the time surrounding a wedding, the congregation expects a certain degree of propriety, as formerly in the *Volkskirche* (state church). If the pair entering marriage were known to be not quite pure, they were marked by certain signs. Thus the *Volkskirche* forbade the wearing of a bridal wreath or gown or the ringing of honorary wedding bells for such couples, dispensing liberal punishments. Allen County preserves the old custom that particularly *wenn's pressiert* (when it is urgent, and a baby is expected), such couples are only allowed to be married during the normal Sunday church service. Virgins and steadfast ones, on the other hand, receive a weekday on which to pronounce affirmative action at the altar. This practice is meant to reward the honest and punish the others.

To make sure the wedding partners are pure, the bishop inquires of them prior to the wedding ceremony whether they have remained chaste. The wedding ceremony takes place a week or two after reading of the bans during a church worship service. It is never on a Friday, for this is the day Christ died on the cross, and never on a Monday, since one is not allowed to make preparations for the wedding on Sunday.

The service often takes place at a neighbor's house, since the host home is being prepared for the wedding festivities. The church may also meet in a barn, for it only "takes one bishop to marry two souls." The worship service on this occasion lasts four hours, but the actual wedding ceremony is concluded in two minutes. The introductory songs are "*So will ichs aber heben an* (Let's set the stage for new beginnings)" (*Ausbund,* no. 69) and "*Nimm deinesgleichen zu der Ehe* (Take for marriage your own kind)."

The bishop then asks the bridal couple whether they want "to enter into marriage partnership at this happy time." They must promise for a whole Anabaptist lifetime to live as husband and wife in Christian order, to mutually take care of each other even "if one should fall into bodily weakness, sickness, or similar troubles," and to bear with each other in love and sorrow until death do them part. The bishop calls them to follow these "marital duties" and thus never have to appear before a judge. Husband and wife hold hands during the ceremony, probably the only time they will ever do so in public.

The sermon spans the whole time frame from the creation of the earth to the seaworthy ark of Noah, with the reminder that in his whole, long life, Noah had only one wife. The preacher explains to the couple why husband and wife were brought together in marriage. "In the beginning, creation was only Adam, but when God saw that it was not good for man to be alone, he gave him a wife" (Gen. 2). Then the sermon includes Isaac, the son of Abraham, and how he married Rebecca; and Jacob, the son of Isaac, who took Rachel to be his wife. Solomon's polygamy is always on the agenda as an example of how not to be married.

Toward the end of the sermon, the bishop asks whether anyone has cause to object to the marriage now about to be covenanted. After the ceremony follows a prayer from the *Die ernsthafte Christenpflicht,* and then hymn 122 from the *Ausbund* according to the melody "*Mensch nun wilst du selig seyn* (Man now holy you shall be)." The congregation sings "Geeeee-looooobt seeeeeeey Goooooooooott . . ." for "*Gelobt sey Gott im höchsten Thron* (Praise be to God on highest throne)."

Amish wear no wedding bands or other rings and exchange no kisses in public: a kiss is passion, and passion is worldly. They use no terms of endearment and do not present flowers. Family and friends give the new wife kitchen utensils, and the husband receives a hammer or a shovel. New couples are not wished a good life together, for such is assumed and goes without saying among the plain folks. In some church districts, along with other tricks, the groom is heaved over a fence after the ceremony, thus symbolically thrown from the youth group into grown-up society. A broom is placed before the feet of the bride; tripping over it represents a poor omen. In a further Amish tradition, acquaintances who pretend to feel slighted at not being invited may appear with a hammer and a saw to bang protestingly against the walls of the building in which the celebration takes place.

The subsequent wedding celebration extends to the end of the day. The bridal couple sits in a corner behind a huge mound of food, the woman to the left of her husband, as in the buggy throughout married life. The Amish make do without musical instruments. While they sing and yodel like true Swiss, it would be totally inappropriate to "fiddle like the Romans." However, this practice did not always go uncontested. When pianos were introduced to some churches about one hundred years ago, the conservative opposition, all keyed up, appeared on the scene. The use of musical instruments was subsequently deemed "unseemly, and also for children's children after us."

The Amish say, "We can read in the Old Testament that Miriam sang and led the women with a timbrel, God ordered Moses to fashion two silver trumpets for worship services, and David played the harp to disperse evil spirits from Saul." But in the New Testament, Paul says, "Sing and play unto the Lord in your hearts" (Col. 3:16). In the heart there is no room for drums or trumpets. Before the great Flood, Cain's line of the children of men sounded out harps and pipes (Gen. 4:21). Musicians attended the golden calf. When the Jewish daughter of Herod danced and asked for the head of John the Baptist, there must have been accompanying instruments, or Salome would not have been able to dance (Mark 6). Finally, the Savior dispersed the pipers from the presence of the dead daughter of Jairus. Therefore, it is up to instrumentalists to prove that the Savior or his apostles ever sat behind a musical instrument or ordered anyone to sit behind one.

Instead of a wedding dance, they play the ever-popular *Eckball* (corner ball). In the yard, youths stand one on each corner of a square and attempt to hit anyone inside the square with a mush ball. Whoever is hit has to get out of the square. When the last one is hit, the groups trade starting positions and continue.

The cooking is done by friends of the family. A rule of thumb has it that for every four hundred guests, a family needs fifty chickens, two bushels of potatoes, thirty-five pies, twenty-five gallons of ice cream, and on and on. . . . Eight cooks—four couples—are the absolute minimum for the preparation of the meat. In some churches it is customary for the groom to chop off all the chicken heads. Potato cooks—three other couples—tend to the vegetables, one *Schnützler* peels and slices apples, and other work is divided out. Potato cooks and *Schnützler* have an advantage in that they can attend at least part of the ceremony. Since everything invariably follows exactly the same pattern, they know exactly at what point in the sermon or Bible references they can leave the church service and return to work. Then eating begins, and this is done in shifts. After the first sitting has been fed, the dishes are washed (but sometimes not, because they will be used immediately in any case), and the next sitting commences.

Wedding ceremonies are particularly exciting for the young. The evening before the ceremony and celebration, the bride arranges seating plans at the tables. Sometimes considerable pressure and manipulations by well-wishers are exerted to influence these seating assignments. The bride places boys and girls together who have been *rumschpringe* (running around) with each other. Some other seating pairs are of particular interest to the older ones and ignite rounds of gossip.

Bridal couples generally spend their first night in the house of the bride's parents. According to Amish tradition, they—"the willing boy and the maiden pure"—are not immediately to engage in marital fervor. Instead, they are to control their lust for the first night and another subsequent two nights and spend their time in prayer like the biblical Tobias (Tob. 8). Only after the first three Tobias-nights, that which was sin previously now becomes duty. In this matter, too, the Anabaptists cling to old European traditions, particularly those of Catholic regions. Thus the couple may now in good conscience get on with the "holy matter of multiplying" (so said Joseph), according to the commission of God: "Be fruitful, and multiply" (Gen. 1:28).

The Amish have no honeymoon. When marrying, the woman is around twenty-three and the man slightly older. Almost everyone gets married; single men constitute the absolute minority. Without a man, an Amish woman does not amount to much in common opinion. Anyone who does not marry should have good reason not to do so, for it is written that people shall multiply and therefore they shall marry—a significant aspect in the religious struggle for survival.

From now on, where the man is, there is glory. In a certain sense, the world of the Amish can be regarded as a man's world, even if not to the same extent as at a Hutterian *Bruderhof.* The man is totally conscious of being the head of the family. He has a feeling of masculinity based on physical strength and established partriachal family relationships. The Amish see the words of the Bible as giving this foundation for a household. While an Amishman honors his mother above all else, he is lord and master in his own house, fully immersed in the myth of masculine superiority. "A woman who wants to rule her husband does not think much of him," says Atlee Miller from Millersburg, Ohio.

In church, a woman may engage in congregational singing, but for the rest of the service, she is meant to keep her peace and not to prophesy as Paul allows (1 Cor. 11:5). Paul and the Amish see the man as a reflection and glory of God and the woman as the glory of the man (11:7). The Amish give comprehensive meaning to verses where Paul advises women to be quiet in church and to submit themselves (1 Cor. 14:34; 1 Tim. 2:11). However, when it comes to marital life, the Amish ignore this selfsame Paul when he says that it is good not to be married, and that this might even be one's gift from God (1 Cor. 7:7-8).

On this matter the Amish accept Luther's statement that woman was created for man's enjoyment. Aside from that, women might speak "confusedly and inappropriately" in public discussions. Although the affirmed marital joy suggests mutual companionship, when it comes to other matters, women's rights are shoved to a back burner on a cold stove. The Amish reject each and every *Regiment* (leading position) of women in worldly as well as in religious matters, even though the Bible does not name even one woman who opposed Christ. God assigned a role to woman which she is meant to occupy. In Amish country, there is first God in heaven, then Christ his Son, then the man, and finally and at the end, his wife (1 Cor. 11:3). Just as Christ was subordinate to the will of his Father, man is subject to Christ, and a woman is to subordinate herself to the man. Yet in the Lord, the man and the woman are interdependent (11:11).

Amish country has women who can ride like a Hun, can exercise like Jane Fonda, are more beautiful than a film star, and can outperform a heavy-duty worker. They nevertheless cooperate in accord with the Amish rules and willingly submit themselves to domestic and child-bearing roles, accepting this position without complaint or hesitation. The principle holds true, as basically formulated by David Kline, that "a marriage in which the woman rules the man is not a real Amish marriage."

After the conclusion of the marriage celebration, it is the principal responsibility of young couples to populate the world with miniatures of themselves. This is in line with the motto of Joseph on Cuba Road: "God has fashioned the world for believers. What happens if we, of all people, do not produce children?" He lived up to his own motto. A believer is worth more to the Lord—so the preacher says—than a thousand nonbelievers. Joseph has fifteen children, which counterbalance 15,000 nonbelievers, although the gray-haired preacher would never be so presumptuous as to make such a claim publicly.

One Moses Burkholder was a master in obedience to God's commission. While he was still alive, children and children's children took turns in filling the cradle until he and his descendants counted 550 people. If a woman refuses her husband in bed, that is breaking the marriage vows. Such matters sometimes surface publicly in church. A marriage also may be stressed if the husband "makes himself guilty" by committing the sin of Onan (coitus interruptus).

The Amish use their commission to fill the earth with their own kind as their way of doing the mission work commanded by Christ. With few exceptions, the Amish engage in no mission work beyond their own congregational activities. Joseph has a plausible reason for this. "To teach one's own boys and girls to fear God and to do right" is missionary work enough, even though this may seem somewhat group centered. Yet the Amish style of life is a light to the world, and this in itself constitutes mission work. If others see the light, they can come to the light. Thus keeping the Amish church community strong is a witness for Christ.

Babies of Allen County are born in hospitals, but more and more are being born at home. In this area, a midwife charges only one-fifth the cost of a hospital stay. An Amish family has an average of six to eight children, which makes them the fastest growing religious group in North America. In time this amounts to a demographic time-bomb, with the total Amish population doubling about every twenty years. Yet families with large numbers of children are not poor by any means.

An Amish woman has no maternity or mother leave, but she always has guaranteed work and the prospect of another baby. She has been born for and into this role. Birth control, chemistry versus nature, is strictly *verboten* (forbidden). The Lord even tends to such matters in his wisdom. He has women age beyond child-bearing capability. When the time has come, he takes the strength from the man's loins, thereby preventing him from following the great example of Noah, who still conceived sons at the age of 500 (Gen. 5:32). Some couples may quietly contest the rule of allowing nature to take its course and use old remedies and new pills. If the mother's life is in danger, they might even take more drastic measures after counseling with the bishop.

Motherhood is no purely personal matter in the church districts. This corresponds, in a sense, to the traditional role of the woman in Old Europe, even if this role has long since been forgotten by most descendants of emigrants. A family I know who lives in the Grabill district definitely wanted to have no more children after number five. *Schluss* (case closed)! Husband and wife were agreed on the matter. However, the lengthy period of time in which the cradle remained empty made the brothers and sisters suspicious: Were they through with sex? Had they resorted to birth control? Then one fine day, they resumed activity and produced another baby to pacify the inquisitive.

The birth of a potential plowman, butcher, *Hausfrau* (housewife), or milker is just as welcome whether the child is wanted or simply could not be prevented. There is always a father, known by name. Amish women don't talk openly about a pregnancy. A mother of five or six still blushes when somebody might realize that the sixth or seventh child is on the way. Like other Christian churches, the Amish regard birth as an original beginning, not a return (in the sense of reincarnation) even if a puckered-up little newly born babe frequently resembles a great-grandfather or his wife. Amish children are unplanned wealth, hoped for, loved, treasured. Biblical names are commonly given to the *Bobblin* (babies) in accord with a simple principle: they are named after good people rather than bad ones.

Small children in an Amish family can do nothing wrong until they have learned to walk. They are thought incapable of knowing the difference between good and bad. Then they slowly have to learn to show respect for their parents, older siblings, and adults in general. Finally, they are taught that things German are closer to being good, while things *englisch* (non-Amish) are closer to being bad. Menno Simons' instructions guide the rearing of children. Boys and girls are expected to work at whatever they are capable of doing, depending on their age and abilities.

Senseless or uncritical love is negative, since it makes parents blind, allowing them easily to overlook the mistakes of their children. "Spare the rod and spoil the child" is the prevailing proverb. Wisely, all punishment is to be administered without anger or bitterness and according to "good measure," if possible on the rear end, which God has shaped and fashioned for the purpose. Mothers teach their children how to pray as soon as the youngsters can formulate words. Fathers teach them "not to disappoint Jesus" and lend the weight of hand and authority to the order. On birthdays, fathers administer a good-natured spanking on boys' bottoms while singing "Happy Birthday," a clap for each year.

Amish couples are allowed to separate only if very good reasons are given—for example, if one spouse departs from the faith. But they can never be divorced, for this would result in immediate banning and shunning. The seventh commandment is thoroughly up to date and modern in its implications in Allen County. Committing adultery as a national pastime is known only to the world. The Amish are immediately to report any extramarital or premarital cohabitation of church members to the congregation, leading to serious consequences for the straying. Marriage is and remains an institution from which one cannot escape unpunished. To keep it holy is a duty taken for granted both in ethical and religious terms. Differences between partners are to be resolved in personal discussions after praying over the matter.

To the outsider, Amish marriages appear to be happy, and certainly many of them are. Some unions may seem to lack deep emotional bonds, with conversations being rather short and abrupt. But one can see that they are held together by loyal friendship, faithfulness to the marriage vows, and the shared task of raising the children. There is not much verbal expression of love because partners count on life commitment being more important in marriage than glib words of worldly romance, which may go with fickleness. As Elam says, the real Christian is known by his deeds rather than his words (Matt. 7:21). Sometimes a wife bothered by a failing of her husband may not feel free to express or discuss it since this would seem to elevate herself above her God-given role. Such a woman may fight depression, but on the whole, she would trust that God has given her the partner for a purpose, even if there are trials. Furthermore, the supportive network of congregation, friends, and *Freundschaft* (kinfolk) wraps around each Amish marriage like a huge quilt.

******

On a Sunday morning in September, we buggy through the early hue of autumn around Harlan, where Joseph's church district conducts an *Ordnungsgemee* (counsel meeting). Held two weeks before communion, this is an attempt to settle differences between members and questions about an obedient lifestyle. The intent is to show the brothers and sisters how they are to conduct themselves with each other and to reaffirm the *Ordnung* (church order, rules). On the Sunday morning between the counsel meeting and the communion, the Amish invariably fast, as they do on Good Friday and Ascension Day.

This Sunday everything starts with a normal church service, except that the families have appeared even earlier than usual at the assigned farm. Benches standing by the walls offer back support and soon all are occupied. The sermon is miles long. After the singing of a song, old Joseph makes the introduction. He has but recently recovered from a bout of illness and is therefore too weak to conduct the main service. Joseph stands like a rock in raging waters between kitchen and living room, between the men's division and the women's, and restricts himself to a good twenty minutes. He is followed by the rather verbose Jacob Zehr, a servant of the poor (deacon). The main sermon is conducted by Henry Zehr, who launches his effort in paradise and makes mention of the absolutely bad role of the snake. Then he turns practical: "That's the way it is even today: a horse always rears up when a snake crawls across the road. And that's why we step on it and flatten it, yes, we flatten it as we should."

After two hours—next to me a brother has fallen into a deep sleep and snores a little until he is nudged by his neighbor—Henry remarks that he has spoken for 120 minutes. But whether he spoke for two hours or even three, he says, what is this fleeting bit of time compared to an entire eternity and the price of saving just one soul from the fire of hell? At 12:00 noon we arrive, together with the children of Israel, at the Red Sea.

Water is passed around in a white tin can, and then chip bags are opened. The small children, again extremely disciplined, have made themselves much at home under the benches, either sleeping deeply or waiting patiently. After four hours of sitting, there is bound to be some human discomfort. Tobi whispers toward me, "*Wilscht mitkumme in de Schtoll* (want to come along to the stable)?" Today one does not go there to look over the animals but for urgent needs. Amishmen are lined up in the stable and between them a *Doktor der Schrift* clothed in one neutral color, all as-it-should-be casual, forming one long row behind the cows and horses. Atmosphere substitutes for comfort. The *Weiber* (women) and small children head for the outhouse or a portable commode in the house, as allowed in Allen County.

Back in the farmhouse, Henry thunders, "We are free and no servants." With regard to servants, he reminds us of the evil scoundrels who flogged Jesus thirty-nine times before they nailed him to the cross. "And did he sweat, our Lord did! Water and blood simply ran down from him" (John 19:34). But even Henry cannot tell everything, and it's not really necessary, for by now everyone knows how much Jesus perspired!

Around 1:30, earlier than usual, Henry is too fatigued to go on. This stalwart servant in the vineyard of the Lord has to leave time for a possible rejoinder. Now it is the duty of the *Ordnungsgemee* to identify and handle any problems before the communion Sunday. Who or what has caused trouble in the church district? After

308

all, "Only those are allowed to partake of the Easter lamb who are worthy of it, just as Israel saw to it that no one unclean or uncircumcised tasted of the Passover lamb. The judgment of Paul would come over anyone unworthy" (1 Cor. 5; 11:27-32).

Only those with a clean record of accord and harmony with their fellows are allowed to celebrate holy communion. If any have a clouded record, then such have no admittance to the great cup of our Lord. The celebration would then have to be postponed until the congregation has been "cleansed." All who break bread to the memory of the broken body of Christ and drink to the memory of his spilt blood, have to be one and united before that event. The congregation thus excludes from holy communion drunkards, arrogant people, idolaters, the immoral, the greedy, and any who have something not right with them.

There is not much to confess today. However, the bishop, wearing a typical otherworldly look, does remind them "that handling a beard with a razor" is forbidden, just like any triangular neckerchief and plaid materials in general. He admonishes all to lowliness and humility, and thus the skirts of women should again become a little longer. Finally he explains—all the while seeking for the Lord who chastises his children—that he has no way of understanding folks who are installing white stoves in their kitchens. Whoever is in possession of such a white stove should immediately paint it black or get rid of it. The kerosene-operated refrigerator is forbidden in principle to church members. Yet it is economically attractive for people who otherwise have to buy ice for $3.25 every second day. Since everyone knows that this matter will appear on the agenda of the *Ordnungsgemee*, they fall into line, some only temporarily, perhaps by turning off the appliance a few weeks prior to communion and then back on again after the holy event. The call is for a few repairs to keep the *Ordnung* more faithfully, and everyone is sure that such will be undertaken shortly.

Two weeks later at the communion service, Joseph takes on all those who were sleeping during the counsel meeting, and he does it with full force. After all, there had been in attendance an *Englischer* from Germany (meaning me), and what would he think of those who had fallen asleep under the sound of God's Word, still claiming to be his children? After all, only such who lack genuine piety fall asleep during the *Ordnungsgemee.*

Elam's Rachel had received the commission this year to bake the bread for holy communion, the remembrance of the table fellowship of the Lord with his followers, sinners responding to the gospel. This is a special honor. Twice every year, once on Easter Day and once in autumn, the holy communion is conducted in the whole congregation. This twofold covenant renewal between God and his people each year was one of the reasons for the Amish separating from the mainstream of Swiss Anabaptists. Jakob Ammann explained that if some believers were incapable of attending one communion service on account of illness, they ought to be given a second chance within the year.

Attendance at the *Abendmahl* (Lord's Supper) means *"Brot breche zu der Gedächtnis des gebrochen Leibes Christi* (to break bread in memory of the broken body of Christ)" (1 Cor. 11:24). Participation is for all who are baptized and willing for the cause of truth to risk everything—personal effects, life, and blood. This we read in the history of the bloody tracks of early martyrs. The Swiss Brethren have retained the symbolic character of the holy Supper but reject the belief that from it comes sacramental or automatic assurance of forgiveness of sins and personal salvation. Holy communion to them is, according to Menno Simons, "a symbol of admonition, which the Son of God has given us through the spotless sacrifice of his guiltless flesh."

On such occasions, for the *Grossgemee* (communion), the Amish leave their children in the care of teenagers, at home, where they "enjoy the most beautiful hours, second only to the school picnic." The semiannual communion services may be regarded as the highest celebrations of the Amish church year. This is shown by the religious ceremony extending from 9:30 a.m. to 3:00 p.m. Only then do they break the bread before proceeding to the washing of feet.

Then they sing their hymn of communion in the slow melody,

> Come now, all humankind,
>   And see what shall transpire.
> Come, all you sinners, come,
>   If Jesus you admire!
> Down in this vale of toil and sin,
>   He stands, the martyr souls to win,

And ready for torment,
For love of faithful kin. . . .

To fill the hours, the preachers engage in longer marathons of sermonizing than usual. Typically the starting line is Matthew 18. Then their proclamation sweeps through a sketch of the whole Bible story, with some painstaking detail here and there.

Anew they all experience holy history right from creation to the end: the Fall into sin through Eve's desire for the forbidden fruit, the "blessed seed of woman" which made Eve the original mother of the human family, Noah's ark as the haven for people and animals, the prophecy to Abraham according to which through him and his seed all tribes of the earth shall be blessed. Then follows the aborted sacrifice of Isaac, the birth of Esau, and Joseph's sojourn in Egypt. Around noon, Moses' last blessing and the prophecy of the coming of Christ has to be completed. The remaining time belongs to Jesus' words and works, the happy tidings of his suffering and death out of love for us all, the warning to the living regarding the world, and an appeal for Amish order.

Whenever a preacher is momentarily lost for words during this mammoth service, he catches his breath with an emergency reminder: "You know these verses yourself. I do not have to repeat them to you again." But then he does just that, having had time to call them up in his mind.

The holy communion is conducted with homemade essentials, *Brot und Wei* (*Wein;* bread and wine) from Amish farms. The servant of the poor (deacon) cuts bread into long strips, and the bishop breaks off the first piece. First he serves the ordained men, then the men in general, and finally the women. After a prayer from *Die ernsthafte Christenpflicht*, the communion cup is handed out.

One of the main ordinances of the celebration is the washing of feet. This is done by the Amish to demonstrate that every single one of them, regardless of position or class, is meant to be the servant of the others, just as Jesus in his day washed the feet of his disciples. Anabaptist foot washing probably stems from Jesus through the tradition of the Waldensians, whose itinerant preachers regularly practiced it. Menno Simons said, "Wash the holy feet; be not ashamed of the Lord's works . . . so that true humility of the divine will be found in all of you."

Yet it is also true that Roman Catholic cathedral and abby churches preserved this ceremony in a representative fashion. The leader of the Maundy Thursday service (just before Easter) would wash and dry the feet of twelve men. Up to World War I, even the mighty Hapsburg emperors in Vienna washed the feet of some pilgrims and older men before they sat down together for the *Liebesmahl* (love meal) on Maundy Thursday. This was representative action, a traditional ceremony to make a political impression. The Amish, however, involve all members in this observance.

After a prayer, one of the ministers reads the account of Jesus washing the feet of his disciples and refers to the ceremony of foot washing as a sign of true humility and lowliness (John 13). Meanwhile, the servant of the poor (deacon) and some lay members bring in tin pails of water and lay out towels. Then the men wash each other's feet while the women do the same in a separate room. During the ceremony, the congregation sings number 119 from the *Ausbund:*

> When Christ was still upon the earth,
> With his disciples dwelt,
> He humbly washed their very feet,
> In love before them knelt.

Each pair of Amish obeys the symbolic ordinance which reaped for them the name of *Fusswäscher* in Europe. After washing each other's feet in turn, they seal their love and fellowship with a holy kiss. At the conclusion of the service, the Amish deposit their alms into the hand of the deacon, who puts it into his pocket without looking at it. This is money for the poor, and each gives according to his means.

******

The Amish are reluctant to call anyone a sinner since all are sinners, and according to the witness of the Gospels, we daily become such, ever again. This is how Elam explains it to me. In principle, every member of the Amish church daily has to fulfill certain obligations, even if just to rise above the world. Each one of them knows what they are allowed to do and what they are meant to do. Indeed, one could regard the Amish as the salt of the earth.

The Amish reinforce themselves both inwardly and outwardly against the enemy, so that "the weeds shall not grow while waiting for the judgment of Christ." They place great importance on church discipline, which comes to bear on anyone of the close-knit group who "does not stay in Jesus." Such are to be cast away like a vine which withers. "Men cast them into the fire, and they are burned" (John 15:6).

These Anabaptists feel obliged to exercise strict order among themselves and to apply suitable disciplinary measures whenever needed. As Jesus said, "If your brother shall trespass, . . . go and tell him his fault between you and him alone . . ." (Matt. 18:15-18). For the Amish, there is a snake in every paradise. The faithful aim always to attempt first to improve the sinner, to convince the straying brother and sister of their wrongdoing, to lead them to healing, and to train them anew in the path of faith. This is to be done gently, remembering one's own temptations (Gal. 6:1).

In addition, discipline and exercises in penitence are used to keep the church holy, as a protection against moral decay, so that "the church will be glorious, without spot or wrinkle" (Eph. 5:27). Thus it is necessary to install a thousand safeguards in the life of the Amish. Among the young, this is relatively simple and uncomplicated. Old punishments are meted out upon young sinners. Parents and teachers subscribe to the words of the risen Lord, "Those I love, I punish and chastise" (Rev. 3:19). For Amish who swim against their own faith stream, the result can be a heavy load of chastisement.

For an imaginary but true-to-life example, let us take Daniel, named after the master of Babylonian wisdom. He may live somewhere west of Cuba Road. One day while in a flea market in Shipshewana, he buys a transistor radio and takes it home. Daniel is a husky fellow built along the lines of a hero in a mountain novel. He has been baptized and knows that he has transgressed the rules of the *Ordnung*. A short while later, Aaron, an acquaintance, hears suspicious sounds emanating from Daniel's buggy when he passes Aaron's yard. At the next opportunity, he takes up the issue with Daniel. He does so quietly, reflectively, and without witnesses, eye to eye. Naturally, Aaron also knows that "we would like to have many things, but we have to crucify our flesh and not love the world."

This talk between two brothers has a purely pastoral quality. Aaron is concerned about the person of the sinner, not about punishment. He intends to draw Daniel's attention to his transgression and advises him to smash the radio and throw it onto the farm's trash pile. The guilty party has escaped the church's penal bench. Daniel seems cooperative and lets Aaron trot home with the biblical feeling that "in this manner you have won your brother" (Matt. 18:15).

A few weeks later Aaron notices that Daniel still keeps hiding the satanic device in his buggy. Now he reports the case to the church leaders, who continue the process of correcting Daniel. Upon baptism, Daniel had agreed to the right of the church to do this. Penance is now due, and it has to be done publicly. To reclaim Daniel, the deacon or one of the bishops might now approach him with a witness—"Take one or two along" (Matt. 18:16). The decision is reached that Daniel has to dispose of the radio and then go before the whole church regarding it. Daniel agrees that he will make confession after the Sunday worship. This means that after the service and before the common meal, in a members-only session, he will declare, "I admit that I bought a radio and have had it for some six weeks. I have gotten rid of it. I would like to ask the congregation to forgive me and please have patience with me." During his confession, Daniel is allowed to remain *seated*.

He is forgiven, for after all, a goodly number of Amish have owned a radio at one time or another during younger life. They trust that with his confession, he has died to the flesh, the devil, and the radio. A few weeks later, however, it comes to light that Daniel owns another transistor. He is called on to trash the radio and again "make confession" before the church. This time he has to *stand* before the congregation. Daniel has not intended to make an elephant out of a mosquito. After the flails of his conscience have had their workout, he explains to the church, "I bought another radio and hid it in the buggy for a while, but I have disposed of it. I acknowledge this and ask for forgiveness, for such is against the order, and I know it." The words of this confession may seem as frayed as an old songbook, but the congregation accepts his profession of being contrite.

Again he is forgiven. Finally, when it again becomes apparent

314

that Daniel and a radio are traveling companions, he now has to *kneel* and ask the congregation, "On my knees, I implore you to forgive me. . . ." And they do, as a sign of God's unlimited grace (Matt. 18:22).

Yet Daniel is warned about the snake, who came to Eve, mixed with falsehood and truth. Furthermore, a brother writes a letter to Daniel, whose reputation has received a bad jolt: "Grace, peace, and mercy from God the heavenly Father. I wish upon you the love of Christ, as well as the ever-present power of the Holy Spirit. When this modest writing arrives at your doorstep, may you then be of the same faith as I am and stand in that faith and be zealously walking according to the teachings of Christ with a faithful heart. With cordial regards. . . ."

When it is established a few weeks later that such a devilish device is yet again in Daniel's possession, things turn ugly. The congregation now intends to have it out with Daniel, to which end "many heads are of common accord." The verdict is tough but in Amish terms quite consistent with the infraction. He is to be banned and shunned for at least six weeks. The punishment of the church is suitable for "all those who have surrendered themselves to the Lord and walk according to his commandments, been baptized into the body of Christ, permit themselves to be called brothers and sisters, and yet stumble and fall into mistakes and sin." During this period, he will taste what it is like to be shunned. He is urged to attend church as a nonmember, meet with the ministers for admonition, but leave after the service and before the fellowship and common meal. If after six weeks he will not submit nor confess to the church, he cannot regain his membership in the Amish congregation.

The Amish do not ban easily or quickly, unless the nature of the transgression permits no other alternative. As far as shunning is concerned, it is meant to be imposed without regard for the person. The spiritual marriage into which the Amish have entered with the heavenly bridegroom (Christ) permits no differences, and the spiritual has precedence over the natural. In this vein, the bishop, ministers, and deacon meet to discuss the case of Daniel. Since he has been warned repeatedly, and after the six-week ban was not ready to submit to the *Ordnung*, his excommunication stands. Even if Daniel joins another church such as the Mennonites, in Allen County he stays shunned until he makes peace with the congregation where he did wrong; this is called "strict shunning." In the La Grange (Ind.) area, however, the Amish quit shunning a person who joins the Mennonites or a "higher" church; this is called "lenient shunning." The Allen County observers think that is why over half of the younger La Grange generation leaves the Amish to join a "higher" church.

In principle, the Amish do not subscribe to doing things halfway. To be a little Amish is just as impossible as to be a little pregnant. To sin against the church is like sinning against God. It challenges the disciplinary powers and holy counseling of the church and its charge to cleanse itself in the name of Christ.

Every baptized brother and sister can have a voice in important decisions, along with the duty to use and to protect the entrusted spiritual gifts. During the discussions regarding Daniel, some advocate might stand up and request a little more patience with the "weak lamb" in order to give it one more chance in the flock of the Lord. During the discussion the sinner is present and allowed to defend himself, and the atmosphere is similar to a funeral. He is only required to leave the room when the matter is put to a vote.

Close and distant relatives of Daniel weep over the calamity which has come upon the family. They suffer "from grief of long duration" and pray to God that he would allow the bitter cup to pass, if at all possible. The excommunication could be postponed, but on this day everyone seems convinced that, after the many words spoken over this matter, action must follow. Daniel is banned from the church. Before the congregation, the bishop officially turns Daniel over to Satan (1 Cor. 5:5). For Daniel, this ban means excommunication from the protective life of the Amish, from "eating, drinking, *Handel und Wandel* (business transactions and social relations, everyday affairs)" within the community—unless and until he truly repents and changes.

The tradition of the ban serves the purpose of impressing upon the sinner the need to repent and goes back a long way into Anabaptist history. When the time is ripe "to sweep the threshing floor," it is applied. Jakob Ammann applied the ban at the very outset against all such who, in his opinion, were not on the right road to eternity. Banning is in effect until this very day if, for instance, someone spreads a false doctrine. A little leaven can cause the whole dough to turn sour (1 Cor. 5:6). Also banned are any former members who live in sin or who bring disturbances into the congregation. This would include homosexuals, since they "commit disgrace like Sodom and Gomorrah." Since the days of the Old Testament (Lev. 18:22), it is written, "Thou shalt not lie with mankind, as with womankind; it is an abomination."

For the Amish, sin includes everything that conflicts with the Ten Commandments. Sinners are those who are old enough to be responsible for their actions and yet do something wrong. Sometimes a "sinner" may feel that a punishment is not fair. But the chastised party bows his head and simply acknowledges everything with a "yes." At this point, it is expected of him, and for the long run he trusts the spiritual wisdom of the congregation.

Nevertheless, the Amish differentiate between various sins in their reclaiming procedure. Indiscreet drinking, visiting a movie house, forwardness, wearing of "the high style of skirt, high hats, or a comb in the hair," a touch of pride—these are small sins, "not unto death," which can be forgiven by a request and a pastoral admonition, if they are not repeated (1 John 5:16-17). Great sins, "unto death," are identified in accord with the Bible and immediately punished by the ban and shunning: committing adultery, being a drunkard, leaving the church in spite of being baptized into it (the most deplorable of all defeats), or the blasphemy of the Holy Spirit (hardly anyone knows what this really means). The prospect of the guilty person not only cut off from the church but also automatically banned from the table of the Lord, is deeply anchored in the religious consciousness of the Amish.

In his day Luther took strong issue with the "great ban," the *excommunicatio maior* (major excommunication), at the time when Christianity as a *Weltanschauung* (worldview) controlled the larger part of the population. The great ban automatically led to punishments by worldly courts. Luther stated, "The preachers ought not to mix worldly punishments into the ban or other spiritual punishments." He recommended the "lesser ban." "Obvious, stubborn sinners should not be allowed to come to the sacraments or into the community of the church until they improve themselves and shun sin."

All Old Order Amish today apply the ban to guarantee the

"holiness of the church." The ban prevented the Anabaptists from becoming a *Volkskirche* (state church, established church), which makes no claim of being a union of the holy since it accepts into its ranks the weak and those in the process of becoming Christian. From their beginnings in the 1520s, Anabaptists wanted the church to be a special community, excluding unworthy and corrupt members, and independent of the state. The ban prevents the Amish from attracting large numbers of people into their churches, even if they wanted to do so. The church depends for its growth almost exclusively on their own children, prepared for membership by rigorous parental training.

It was precisely the ban and the practice of it that frequently led to quarrels and schisms among the early Dutch Anabaptists and later among the Amish. A strict use of the ban was already promoted by some Dutch Anabaptists in the 1530s and 1540s, leading to the first division (1556) between the main Frisian-Flemish group (demanding avoidance even in marriage) and the Waterlanders (favoring a milder form of banning). Menno Simons defended avoidance in marriage, but called for Christian kindness in applying the principle. Various meetings of Anabaptists rejected marital avoidance (1557, Strassburg) or affirmed it (1554, Wismar; 1607, Strassburg). The Dordrecht Confession of 1632, still used by the Amish, calls for shunning with moderation and Christian love, exhorting the backslidden as brothers and sisters (2 Thess. 3:14-15).

Jakob Ammann (1693) insisted on marital avoidance and refusal to eat with those banned—the position of the Amish. Hans Reist and others (1694) claimed that shunning applied not to social relations but to communion (partaking of Christ, the passover lamb; 1 Cor. 5). The strict stand was signed by the ministers of Amish congregations in 1779 in Essingen in the Palatinate. The Amish debated over how far shunning should be extended to "the natural" and social relationships, such as eating at the same table, business dealings, or cohabitation of husband and wife when one of them is under the ban. Is this not the unequal yoke, which brings defilement (2 Cor. 6:14)?

Strict as well as benevolent representatives of church discipline were ever present. The early conservative leaders generally held the position that if the ban is to be applied, then do it with

318

full force. This meant that "the natural" followed along behind the spiritual principle. At the great ministers' meeting in Wayne County, Ohio, in June 1862, voices were raised that Amish congregations should rather ban according to Christian moderation. Frequently the banned were simply being cast out too far; after all, believers were to hate the evil deed and not the perpetrator. Some argued that concessions should be made particularly regarding married couples. For example, a wife—"who is, after all, the weaker vessel" (1 Pet. 3:7)—was disciplined after she had again been "natural" with her husband, meaning that she had joined him in bed. When she separated from him, she was punished yet again, this time on account of spiritual adultery. The same debate could again be repeated in Allen County today.

When imposing the ban and shunning, the Amish stick to the Word as only the most radical Anabaptists do: anyone banned may no longer eat at the same table with his or her family, but sits isolated or together with unbaptized children. One becomes a nonperson, unclean, almost as in old Israel after touching a dead person. The backslidden spouse has to leave the common bedroom. No Amish is allowed to use the services of a banned person, such as riding with one in the same buggy or car or van. In the course of time, a banned youth has to leave the living quarters of his own parents since his evil influence on the rest of the family is feared.

Anyone who does business with a banned person is punished. Someone who knowingly eats or dines with a banned person is likewise susceptible to banning, according to Amish interpretation of the biblical word: "But now I have written unto you not to keep company, if any man that is called a brother be a fornicator, or covetous, or an idolater, or a railer, or a drunkard, or an extortioner; with such an one no not to eat" (1 Cor. 5:11).

Things become somewhat difficult when an Amish person goes to a restaurant as to the Just-a-Bite Tea Room in Grabill and is served by, of all people, an ex-Amish waitress. If such a person was already baptized before leaving the church, the Amish are required to decline her services. On the other hand, dining at a common table in a restaurant with banned parties is permitted. In such cases, one does not eat out of the biblical "common pot," as would be the case at home.

In Sarasota, Florida, the secret retreat for a real Anabaptist vacation paradise, I chanced upon Christian Kurtz from Holmes County, Ohio. In summer, he lives in his church community, but when the north casts longer shadows in the fall, he and his wife hop on a bus and head for the sunny south. Officially he does so with the excuse that he has the "sniffles," which cause him particular problems in autumn and winter of the year. In Florida, Christian's wife bakes lime, pumpkin, coconut, and raisin pies for Yoder's unlicensed restaurant on Bahia Vista Street in Pinecraft. Christian likes to sit at a "table of temptation," close to his wife's pies. For a beverage, Christian drinks orange juice. But strictly speaking, both supplying and patronizing that eatery are forbidden since the Yoders are Amish turned worldly and therefore banned.

However, the Amish of some churches are prepared to make exceptions. Christian informs me that from his perspective, while the Yoders are banned since they have left the church in Nappanee, Indiana, they are, after all, fairly good Christians. Jakob Ammann would turn over in his grave at all this, but the Amish vacationers who with gusto *schmeck* (taste) cabbage rolls and fried liver at the Yoders or work for them, have taken the ban from the banned. Precisely because of such situations, not many Amish congregations allow their members to make the trip to Florida.

The church does not only punish, however. It also comes to the assistance of those under the ban, as, for instance, if Daniel's barn were to burn down. The ban has nothing to do with hatred. Instead, according to the understanding of the Amish, it is seen as an act of love, to reclaim the erring one. Whenever the banned party desires to return to the bosom of the church, the doors are generally flung wide open to receive the repentant party. If he had been a great sinner, much discernment would be needed. The returning party has to ask the church for forgiveness and make peace with the brothers and sisters. The Amish assist the penitent to reenter the circle of the chosen. All along, his family and friends have been trying to soften him to take such a step by continually praying for him. The church can then again receive him into their circle, according to the authority of the Scriptures: "Whose soever sins you remit, they are remitted unto them; and whose soever sins you retain, they are retained" (John 20:23).

Thus it is possible for Daniel again to stand before the church, for only the lost are truly lost: while the sinner lives, there is still hope for repentance. Daniel does, in fact, throw away the radio even before he grabs the manure fork in shame before the congregation. He pleads for forgiveness. After reading to him from Luke (15), the bishop admonishes him: "Now, fallen brother, you are appearing before us in the hope that our Heavenly Father will approach you and be merciful unto you. You may fall on your knees in the name of God. Do you confess that you deserved this punishment and that it came upon you according to Christian *Ordnung?*" (Yes.) "Do you promise before God . . . as you have promised at baptism before God and many witnesses?" (Yes.)

Now Daniel is again a member of the congregation, a totally renewed Amish believer, just as he had previously been upon baptism. The bishop confirms this with a handshake, a brotherly kiss, and the command, "Go and sin no more!" Daniel is of serious intent in his decision to sin no more.

An Amish member can be placed under the ban several times and be readmitted. It has even happened that a banned person has turned to a worldly court to sue the church, and that a worldly judge has agreed with him. At times a whole church has been placed under the ban, for instance, when it decided to build a house of worship. Also, cases are on record of individuals or entire families deliberately provoking a church district in order to facilitate their departure. Such action is easily recognizable if a couple fails to attend several worship services without adequate excuse or if an Amish driver trots his buggy with *rubber* tires through the countryside for all to see. In such cases, the brothers and sisters are quick to take action.

As I write, new troubles are brewing in Allen County. The unthinkable has become public in the Amish country. Several young men from Tobi's church got together and bought a restaurant in Jamaica! They obviously wanted to take a firsthand look at their investment, so they went by airplane, which is invariably a sign of ultimate pride. The sinners were placed under the ban. Whether they will ever find their way back to church is an open and widely discussed issue.

******

An autumn day at the Amish cemetery of Allen County. This *Totengarten* lies by Roth Road, that tree-shaded street named after the Swiss Anabaptist family Roth (also Rott, Rod) from Diessbach and Steffisberg in the canton of Bern. It is a fitting resting place for people who, in life, were used to being different from the world. They lie before me, row on row, awaiting the day of resurrection and judgment. Some 600 final resting places have accumulated here over the years, among them graves of Grabers, original pioneers who migrated into these parts with little but axes and Bibles.

Each grave is unmarked except for a sharpened, raw piece of pine, gray with age, reminding one of the ancient stakes to which martyrs were tied. Every Amish church keeps its own records as to who rests under each peg. The plain folks know this, and the world doesn't care. Here the Amish never clear a grave, as done in crowded Old Europe. They also do not tend or lay flowers on them since one is to present flowers to people during their lifetime and not after they have died. Eventually the wooden marker at the head of the grave weathers into obscurity. Only then is a new one inserted in respect for those who have entered heavenly rest.

The Amish lay aside their pilgrim dress when the appointed hour and day has come. Then the Lord "needs such people as David or Rebecca" and holds the death of a devout Amish person to be more valuable than the life. Death as a result of Adam's sin is as expected as the birth of a child, a gift of God, who will one day return to God. This is according to the rhythm of farm life, seed-growth-harvest. Death exists because the Lord "formed a claylike clod of earth into human form, and gave that form living breath, a complete consciousness, and a discerning soul." But then human beings fell under penalty for sin (Gen. 2—3).

Each person enters the world as a mortal and then one day dies, like the Oma of the Schmucker clan. Her family chose four *Grabmacher* (gravediggers) from friends and family. They dug out a grave that very evening by Roth Road. The Schmuckers do not have to look after the *Totelad* (coffin). Every church district always has a complete set of coffins ready, and in five sizes: big, middle-sized, some for twelve-year-olds, others for six-year-olds, and finally a small size for babies. They are always available at prices from $50 to $75, although they may be used for other purposes pri-

322

or to the last. Sometimes apples or potatoes are stored in coffins, to help the living before the dead.

The church takes over the funeral, young boys volunteer for stable work, and girls look after kitchen duties in the house of the bereaved. A problem arises as to how most efficiently to get the word out to those who must be informed. The Amish of Allen County go to a worldly neighbor who has a telephone or use the public pay phone in Grabill. They ring up worldly neighbors of the Amish, who in turn pass on the message.

The Amish are afraid of death even though they view life as a more or less uneventful episode, a necessity on the way to eternity. Elam's Rachel, a member of a society in which the men often outlive women, claims it would be easier to die if one were certain that a paradise was waiting on the other side. However, not even the Amish know this, although they live in the assumption that after a righteous life, they have the "living hope" of a place reserved at the Lord's table. Without it, the days on earth sometimes seem to be a dreadful mistake. Their fear of death is only this uncertainty and not terror arising from a life poorly lived. And yet, the brothers and sisters have never quite managed to resolve the taboo of death.

In general terms, death has occupied the farmer more than it has the urbanite. He has lived all his life with the coming and going in field and stable. The close personal relationships kept up in the church district also bring the Amish to see or visit graves more frequently than do the worldly. They keenly feel the loss of their loved ones.

The plain folks keep praying every day as if they were to die today, while living and organizing things as if their sojourn on earth would be eternal. The Amish believe that there will be a God-given further chapter after this life, but that does not necessarily mean that the older ones are prepared for death when their call comes. It is touching to observe how they stock the autumn shelves of their life in the knowledge that winter is coming soon. At the same time, the Amish do not leave everything to Providence. In their houses one finds more remedies than expected, diet aids, "make fit" vitamins, and herbal concoctions for and against more serious matters. If possible, the Amish prefer to die at home rather than in a hospital.

Death, that day which knows of no evening, does not care how one dies. Yet it does not hit these families as hard as it does those in the world who, according to Amish opinion, "live like devils and bid farewell like angels," with the body painted to deny death. They "sorrow, but not as others who have no hope" (1 Thess. 4:13). Regarding resurrection, the brothers and sisters know little more than that the good are in for an eternal life while the bad are headed for judgment (John 5:29). There are unanswered questions, yet with God all things are possible. It is, therefore, impossible to make exact predictions in the matter. When the Amish are dying, if there is enough time, they bid those remaining behind *"auf Wiedersehen!"* meaning *"auf Wiedersehen,* hopefully, in a better land!" In the heavenly Jerusalem, I'll see you again, around the throne of God and of the Lamb, where there shall be no more death, nor sorrow, nor pain (Rev. 21-22).

Hopefully. Hopefully.

When Oma Schmucker is dying of a heart attack, she is granted a few hours of grace. Everyone who gathers around her deathbed can be sure that they will receive a stern warning or two. From the whole neighborhood, people are coming to the sickbed, even if only for a few minutes. Soon talk of "what Sister Schmucker saw or said when she was deathly sick" makes the rounds of Allen County. She is ranting against the plants of the field which were not all of the Lord's making (hybrids), against the striped ostentatiousness of worldly style, against pride which separates from God, against lightning rods and photos, used to carry around likenesses of those fashioned in God's image. Businesspeople ought to be careful of the merchant trade, for after all it was the Savior himself who threw traders out of the temple. Young people should exercise care, refrain from slander and gossip, and stay away from places selling strong drink, so that no false doctrine would be cropping up. . . .

Then Oma Schmucker, who has so honestly earned her rest but never found a suitable earlier age for dying, takes her leave. Since childhood she has known that she intends to leave this world with the words, "Lord, be merciful to me a sinner." This is exactly what she now does. Those present kneel while a prayer from the *Geistliches Lustgärtlein* (Spiritual happy little garden) is read for the ear of the Lord, asking for his mercy upon them all.

Then they reach for their white handkerchiefs. There is no doubt that Oma Schmucker during her life managed to overcome the world, and this now brings emotional relief to her relatives. This is a spiritual victory. The older and smaller she became through age, the larger she must now surely appear before God, her oldest friend still living. Now the time has come that God should claim his own. Born human, died holy—she now rests in the roughly hewn coffin lined with white foam rubber.

Consternation stirs sufficient hands when death strikes. Many wheels roll for the deceased and her relatives. Otherwise a deep peace surrounds the home of the departed. Four men assume the wake during the first two nights, while four others—those who dug the grave—sit by her during the last hours in the farmhouse. By kerosene lamplight, friends and relatives come to observe the corpse clothed totally in white and sit by her until the entire family is together. "They shall walk with me in white, for they are worthy" (Rev. 3:4). In some churches the deceased person is dressed in deep black colors or simply in whatever is left of her bridal dress. The latter comes from that part of the closet where the best Sunday dresses hang.

Beyond that, each district has definite ideas of what the departed ought to wear on that last mile. Great excitement once ensued in Allen County when it was established that a deceased was buried without suspenders. The relatives insisted that he be exhumed, but the bishop told them he didn't think the matter was that important, so the dead was left to rest in peace. Church districts vary regarding what else happens to the deceased before the funeral. Some Amish turn to the world at such times, have a funeral parlor tend to the corpse, and then return it as soon as possible to the farm. For others, again, this procedure is too modern or simply too expensive. They place the corpse on ice in their own homes until the funeral and rub it with alcohol at regular intervals.

On the day of the *Abdankung* (funeral service), a *Leichred* (funeral sermon) is given, lasting ninety minutes. The coffin is either closed or open, depending on the church district. Allen County has dropped the custom of sisters crying into a specially fashioned "grieving hankie," a black hankerchief. A service like the one for Oma Schmucker is frequently held in the afternoon and is called an *amische Leicht* (Amish funeral). On this occasion hymns are spoken and not sung, and a minister reads suitable selections from a prayer book.

Before the last trek to the cemetery, a brief obituary is read, making little reference to the departed and the past. All that is mentioned is her name, her age, and the number of offspring. Her judgment is left to God, as written in the *Handbook for Amish Preachers*: "The good characteristics of the deceased can be cited as an example and as role model, but this does not take much time. Even the most pious person has too many shortcomings for him to be set up as a perfect example." Instead, the word of the gospel directly addresses the mourners: "All flesh is grass, and all the goodliness thereof is as the flower of the field: The grass withers, the flower fades, . . . but the Word of our God shall stand for ever" (Isa. 40:6-8). Then the preacher commonly reads John 5:24-34, reminding all once again that humans are made of dust and will return to dust, and to be ready for God's judgment day at the resurrection.

The funeral procession is sometimes up to a mile in length. On the way to the cemetery, great care is taken to carry the dead out of the house headfirst. Likewise, in burial the body is always placed with the head to the west, facing the east for resurrection morning. When the coffin is carried out of Oma Schmucker's house, the brothers doff their large black hats to signal a final *auf Wiedersehen*. Then the Amish buggies form a long convoy. The coffin rests in one of the simplest buggies, for the Anabaptists will never understand a world that wants to transport its dead to Jesus in a Cadillac.

At the end of the day, a great dinner is served at which hundreds of Amish are present. Young and old partake of the opulent meal and console each other with talk of the resurrection. If this is to happen, then dying comes first. Thus it all has much in common with the death of a kernel of wheat as it sprouts to new life. The planted body is mortal, but God's Spirit will raise it up. The body is sown in weakness, to be raised in power. Just what the resurrection will be like is not for us to know, for God gives a body as he chooses (1 Cor. 15).

The women of Oma Schmucker's immediate family wear black for a year, similar to German traditions of grieving. Nieces wear black for only three months. In any case, men wear dark clothes practically all their life long. Grandchildren of the deceased, according to tradition, are to wear black upon certain occasions for up to six months.

After the wake and the great dinner, the older women friends of Oma Schmucker spend the next weeks doing little else but sewing. They work ahead just in case they should be called home first, ensuring that their spouses have enough reserve clothes to wear in such an event.

9

God's Second Choice

In the French Couthenans, on the main road close to Montbéliard, is an area where old farmhouses determine the landscape. There lies the historical Graber farmyard. Descendants of these Grabers still live in the vicinity, even though the door sign designates the owners as Hückels. Jean Hückel's mother was a Graber by birth. In the middle of the eighteenth century, this farmyard served as a focal point for the ancestors of those Grabers who migrated to America and today populate the land around Allen County, and those Grabers who remained in Old Europe.

A bundle of documents with dates referring to the history of this Anabaptist family is in the hands of the *Bürgermeister* (mayor). Pages yellowed by age report dates of births, weddings, and deaths, leaving no doubt that the Grabers of this area once were people of class and standing, as their descendants still are. However, the Hückels, with the exception of one son, no longer belong to an Anabaptist church. They have migrated out of the family history of faith. For a long time now, new life inhabits the frame house.

To this day the larger area around Montbéliard in eastern France, close to the Swiss border, is home to Anabaptists. It has been their refuge ever since the days when dispersed religious refugees from Bern—mainly via Alsace—found religious asylum here. Yoders still live in Florimount, Roths in Hericourt and Saint Louis, and Widmers in the city of Montbéliard proper. All these are everyday names in Allen County as well.

Above the entrance door to the Graber house in Couthenans, the year 1751 was hammered into stone as a stamp of history. This date resurrects the past. Located further back in the house is the great kitchen, where in times long past Anabaptists cooked the *Liebesmahl* (love meal), a traditional bean soup served in huge bowls and eaten in common by the believers, eight to a vessel. In addition, milk and bread were served. Alongside is the living room, still pervaded by the religious warmth of the past: discussions fed by fear and hope, words of the bishop emphasizing the end times "to strengthen hearts and ears against the evil one." Then he sent the congregation on its way in the beggars' dress of the early Anabaptists, accompanied by the blessing of Aaron.

At one crossroads in Couthenans, not far from the Graber farmyard, stands a monument for one Paul Graber, killed in action while wearing a French uniform during the occupation of the German Ruhr Valley. The uniform is proof that Grabers had given up the nonresistant status of their forebears during the French exile after Montbéliard had become their new home. Probably the newly introduced national army did not grant them special status. The last World War brought with it something unthinkable for early Anabaptist martyrs, one soldier fighting against a related soldier on an opposing front: French Grabers from the region of Montbéliard against Alsatian Grabers from the German *Wehrmacht* (army). Both descended from the same family tree dating back to their origins in the Swiss canton of Bern.

In 1707 the master weaver Peter Graber and his wife Elisabeth from Huttwil are mentioned in documents of Jebsheim in Alsace. Old documents, now stored in Colmar, reveal that on December 12, 1707, in Jebsheim, one Hans was born "son of Peter Graber, the Anabaptist," and Elisabeth, his wife. This couple had arrived only fourteen days prior and found accommodation at the castle of the *majer* (a ranking official). At that time the *majer* of the Jebsheim castle was one Felix Kleiner, an Anabaptist, to whom Christian II of Birkenfeld had leased the premises.

Two World Wars have taken their toll on Jebsheim, and the church records are practically the only reminder of the emigrating church of the Anabaptists in Jebsheim. Anyone on the lookout for Swiss Brethren will likely find traces of them sooner in the Vosges Mountains of the Alsatian north than in the area around Markirch. Precisely in Jebsheim the evangelical Lutheran church once spent much time trying to "convert" the Anabaptists, who resisted assignments to "occupy trenches and watchtowers on the Rhine" nearby. Judging by the standards of the time, they were undesirable citizens. Old church records confirm in black and white that no efforts were spared to convince these Anabaptists of the "right" way.

Sometimes they were successful. A 25-page entry from 1679 confirms the transfer of an Anabaptist. The cleric in charge proudly announced that one Jacob Baumann was finally converted. "Can you pray?" he had actually asked Jacob. "What do you pray? . . . Would you like to rid yourself of your errant ways?" To which Jacob replied, "It is a mistake to which the Anabaptists subscribe, and among their many errors, they deny holy baptism of small children and so conduct themselves contrary to the teachings of Jesus."

Such capitulation was not true of the Grabers, Peter and Elisabeth. Still Swiss Brethren but already rather Amish, they had arrived in Frédéric Fontaine from Jebsheim in 1708 with their son Hans because of the constant pressure exerted by the established church. At the time Leopold Eberhard was count of Mömpelgard (Montbéliard), and Peter was now engaged in his service. With the Grabers came others originally from Switzerland: Schmuckers from Grindelwald, Roths from Diessbach and Steffisberg, Kauffmanns from Steffisberg and Grindelwald, Hochstettlers from Schwartzenburg, Zimmermanns from Zollikofen, Lichtis from Biglen and Eggiwyl and Heimeswill, the Bachmanns from Röthenbach, Augsburgers from Langnau, Klopfsteins from Laupen, Hildebrands from Ober-Oenz, and Eichers (Eichners) from Schwartzenegg and Diessbach.

They settled in a strip of land still suffering from the consequences of the Thirty Years' War. The Anabaptists, experienced and successful in matters of agriculture, now became desired tenants. Initially they were merely tolerated here and received no written permission of residency. Their church, rapidly growing, was permitted to establish its own graveyards and schools but at first prohibited from constructing churches or purchasing their own land. These folks, persecuted for decades, nevertheless were grateful for this opportunity. They introduced the potato to Mömpelgard long before it was common in France.

Peter Graber, destitute as a result of two migrations, requested credit from the governing officials to buy seed grain for that first year. He earned additional income in milling, woodcutting, and producing charcoal. Peter died at the age of forty-five and left behind a wife and six children. One Sir Berdot, physician and adviser to the lords of Württemberg, soon took note of his son Hans. He was to become a most efficient agriculturist on the doctor's farm in Couthenans.

In 1793 the principality of Mömpelgard was occupied by France, and eight years later at the Peace of Lunéville, it became part of France, renamed Montbéliard. This was only a few months after Peter Graber, son of Hans, had purchased the farm by the present main road. According to the principles of the French Revolution, everyone living in France was counted as a citizen. This now allowed Anabaptists to purchase land. Another Graber was able to purchase a farm in Monteprevoir in the district of Montbéliard, still in operation today. One Graber at the time barely managed to escape the guillotine, the razor blade of the French Revolution. In the tradition of the Anabaptists, now all the Grabers together not only added to themselves but multiplied. Many children in that time and place were a virtue, just as they have remained to this day in Allen County.

God was the best farmer, but the Anabaptists followed a close second, assisted and aided, no doubt, by their religious convictions and Swiss individualism. At that time they belonged almost exclusively to the farming class and worked the very earth from which the first people had been fashioned. They bred the so-called Anabaptist horse, an animal with all the qualities to help their preachers get around fast. Joseph Graber from Couthenans became a particularly successful farmer. He crossed the Simmental cow with another breed to produce the Montbéliard strain, which by 1870 became a great success. In those parts even today, they still speak about the "Mennonite cow," even if for a laugh.

For this achievement, Joseph was made an honorary officer in the French Legion. He had brought honor to his country, not only because his breed produced and still produces outstanding milk and meat. Before the Franco-German War (1870), Graber had patriotically intended to name his cattle breed Alsatians. After the war started and Alsace had again become German, he named his breed Montbéliard (not the German name, Mömpelgard), to eternalize the French in his bovine breed.

The Grabers from the region of Montbéliard are attested in surviving church books of the early Anabaptist churches. They preferably married into such families as the Widmers, Roths, Kauffmans, or Schmuckers, just as they do today in America. A problem arose as it had previously in Alsace. Their neighbors and employers respected the Anabaptists around Montbéliard as workers much more than they loved them as people. This was one of the reasons why part of them, including some Amish members of the Graber clan, now moved "on the Danube to Vienna and further," to Volhynia in western Russia. There they settled in Eduardsdorf under the guidance of their preacher Samuel Stoll. Family members can be traced back to 1790 in Einsiedl, Austria; 1797 in Michelsdorf, Poland; and in Volhynia, 1837 in Horodyszcze and Waldheim, and 1861 in Kutusowka.

The majority of these pilgrim families emigrated to America in 1874 as a reaction to general Russification, which required military service. Today this branch of the Graber clan is mainly to be found in Kansas and South Dakota. By now, Grabers live much beyond Allen County. Based on a 1988 count, in the entire USA live some 10,000 people from 1,200 Graber families, all traceable to the same Swiss Anabaptist family.

The consequences of the French Revolution hit hard upon the Anabaptists who remained behind in the Montbéliard region. Their members refused to swear the oath, give up their German language, or be registered for service in the national guard. A major problem then developed when Napoleon made his call to arms. Wherever the general marched in victoriously, he revoked the Anabaptist exemption from military service. The Anabaptists sent a small delegation to Paris, but the great general refused to receive them. Some members of the congregations managed to receive permission to serve as wagon drivers for the army. They gradually became tired of all the business of wars in Europe. In 1818, several Anabaptist preachers meeting in Schlettstadt in Alsace decided to follow their brothers and sisters to America. It had become simpler and less expensive to finance a voyage than to buy freedom from military service.

Several Grabers followed the lead of these ministers. The first departed in 1819. In 1834 one Daniel Graber arrived in the New World with the sailing ship *Troy* and made his way to Ohio with little more than hope in his pockets. Katharina Graber and her husband Peter Stoll from Couthenans undertook the voyage across the ocean in 1837, while Christian Graber followed in 1852. Daniel had joined the Amish church on August 31, 1794, in order to marry Maria Frey. These two became the progenitors of most of the Grabers who still live in North America as Amish. He and his descendants were exceptionally diligent in the holy endeavor of multiplying. In the genealogical book of Joseph, Elam, or Rachel of Cuba Road, is an entry made by one Rosa Veronica Graber, with the maiden name of Schwartz. She had given birth to twelve children in the middle of the previous century. Then came her son Christian, who had fifteen children, son Peter with fourteen, whose son Aaron again had eighteen, and so on and on.

Daniel's son Peter, one of eleven children, married Anna Müller (Miller) in Wayne County of Ohio. He and his brothers Jakob and Johann made their way by oxcart in November 1852 to the Bible Belt, the Corn Belt, what was then called the Midwest of the USA. However, these Grabers did not leave voluntarily. Early in the 1850s in Ohio, the so-called "great disturbance" raged among the Amish. Initially the problem revolved around which mode of baptism was more biblical, "in the water" or "with water." Was a baptismal candidate to be led to a brook, or baptized at home with water—which might indeed be from the same stream? Finally a compromise was reached in the matter. One group stated that they "were prepared to exercise patience with the others."

Things became critical when bishop Jacob D. Yoder made the claim that the chief sin in paradise was lying by Eve and Adam rather than disobedience of God' command and defiance of the Creator. Christian Graber, himself a servant of the Word (minister) in the same congregation, approached Yoder and asked him to explain himself on the matter. According to a report of the time, he told Yoder, "If you teach this and claim it to be fact, you are an angel of the underworld." Graber was banned. A meeting of the ministers called to resolve this quarrel was unsuccessful, leading to a huge split right through the congregations in Ohio.

The split was said to show the difference between the "gentle" and the "coarse, heathen, money collectors." This was nothing exceptional in a group which had seen or experienced practically everything that could happen in a religious movement. Disparity repeatedly challenged the total commitment of individual churches as they sought to understand life on the basis of Christ's teachings and their own traditions. Such controversy here and there led to factions, second migrations, new beginnings. Although the divisions marred unity "in the same mind and the same purpose," they also clarified who was courageous and constant (1 Cor. 1:10; 11:19).

Close to where the yard of Preacher Joseph is presently located, Peter bought forty acres of land, backwoods at the time. He paid one dollar per acre when wheat still commanded thirty cents a bushel and corn ten cents. Here the first log cabins were erected, then the summerhouses of the Amish, and finally the buildings of later generations. After the clearing of the land, changes came slowly. South of Grabill, Peter's house still stands, even if a little worn. Aside from Graber Road, no monument marks the place of these pioneers. It is not a large building, but no matter.

According to the records, in that house Peter preached with the voice of a trumpet, and the overflow of the congregation, sitting a hundred meters away in the barn, could easily hear his mighty words. When casting about for construction sites, the Amish families opted for elevated ground in case of wet years, preferring wooded areas with ash, oak, or maple. The soil under and around these trees was slightly oily and rich. In Allen County, the Amish were pioneers. Their farms, like those of their fellow Amish in Lancaster, were not meant as speculative sources of income but as homesteads for innumerable descendants.

In this Indiana, "Land of the Indians," the Grabers as German-speaking immigrants were no exceptions. Since the War of Independence, German settlers had been attracted by the fertile soil. The non-Anabaptist pioneers engaged in the skirmishes with the Indians with enthusiasm, but the Anabaptists opted for peaceful coexistence. From 1838 Swiss Anabaptists of Mennonite persuasion were arriving in Adams County, Indiana, from Ohio. By the 1850s others came to this Berne area, mainly from the Jura, but also in growing numbers from the Emmental (valley of the Emme), particularly from the area around Langnau. From 1839 Mennonites were also settling in the Yellow Creek area of Elkhart County.

The first Amish in Indiana immigrated from Somerset County of Pennsylvania and from Ohio in 1939-1940 and located at or near Nappanee in Elkhart and Marshall counties. The earliest were fairly recent immigrants from the Palatinate, of Swiss origin. Beginning in 1941, more Amish from Somerset County settled east of Goshen in Elkhart and LaGrange counties. In addition to Yoders, Hochstetlers, and Millers, from Pennsylvania; Borntragers, Schrocks, Schlabachs, Masts, Troyers, and Christners came from Ohio. From 1850 the vicinity of Berne in Adams County attracted Amish families from Alsace and Lorraine, among whom were Eglys, Liechtys, Schindlers, and Stuckeys. While the Grabers were clearing soil around Grabill, families named Kurtz, Lantzes, and Hartzler tried their farming skills around Topeka. Around the Amish of Indiana, settlements sprang up like New Alsace, Mühlhausen, New Oldenburg, Luzern, Elberfeld, Hamburg, Bremen, Berlin, or Lippe.

Fort Wayne became the capital of German churches. The Swiss introduced vineyards into Indiana. The religious communist settlement of New Harmony, a church splinter group from Württemberg called the Rappists, located near Evansville and started the first large commercial agricultural model in the Midwest. In the capital city of Indianapolis, the presidential candidate (1900-1920) of German background, Eugene V. Debs, held high office. During the American Civil War, Indiana provided the 32nd Voluntary Regiment, totally German and repeatedly decorated, under the command of Colonel August von Willich. At one time, thirty German newspapers were printed, and German life thrived in some 176 clubs and societies.

While the Amish were German, they never regarded themselves within the framework of the general German migration. Their world turned inward, to the ethnic isolation of family and church. Other Germans were much more for looking outward.

The young generation of Indiana pioneers in Hanover or Hesse-Cassel quickly became Anglicized, and other church bodies gave up their language and traditions as well. Yet the Amish, who rejected things new, maintained their German ways and language. They remained simple folk.

In the first generations they often had a command of four languages. Swiss-German was the language of their homes, High German was for church and school, French was retained from their sojourn in France, and English was the language of their new home. The *Dütsch* (German) helped them to stay in dialogue with their forebears, guard against assimilation, and preserve their form of Christianity.

The Graber brothers, Peter, Jacob, and John, were all chosen to become bishops of the Amish church. This meant that according to Anabaptist regulations, they knew how to keep their physical bodies in check. They felt the fruit of the Holy Spirit within, and thus strengthened and equipped, they taught the way of truth. Through them the Word of God produced the right kind of fruit. However, just as in the Amish settlements before and after, serious differences cropped up among the plain folks of the Grabill region. As a result of these frictions, they split into three different groups: the traditional Old Order Amish, the change-oriented Amish Mennonites (most of whom merged with Mennonites in the twentiety century), and the progressive Mennonites.

Jacob Graber contributed to all this when he took a strong stand against new customs and innovations within the church at a meeting of the ministers in June 1864. One of the points he argued forcefully was that members should not marry outside their own church. After all, no less than an apostle stated clearly, "What concern are those outside to me?" (1 Cor. 5:12). The conservatives insisted on old traditions and therefore rejected prayer meetings or Sunday school, opposed things *englisch*, and retained the heavy half-linen garb. The "liberals" wanted to try the new *Springweisen* (quicker-paced melodies) instead of the slowly sung style used with the *Ausbund* hymnal. They also gradually accepted "flashy external dress." While some fought against the devil in general, others in addition also fought against the wider world.

The Anabaptist factions of Allen County gradually grew apart. Grabers were soon to be found in all three groups. By 1880 they had made a name for themselves as spiritual leaders among the conservatives as well as men who knew how to assert themselves in the world of commerce. Others moved out from there in every direction, and the plain folks, with groans of sorrow at the separation, founded new church districts in the country around them. Some simply became part of the world.

Anabaptists generally have a strong sense of family history. Whatever is considered to be important, they write on special record pages of Bibles and songbooks in order to save it for posterity. Since Mennonite archives like to keep records of the Anabaptists, whole volumes of up-to-date and complete chronicles of Amish families are available. Based on such information, one can conclude that the Grabers of Huttwil became totally "genuine" Amish only after they came to America. To be only "a little bit Amish" meant to be of family splinter groups, according to the Graber grandson Hückel in Couthenans of today. This was already true in Old Europe, but splinter groups also was a term for Swiss Brethren who had opposed Jakob Ammann at any time.

In the area around Montbéliard, the descendants of the Amish have been squeezed out by the competition of the religious giants. They consequently can be found only in other churches, since there is no status for half-Amish. However, stories of the early Grabers have certainly been preserved in the widely networked family circle. There is the tale of one Maria Graber, so powerful that she could carry three bags of potatoes at one time. Then there was the Peter who just barely managed to escape the Jacobites by the skin of his teeth, and another Peter who, like Joseph, had the talent to dismiss the pain of his fellows or remove warts "in the name of the Father, the Son, and the Holy Spirit."

Exceptional happenings are being told in Couthenans to this day. Recently an Amish of conservative persuasion, a direct descendant from Jakob Ammann's remarkable followers, arrived to visit the house of his forebears. He obviously was traveling incognito. Not even his own church knew about this trip, nor is it ever meant to know. Occasionally, but rarely, an Amish person ventures a little sidestep, too.

******

Trubach in Trubtal (valley of the Trub), the Trub principality in Switzerland, is like every other place in the region. The surrounding mountains are so high that they swallow the sun. Highway traffic is so distant that forests all around will probably sigh and rustle for all time. People on surrounding farms belong to their land as do the mountain cattle to the slopes on which hangs the house of Hinter-Hütten, at the Hütten ravine. There is nothing exceptional to it all. When hiking through the valley, not one in 10,000 tourists pays attention to the old farmyard hard by a nature trail close to the basin. Yet that site hides something important and noteworthy. The farmyard and neighborhood of the Schwartzentrubers has given its name to one of the most conservative of all Amish groups, though the name has been slightly Americanized.

The Hinter-Hüttenhof once was a reliable hiding place for the Anabaptists in Trubtal, part of the Fankhauser family, when they still spelled their name Fanghauser and were certainly rebellious in matters of faith. One Fanghauser was imprisoned in Bern in 1709 on account of his faith, another was banished and migrated to Pennsylvania. Living quarters, stable, and barn are all under one roof. One of the heavy supporting beams has the year 1608 carved into it. This building once offered refuge to the devout of the area who were on the run from the *Täuferjäger* (Anabaptist hunters). The system of hiding the refugees was as simple as it was effective. "*Die Töfer* (Anabaptists)," so runs the commentary of Hans Fankhauser, were at his farmhouse-barn one second, and when forced to flee, they simply disappeared.

When catchpoles surfaced, sympathizers sounded a warning by blowing into a cow horn. Then the persecuted ran up the entrance to the threshing floor of the Hinter-Hüttenhof, stepped on a tip board (hinged like a seesaw) called *Gampfilade* in the Trubtal, and fell into a camouflaged dungeon measuring seven feet square. The tipping board returned to the floor and stopped vibrating just in time. The hunters noticed neither that board nor the hiding place. The Anabaptists had sufficient fresh air in the hole and stayed there until the chamberlords of the Anabaptists or their catchpoles had moved on.

The Anabaptists of the canton Bern, honed in survival skills, have to this day managed to remain in the tradition of the Swiss

Brethren, even if in small numbers. Their church in the area of the Emme has never quite died out. During and after the actual persecution of that time, church services and children's protection meetings were held in up to thirty-eight places in the valleys and foothills of the great surrounding mountain ridge. They met at the Röthlisbergers in the Mättenberghüsli, at the Gerbers in Stock, or at the Mosers in the *Pfaffenbachscheuer* (barn of the pastor's brook), and occasionally they still meet to this day. The group is small, and yet Anabaptists from the Emmental are active as missionaries today in China, Angola, the Philippines, and the Cameroons.

There never were real Amish in the Emmental. Foot washing and shunning in the spirit of Jakob Ammann were never practiced there. The Emmentalers, whose descendants live in America, chanced upon the radical Amish Anabaptists in the diaspora. Yet some of their spirit seems to have survived to this century. There are new Anabaptists today in Langnau who separated from the old Anabaptists in 1835, then split again, and now follow a strict church order within their congregation. The women, like the Amish, are not allowed to cut their hair, and if the situation calls for it, they practice shunning.

Hans Rüfenacht from Emmenmatt, the confluence of the Emme and the Ilfis, is the bishop of the 550-member church of the *Alttäufer* (old Anabaptists). He calls this new group *sektierisch* (sectarian), just what others had called the followers of Jakob Ammann or, earlier, the Anabaptists in general. Since World War II, the old Anabaptists of Rüfenacht are also known as Mennonites, but in the Emmental they do not approve of this term, imported from the north. Here they strongly maintain that "the church shall be named after no man and after no place." The Emmentalers prefer to be *altevangelisch* (old evangelical) Anabaptist and explain that in the course of their own history, much has been deliberately destroyed in their homeland.

Not only in the Emmental is this so. Anyone who wants to get to know the Amish today has to go to America. In Europe at one time, some forty churches observed their religious style. Now remaining are no followers of Jakob Ammann and only a few witnesses and records of their history, often intertwined with the accounts of other Anabaptists. Before the departure of the last congregations, they held that no state could be maintained according to the standard of the Sermon of the Mount (an opinion shared by Bismarck). The Amish disappeared from Switzerland, Germany, France, Holland, Poland, and Russia; families that stayed have long since lost their Amish innocence.

In the original home of the old evangelical Anabaptists, in Switzerland, there were two churches left some one hundred years ago which practiced foot washing but did not call themselves Amish. The French Revolution had temporarily instituted freedom of conscience and religion when the old church regiment was abolished. After Napoleon was overthrown, sharp confessional battles between conservatives and radical groups broke out. The Anabaptists were again seriously restricted in their practice of faith. Total religious freedom was finally guaranteed as a result of the special status war leading to the Swiss federal constitution of 1848, and extended in 1874. This benefited the 3,000 Mennonites who live in the Emmental and in the Jura today. In 1963 an Old-Evangelical Anabaptist congregation was again called to life in Bern.

The present Mennonite church in Basel on Holee Street was originally Amish. The members trace their history back to 1777. Up to recent times they were nicknamed *Häftligemee* (congregation using hooks and eyes) as opposed to the completely Mennonite *Schänzligemee* (congregation in the Schänzli suburb of Basel). These names date back to the days when the Amish separated themselves from the Mennonites, the *Knöpflern* (button people). The Amish identified the difference in a little jingle:

> Die mit Haken und Ösen wird der Herr erlösen.
> Die mit Knöpfen und Taschen wird der Teufel erhaschen.
>
> Those with hooks and with eyes, the Lord will save.
> Those with buttons and pockets, the devil will seize. *(literally)*
>
> Those with eyes and with hook, will be saved by the Book.
> Those with buttons and pocket, will be Satan's locket. *(freely)*

However, Jakob Ammann's rules have been dead for a good while in these parts.

Hard by the Swiss border, one Jacques Graber is the bishop of the Alsatian Mennonite church of Altkirch-Birkenhof. There communion was celebrated up to 1957 with foot washing following. The congregation is bilingual, German and French, and yet the old church members there, like their Amish counterparts in North America, still believe (according to Graber) that God speaks German, and therefore their church services are conducted in German. In the community of Altfeld-Birkenhof, the Montbéliard or Mennonite cow still is regarded as original only if the mandatory three red spots on its hide do not touch each other.

Jacques Graber also says that his family in 1711 was subject to an order of the Bern government striking down "land and people's rights for him and his descendants for all times." Now, however, they again enjoy full rights of home and country in Huttwil, canton of Bern.

Today 3,000 Mennonites in Alsace and Lorraine are to a large extent of Amish origin but have not held to the old ways. After the early believers had been dispersed from the area around Markirch, their preferred destination was Montbéliard, Lorraine, and the Palatinate, and from there to the USA. Larger concentrations of Anabaptists are also to be found on the Geisberg (Goat Mountain). This is quite near the site where in August 1870 the French suffered one of their first major defeats in the Franco-German War. Huge Pentecost celebrations are still held on the Geisberg annually. Below, in the valley, Protestants speak about the deep faith of the Anabaptists on high.

Memories of early Anabaptists are to be found in the Täufergässl in Birlenbach, in the municipality of Drachenbronn. Here older citizens still have much to say about early Anabaptist neighbors. It is assumed that the great meeting of the Amish ministers took place in 1752 at the *Mahlstein der Mühle* (grinding stone of the mill) in Steinselz. Old Anabaptist farmyards are still to be found in places like Nehweiler, Riedseltz, Dornbach, and in the congregations at Windstein, Lembach, Reichshoffen, or Gundershofen, and particularly in the valley of the Leber.

In Germany, the Amish settled especially in the Palatinate. During the best times, their church had between 6,000 and 7,000 members. Problems arose because of the worldly and the Amish living side by side. Constant reprisals came from the world and from other churches. In addition, there were considerable distances between Amish homes since the group was not allowed to purchase adjoining plots of land, as later in America. The Amish were quite active and managed to survive a relatively long time in church districts around Kaiserslautern, by Essingen close to Landau, or around Zweibrücken. In the latter area, the Amish became part of the Mennonite church in 1937.

The Palatinate group which went to Bavaria intermixed with fellow believers from Alsace-Lorraine. They were in the regions of Ingolstadt (where an Amish group lasted until 1912), Regensburg (until 1908), and Munich (until 1892). Descendants are to be found on various farms of these areas. Large groups of immigrants to Canada originated from these areas in the nineteenth century. The tracks of the Bavarian congregations were obliterated by history around the turn of the century. In Regensburg and in Munich, the last of the Amish joined the Mennonites. In Luxemburg, ten Amish families were counted in 1935.

Smaller Amish congregations lived on the Eifel plateau and in the area of Neuwied. In 1730 a group of Amish settled in the region of Hesse-Cassel in Wittgenstein (later Waldeck). Around 1800 there were more groups, as for instance in Nassau-Siegen and Nassau-Weilburg, Lemberg, and Marienberg. Amish were to be found around Wiesbaden, Marburg, Darmstadt, Mainz, and Worms. Around 1900, however, their congregations had been dissolved. "Hessian" Amish are today found concentrated in Somerset County, Pennsylvania; Garrett County, Maryland; and in Butler County, Ohio. In Baden (Germany), in the area of Bruchsal, the congregations had already disbanded in the eighteenth century.

A small Amish group which left the Palatinate, together with other Anabaptists from Montbéliard, headed for Galicia and Volhynia. There rich landowners had been alerted to them and were eager to use their agricultural skills. These Amish lost part of their identity by living close to the Mennonites. The end of their Amish history was sealed even before they moved on in 1874 to Freeman, South Dakota, and Moundridge, Kansas, as Mennonites.

The longest surviving Amish group of Europe was the church district of Ixheim near Zweibrücken. Shortly before the Second World War, their own *Bethaus* (house of prayer) was given up, and the congregation attended the Mennonite church in Ernstweiler. On January 17, 1937, the two congregations, which shared a common tradition, shook the hand of membership in the Mennonite church of Zweibrücken. Already at that time, the German Amish were no longer in step with their brothers and sisters in America since the Amish of Europe were much more open to technology. In Europe, many teachings and religious guidelines were diluted up to a point, and many *Ordnungen* (sets of rules) there regarded as of little consequence were still held as important in the New World.

The old house of prayer of the Amish was rebuilt into living quarters. There are still typically Amish names left in this area such as Stalter, Oesch, Gingerich, Guth, Hauter, Naffziger, Reidigers, and Schertz. On the Schmalfelder farmyard close to Marnheim in the Palatinate, lived one Emil Guth up to a short time ago. He liked to describe himself "as the last German Amish." Guth came from the congregation of Ixheim.

In Germany, many old, practicing Mennonite churches have survived, such as those at Emden (since 1530), in Leer-Oldenburg (since 1540), in Krefeld (Crefeld; since around 1600), in Hamburg (since 1601), at Friedelsheim in the Palatinate (since 1650), or in Worms-Ibersheim (since 1660).

The Amish moved from place to place in Europe as "strangers and pilgrims" (Heb. 11:13). In addition to coping with religious restrictions, they had to make do with too little land and put up with too many people. In the New World, they are allowed to practice their ideals without serious interference from worldly authorities. They were never able to realize this in their old home prior to their emigration. However, in North America their history is also shaped more and more by restlessness, a search for land, a quest for a peaceful place, close to nature and God and their family.

In the future it will be difficult to find the new farmland they need since their population doubles every twenty years. Always there is a race between stork and plow. The Amish church family has to expand, and yet acreage is most expensive precisely where their settlements are located. Still surviving are congregations in three Amish settlements begun in the 1700s: Lancaster-Chester counties (Pa.) by the 1740s, southern Somerset County (Pa.) and northern Garrett County (Maryland) by 1767, and Mifflin County (Pa.) by 1791.

In the early 1800s, when the push toward the West commenced, twenty-two church districts were counted. In 1993, the count stood at 918 districts, among which are the newer Amish settlements in Missouri (since 1947), Wisconsin (1925), Minnesota (1972), Montana (1975), and Texas (1982). A number of districts were dissolved, some in good old tradition because of internal dissensions, others because they objected to school laws of the new area, and a few because of an unsuitable climate. Sometimes they moved back and forth, for instance, from one district in the USA to Ontario, Canada, only to return to the USA after it became law in Canada that in order to sell milk, it had to be cooled in specified containers. (On migrations, see pages 13-16.)

When the Amish move, they do not move alone, but in family groups, planning to settle within horse-and-wagon distance of each other. This guarantees them the right kind of living together, harbored in their church and family, strange to the world and different from it. Today three out of four Amish live in the states of Pennsylvania, Ohio, and Indiana.

The world expects no wonders from such conservative Anabaptists of North America, who have no ecumenical connections to other groups. Yet after World War II, some Amish did give generously through the Mennonite Central Committee to help resettle European Mennonite refugees in South America. The times are long gone when, for instance, the Hutterites in Europe "invented" the kindergarten, long before it was known in Germany. They operated bathhouses in Moravia and Slovakia, convincing the relatively unsanitary world of the time of the virtues of cleanliness. The Swiss Brethren were trailblazers in matters of looking after the poor.

The fact that tens of thousands of young people save the churches from the danger of succumbing to old age surprises only those who have never bothered to take a closer look at the Amish of Allen County. Their lifestyle is a challenging model and one of the most unusual alternatives to the modern world, if the worldlings would ever take it seriously. However, the Amish know that hard times lie ahead and that there is no permanent guarantee of customary harvests. The same holds true of the Hutterites and Old Order Mennonites. At the same time, the record shows that Anabaptists have always fared better in hard times than in good.

On principle, the Old Order Amish practice no missionary

work beyond their own church activities. Yet they are a Christian presence and in touch with many people through their far-flung settlements and the tourists and visitors who seek them out.

Today a few Beachy Amish members, however, attempt to reclaim long-lost terrain in Europe. Some with names of Yoder, Miller, and Bontrager are presently in northern France, close to the Belgian border, attempting to start a congregation. Thus far the effort has been unsuccessful.

From the 1960s, the Beachy Amish also have been doing mission work in Central America and now have three congregations in Belize, three in El Salvador, and five in Costa Rica. Various attempts to organize congregations in Mexico or Honduras have been terminated. They do have an experiment in East Paraguay, where live some twelve to fifteen families, transitional Amish products of a more progressive bent. Beachy Amish, some of whom had earlier settled in the Chaco of Paraguay, organized this Colonia Luz y Esperanza (Light and Hope Colony, 1967) and see their life as farmers and missionaries. In addition, a Beachy Amish group is at Asunción.

Old Order Amish were also in the Chaco, the so-called "Green Hell," in 1967-78. Their sojourn, close to the Mennonite colony of Fernheim, was of short duration. These Mennonites of Dutch and North German ancestry and Low-German language had emigrated from Prussia to Russia (beginning in 1788) to South America (in the twentieth century). They had a more liberal style of life, and the Amish quickly decided that this neighborhood jeopardized their youth remaining Amish. In many respects, the two groups were too similar for them to call each other satanic. There the Amish laid aside suspenders and wore the belts of the Mennonites. In short, some became what they had always been, Mennonites.

Others of these Amish moved on to a world with more clearly contoured sins, to East Paraguay, or even to Pennsylvania. At Asunción are the remnants of an Old Order Amish settlement, according to David Luthy, Amish historian of Aylmer, Ontario. The ten families include some of native background, are called Amish, and have no motor vehicles. But they use Spanish in their services rather than German and ordain their own ministers with no wider Amish counsel.

Today Mennonites, including Amish and Brethren in Christ, live all over the world and number almost a million. In Germany, reinforced by immigrants from the former Soviet Union, are about 75,000, in the Netherlands are about 25,000, in North America about 400,000, in Zaire over 100,000, in India over 75,000, and in Indonesia almost as many. The majority of them are open to the world.

Mennonites live "in the world" and mingle with it more freely than the Amish. Most of them use modern technology, but they try to abstain from the sin of the world. Their Anabaptist status has become routine. With such a lifestyle, they recognize what their forebears in the age of the Reformation of Luther or Zwingli failed to see: the world changes. The biblical life of the first Christians in old Jerusalem is an important model, but it cannot for all times be rigidly copied by the church today which still identifies with those early believers. To the Mennonites, new and changing times demand the same kind of Christianity, but becoming Christian and remaining such depends on the zeitgeist, on the spirit of the times. Thus many non-Amish Anabaptists accept the modern world as home. But Jakob Ammann spoke for and to a different century. He would have had difficulty in providing helpful counsel to such followers of today.

10

The Hard Search for Paradise

At Zehr's Store we buy the knife for the job ahead. The pincers, the twitch (restraining device), and tetanus needle are in the plastic pail beside me. On this moody autumn morning, we, with equipment and all, set out by buggy for Paul Eicher's farm. His stallion, a Standardbred aged eighteen months, is to be converted into a gelding. David would have preferred the stallion to be a few weeks older for the operation ahead, but then, business is business.

David Nolt and Teacher John Zehr are masters of this cutting craft in Allen County. David prefers to castrate in spring or in late autumn, before or after the mosquito season. Each year some seventy-five stallions fall prey to his knife and pincers during these seasons. The Amish neuter every stallion not used for breeding purposes. The operation results in the male losing aggressiveness and sex drive, and thus becoming a usable horse for farm and farmer. Also, one can trot a gelding to church, but not stallions. They have little sense of occasion, as the all-out war between King and Constable recently demonstrated. More than enough mares are lined up at the churchyard for stud and stallion to get excited about. Another consideration enters into the deliberations: its meat will be tastier if one in good time is prepared to pay the price of an incision there, you know where. The Amish never eat horse meat; they leave such delicacies to others.

When it comes to castrations, David has a simple, common-sense approach. In former times a horse was forced to the floor for the purpose. Today he is castrated standing up, backed against a fence or a wall. Four tools are necessary for the job ahead: the cutting knife, razor-sharp; a relatively simple pincer-pliers, doubling as a wire cutter; a loaded tetanus needle; and a twitch, a length of chain pulled through a horse's mouth and twisted, rendering any horse docile, even without a tranquilizer. When David goes about his job, the owner is required to engage the twitch sufficiently for the horse to stand still long enough for "him" to become "it." The brothers naturally call this kind of restraint "natural."

David approaches Eicher's stallion with the new knife from Zehr's store. With a quick incision he severs skin and flesh right to the testicles. He is always on a bit of a jump since he cannot predict the reaction of the animal with total accuracy. Then he activates the pincers to cut off both testicles. A few more corrective measures to clean up dangling spermatic cords, and the procedure is over, even before the horse has had time to determine the greater irritant, the pain between teeth or that between legs.

The farmyard dogs devour the parts cut off, David hums the song of an Amish gray-weather poet, Paul Eicher goes for his checkbook, and the children, who have witnessed what they were not meant to see, now leave their peeping knotholes. The patient will probably be a little sore for a day or two. Thus prepared, the gelding will soon be ready for a life of work between the shafts of a buggy or teaming up to help pull a seed drill or a plow. Eicher's sorrel would be broken in at age two, have its most productive years between five and twelve, and after fifteen be on a gradual decline, similar to a human in his fifties.

From the Eichers we make our way to Ora Schwartz, who is surprised that I, the *Englischer*, can speak German, meaning "Amish." Then we're off to his brother . . . and always the same procedure. This goes on all forenoon until we run out of tetanus. For David, it is a job like all the others, part of the everyday life of a farmer, which starts early and ends late. It also is a day in the life of an Amish horse.

On the way home, David admits that he is thankful to heaven

for having been born a human being and not an animal, and I know why. Then we stop briefly for a drink of water at John and Lilian Graber's farm. They live in a remote and sleepy hollow where the road leads over some topographic hunchbacks from Grabill to the northeast. As in the Grabill area itself, the sun is about to change time and seasons; autumn is in the air. At this time of year, everyone works from sunrise until much after sunset. The day is not long enough to finish necessary things, although the entire family works in accord like a great orchestra. John's oldest turns over seams of earth by plow, his brother pumps the well for watering the cattle. For Lilian, it's laundry day, as for all Amish womenfolk on Mondays, after putting the clothing to the spot-and-whiff test. One of the daughters harrows the garden by horse, which responds to her cool command clicks, and the small ones practice the long jump in the stable.

On the farm, legs of animal or man constitute an important means of transport. John, a man cast for his role in life, operates a sawmill. He is firmly anchored in the waters of a deep past. John appears to be German, and he acts the part. It comes as little surprise that John knows of only duty in life: he is Amish by conviction. Ammann's Jakob would have been happy with this man.

All the many orders issued by Ammann and his successors over the centuries are routinely followed by John Graber, his family, his wider family, and their relatives. In practical terms, this does not mean picking out the raisins and ignoring the bitter dough. The Amish church challenges the whole of the person to obey standards and avoid the snares it has flagged.

Take Lilian and her daughters as examples. The guidelines for the simplicity of their dress go back to 1568 in Strassburg. In 1779, the servants in Essingen in the Palatinate forbade them to wear anything red. In 1809, the bishops at a meeting in Pennsylvania brushed clasps from their hair. In 1865, the Amish in Ohio added to the list of things *streng verboten* (strongly forbidden) anything checkered, striped, or flowered according to the *Weltmode* (worldly style), or an outer rubber skirt or oilcloth. The same year a decree was issued forbidding the display of pictures of *Menschen* (human beings) or carrying them about in secret. There are some one hundred orders of which the Grabers have to be mindful every day in order not to stray from the right path. These orders include thou-shalt-nots for the woman, the man, the boys, the girls, the old, John the farmer, and John the businessman.

The Amish, caught in pressures for technical and industrial development, have land for seeds and land for weeds. The plain folks attempt to compensate for their quiet, passive patience with agrarian and cultural achievements, at least in their understanding of culture. The dependence of man on the soil he cultivates, plus the seasons, and climatic conditions—all these correspond to his relationship of dependence on God. The Amish, producers in a consuming world, pray for what they want and work for what they need. They offer their hands for the day's work and their hearts for God in the attempt to conduct life in accord with Jesus' commission, "Occupy till I come" (Luke 19:13). This indeed is not a bad concept for people of yesterday who intend to make it today. If the crop one year turns out to be poor, there still is hope for the next year.

Hope, living hope is the philosophy of the Amish for this life and for life after death. They cling to this outlook even though their simple way is becoming ever more bumpy and more difficult to travel. There is deceptive ease in the way their swift trotters glide down Cuba Road, or young girls work the fields with a team of eight, guiding many tons of muscle with a gentle command in Bernese German. Amish prosperity is the product of sweat, thrift, and a sense for profitable products or enterprises. An Amish farm is an El Dorado for employees since no unemployed can or will ever exist on it.

Amish people like Lilian and John are first and foremost farmers and are equipped better than average for this kind of life. Work on a farm, large enough to remain independent of state subsidies even in hard years, is an American way of life that fits them well: butchering in January, plowing in March, planting in May, harvesting hay in June, threshing in July, and filling silos in September. A farmer, dependent on no one, can live a more Christian life than a salesman, in their opinion. Poor farmers can serve God better than learned philosophers.

Organic self-preservation on the farm strengthens the traditional family order. Up to now, Amish moralists are not at all clear about whether or how life after farming might exist for them when there will not be sufficient land in America. Ever more farms are needed on which the rapidly growing and environmentally sensitive community can expand while still maintaining a symbiosis between work and worship. Up to this day, it has been precisely their self-sufficiency which has enabled them to remain economically independent and has protected them from outside cultural control.

Yet this Anabaptist movement is and was never entirely comprised of farmers. During the difficult centuries of persecution, Amish of every class fled to remote areas where they isolated themselves and had to look after all their own necessities. There they developed agricultural practices which soon marked them as model Anabaptist farmers and Christians—*der Herr sei dafür globt und prise* (the Lord be honored and praised for this). Already in spoiled old Europe, the Amish managed to convert poor soil into producing land by their revolutionary agricultural methods such as rotating crops and applying gypsum and manure to the soil. Their success in breeding cattle is well documented. The Amish as farmers stand for the ability of a class of people and its culture to assert itself against all odds.

Here is farmwork, original agrarian production without any technological nonsense, the care for the temporal without deviating from the eternal. This remains for families such as the Grabers a *Weltanschauung* (worldview), the natural way to fulfill the biblical commission to tend the earth. The Amish work hard and if at all possible, hand in hand with nature. They brought along from Europe the rotation of crops resembling the three-field system of the Middle Ages.

The Amish depend on all of them earning their keep by the sweat of their brow, in accord with the Bible, just like a woman having to bear her children in pain, ever since Eve's unfortunate bite of the forbidden fruit (Gen. 3). They work for themselves, for their families, for their community, as well as for nature, which is of divine origin and therefore good and shall remain so. The old way of doing things sees to it that nothing on a farm is rationalized away and that the farm harbors no loafers.

Amish may appear to be backward in some respects by the ever-modern bound, as in North America. But there are many countries, such as in the third world, to whom Anabaptists would appear to be thoroughly modern with their effective methods of farming. Indeed, Amish farming may be more sustainable over the long run than commercial North American agriculture. The latter uses big machinery, much fertilizer, and nonrenewable fuel, consuming about ten calories of energy input for each calorie of food placed on the table, according to Art and Jocele Meyer in their book *Earthkeepers*. But Amish horse power is indefinitely renewable.

The Amish are torn between profit and God's commission to care for creation. They have organized their farms to manage the work with old methods and the manual labor of their own families. In so doing, some small adjustments of older biblical interpretations and orders are permitted. This means that the plain folks of Allen County are even allowed to sell milk on Sunday, the day of the Lord. According to Elam, their reasons are simple: "not to misuse the cow which is to be milked" and not to impose a double amount of Monday work on the worldly who come every morning for their milk.

This little concern for the worldly may well be an emergency exit from earlier regulations. In Lancaster County the Amish responded to milk boards demanding delivery of milk every day, including Sunday, by building their own cheese factory. Milk production is popular since a little fodder from a relatively small tract of land can be transformed into some year-round cash flow. Amish farms in Pennsylvania average seventy acres, while in Indiana they are somewhat larger and yet considerably smaller than those of typical *Englischers'* farms. Where tobacco grows, the Old Order Amish tend to give it preference since it provides work for young and old much of the year and brings more cash return per acre than most other crops, allowing for smaller viable farms.

The Amish have always assumed a nonexploitative attitude toward their land since it must one day provide for children and children's children. To damage the earth would mean to abandon one's own offspring. With their attitude, the Amish might well be a leading symbol for modern environmentalists. It is a rare exception for Amish to sell their land to the worldly. Yet this has happened, as for instance in Kansas, when oil was discovered on Amish land. The plain folks quickly packed their earthly effects and sold the land. To sit on oil wealth was too worldly for them.

In principle, their land is not meant for speculative purposes;

it is bought and cultivated as though "for eternity." Whenever they purchase land, they try to keep payments as low as possible. Coming generations can pay off the mortgage since the land is, after all, meant for them. Divorces, which could force a farm to be divided and sold, are nonexistent. It follows that these Anabaptists have a particularly intimate relationship to their estate since God has granted it to them for their administration. Nothing gives them a greater sense of satisfaction, self-confirmation, and security than to view their land holdings and know that they are on the right path.

This does not mean that all Amish are necessarily ideal alternative bio-farmers. Among them also, forces collide and interplay between environment and civilization, traditional methods of production and new methods of utilization. The Amish harvest the same crop quantities per acre as the worldly farmers but manage to do this by using only 200 pounds of fertilizer instead of the 800 pounds his worldly counterpart applies. Many church districts categorically reject newfangled chemistry, genetic engineering, and biotechnology as ecologically irresponsible agriculture. Subsidies by the state are taboo since "not the government but the cow that gives milk shall support the farmer."

Whatever the land produces is not used for the accumulation of wealth nor to buy luxury articles nor to go on trips. The churches take great care to prevent members from becoming *zu gross* (too big). They despise the frenzy for *Geld zmache* (making money), the typical American way of driving for success with blinders on. An Amish person is to buy nothing for self that is not absolutely necessary. Today the Amish are no longer as completely self-sufficient as in the hiding places of Europe, where they grew or made practically everything they needed. However, if need be, they could do it again.

Buying and selling, for instance at the great horse auctions, is an occasion when the Amishman comes closest to the world and the worldly. However, huge contracts, credit cards, and signatures under oath are nothing for him. Business is closed by "I, John Graber, herewith confirm that my yes means yes" and sealed by a handshake. He buys what he does not manage to produce himself, and he sells what he has extra. Any profits realized stay in the family, except for their giving through the church to help those in

353

need. At this point the Amish part ways with the Hutterites, who believe that *ein Reicher* (a rich man) can attain heaven only with great difficulty since it is repulsive to the Savior for people to possess an excess of earthly goods. The Amish *Kleinkapitalisten* (small capitalists) generally have more compassion for the human aspect in Christ. They believe the thorn in God's eye is not so much the rich as those whose hearts are committed to riches. Whoever has been chosen by God to give, must first have something in order to distribute.

Up to World War I, the farmers in Allen County, whether worldly or Amish, still had practically equal chances. In the ensuing decades, complex machines replaced horse power among the one group. For the Amish, that new source of energy was counter to nature. Working with the latest machines was unspiritual and therefore not permitted. Amish farming started becoming different from their worldly neighbors, or better said, the Amish stayed mostly as they were while their neighbors changed. Since then, the Amish struggle with the problem of how best to make their farms more productive without destroying God's creation and without surrendering their own style of life. The motto of *Martyrs Mirror*, "Pray and work," does not always help.

Individual groups among the Amish do accept selected technical innovations on account of economic pressures. But in general, the congregations live by the concept that the more modern an Amish becomes, the more he will depart from the simple way of the life of Christ. "*De Traktor zieht di aus dem Paradies* (the tractor pulls you out of paradise)," the Amish of Allen County say of those who change. The same holds true of automatic milking machines, even though Amish users generate the needed electricity on the farm. One might think that Anabaptists who milk automatically or use tractors realize higher incomes, and therefore their youth could remain on the farm more easily than those of the very conservative. Yet actual experience shows that the most conservative Amish milk by hand and are more likely to make a living from the farming. Machinery tends to beget more machinery and may ween youth away from as much direct contact with earth and animals. It is also obvious that the overhead cost of technology has overwhelmed some worldly farming operations.

Highly technological worldly competition with its rapidly

growing industrial economy is of greater concern to the Amish than ever before. Sometimes the modern neighboring farmer has his harvest in the bin prior to the heavy rains while the Amish with his horses is left to trust in God. Yet, the old ways have positive sides to them which one must learn to observe. In a wet fall, the Amish who husk corn by hand can get the crop in earlier than those who have to wait for freeze-up to use tractors and pickers. In the spring, farmers with horses can work the land earlier than those with huge tractors and machinery that would pack the wet ground or even get stuck in the mud. The plain folks use horses and know it takes longer to do the field work, so they plan for that and start early. Sometimes those using big equipment wait to start an operation because they know they can do it fast, but a change in the weather may catch them because of that delay.

The Amish have no radios or TV and do not listen to weather forecasts. Elam claims they are never plagued by excessive fear of bad forecasts which may later turn out to be false. Yet they do not completely ignore worldly knowledge. There are scientific reasons why chickens since 1935 lay eggs throughout the year even on Amish farms, something unthinkable for oldsters of yesteryear. Or that one cow produced 925 gallons of milk in 1900, but now one produces an average of about 3,000 gallons a year, and high performers even produce over 5,000 gallons. As for worldly medicine, any farmer in Lancaster County knows what it can do and what it means. It is well-known and documented what havoc tuberculosis inflicted upon Amish herds between 1915 and 1936.

The Amish are allowed to work at many trades under certain conditions, if such work has a clear connection to Amish life, such as blacksmiths, cabinetmakers, apiarists, wagon-builders, or millers. Approximately half of all Amish are pure farmers. For the more than 3,500 Amish who live around Arthur, Illinois, the past thirty years have been a transition period with many changes in their lifestyle. No longer able to buy land and expand in farming due to ever-rising land prices, the Amish moved into crafts and woodworking. Today close to 160 rural businesses are owned and operated by Amish families on their own homesteads, most using no electricity. Among their products are handmade cabinets and furniture, quilts, harnesses, buggies, homemade jams, jellies, candies, and baked goods.

The Amish see no contradiction in a member farming and raising horses for the racetracks of the world in order to achieve a higher income. In Allen County, Amish have built roads and railroad tracks. Their wives do needlework from old patterns, as in the famous quilts and bright patchwork throws, marketed even in Europe. A specialty has recently opened up for handymen or inventive sorts to supply repair parts for old, horse-drawn farm machines. Without these repairmen, the typical Amish life is unthinkable. Hence, some brothers specialize in manufacturing parts and remodeling old machines which the world has long since forgotten.

Conservative Amish cannot be found working in industrial complexes with work gangs, where the individual risks dissolution of his faith. Also, they are not found in general working conditions that would tend to make them into human wares or cogs in a machine. A parental couple like John and Lilian Graber would stop at nothing to provide an economic starting base for their children so that they would never have to earn their bread in a worldly place of employment. Economic stability is the only thing guaranteeing that the youth would have a future on the farm and thus in the church community of the Amish.

The Amish pay taxes like any other American but make no payments to social security, since they reject all forms of insurance. The state is not to bear any responsibility for the Amish families, and on the Amish farms they work hard so that they will never need assistance from the state. One problem exists in Allen County: a sizable number of Amish operate businesses in addition to their flourishing farms. In these operations, they almost exclusively employ Amish, which amounts to discrimination in the workplace. Yet these Amish technically are not employees but instead are all independents, classed as self-employed, who do not have to pay any deductions to the state. Consequently, there also are no payments for accident insurance. If something happens to a worker on the job, the Amish church assumes full responsibility for the employee. Amish do not belong to unions and, according to John, are capable of working considerably harder than their worldly competitors.

Those of Allen County are, nevertheless, competent businesspeople. In their place of employment, they tend to outperform their neighbors, probably a German trait not lost in the long historical process. In addition, they have a Christian perspective from Jesus: "Behold, I send you forth as sheep among the wolves; therefore be wise as serpents and harmless as doves" (Matt. 10:16). Amish are prohibited from entering a partnership of any kind with the worldly, according to the word of Paul: "Be not unequally yoked together with unbelievers: for what fellowship has righteousness with unrighteousness? and what communion has light with darkness?" (2 Cor. 6:14). This does not mean, however, that they do not engage in arm's-length business dealings with the world or its organizations and institutions.

Among the Anabaptists of Allen County are quite a number of persons blessed both in spiritual as well as earthly terms and who could be classified as wealthy. As a rule of thumb, the bigger the manure pile, the richer its owner. In principle, the Amish always intend to communicate the impression that they follow the apostles, whom Jesus admonished to be poor when he sent them out (Matt. 10). Whoever is wealthy on Cuba Road does not show it, for self-display and self-praise in these parts stinks more than anywhere else. Any Amish who would seem to puff themselves up would in the sight of their brothers and sisters shrivel just as much.

Another matter important is to survive in the right faith by "bending to those of little station" rather than setting one's sights on riches. Thus John's father, a servant of the Word (preacher), not only has his farm but also owns, together with his sons, a sawmill with an annual turnover of approximately one million dollars. However, there is no sign near his house which points out the sawmill. Instead, at the entrance to his office is a motto inscribed in huge letters on the floor: *BETE TÄGLICH* (Pray daily).

Amish people like John and Lilian Graber see no reason to take it easy for once, drop out of a life of work for a while, and vacation with wife and child but without horse and buggy. They would rather *hi sitze* (just sit here), as the plain folks of Allen County say, or *hi hocke* (just squat here), as those in Pennsylvania would say. A farm needs its man every day of the year, while tourism is worldly and costs money. However, now there are some exceptions; otherwise it would not be Amish. In some churches, the secret word *Florida* is now circulating. The bishops are opposed to it, as are the preachers and the servants of the poor (deacons). The parents forbid the tainted fruit of southern travel, and the teachers warn about it.

Even so, in the area around Sarasota, an Amish church has been founded, a mediating solution between the church districts of the north and the worldly world. There are no buggies in this district since they live on the edge of a great city which cannot tolerate the trot of horses. Where one expects trotters and buggies, the Amish coast about on bicycles and adult-sized tricycles, to which are attached yellow warning signs that give testimony to conscientious conduct in traffic. Once in a while the plain folks put a little extra weight to the pedal to get there more quickly and take a better look at the Gulf of Mexico located hard by. There they go fishing with friends, play checkers and shuffleboard, or exchange their pilgrim smocks for a modest bathing suit. In Florida, the Amish develop new hobbies. One Levi Miller grows plants which he calls "Moses in the reeds." Some sweep streets or renovate gray-with-age houses for a minimal fee.

Florida has become their destination for winter trips just as for the worldly. In high season some 1,500 Amish travel annually to follow the sun. There they rent a modest house for little money, and since they are vacationing, they are even prepared to put up with electric light and a water toilet. For a proper church service, Bishop Swartzentruber assembles the holidaying Amish in a meetinghouse since the rented apartments are too small for the purpose.

Wherever the Anabaptist tourists congregate, one can quickly find streets named Stoltzfus, Wagler, or even Graber. The houses lining the streets display mailboxes bearing typical Emmental-Anabaptist names. Soon automobiles have a way of sneaking into their garages. The warm southern breeze disperses the draft from the cold north, sets the scene for dolce far niente (sweet doing nothing, pleasant relaxation) in territory not securely Amish, and changes not only the weather but also relaxes the church rules for some. Amish fall like overripe apples, . . . and this is why John and Lilian, Elam and Rachel, and Joseph and Rosanna all their lives will have to make do without Florida.

******

358

The day is beautiful, but the nights are occasionally rent with questions, puzzles about that stage in life when "colt becomes stallion," boys become men, and girls become women. The Amish youths, too, have their moments of straining at the code. There are great tensions between the desire to live one's own way and the pull of obedience to Christian faith as defined by church and parents. On such occasions, God is willing to take the chance of allowing free choice. Sometimes God does so in a way that makes those of Allen County regard him as a spoilsport.

It is a Sunday afternoon south of Grabill, shortly after the church service. A highly polished buggy carries three schoolgirl beauties in thoroughly proper attire down the straight and narrow part of Graber Road. The horse has thrown back its head, the girls on the buckboard sit chastely, hiding legs and hair. Instead of wearing black leather shoes, the traditional match for their old form of dress, they wear the popular sneakers of the world.

What really surprises even the horse, however, is the accompanying music: not the click or clack of a teenager's tongue with the slap of the reins, nor a primeval sound in Bernese German, nor the snap of a whip. Under the seat of the buggy, the girls have hidden a radio, broadcasting "satanic" messages in full volume, rock music from the hit charts of the late 1970s. Rock music, of all things, which relates to Anabaptism as the Lorelei to Rhine sailors, or a billy goat to gardens, or Dracula to hemophiliacs! Music not *for* the Lord is *against* the Lord.

Under their skirts the teenagers tap their feet to the rhythm and react to it in the same carefree style of other girls their age. Yet they cannot afford to get caught. There is agreement in the pack, and horses don't talk. The girls surely are unbaptized, and these are chapters in the book of life during which all people make mistakes, even though they have not the slightest doubt about good and evil. The church has no direct control or authority over the unbaptized, and so it is up to the father to lay down the law, that *"der Saton stork, aber Gott nuch stärker isch* (Satan is strong, but God is much stronger)."

Even in a community in which God is particularly strong, generational conflicts surface and the world's attacks sometimes leave scars. The Amish way of life is shaped and formed by morals and the gospel. Their rigorism is never above criticism from their own, particularly the unbaptized youth. The most serious competition Jakob Ammann faces are the revival evangelists who sprout everywhere in the fertile soil of North American fervor. The Amish servants of the Word not infrequently have to remind their people that things happen in the body of Christ which dishonor the Lord.

The main conduct problem is one which the Anabaptist group has had to face ever since its founding and which they have contested in written form: *"dass d'Buwe mit d'Menscher in die Better gehn* (that the boys go to bed with girls before they are married)." "Oh, what terrible sin it is if possibly mothers even help to make such a bed!" How often do the Amish have to be reminded that "adulterous cohabitation is whoring" and will be punished as prophesied in the books of Samuel (1 Sam. 2—4)? Alcohol consumption of some of the young set also causes much grief to penitent hearts. Also, cause for heaviness of heart is some teenagers' "desire to please," going along "with the pride of the world" for a few hours by stroking their eyelids, rouging their lips, or applying a few drops of eau de cologne with the brand name Making Love.

In remote places one can detect an Amish boy behind the wheel of a car. Somewhere, far removed from their own past, in a place for bad experiments, one might witness young Amish entering a disco or smoking pot. Buggies in the Shipshewana area sometimes have suspiciously thin whip rods which double as antennas for battery-powered stereos or even TV sets. Some of the young people allow themselves to become religiously warped. However, these episodes are exceptions to the rule, variations on religious cravings. They demonstrate that children of believing parents, even in Allen County, do not automatically remain at Jakob Ammann's side.

No doubt, not all parents stand firm either, and "when the fathers eat sour grapes, the children's teeth are set on edge" (Jer. 31:29). The Amish are not perfect people even if the outside world expects such of them. For some of them, the pressure of being good is simply much too great. There are cases where the effort to be holy has caused not only spiritual damage but even mental breakdowns. On the other hand, some Amish attempt to leave the group to find their own niche of holiness in order to be more perfect than the perfect. There can be no doubt that it is a heavy burden on the brothers and sisters to be as good as Christ.

This is most certainly true for the young people now growing up more educated than in the past. On their own they can read and interpret the demands of the gospel as well as its promises. How do you explain to a sixteen-year-old boy that humility is still the most beautiful of all virtues? That he is supposed to keep himself outwardly and inwardly "humble at all times," since everything elevated among others is an abomination unto the Lord? No doubt they believe in God, but they think God does not yet believe in them.

True humility becomes the stance of poverty for the Anabaptists on earth. Yet these maturing youth are regarded as quite mature when it comes to putting their shoulder to the wheel in manual labor. Caught between humility and self-respect, they look for their place in the scheme of things and may rebel now and then. This is particularly true for the weekends, during which one or the other likes to live like one of the worldly. For that he simply has no time during the week. Thus an Amish youth may find a stroll through the city of Fort Wayne to be particularly attractive. He can look at television sets in display windows and watch sports on TV through a separating pane of glass. This is a break for Amish ready to kick up their heels.

Some even leave the church if the last sparks of an Amish conscience have been extinguished in them and they can no longer be controlled by their families and tradition. "The ways of the world are about to become the ways of our youth, and that is regrettable. Young people meet lusting men who have long hair and drugs and want others to imitate them. . . ." So Joseph of Cuba Road comments on the topic. Other teenagers have already decided to remain faithful to the Amish church. Some of these, ironically, may briefly go over the barricades. Baptism represents not only one of the main steps between birth and death but also a framework of restrictions in the adult life of an Amish individual. Just prior to their baptismal pledges, some may try out selections from the catalog of sin for the last time. One really does not quite know how good Christians will react to good challenges.

Four young Amish from the vicinity of Canton in Minnesota broke into a farmhouse in the mood described above, not in order to steal but to watch a football game on television. These four were the first Amish to have a brush with worldly law, aside from all the usual wrangling about traffic safety. Curiously enough, the church had no opposition to the sentencing of the four by a worldly judge. Close to the vine invariably also grow weeds, and the Amish know this. However, the servants of the Word did request that during their incarceration the boys be prohibited from watching television and that they be spared wearing the red prison garb, since red is the color of the spilled blood of Christ. The saying, "Amish always go to church but never to jail," no longer applies, at least not in the state of Minnesota.

Yet the young represent Amish survival. The old know full well that in the search for paradise, a completely isolated life is as unhelpful as calm seas in producing good sailors. Girls and boys, therefore, receive a certain degree of independence in order to prepare themselves for the most decisive question of their lives, to be baptized or not. Amish parents are occasionally prepared to go easy on the inability of the young to recognize the cross and suffering as the only lesson in life. They will let the teens engage in a bit of precarious fence-sitting between the farm and the world.

For entertainment, the Amish youth of Allen County do not have to go to Fort Wayne, the nearby city with back doors and trapdoors, where they could listen to yodeling by the Alpen Echo band or pay to watch flesh at one striptease joint or another. Within the limits of their modest way, youths of the Amish celebrate in their own parties, with up to 400 young people assembled in some remote bower. Word quickly spreads in Allen County when a get-together is in the wind. This may mean that some teens dance in an isolated barn with the innocent charm of their early years, or that a group of Amish girls gets together, or that somewhere rock and country music with Alpine yodelers can be heard. On such occasions the boys brush their hats, spruce up their buggies, and away they go, with the sixteen-year-olds in the slipstream of the seventeen-year-olds, and these in the slipstream of the eighteen-year-olds. Not far behind are immaculately dressed girls, but without ornamentation.

In Allen County four gangs of Amish youngsters meet regularly as individual groups or all together. They have names like Wild Turkeys, the Feathers, or the Hermanns. Elam's son Chris belongs to a group that counts some 200 boys and girls who like music, like to listen to the radio, and probably even own some musical instruments without going crazy from indulging their interest. If there is one item in the Amish system which Chris would like to change, it would be to tolerate some worldly music. He claims that anyone who works hard has little spare time to learn any instrument hidden somewhere, and therefore such a venture would remain amateurish. An Amish musician is condemned to remaining an undiscovered talent all his life long.

I try to get invited to the youthful party à la Allen County, only in the friendly spectator spirit, naturally, and just to have been there. Chris is quite prepared to take me, but his group refuses because they fear that I might be a "spy" after all. Once again, I detect a hint of unhealed wounds of Old Europe: the spy. But then again, possibly they suspected that I was an agent of their parents.

Whenever a son or a daughter goes on a rampage and their lifestyle threatens to become ruinous, an Amish father is perfectly capable of becoming a tyrant, and a petty one at that. Among the Amish, power comes from the father, and he will use that power of authority and punish as long as the candle flickers to promise improvement. Fathers have Scripture on their side when they issue rebuke to inspire obedience (Proverbs 19:18). "*Du bleibsch dütsch* (you stay German)!" which means "Behave yourself, or else. . . ." Do not become *englisch*, for what they are up to is no good. The heavenly Father will find you and find you out. The form of the vessels may vary, but the content always has to remain the gospel.

This generally keeps a teenager in the *Ordnung* (church order), so that faith will look farther than the temptations from outside. Sometimes it also goes beyond reason, for in general terms, the Amish youth is much better prepared, religiously tamed, and regulated to be Amish than to become worldly. A young Amish chap who makes his home on Highway 515 close to Walnut Creek, Ohio, once told me about receiving a sturdy lesson. For weeks afterward, he was convinced during every thunderstorm that the very earth would open up before him and the destructive rage of the Lord would devour him.

Yet Amish methods of rearing do not always work. This can be demonstrated in the case of John Dillinger, that infamous gangster in the Midwest of the USA in the twenties and thirties. John was not Amish, but his father grew up with his adoptive Amish

363

parents, the Troyers from Holmes County, Ohio. Dillinger's father left the Amish at age eighteen. He had obviously not learned much, at least not much which he managed to transfer to his son.

Darvin Ray Peachey is another example of persons of Amish heritage turning worldly. According to the Associated Press, on one 1992 night of terror in the Amish country of Belleville (Pa.), 23-year-old Peachey set fire to six Amish barns in 90 minutes. He caused one million dollars worth of damage and killed 181 head of livestock. After he was caught, he admitted his part in the burning rampage, using a propane torch, but told the judge that he couldn't explain why he did it. Though his grandfather is an Amish bishop, Darvin himself is not Amish, and his father spent three months in jail for burning an Amish barn. The proposed plea bargain for Darvin includes the requirement that he make restitution. The Amish farmers quickly rebuilt and restocked their barns with widely contributed support. They threatened no lawsuits and only asked that Peachey write letters to editors of local newspapers, apologizing for his fiery deeds.

******

Amish school plays an important role in protecting the Amish from the threatening enticements of the world. Here the children are trained first for heaven and then for an adult life on the farm. The parents and teachers truly believe that "the fear of the Lord is the beginning of knowledge" (Prov. 1:7). On the other hand, "worldly wisdom makes proud, like the antichrist" (1 Cor. 2). The most prominent subjects are reading, writing, and arithmetic, offering basic tools for everyday use. The school is better for preparing a simple Amish life than for training according to a worldly model, "which has scientific explanations for more things than it ought to have" and is regarded by the plain folks as a sidetrack from Anabaptist ideals.

In former times the rising generation of the Amish mainly attended public schools, but their own small schools began to appear in the 1930s. Generally these Amish schools have only one room and one teacher for all classes, just like the rural schools of the USA in former times, which emphasized oral instruction, example, discipline, and basic skills. The Amish loved this kind of instruction since it corresponded with the local and family character of their church. In the 1930s, however, the state gradually closed all rural schools, sending pupils to larger, consolidated schools and teaching them anti-Anabaptist material like sports, music, and natural sciences. In addition, the Amish did not agree with the school year being extended and interfering with busy farm seasons.

Public schools became a thorn in the Amish eye since they taught too much worldly material such as theories on the origin of humans and unwomanly gymnastics. The longer school year meant less time spent helping on the farm. More school attendance meant learning things which an Amish person would not need during a whole lifetime. However, not all Amish can afford to send their numerous children to Anabaptist private schools. The public schools are supported by tax dollars which the Amish pay even when they also foot the bill for their own schools.

There are three schools owned by the Amish in Allen County today, including the one built in 1957 on Cuba Road in which John Zehr instructs. Here he chased me around the bush of Galatians. Some 200 pupils attend school, and therefore the one-room format is not adequate. There are now four units, meaning that grades one and two are instructed together, as are grades three and four, and so on. John's classroom has forty-four pupils. Parents pay $15 per child or $40 for an entire family per month. A school board keeps watch over teachers and pupils. This school board does the secretarial jobs as well as functioning as "tax collectors" or cleaning personnel. Their work is voluntary, but the teacher gets paid. School administration, teaching personnel, and parents discuss school problems together, such as whether two pupils of opposite sex are allowed to sing out of the same songbook, and what could or should be said all day long in German or in English.

A man like John, brainy and bright, instructs everything as outlined in the teaching guide for the seventh and eighth grades. When he is not teaching, John is busy constructing wheel spokes and wheels for Amish buggies or out at farms castrating horses. In winter he fires up the giant *Hitzer* (woodstove made in Fort Wayne), and in summer he cuts the grass on the schoolyard with horses and mower. For a long time I have regarded John as a thorough scribe who has managed to outwit the Amish motto "By learning hook-ed, makes you crooked." The suspicion toward higher education seems no longer to be as great as it formerly was. John has no special training for his teaching profession, and like Elam, Tobi, or Rachel, he has to rely on his eight years of basic schooling.

Tietscher or schoolmaster is a profession attained among the Amish if the church in question approaches you to teach and you answer yes. Most of the teachers around John are young Amish women, not yet married. A mother cannot be a teacher since her place is by the kitchen stove and her family, not in a profession outside her home. By now the language of instruction is English, while German is spoken on certain days—in John's classroom on Wednesdays—or whenever religious themes are to be discussed or certain songs sung. This includes the school song, sung to the melody, "*Ach Herzensgeliebte!* (Oh, love of my heart!)"

> We come to the school, by parents' decree.
> They give their support and pay for the fee,
> To hone our five senses, to seize all things good,
> To shun all things evil, flee sins as we should.

The teaching material is selected by the Amish themselves. If it comes from outside, they black out certain passages to which they object. For some subjects they have purchased the printing plates of old textbooks from days gone by, when the air was cleaner, sex was dirtier, and there was no new technology like television. As a result, arithmetic comes to a stop in 1940 when eggs still cost a few cents a dozen. Generally, the Amish prefer lessons from the practical world to "book learning." Instruction in German is an exception. Then such books as *Let's Learn German* and *Let's Read German* take over as well as *Das Neue Testament* and Johanna Spyri's *Heidi*. To learn to read Luther's German Bible is of particular importance. Other edifying literature in the German language is printed by their own Amish publisher. As well, always at the ready is the *Ausbund*, blessed with hymns of many verses.

Of course, John is also a German teacher although his *Dütsch* is regarded as slightly too *schwyzerisch* (Swiss) even by the standards of the Amish church. Gaps exist between it and High German, and therefore it is not always in line with that standard. This is not necessarily a disadvantage. In Allen County, everyone claims to prefer to *schwyzerschwätze* (chatter in Swiss German), a relaxed form of Bernese German. To the Amish, their dialect is synonymous with being different and is therefore welcome. This is the language of the child before making contact with the world and before learning High German in church services and some school instruction. It is dialect as mother tongue, as gratitude spoken to the ancestors who have preserved their faith and brought their religious group into a country which offers them religious freedom to this day.

The Amish spare no effort in trying to maintain this linguistic inheritance. Anyone here who can also speak High German, in addition to a rather pedantic form of English, is awarded a bonus. However, their skill in the German language has suffered considerably because of *Dütsch* (the dialect) and English. It thus is a dying part of their tradition. Hardly one Amish person in Allen County has a sound command of written German. It was inevitable that, at least once during my "school days" in John's classroom, my German would collide with his *Dütsch*. Along the way, there were already several minor accidents in this direction. That day the teacher positions himself in front of the class and states, "Now we shall ask the German what *rüschte* (to arm, prepare, get ready) means."

"*Rüschten, rüsten, Rüstung. . . .*" I name the example of the military of a country arming itself.

John, the pacifist incarnate, is beside himself. This is too much, an attempted murder of his mother tongue. The German Bible states how the church of God is to prepare—or arm—itself for the kingdom of heaven, and I, as the *Doktor der Schrift*, am implying that in the preparation thereof, it is arming itself with physical weapons. "*Rüschte,*" so says John with pitying eyes directed at me, "means preparing yourself, getting ready for heaven." At the same time one is preparing for the second coming of Christ.

A second collision follows soon afterward on account of the word *Schnur* (a piece of yarn; also, a daughter-in-law). As with the Hutterites, the term *Schnur* among the Amish means a daughter-in-law, and this they have on biblical authority. If the Germans today use a different term for it, then they no longer speak the language of Luther. "*Nebehocker* (side-squatter)?" This is no more and no less than a person who functions as a witness to an Amish wedding. By now John no longer believes in the *Dütschen* in the German me, and his opinion is probably shared by most of those in grades 7 and 8 in the Amish school on Cuba Road.

A day like this in Allen County starts with the children marching in. They have arrived in large groups with sizable lunches under their arms. During inclement weather, they sometimes come by cutter or sleigh. In any case, parents and teachers see to it that the young set is properly dressed. Short pants or T-shirts are not permitted, but the American sneaker craze has managed to infiltrate their ranks. Pupils wear subdued colors, brown, blue, black, or gray. Some of the boys have the collars of their jackets turned up rather nonchalantly. In contrast to Sunday jerkins, school jackets have collars. Every boy wears a hat. The girls wear their school dress, called *Scharz* (probably an abbreviated form of *Schürze*, meaning apron). Aside from this, the genders resemble each other, particularly in their hairstyle. The boys look as if an oval pot has been placed on their heads and whatever hung out was cut off. The girls have bundled their hair tidily, parted it in the center, and finished off the hairdo by placing a comely bonnet on it.

The school building is small and rather inconspicuous. It is built to capture as much light as possible so that they can make do without electricity. *Hislis* serve as outdoor toilets. From their arrival at the school until the start of instruction, the pupils like to spend their time playing Ping-Pong, girls against boys, without the game becoming seriously competitive, in which case it would be poor schooling for the teenagers becoming adults. The teacher as always is dressed in somber black and white. When he enters, he extends a greeting, "*Guten Morgen, Jungen und Mädchen* (good morning, boys and girls)." The class answers with, "*Guten Morgen, John.*" They are all on a familiar first-name basis.

Now follows a prayer and then a school song, such as

> We come to the school, arrive happily,
> Each other to help, to keep company.
> We follow the teacher, to please him we try,
> Since we're at his heart, on him we rely.

Then the teacher reads from the Old or the New Testament. Next comes other instruction: the seventh grade begins with arithmetic, while the eighth grade starts reading, or vice versa. The younger children thereby learn from the older, while the older ones listen once again to what they took the year before. Also, they learn how to get along with each other, which in this setting is just as important as the simple reading, arithmetic, or writing. Instruction in writing is becoming more important since the Amish are not allowed telephones. When doing business with the world, they depend largely on correspondence.

During the first two hours, John occupies himself mostly with the eighth grade, and then a short recess follows. After that, it's the turn of the seventh grade. In between, he once addresses both at the same time, practicing spelling. He calls out a word to the right or the left, depending on the skills of the two classes. On the schedule before the lunch break, both age-groups practice a bit of science, using a practical lesson involving the multiplication table in terms of humanity, in this case, their own Amish population.

Whatever John instructs invariably ends on the farm right in the center of Amish life. When teaching arithmetic, he has the pupils add hay bales to hay bales, or multiply glasses of preserves put up in a day times days of canning, or he has them add milk cans to more milk cans. The pupils subtract hourly wages from the value of amounts harvested and arrive at the conclusion: better effort on the farm amounts to greater profits. When they one day retire from farming, their land and buildings should be in a better condition than when they took over.

Then the hour of science strikes. John asks whether it is possible to make a solution of sand and water, whether weeds harm the soil, and why rotation of crops is so important. With quiet discipline, the children volunteer to answer by raising their hands. Sometimes to egg them on, John plays a role of despair: "What? We intend to be good farmers and don't even know how to properly cultivate the land or add hay bales to hay bales?"

John has no use for foul play. In school also, the Amish conduct themselves in keeping with the biblical standard: "As many as I love, I rebuke and chasten" (Rev. 3:19). Barbara Ann is punished by having to change her seat although she absolutely insists she has not disturbed class instruction. A young fellow has to stand in the corner with a wad of gum on his nose because he chewed during schooltime. Once in a while, the seat of the pants or a skirt gets a good dusting. News of such discipline spreads rapidly around Allen County since it is dreadfully embarrassing for both pupils and parents. In an Amish class, there are no disturbing or disturbed children, and not only because a visitor from the world is present. This is in dramatic contrast to many public schools.

John also speaks about AIDS (*acquired immunodeficiency syndrome*), the fact that today illicit sexual relations can bring death. Naturally, he handles the problem as if it were a purely worldly one, a result of dissolute living out there. But he does speak about it, and the children know what he is talking about. As John holds forth, he explains, he gesticulates, but he never invents. When the upright schoolmaster gives the pupils assignments which have to be answered in writing, he has each pupil correct the work of another after passing one's answers to the child sitting behind. John admits that in so doing he has to supervise a bit. Yet this practice is both rational and educational.

The first recess is at 10:00 a.m. The pupils again play table tennis and other games such as round the clock, or bear: one is the bear, and the others try to catch him. One can see how the school system prepares Amish children for life: whether in the classroom or on the schoolyard, a pupil is never to be alone but always part of a group structure, thereby cultivating a spirit of community. When Elam's daughter, Barbara Ann, has a birthday, she brings along a little something for each member of her class, not the other way around. A granddaddy walks in and unloads homemade goodies for the noon meal, and another supplies things American, like hot dogs or burgers. All in all, the interest displayed by the adults in the school is considerable. Parents simply walk into the classroom unannounced, if for nothing else than to demonstrate how important school instruction is to them. They come to help the teacher if he requests it, and they vote him out of office if he introduces some piece of wrong material into the curriculum.

School lessons stop at 11:30, when it's time to wash hands, say grace, and eat. To prevent them from wolfing down their lunch, eating is to take at least ten minutes. At the stroke of 12:30, school starts again until about 3:30. They have longer holidays when field work interrupts the joy of school, and school-free days are given when warranted by a special occasion. The high point of a school year is the annual picnic.

Children of the Amish attend school for eight years and not a day longer since they believe that the tree of knowledge far too often soaks up the water of disappointment. By their fifteenth birthday, Amish children are to learn the basic school subjects needed for life. Higher education is regarded as totally superfluous. This leads to the world's charge that the Amish deliberately want to keep their community on a low educational level since higher educated young would be more difficult for them to discipline. There is some truth to this claim. Gideon Fisher from Intercourse (Pa.) admits that people who know more simply do not want to be farmers in the style of the plain folks.

In some states, Amish parents have gone to prison because they categorically refused to send their children to school any longer than eight grades lest they become "too educated." When summoned to court, they did not appear because these Amish did not recognize worldly judges. Preacher Joseph and his wife Rosanna were once sentenced to imprisonment for a totally different reason: they refused to send their daughter Barbara to school because after physical education class, the students had to take showers together, boys with boys and girls with girls, of course. But "exposing one's shame" went too far (as Exodus 32:25 states) and did not correspond to Amish ideas about body hygiene.

For several decades a quarrel raged in some states regarding how many years of schooling were required for the Amish. Eventually America realized that fifteen-year-old Amish children learned proper farming, and this was equivalent to a school education. This does not mean that the Amish took the initiative in this matter. In 1967, one William Ball, an attorney from Pennsylvania, and the Lutheran pastor William D. Lindholm from Michigan became aware that the Amish were having problems with the officials in Iowa with regard to their schools. At the University of Chicago, some interested parties founded a Committee for Amish Religious Freedom, which became involved in the Wisconsin case of "the State versus Yoder."

Various courts deliberated on the fact that these Yoders no longer sent their fifteen- and sixteen-year-olds to school, and finally the case was taken to the Supreme Court in 1972. There the justices decided that the practice of religious freedom was a higher right than mandatory school attendance. This also was an important mix in the basic political conflicts of the time, when white parents resented sending their children to racially mixed schools. America's highest judge, Warren Burger, recognized that the young Amish in their schools were being prepared for a good life even if not an intellectual one. They were trained for wisdom instead of technological education, for care instead of competition, for separation instead of intermingling with the world. Yet Justice Burger left no doubt that he was concerned about the children who might one day leave the Amish community, whether their education would prepare them to cope with life on the outside.

The court made it clear from the outset that this judgment pertained only for a sect as old as the Amish and excluded new sectarians. This did not mean unequivocally that the Amish would be permitted to resolve their own school questions from then on. Again in 1978, new difficulties cropped up when in Nebraska the state tried to prescribe a high school education for Amish teachers. However, before this new dispute came to the Supreme Court, the Amish families in question had migrated to other states in 1982.

The Amish school system is successful and in the earlier grades even excellent. This is true if one applies the gauge that these plain people intend to rear their children "only" to become good human beings and good workers according to their own Amish self-understanding. The system produces geniuses and catastrophes, but if a pupil on the Cuba Road does not make it with his head, then the community accepts his hands, his ability to work. On the farms around Lancaster, they have a handy excuse in Pennsylvania-German for such persons: "It's not that he can't learn, it's just that he forgets too soon." Intelligence is not something the Amish praise, and stupidity is not something the Amish scold, for both are of God. Knowledge is not something to show off. Anyone who knows the Bible is highly regarded. But anyone who knows it and learnedly quotes from it, is regarded as a *Stolzer* (a proud one). New knowledge is generally rejected since these conservative Anabaptists base their thinking on the fact that everything intelligent has already been thought of.

The Amish school cannot accommodate exceptional "head knowledge." In the Grabill area, there are more than enough pupils who do not understand the Luther Bible of their family tradition and instead read the English of the King James Version. A recently ordained preacher in Indiana did not know any German at all, and so he had to take a crash course in it. Some Amish have problems with the English as well as with the German language; in later years they may notice that they have been using some words wrongly all their life.

The Amish have general knowledge of the outside world, but I did find an exceptional case: a successful and upright farmer beat his thighs black and blue when I explained the difference between Martin Luther and Dr. Martin Luther King. He found it hard to believe that a difference existed between the two. Occasionally an Amish person's Bible beliefs stand in the way of accepting information gained through science. Thus, for example, one time I was unable to convince a servant of the poor (deacon) that our earth is round. He always held to the opinion that it is square, because indeed it stands written in the Bible that "all the ends of the earth shall see the salvation of our God" (Isa. 52:10). Whatever has ends, cannot be round!

In their schools the Amish have no religious instruction as a separate subject. Yet here everything is geared to transmit to the children a secure knowledge and sensitivity for the faith. The parents have first responsibility to nurture a feeling for things Amish and to provide Bible teaching and the necessary guard against false doctrines. In the Amish child, one recognizes the father and the mother. The parental home is a safe place for a child to learn to swim without fear of sinking. Here is laid the foundation for what shall one day shine in their church.

As long as the child is as pliable as a blade of grass, the family life provides the setting for that child learning to enter into the childhood of the parents. In the young child, parents seek to develop religion, the golden rule of humility and being good. This for the child is much like a feeling of love or sorrow, a spiritual stirring, instinctive. As the child grows into an age of knowledge, some doctrinal teaching is mixed in. Only thus can the individual always assure oneself of one's own identity. The inner dialogue between religion and being Amish is in fact only concluded at death, when people are totally muted who have never been heard in the worldly theater.

******

Between Christmas and Three Kings' Day (Jan. 6), the Amish in Old Europe experienced windy, raw nights proclaiming blessings or woe. Now in the New World, they listen to the wintry rigid land, observe weather, wind, and blowing snow in order to compare all of these with their farmers' maxims. Last autumn the "woolly worm" had been black. For the Amish of Allen County, this means that the winter will be long and cold. They can only find this worm for a few days late in the year. The previous year it was black at the head and the tail but brown in the middle. This meant a cold winter at the beginning and the end, but milder weather in between. The Amish go by this, and I cannot hold it against them.

However, if this winter were merely cold, it would be the greatest understatement since Noah looked out of his ark and proclaimed, "It's raining." The frost penetrated the ground for more than a yard. In short succession five and then six inches of snow fell, and the wind blew constantly, making a white desert out of all of Allen County. The land froze, hoarfrost covered the yards along Cuba Road, trees covered by hundreds of pounds of ice fell crashing to the ground, barn roofs caved in. A cow which had become wet quickly turned into a block of ice. The barometer dropped, then dropped some more, and it turned so bitterly cold that somewhere a buggy horse with frozen nostrils dropped and died.

The brothers and sisters know that when it's colder than minus 13 degrees Fahrenheit (-25 Celsius), they need to protect the lungs of horses by not asking great exertion of them. But the Lord who threatened them with the cold also saw to it that horses survived the cold. All of Allen County now resembled an area which the loving Father had created for polar bears and not for the open buggies of the faithful.

The Amish celebrate Christmas—the "great joy"—without St. Nick, Santa Claus, or a Christmas tree, but with "Jingle Bells" and *Stille Nacht* (Silent night)." They exchange small presents, but it would be un-Amish to display much pleasure when receiving them. On Christmas Day attention is drawn to the birth of our

Lord, to his return, and also to the fact that according to the old (Julian) calendar, the birthday of Jesus was actually on January 6, which should be celebrated as the oldest Christian festival. However, those of Allen County have become used to the December 25 event of the Gregorian calendar. In other churches, as for instance some of those in Wisconsin, they prefer to play safe and celebrate on both days. No one is quite sure on the matter. Even the Amish livestock seem to agree with their masters that Christmas is holy. The Amish are habitually in communication with their animals, and occasionally one of them claims to have heard the cattle talking on Christmas Eve.

After worship, the congregation indulged in a big spread before the *Psalmenstechen* (piercing the Psalms). This tradition goes back to the Emmental (Switzerland), where it was still practiced in the 1800s. In the *Psalmenstechen*, a woman supplies a pin from her dress to be inserted between the pages of a Luther Bible at the Psalm section. Then they open to the page where the needle has penetrated and find the Psalm to which it points. Now everyone reads it and gives it some significance for the coming year.

The Amish of Allen County today have considerable difficulty with measuring the temperature. Up to a few years ago, they were well acquainted with the Fahrenheit system, but then the *Englischers* came along to impose their metric temperatures. The farmers read the scale on the Celsius thermometer in centimeters, announcing that it is ten "centimeters down." Ten above is recorded by them as ten "centimeters over." They do not know what this change could mean aside from being further proof for the instability brought about by the ever-new, a world dehumanized by modern things.

When winter descends on Allen County, the day in Elam's house begins later than usual and yet quite early by the standards "out there." Problems of the Amish variety start with their *Kackhisli* (outhouse), which is rather defenseless against the blasts from nature's north. During blizzards the Amish run a cord from the house door to the *Kackhisli* so the children will not lose their way toward relief. In their carriages or sleighs, the Amish install stoves burning wood, while others place hot bricks under their seats. So equipped, they trot down Cuba, Grabill, or Graber roads over trackless winter snow.

An umbrella with a plastic peephole sticks out of every buggy and has to serve the purpose of a roof. It demands quite a bit of skill to poise it against the wind just right so it doesn't fold over the wrong way. If this happens, the horse turns skittish and becomes rebellious. If the steed rears or kicks, worldly car drivers panic and step on the gas, blow their horns, or simply lose their nerve. Yet, during the last few days—"Let us do good unto all men" (Gal. 6:10)—we with Amish one-horse power have pulled many cars out of snowbanks.

The rooms on the main floor are warm, regardless of how cold it is outside or how much the wind blows, although like the other Amish, Elam rejects central heating. Life plays itself out in the immediate vicinity of one of the two stoves, unless there is work to be done in the stable or on the fields, now being spread with manure or wood ashes to keep the spring worms busy. Producing manure is now the main business of the heavy Belgians surrounding their boss Constable. The two girls are busily fetching coal or wood from the sheds, while Rachel stokes the fires and cooks or bakes pies on the stoves.

For the guest of the house, the whole matter of going to sleep becomes more serious since the Amish have retained old European customs of not heating the upstairs bedrooms. The room in which the two boys sleep has a register in the floor so that some of the warm air from below can heat this room a bit. "You've got a fur coat along?" Elam asks ever so frequently. "Got mitts?" Youths courting girls of marriageable age in their rooms might now think bundling necessary, although it is forbidden here.

Elam's household does have some homemade dandelion wine, but it is dispensed with great thrift. This variety of Amish champagne is made from dried dandelion blossoms, water, sugar, a few grapes, and some lemons; it is not regarded as alcohol but as medicine. In some areas it is also used as an aphrodisiac. With a recently married couple whom I know quite well, the grandfather of the wife insisted that she drink a glass of dandelion wine every evening before going to bed. The grandfather was of the opinion that the two had been married long enough finally to have a child. As a result of the wine, or in spite of it, the two one day became three.

A winter day in the farmhouse calls for stories like Joseph W.

Yoder's *Rosanna of the Amish*. When I tell fairy tales such as *The Three Bears* and *Snow White* or *Hänsel and Gretel*, using the Amish dialect, the girls are fascinated. They even sing, "*A, a, a, der Winter der ist da* (a, a, a, winter's here to stay)." Of course, religious instruction also helps to fill the evening's agenda. After the descent of early darkness, when the storm blows the winter against the windowpanes, the old pull out the *Katechismus für kleine Kinder* (Catechism for small children), "compiled by some brothers upon the advice of many brothers" and now applied for the use of upcoming generations.

The plain people here are especially interested in the catechism's "Nine Items for Salvation," called the spiritual ladder to heaven or the ladder to the kingdom of heaven. In order to climb this ladder and attain the topmost rung, one has to—just like the chickens in the henhouse—start at the bottom rung with "Blessed are the poor in spirit" (Matt. 5:3). Then up it goes step by step. Rung two: "Blessed are those who mourn" (Matt. 5:4). Rung three: "Blessed are the meek." And so forth, till the ninth rung: "Blessed are you, when men . . . say all manner of evil against you falsely, for my sake." With the help of the catechism, parents teach children patience, love of neighbor, and pacifism, yet taking care that their offspring are always mindful of the terrors of hell.

Winter evenings are suited to the telling of ghost stories, and Joseph is good at it. While the stove rumbles and roars, he reminds everyone of times when son Ben heard the cows talking or Tobi saw a white ghost flashing across the yard. Joseph tells of dreams, ancient fantasies, and strange things happening at the same time. One may attribute some of this to the prescientific worldview of the Amish. They know of benign and malignant premonitions, not out of the Bible but from imagination and yet a daily part of life around here. The general backdrop for these tales is a traditional view of heaven and earth. There is the yarn about a haunted house near Grabill which devours its inhabitants. Someone repeats a legend about the unfortunate Pilate, who according to the Amish is buried somewhere in Switzerland. The circle likes to dish up some horror story, and everyone lightheartedly tries to add a spoonful of mustard to it. If, however, anyone in the world out there should claim that the Amish are superstitious folks, . . . well, they have the wrong end of a manure fork in their hands.

Outside, the street is as slippery as a half-sucked candy, and the snow-covered lane to the farmhouse humps up and down like a seesaw. Amish taxis are in top demand. The plain folks rent a worldly neighbor and his vehicle to take them to Grabill or to a relative. Since this practice lies on the edge of the permissible and also costs money, a good number of the Amish prefer to ride in their own carriages or in a sleigh. Yet the road to the church service puts everyone to a great test, with a minus-forty windchill factor, just as miserable by Fahrenheit or Celsius.

The house of Elam has given the whole matter some thought and come up with three possibilities: the first is to avail themselves of the Amish taxi but get to the service first, early enough to avoid all witnesses. The second option is to take a taxi and tell the brothers and sisters that the *Dütscher* (I, Bernd) was simply not up to handling the cold. Elam, as lord of the house and in this capacity as flexible as tar in December, picks the third possibility: he has Nancy hitched up. In accord, we settle into the sleigh, and a few years before the twenty-first century is to begin, we take off for the church service, teeth clenched, blankets tucked, umbrella unfurled—just like all the others. When we arrive, everyone shakes the cold out of their bones and confirms the preached word of Christ: "Whoever will come after me must deny self and take up one's cross daily and follow me" (Luke 9:23). At minus thirty, with a windchill of minus forty or even minus forty-five, it indeed is a cross to travel cross-country in a one-horse open sleigh.

Yet the temperatures of the season are nothing to Elam's son Chris, who has become quite active at nights. In the evening after a hard day's work, he swings himself into his fiberglass buggy and travels out to survey the beautiful girls. Because of its frills, he refers to this luxurious craft from Bishop Victor's shop as his sports car. He has received his ultramodern buggy as a birthday present, just like all sixteen-year-old boys of Allen County receive a buggy, known in these parts as a courting carriage. Chris is old enough for it. To the buggy belongs a new horse, a long-bodied Standardbred with spiked horse-shoes designed for icy winter conditions. Horse and carriage are just right. Among the young male set, prestige is expressed in horse power, even if such is without chrome or varnish. The unattainable makes Chris happy with the attainable.

Mother Rachel shows great interest in guessing whom her boy

takes for a homeward ride during the long dark evenings of winter. Such is of consequence in the Amish community, and yet she would never inquire of him since Amish parents respect the private lives of their children too much.

Shortly after Christmas, on a particularly cold day, butchering time arrives. Chris shoots a fatted sow with his twenty-two caliber gun, then Elam sticks it in the artery. The mountain of flesh is still quivering when it is already scalded with boiling water, making it relatively easy to scrape off the bristles with sharpened old spoons. When the sun rises, the pig hangs, half-open and suspended from a beam. Intestines and belly are bulging forth, then removed and cleaned by Rachel. The family helps with knives, cleavers, and bone saw. They gather the fat and deposit it in tin containers even before the heavy pieces of meat freeze. After the pig has been finished, Rachel Mae's tender-eyed bovine, her favorite cow, is put on the chopping block. During the following hours, belly, hocks, filet, spare ribs, and back bacon become the center of attention and of manufacture. What was a pig or a favorite cow now lies or hangs in pieces, frozen hard as rock and covered by snow, with the exception of a liver now steaming in the oven.

The Amish are careful not to allow any female animal close to the place of slaughter. According to ancient lore, such precautions help to avoid miscarriages.

******

That spring with Preacher Joseph, the immortal Amish man, I stand on the edge of his yard on Cuba Road and watch as the horned cattle come home. In the kitchen Rosanna is preparing pie while simultaneously engaged in the futile battle against insects with her flyswatter. In front of the barn, Tobi is hitching up a trotter. In the stable, the woman of the house, Naomi, in cornflower-blue and a lady all the way even on a milk stool, strips the last milk from her third cow. Ruth, who has just finished doing her family duty by giving birth to a new baby, carries a pail of water together with her squealing child. Barbara is inspecting apples for rot, and monotone Amish laundry hangs on the line. Young cattle munch grass, a sow scratches her ruddy hams against a railing gate, another pig fattens itself on some garbage, while from the neighboring yard comes the news that David's saddle horse Max has gained sire status. All around, the land lives, loiters, and quakes.

In the sky above Allen County, jets sketch patterns with their vapor trails, and on the highway to Grabill, cars streak by. From somewhere wafting toward us are fragments of a song, "Release, oh Lord, these lips of mine, To sing to you a song so fine." A rusty door screeches. This is Amish country in the year of our Lord 1988, *Gelassenheit* (yielded to the Lord) in black, no flat folklore in a modern world, but present, in which the past is not dead, not even really past. The Amish are a tribe unto themselves, with quite original abilities and characteristics. People with taboos and problems, but biblical Christians without any kind of secret wisdom. Around me is a world with a unique style of life, still so real that their people never have the feeling of being superfluous or out of place.

There can be no doubt about it: small groups with their own defined character have always existed and will always exist. But as the years pass, they change from time to time or they go under. Not so the brothers and sisters of Allen County, God's second choice as a chosen people, after Abraham's descendants. Their farms are not preserves of natural resources; the Amish constitute no relics. This is the world of Joseph, whose firm hold on traditions prevents a more contemporary lifestyle. Joseph's Christianity places faith and human values above those of technology. The German world of Allen County has made a few compromises with the American world, so that the preacher claims: "We are German because we have been raised German," but German without *Lederhosen* (leather breeches), Christmas trees, and umpapah music.

Joseph in his natural, countercultural serenity has the encompassing gaze of a practiced prophet. A man and his clan. The kingdom of God not as a distant promise but as an obligation to obey on earth. A man whom you can see as a lifelong prayer. The Amish are like a race, a humanly refreshing society, in spite of the sense and the occasional nonsense as they apply their old writings. They are people who no longer want to reform society, but simply request understanding for their own reform, holy people who never led holy wars. I could not become such as they. Con-

380

versely, why should they become like me?

The Amish appear to me to be more satisfied than the average *Weltmensch* (person of the world). Certainly they are more carefree and future oriented, even if this future is found in God's eternal timelessness rather than in the limits of secular history. This in itself compensates for their refusal to be completely at home in this world. Thus they do not have to change as long as their insular style of life does not force them to do so and as long as God does not wish it otherwise. Joseph's lifestyle is not directly threatened these days. His manner of living does not come into question even if one accepts the premise that alternate communities like the Amish are acceptable to the world and in the world only in small doses, and this will not change. Yet their quiet significance for whole geographic areas of the USA is a fact of life; their disappearance would leave a vacuum behind.

This servant of the Word (preacher) stands before me like a mat oil painting of a *Mensch* (real human being), the Reformation personified, framed by a life of farming, family, and God. Love for all three shapes his bones, his muscles, and the very marrow of his bones.

"So you want to fly with the airship?" he asks, knowing it is a foregone conclusion. He says nothing more. He lacks the confidence to use big words. Flying as heavenly enjoyment! I knew that deep within, he was beside himself, uncomprehending. Anyone who flies has no credibility, and as far as the preacher before me is concerned, such a person has as much chance for a spot in paradise as a snowball does in hell. Then the patriarch trots away to see "how the growth is doing, whether everything is in good order."

For Tobi, also, the airplane is the most worldly and unchristian means of transport in existence and therefore the stupidest human project since the Tower of Babel. Why couldn't I simply see the discrepancy between technology and Christian morals, even if I might doubt his interpretation of the Bible? This airship has destroyed an age-old *Weltbild* (worldview) and confused the concepts of the Amish, who for long believed that behind and beyond clouds and stars one would find heaven, the absolute Amish limit. From the Lord's spot on high, he directs the transient small life on earth and the life of humans, who daily thank their Creator that they are, after all, men like Joseph, Elam, and Tobias, and women like Rosanna and Rachel. Nevertheless, recently someone from Allen County was allowed to fly. After gaining the approval of the church leaders, one family sent an Amish woman with cancer on a plane to see a well-known doctor in Mexico.

On the next to last day of my stay, my Amish friends of Allen County get together again, Elam and Tobi, David and Barbara, Rachel and Ruth. The brothers and sisters are humble and in good spirits like the first Christians, just as I have come to know them over the last few years. We sing a few Amish favorites like *"Müde bin ich, geh' zur Ruh'* (Tired I am, I go to rest)" or *"Mein Lebensfaden läuft zu Ende* (My span of life comes to a close)." Then they congregate in Joseph's farmhouse, giving their thanks to God that everything has gone well, and praying together as Jesus had taught them to pray, ". . . Thy kingdom come." When the Amen is spoken, I do not doubt for one second that they wait hourly for this kingdom promised in the Gospels. With God everything is possible, for God is a great God.

Finally Tobi and Rosanna yodel once again, and when the Amish of Allen County yodel, the very land smiles. At the conclusion and "to my honor," they serve milk soup with crumbled crackers, prepared in Tobi's style, then choice cuts of ham, mashed potatoes, and green beans.

When farewells are exchanged, my Amish friends do not give me a brotherly kiss since I am not one of them but just an *Englischer* from Germany who felt other feelings and dreamed other dreams. But they do give me a firm handshake. Their parting words are not *"auf Wiedersehen"* but *"seh di wieder* (see you again, on this earth, we hope)." Barbara then gives me a sealed jar of red beets for the way home. Tobi's Naomi mentions in passing that in Amish country, Bernd is no real name for people, but they will probably name a horse after me. They cannot comprehend that I will return to my earthly individualism and write a book about them, that I will put into the letters of the alphabet, things and events about them for the Old Country, and now for the New. What is significant to write about them that has not already been written in the Book of books? If I obstinately persist in writing, says Joseph, I ought to have it printed in their *Dütsch* (Swiss-German dialect) so that they too can read it.

Dütsch or *Deutsch?* It was of no further use to the old preacher. Shortly before this book was first published in German, he walked the Amish way, not from life to death, but from life to eternal life. A man who, in accord with Paul, did not unequally yoke himself to the world (2 Cor. 6:14) and had been obedient to God's commission to be fruitful and fill the earth (Gen. 1:28). A pious servant, who acted according to Acts (4:32) and became as one heart and one soul with his fellow believers, who cultivated his land by the sweat of his brow (Gen. 3:19), who did not love the world nor the things in the world (1 John 2:15), who was seeking the righteousness of the kingdom of God (Matt. 6:33), who never sowed according to the flesh like—well, Galatians 6 has much to say about that topic. And finally, a family father who was not afraid of the world. Possibly because he knew the world too well.

Big words of farewell? Joseph would not have wanted them. An Amish servant of the Word had taken his leave, one who never missed putting his earthly house in order. He did this daily, in keeping with his *Weltbild* (worldview), with pity toward the world and oriented toward the Word. Such was Joseph Graber of Cuba Road.

Timetable

A.D. 70 Scattering of the early Christian church after the destruction of Jerusalem

Ca. (around) 1175 Founding of the religious lay movement of the Waldenesian Society for Atonement and Poverty, which rejects all sacraments such as oath, purgatory, and military service, while retaining only the Lord's Supper, baptism, and penance

1414-1418 Reform Council of Constance. The Czech reformer John Hus burned as a heretic (1415)

1516 Huldrych Zwingli (1484-1531) people's priest in Einsiedeln, attracted to Erasmus. First edition of the New Testament in Greek by Erasmus of Rotterdam (ca. 1466-1536)

1520 Luther banned at Worms, sojourn in the Wartburg. Publication of Luther's translation of the New Testament

1522 Zwingli objects to church abuses in Switzerland, introduces Reformation in Zurich with his Disputation Theses, "67 Final Speeches." Zwingli's followers break Catholic fasting order. Conrad Grebel is among the radical champions of the Reformation in Zurich

1523 Thomas Müntzer (1489-1525) assumes preaching office in Allstedt and proclaims first social-revolutionary thesis. Johannes Oecolampadius (1482-1531) starts the Reformation in Basel. Zwingli introduces the Reformation in Zurich through the city council. Open break of Grebel's group with Zwingli

1524 Grebel's letter to Thomas Müntzer. Start of the German Peasants' Revolt (1524-1526) in the southeast edge of the Black Forest, rebellion in Thuringia under the leadership of Müntzer, expansion within Upper Germany, Austria, and Switzerland. Luther opposes peasants' rebellion in spite of partial identification of the Protestant movement with the rebels. Martin Bucer (1491-1551) reforms Strasbourg

1525 The order by the city council of Zurich to disallow discussions regarding baptism leads to first adult baptism (Jan. 21). Grebel, Manz, and Blaurock lay the cornerstone for the Anabaptist church (experience of salvation, baptism), and thus the foundation of the evangelical free church. Rebaptizers are threatened with banishment. Founding of the first Anabaptist congregation of Switzerland in Zollikon. After public disputations with Zwingli in Zurich, Anabaptists go underground. Grebel in custody. Thomas Müntzer beheaded at Mühlhausen. Eberli Bolt becomes first Anabaptist martyr burned at the stake. End of 1525, Anabaptists found throughout German-speaking Switzerland. Mandates against Anabaptists, 1525-1761, in various parts of Europe (*The Mennonite Encyclopedia*, 3:446-453)

1526 Zurich threatens followers of Anabaptists with penalty of death, Basel prohibits adult baptism with threat of banishment, Graubünden prohibits Anabaptism. Lesser nobility, of Protestant persuasion, offer Moravia as an asylum for Anabaptists. Conrad Grebel (born ca. 1498 in Zurich) dies in Maienfeld from the plague. Anabaptists in southern Germany, Tirol, Moravia, and Austria

1527 Religious talks between Catholic Church and Anabaptists in Bern. Felix Manz (born ca. 1498) drowned in the Limmat River. First synod of Swiss and South German Anabaptists formulates articles of Schleitheim Confession under the leadership of Michael Sattler. Margrave Philipp of Baden forbids adult baptism upon punishment of body and life, Strasbourg accommodates Anabaptists. Regensburg, Augsburg, Nuremberg, Bamberg, and Salzburg attack Anabaptists. Concordat of cities of Bern, Zurich, and St. Gallen against Swiss Brethren. First Bern Mandate against Anabaptists. Michael Sattler (born ca. 1490) burned, Melchior Hofmann moves to East Frisia. Death of Hans Hut (born ca. 1490) and Hans Denk (born ca. 1495)

1527-1581 223 Anabaptists executed in Bavaria

1528 The Union of Swabia organizes roving gangs against Anabaptists. Introduction of Reformation in Bern. Zwingli engages in disputes with Anabaptists in Zurich. Mandate of Bern is intensified. First death penalties in Bern. Balthasar Hubmaier (born before 1485) burned in Vienna, Blaurock banished from Bern. Anabaptists from Austria, South Germany, and Switzerland taking refuge in Moravia divide into two groups, the sword-bearers and the staff-bearers

1529 Founding year of Hutterian Brethren in Moravia. Adult baptism now punishable by death, by imperial decree at Speyer. Life imprisonment or death penalty by drowning for backsliding Anabaptists in Basel. Blaurock (born ca. 1492 in Bonaduz of Grisons, Switzerland) burned as a heretic in Gufidaun, South Tirol. Inconclusive religious debate between Luther, Melanchthon, and Zwingli in Marburg
1530 Zurich orders death penalty for anyone harboring Anabaptists. Bern, Basel, Constance, St. Gallen, and Zurich align themselves against Anabaptists. Ca. 2,000 Anabaptists executed to date. Founding of the Anabaptist church in Emden by Melchior Hofmann (ca. 1495-1543)
1531 Bern threatens to drown banished Anabaptists who return (later penalty was beheading). Forty executions until 1571 in the city. Bullinger's first book against Anabaptists appears. Melchior Hofmann is in the Netherlands. Zwingli dies in the battle of Kappel, succeeded by Heinrich Bullinger (1504-1575)
1533 Life imprisonment for Anabaptists in Bern. Exodus of Anabaptists to Moravia
1534 Founding of the Jesuit Order to combat heretics. Introduction of Reformation in Württemberg
1534-35 Revolt of Anabaptists in Münster, Westphalia ("Kingdom of Zion"). Jan Bockelson, follower of Melchior Hofmann, proclaimed as "King of the Anabaptists." Defeat of Münsterite Anabaptists
1535-1537 Imprisoned Anabaptists in Passau (Bavaria) compose songs of faith forming the base of the *Ausbund*, hymnal used by the Amish
1536 Menno Simons (ca. 1496-1561) declares himself an Anabaptist. Frisia proclaims the death penalty for anyone harboring Menno. Jakob Hutter executed in Innsbruck
1537 Mandate of Bern against Anabaptist teachers
1545 *Men(n)ist, Mennonist, Mennonite*, named after Menno Simons, appears for first time in an East Frisian mandate of Countess Anna
1564 Bern threatens Anabaptists with financial and physical punishments. First edition of the *Ausbund*
1571 Hans Haslibacher is the last Anabaptist to be executed in canton of Bern
1578 Mandate of Cologne threatens Anabaptists with death penalty
1579 Bern again threatens Anabaptists with confiscation of property and death penalty
1587 Bounty in Bavaria for capture of Anabaptists
1599 Bern proclaims Anabaptist holdings to be property of state
1632 Dordrecht Confession signed in the Netherlands, adopted in Alsace in 1660, in Pennsylvania in 1725, used by the Amish today
1637 Zurich banishes Anabaptists
17th Century Swiss Anabaptists flee to Alsace, which becomes French in latter half of century
1640 Swiss Anabaptists in Markirch (Alsace), later home of Jakob Ammann

1643 "Anabaptists, here called Menists," on Manhattan Island (New York), on Long Island (New York) in 1657

1648 Galley-slave punishment for Bern Anabaptists. Swiss Brethren arrive in area of Zweibrücken (Palatinate, Germany). Peace Treaty of Westphalia (at end of Thirty Years' War, 1618-1648) confirms religious freedom of the 1555 Peace of Augsburg for Reformed princes and cities. Anabaptists excluded

1659 Bern institutes a special office for dealing with Anabaptists

1660 Meeting of Anabaptist ministers at Ohnenheim (Alsace) accept the Dordrecht Confession of 1632

1663 Mennonites from Holland in Plockhoy settlement at Horekill on the Delaware River (America)

1664 Law of tolerance to Anabaptists in the Palatinate. Anabaptists introduce clover to the Palatinate

1669 Bern offers bounties for capture of Anabaptists, leading to the police agency of the *Täuferjäger* (Anabaptist-hunters), active in the first half of the 1700s

1671 Oath of Homage introduced in Bern to smoke out Anabaptists, who refuse to swear. Up to 1711, increased migration of Swiss Brethren to Alsace. Holland scuttles Bern's plans to deport Swiss Brethren to East India

1683 First German group settles in America, among them Mennonites. Founding of Germantown in Pennsylvania

1690 Children of Anabaptist marriages are refused rights of inheritance in Bern

1692-93 Jakob Ammann (from Switzerland) appears in Markirch, beginning of divisions among Anabaptist churches in southern German-speaking areas. Founding of the Amish church (1693 to 1698), with strict church discipline, banning, shunning, twice-a-year celebration of communion and foot washing, new dress codes

1695 Old legal regulations in Bern regarding Anabaptists nullified, life imprisonment for Anabaptists threatened

1707-1756 Ca. 3000 Anabaptists migrate to North America. The canton of Zurich is "free of Anabaptists"

1710-1711 Switzerland expels Anabaptists to Holland, down the Rhine

1712 Louis XIV declares expulsion of Anabaptists from Alsace. Numerous Amish move to areas of Mömpelgard (Montbéliard), Lorraine, the Palatinate, and elsewhere

1720 Bern begins branding Anabaptists. Numerous Swiss Brethren locate in the Margrave Baden-Durlach

1730 Amish in area of Hesse-Cassel

1735-1755 First Amish migrations to North America, some perhaps earlier

1737 The *Charming Nancy* brings a group of Amish to Philadelphia. Amish in 1738 found the first Amish settlements in Pennsylvania at Northkill, Berks County; and Upper Mill Creek, Lancaster County; and in Chester County

1742 *Ausbund* first published in America

1743 Dissolution of the Bern Anabaptist office (*Täuferkammer*)

1750 and later A series of Amish families from Berks County flee from the Indian Wars into Lancaster and Chester counties (Pennsylvania)

1752 Meeting of ministers, regulatory letter from Steinselz, Alsace, gives rules for beards of Amish. Only three Amish congregations left in Switzerland

1759 Regulatory letter from Essingen, Palatinate, includes dress code for the Amish

1760 Founding of Amish church in Lancaster-Chester counties (Pennsylvania)

Ca. 1770 Several Amish churches in Hesse, migrate in 1817 to Ohio, mainly to Butler County

1777 Amish found present-day Basel Mennonite church on the Holee Street of Basel

1779 Meeting of Amish ministers at Essingen, Palatinate

1790 and following Amish from Mömpelgard (Montbéliard) migrate to Eastern Europe

1797 Amish migrate from Alsace-Lorraine (France) and the Palatinate (Germany) to Bavaria. Founding of congregations at Regensburg, Ingolstadt, and Munich

1798 French-influenced freedom of religion is introduced in the canton of Bern. Compulsory infant baptism in the Emmental till 1812

1799 Meeting of Amish ministers and regulatory letter from Essingen, Palatinate. Anabaptists receive equal rights in the Palatinate

1800 Some Pennsylvania Mennonites migrate to Canada

1806 Napoleon terminates nonmilitary status of Anabaptists

1807 The first Amish in Ohio. The Grand Duchy of Baden grants military dispensation to Anabaptists for payment of fee

1811 Bavaria extends right of handshake instead of oath to Anabaptists

1815-1860 Migration of Amish from Montbéliard, Waldeck, Bavaria, Hesse, and the Palatinate to America, especially to Ohio, Indiana, Illinois, Maryland, New York, and Iowa

1822 Amish scouts in Ontario (Canada), leading to 1823-24 concentrated immigrations of Amish from Germany

1824 First Amish congregation in Ontario (Waterloo County, later in Perth County)

1830 and following Amish Mennonites in New York State (Lewis County)

1839 First Amish settlement in Indiana, at Nappanee in Elkhart County, and in 1840 lapping into Marshall County

1841 Amish settlement in LaGrange and Elkhart counties, Indiana. Amish in Lancaster County start tobacco plantations

1846 Amish in Iowa (Johnson-Washington counties)

1850 Amish in Maryland (Garrett County), at Berne (Adams County, Indiana)

1852 First Amish in Grabill (Allen County, Indiana)

1862-1878 *Dienerversammlungen,* Amish churchwide conferences which lead to split between Old Order Amish and Amish Mennonites (who later merge with Mennonite conferences)

1864 Amish in Illinois (Douglas-Moultrie counties)

1866 Split among Egli Amish in Indiana

1867 and following Attempts by European Anabaptists for reconciliation between Amish and Mennonites, in Offenthal (near Wiesbaden), Kaiserslautern (1871), Sembach (1872), and Weierhof (1873)

1872 Split of Stuckey Amish (Mennonites) in Illinois

1874 Swiss federal constitution guarantees full religious freedom to Anabaptists

1877 Amish in Pequea (Lancaster County, Pennsylvania) area split into Old Order Amish and an Amish-Mennonite church

1881 Split of Nebraska Amish

1883 Amish in Kansas (Reno County)

1890 First edition of *The Budget*

1910 Amish congregation in Oklahoma (Mayes County) and in Michigan (St. Joseph County)

1915 Amish in Delaware (Kent County)

1925 Amish in Wisconsin (Taylor County)

1927 Split of Beachy Amish in Pennsylvania. Amish in Florida (Sarasota County)

1937 In church district of Ixheim, the last Amish congregation in Germany joins the Mennonite church

1944 Amish in Lawrence County, Tennessee

1947 Amish in Pike County, Missouri

1949 Amish in Cattaraugus County, New York

1955 The musical *Plain and Fancy,* with Amish theme, becomes a Broadway hit

1958 Amish in Todd County, Kentucky

1966 Split of New Order Amish

1967-1978 Amish church in Fernheim Colony, Paraguay

1968-1979 Beachy Amish in Guaimaca, Honduras

1972 U.S. Supreme Court in school quarrel of Wisconsin versus Yoder decides in favor of Amish. Amish in Wadena County, Minnesota

1975 Amish in Lincoln County, Montana, and White County, Arkansas

1978-82 Amish church at Pawnee City, Nebraska

1982 Amish in Gonzales County, Texas

1984 Filming of *Witness.* 175 Amish settlements

1990 Minnesota court approves Amish use of reflective tape on buggies instead of the slow-moving-vehicle sign

1993 Amish settlements in 20 U.S. States and in one Canadian province, with 918 districts listed in Ben J. Raber's 1994 *Almanac.* Beachy Amish continue in Paraguay

Biblical Principles of Amish Faith

Banning and Shunning

1 Cor. 5:13: "Put away from among yourselves that wicked person."
2 Thess. 3:14: "If anyone obey not our word by this epistle, note that one, and have no company with such a person."

Baptism Based on Faith

Acts 2:38: "Repent, and be baptized every one of you."
Acts 8:37: "If you believe with all your heart, you may [be baptized]."
Rom. 3:22: "The righteousness of God through faith in Christ Jesus is for all who believe."

Choice of Servants, Leaders

Prov. 16:33: "The lot is cast into the lap; but the whole disposing thereof is of the Lord."
Acts 1:24, 26: "They prayed and said, 'You, Lord, who know the hearts of all men. Show which of these two you have chosen'. . . . And they gave forth their lots."
1 Tim. 5:2-8: "A bishop (or minister) must be blameless. . . . Likewise must the deacons be grave."
Acts 6:5: "Full of faith and of the Holy Spirit."

Community, Unity, Uniformity

Matt. 5:24: "First be reconciled to your brother or sister."
James 3:18: "The fruit of righteousness is sown in peace by those who make peace."

1 Cor. 1:10: "Be perfectly joined together in the same mind and in the same judgment."

Acts 4:32: "Those who believed were of one heart and of one soul."

1 Cor. 12:4: "Now there are diversities of gifts, but the same Spirit."

1 John 1:3: "You also may have fellowship with us: and truly our fellowship is with the Father, and with his Son Jesus Christ."

Discipline in the Church

Matt. 18:15-18: "If another member of the church sins, . . . go and point out the fault when the two of you are alone. If the member listens to you, you have regained that one. But if you are not listened to, take one or two others along with you. . . . If the member refuses to listen to them, tell it to the church; and if the offender refuses to listen even to the church, let such a one be to you as a Gentile and a tax collector. . . . Whatever you bind on earth will be bound in heaven, and whatever you loose on earth will be loosed in heaven." (NRSV)

Luke 17:3: "Rebuke the offender, and if there is repentance, you must forgive."

Gal. 6:1: "Restore such a one in a spirit of gentleness."

1 Cor. 5:7: "Clean out the old yeast."

Foot Washing

John 13:14: "You also ought to wash one another's feet."

1 Tim. 5:10: "Good works, . . . if she has washed the saints' feet."

Holy Kiss

1 Cor. 16:20: "Greet one another with an holy kiss."

Humility and Holiness

Phil. 2:5-8: "Let this mind be in you, which was also in Christ Jesus, who . . . humbled himself, and became obedient unto death, even the death of the cross."

Matt. 5:5: "Blessed are the meek, for they shall inherit the earth."

1 Peter 1:16: "It is written, Be you holy; for I am holy."

Rom. 12:3: "Do not think of yourself more highly than you ought to think, but think with sober judgment."

Eph. 5:25-27: Christ is making the church "holy and without blemish," "without a spot or wrinkle."

Kingdom of God

Matt. 6:10: "Thy kingdom come. Thy will be done on earth as it is in heaven."

Matt. 6:33: "Seek first the kingdom of God, and his righteousness."

Acts 5:29: "We ought to obey God rather than any human authority."

Lifestyle

Luke 9:23: "If any will come after me, let them deny themselves, and take up their cross daily, and follow me."

Matt. 5:48: "Be perfect, therefore, as your Father in heaven is perfect." (NRSV)

2 Cor. 6:14—7:1: "Be not unequally yoked together with unbelievers. . . . You are the temple of the living God. . . . Come out from among them, and be separate, . . . and touch not the unclean thing."

Marriage

1 Cor. 7:9-11: "It is better to marry than to burn. . . . Unto the married I command, yet not I, but the Lord, Let not the wife depart from her husband, . . . and let not the man put away his wife."

1 Cor. 7:39: Marry "only in the Lord."

Gen. 1:28: "Be fruitful, and multiply."

Preaching Without Notes, Freely

Matt. 10:19: "When they deliver you up, take no thought how or what you shall speak: for it shall be given you in that same hour what you shall speak."

Acts 4:8: "Then Peter, filled with the Holy Spirit, said unto them. . . ."

1 Cor. 12:3: "Speaking by the Spirit of God. . . ."

Rejection of Insurance, Pensions

1 Tim. 5:8: "If any provide not for his own, and especially for those of his own house, he has denied the faith, and is worse than an infidel."

Gal. 6:2: "Bear one another's burdens, and so fulfill the law of Christ."

Acts 4:35: "Distribution was made to each as any had need."

Rejection of Military Service

Romans 12:17-21: "Recompense to no one evil for evil. Provide things honest in the sight of all people. . . . Overcome evil with good."

Matt. 5:39: "Resist not evil: but whosoever shall smite you on your right cheek, turn to him the other also."

Matt. 5:44: "Love your enemies."

John 18:36: "If my kingdom were of this world, then would my servants fight."

Rejection of the Oath

Matt. 5:33-37: "Swear not at all. . . . Let your communication be, Yea, yea; Nay, nay: for whatsoever is more than these comes of evil."

Rejection of Photography

Exodus 20:4: "You shall not make unto you any graven image, or any likeness of any thing that is in heaven above, or that is in the earth beneath, or that is in the water under the earth."

Rejection of School Beyond Grade 8

1 Cor. 3:19: "For the wisdom of this world is foolishness with God."
Deut. 6:4-7: "Teach the Lord's words diligently to your children."
Prov. 1:8: "The fear of the Lord is the beginning of knowledge."

Rejection of the World

John 17:14: "They are not of the world, even as I am not of the world."
2 Cor. 6:14: "Be not unequally yoked together with unbelievers."
James 4:4: "Whosoever therefore will be a friend of the world is the enemy of God."

Rejection of Worldly Fashions

Rom. 12:2: "Be not conformed to this world, but be transformed by the renewing of your mind, that you may prove what is that good, acceptable, and perfect will of God."

1 Tim. 2:8-9: "I will therefore that . . . women adorn themselves in modest apparel, with shamefacedness and sobriety; not with braided hair, or gold, or pearls, or costly array." Also 1 Pet. 3:3-5.

Lev. 19:27: "Do not round the corners of the hair on your head nor mar the edges of your beard."

Deut. 22:5: "The woman shall not wear that which pertains unto a man, neither shall a man put on a woman's garment: for all that do so are abomination unto the Lord your God."

1 John 2:16-17: "Love not the world. . . . For all that is in the world, the lust of the flesh, and the lust of the eyes, and the pride of life, is not of the Father, but is of the world."

Rejection of Worldly Litigation and Courts

Matt. 5:40: "And if any one will sue you at the law, and take away your coat, let him have your cloak also."

1 Cor. 6:1-8: "Dare any of you . . . go to law before the unjust? . . . Rather suffer yourselves to be defrauded."

Roles of Husband and Wife

1 Tim. 2:12: "I do not allow a woman to teach, nor to usurp authority over the man, but to be in silence."

Col. 3:18: "Wives, submit yourselves unto your own husbands, as it is fit in the Lord."

Eph. 5:25: "Husbands, love your wives, even as Christ also loved the church, and gave himself for it."

Submission

Eph. 5:21: "Submit yourselves one to another in the fear of God."

1 Peter 5:5: "Likewise, you younger, submit yourselves unto the elder."

Col. 3:20: "Children, obey your parents in all things."

Rom. 12:10: "Love one another with mutual affection; outdo one another in showing honor." (NRSV)

Wearing of Aprons

Gen. 3:7: "They sewed fig leaves together, and made themselves aprons."

Wearing of Head Coverings

1 Cor. 11:5: "But every woman that prays or prophesies with her head uncovered dishonors her head."

Workplace, Tilling the Soil

Gen. 3:19: "In the sweat of your face shall you eat bread."

Gen. 3:23: "The Lord God sent him forth from the garden of Eden, to till the ground from whence he was taken."

2 Thess. 3:10: "Anyone unwilling to work should not eat." (NRSV)

Rom. 12:11: "Not slothful in business."

Worshiping in Homes, Not Church Buildings

Acts 2:44-47: "Breaking bread from house to house, . . . praising God."

Acts 17:24: "God . . . dwells not in temples made with hands."

Heb. 10:25: "Not forsaking the assembling of ourselves together."

Phile. 1-2: "To Philemon . . . and to the church in your house. . . ."

Bibliography

Almanac, The New American, for the Year of Our Lord 1994. By Ben J. Raber. Annual. Baltic, Ohio: Raber's Bookstore. (Lists Scriptures and hymns for services, Amish districts and ministers, and books for the Amish.)

Amish Cooking. Compiled by a committee of Amish women. Aylmer, Ont.: Pathway Publishing, 1980. Deluxe ed. Scottdale, Pa.: Herald Press, 1992. Pathway books are available in USA from Pathway Publishers, LaGrange, Ind.

Anabaptisme bernois et Réformation face à face. Bern, 1988.

Artikel und Ordnungen der Christlichen Gemeinde in Christo Jesu. Aylmer, Ont.: Pathway, 1964.

Ausbund das ist: Etliche schöne Christliche Lieder, Wie sie in dem Gefängnis zu Passau in dem Schloss von den Schweizer-Brüdern und von anderen rechtgläubigen Christen hin und her gedichtet worden. First ed., 1664. 13th ed., Lancaster Co., Pa., 1981.

Beck, Dr. Joseph. *Geschichtsbücher der Wiedertäufer in Oesterreich-Ungarn von 1526 bis 1785.* Vienna, 1883.

Bender, Harold S. *Anabaptist Vision, The.* Scottdale, Pa.: Herald Press, 1944.

_____. "An Amish Church Discipline of 1781." *Mennonite Quarterly Review* 4 (1930): 140-148.

_____. "Amish Church Discipline of 1779." *Mennonite Quarterly Review* 11 (1937): 163-168.

_____. "First Edition of the Ausbund." *Mennonite Quarterly Review* 3 (1929): 147-150.

_____. "Some Early American Amish Mennonite Disciplines."

Mennonite Quarterly Review 8 (1934): 90-98.

Blackboard Bulletin, The. Monthly. For teachers. Aylmer, Ont.: Pathway.

Borntrager, Mary Christner. *Ellie* (and other novels). Ellie's People Series. Scottdale, Pa.: Herald Press, 1988 (and later).

Braght, Thieleman Jansz von. *Der blutige Schauplatz oder Märtyrerspiegel der Taufgesinnten oder wehrlosen Christen.* German ed., Aylmer, Ont.: Pathway, 1973. English ed., *Martyrs Mirror,* Scottdale, Pa.: Herald Press, 1938. First ed., Dutch, 1660.

Braitmichel, Kaspar. See *Chronicle.* . . .

Budget, The. A weekly newspaper serving the Amish and Mennonite communities. Sugarcreek, Ohio.

Bullinger, Heinrich. *Von dem unverschampten frävel, egerlichem verwirren und unwahrhaften leeren der selbstgesandten Widertöuffern.* Zurich, 1531.

_____. *Der Widertäufferen Ursprung, fürgang, Secten, wäsen fürnemme und gemeine ihrer leer Artickel.* Zurich, 1560.

Chronicle of the Hutterian Brethren, The. Trans. and ed. by the Hutterian Brethren. Rifton, N.Y.: Plough Publishing House, vol. 1, 1987. Vol. 2 forthcoming.

Denlinger, A. Martha. *Real People: Amish and Mennonites in Lancaster County, Pennsylvania.* 4th ed. Scottdale, Pa.: Herald Press, 1993.

Dyck, Cornelius J. *An Introduction to Mennonite History: A Popular History of the Anabaptists and the Mennonites.* 3d ed. Scottdale, Pa.: Herald Press, 1993.

Ein Riss in der Mauer. Anonymous treatise on courtship, undated except as reprinted, 1984. Available at Raber's Bookstore, Baltic, Ohio.

Ernsthafte Christenpflicht, Die, enthaltend Schöne geistreiche Gebete, womit sich fromme Christenherzen zu allen Zeiten und in allen Nöten trösten können. Devotional book. First ed., Kaiserslautern, 1739. Scottdale, Pa.: Herald Press, 1915. Aylmer, Ont.: Pathway, 1992. Selections in English: *A Devoted Christian's Prayer Book.* Pathway, 3rd printing, 1984.

Family Life. Monthly. On Christian living. Aylmer, Ont.: Pathway.

Fisher, George. *The Making of Pennsylvania.* Philadelphia, 1899.

Fisher, Gideon L. *Farm Life and Its Changes.* Gordonville, Pa.: Pequea Publishers, 1978.

Fisher, Sara, and Rachel Stahl. *The Amish School.* Intercourse, Pa.: Good Books. 1986.

Fox, John. *Allgemeine Geschichte des christlichen Marterthums.* 1831.

Friedmann, Robert. *Mennonite Piety Through the Centuries.* Studies in Anabaptist and Mennonite History, no. 7. Scottdale, Pa.: Herald Press, 1949.

Geiser, S. H. *Die Taufgesinnten-Gemeinden.* Karlsruhe and Bern, 1932.

Geistiches Lustgärtlein. Lancaster, Pa.: 1984 reprint. Devotional book. Available at Raber's Bookstore, Baltic, Ohio.

Gingerich, Melvin. *Mennonite Attire Through Four Centuries.* Breinigsville, Pa.: The Pennsylvania German Society, 1970.

Gingerich, Orland. *The Amish of Canada.* Kitchener, Ont.: Herald Press, 1972.

Glaubensbekenntnis des wehr- und rachlosen Christentums. Baltic, Ohio: B. J. Raber, 1983. (The 1632 Dordrecht Confession in German. An English translation is in Braght's *Martyrs Mirror.*)

Gleysteen, Jan. *Mennonite Tourguide to Western Europe.* Scottdale, Pa.: Herald Press, 1984.

Gratz, Delbert L. *Bernese Anabaptists and Their American Descendants.* Studies in Anabaptist and Mennonite History, no. 8. Scottdale, Pa.: Herald Press, 1953.

Gross, Leonard. *The Golden Years of the Hutterites: The Witness and Thought of the Communal Moravian Anabaptists During the Walpot Era, 1565-1578.* Studies in Anabaptist and Mennonite History, no. 23. Scottdale, Pa.: Herald Press, 1980.

Guth, Hermann. *The Amish-Mennonites of Waldeck and Wittgenstein.* Elverson, Pa.: Mennonite Family History, 1986.

Goertz, Hans-Jürgen, ed. *Die Mennoniten.* Stuttgart, 1971.

Handbuch für Prediger. Baltic, Ohio: B. J. Raber, 1986.

Handlung oder Acta gehaltener Disputation zu Bern 1528. Zurich, 1528.

Hege, Christian. *Die Täufer in der Kurpfalz.* Frankfurt am Main, 1908.

Heritage Review. Ohio Amish Library. 1990.

Horsch, John. *The Hutterian Brethren, 1528-1931.* Studies in Anabaptist and Mennonite History, vol. 2. Scottdale, Pa.: Herald Press, 1931.

Hostetler, John A. *Amish Children: Their Education in Family, School, and Community.* New York: Holt, Rinehart, Winston, 1992.

_____. *Amish Life.* Scottdale, Pa.: Herald Press, 1983.

_____. *Amish Society.* Baltimore: Johns Hopkins, 4th ed., 1993.

_____. *Hutterite Life.* Scottdale, Pa.: Herald Press, 1983.

_____. *Mennonite Life.* Scottdale, Pa.: Herald Press, 1983.

Hubmaier, D. Balthasar. *Von dem christlichen Tauf der Gläubigen.* Waldshut am Reyn, July 9, 1525.

Hueckel, Jean. *Les peregrinations de la famille Graber.* Couthenans, 1988.

Juhnke, James C. *Vision, Doctrine, War: Mennonite Identity and Organization in America.* Mennonite Experience in America, vol. 3. Scottdale, Pa.: Herald Press, 1989.

Katechismus für kleine Kinder: Zum Gebrauch für Schulen, Sonntagsschulen und Familien. First ed., by Amish, 1888. Baltic, Ohio: B. J. Raber, 1983.

Keim, Albert N., ed. *Compulsory Education and the Amish: The Right Not to Be Modern.* Boston: Beacon Press, 1975.

Keller, Ludwig. *Zur Geschichte der altevangelischen Gemeinden.* Berlin, 1887.

Kerssenbroick, Hermann von. *Geschichte der Wiedertäufer zu Münster in Westphalen.* First ed., 1568. Münster, 1881.

Kline, David. *Great Possessions: An Amish Farmer's Journal.* San Francisco: North Point Press, 1990.

Kraybill, Donald B., ed. *The Amish and the State.* Baltimore: Johns Hopkins, 1993.

——————. *The Puzzles of Amish Life.* Intercourse, Pa.: Good Books, 1990.

——————. *The Riddle of Amish Culture.* Baltimore: Johns Hopkins, 1989.

Längin, Bernd G. *Die Hutterer: Gefangene der Vergangenheit, Pilger der Gegenwart, Propheten der Zukunft.* Hamburg, 1986. Munich, 1991.

——————. *Germantown—auf deutschen Spuren in Nordamerika.* Berlin, 1983.

——————. "Die Mennoniten in Paraguay." *Globus,* Feb. 1989.

——————. *Die Russlanddeutschen unter Doppeladler und Sowjetstern.* Augsburg, 1991.

Letters of the Amish Division: A Sourcebook. Trans. and ed. by John D. Roth and Joe Springer. Goshen, Ind.: Mennonite Historical Society, 1993.

Lohmann, Martin. *Die Bedeutung der deutschen Ansiedlungen in Pennsylvanien.* Stuttgart, 1923.

Loserth, Johann, ed. *Quellen und Forschungen zur Geschichte der oberdeutschen Taufgesinnten im 16. Jahrhundert.* Leipzig und Vienna, 1929.

Luther, Martin. *Von der Wiedertauffe an zween Pfarrherrn: Ein brieff Martin Luther.* Wittenberg, 1528.

Luthy, David. *The Amish in America: Settlements That Failed, 1940-1960.* Aylmer, Ont.: Pathway, 1986.

——————. *Amish Settlements Across America.* Aylmer, Ont.: Pathway, 1985.

MacMaster, Richard K. *Land, Piety, Peoplehood: The Establishment of Mennonite Communities in America, 1683-1790.* The Mennonite Experience in America, vol. 1. Scottdale, Pa.: Herald Press, 1985.

Mann, W. J. *Die gute alte Zeit in Pennsylvanien.* Philadelphia, 1880.

Martyrs Mirror. See Braght.

Mathiot, Ch. *Recherches historiques sur les Anabaptistes de l'ancienne Principauté de Montbéliard, d'Alsace et de Régiones voisines.* Belfort, 1922.

Mennonite Encyclopedia, The. Scottdale, Pa.: Herald Press, vols. 1-4, 1955-59; vol. 5, 1990.

Mennonitisches Lexikon. Ed. by Christian Hege und Dr. Christian Neff. 4 vols. Karlsruhe, 1913-67.

Menno Simons. *Dat Fundament des Christelycken Leers, opniew uitgegeven en van een engelse inleiding voorzien von H. Meihuizen.* The Hague, 1967.

——————. *The Complete Writings of Menno Simons.* Trans. by L. Verduin. Ed. by J. C. Wenger. Scottdale, Pa.: Herald Press, 1956, 1984.

Meyer, Art and Jocele. *Earthkeepers: Environmental Perspectives on Hunger, Poverty, and Injustice.* Scottdale, Pa.: Herald Press, 1991.

Miller, Levi. *Our People: The Amish and Mennonites of Ohio.* Rev. ed. Scottdale, Pa.: Herald Press, 1992.

Müller, Ernst. *Geschichte der bernischen Täufer.* First ed., Frauenfeld, 1895. Nieuwkoop, 1972.

Nolt, Steven M. *A History of the Amish.* Intercourse, Pa.: Good Books, 1992.

Peachey, Paul. *Die soziale Herkunft der Schweizer Täufer in der Reformationszeit.* Karlsruhe, 1954.

Raber, Ben J. See *Almanac.*

Sachse, Julius F. *The German Sectarians, . . . 1708-1742.* Philadelphia, 1899.

Schlabach, John F. *Begebenheiten von die Alte Amische Gemeinde von Holmes und Wayne Co., Ohio, und Adams Co., Indiana.* Gordonville, Pa.: Pequea Publishers, 1986.

Schlabach, Theron F. *Peace, Faith, Nation: Mennonites and Amish in Nineteenth-Century America.* The Mennonite Experience in America, vol. 2. Scottdale, Pa.: Herald Press, 1988.

Schleitheim Confession, The. Ed. and trans. by John H. Yoder. Scottdale, Pa.: Herald Press, 1977.

Scott, Stephen. *The Amish Wedding.* Intercourse, Pa.: Good Books, 1988.

_____, and Kenneth Pellman. *Living Without Electricity.* Intercourse, Pa.: Good Books, 1990.

_____. *Plain Buggies.* Intercourse, Pa.: Good Books, 1981.

_____. *Why Do They Dress That Way?* Intercourse, Pa.: Good Books, 1986.

Sources of Swiss Anabaptism, The. Ed. by Leland Harder. Classics of the Radical Reformation, vol. 4. Scottdale, Pa.: Herald Press, 1985.

Souvenance Anabaptiste: Bulletin de liaison des membres de l'association française d'histoire Anabaptiste-Mennonite, 1987-88.

Stucky, Joseph. *Eine Begebenheit, die sich in der Mennoniten-Gemeinde in Deutschland und in der Schweiz von 1693 bis 1700 zugetragen hat.* First ed., Danvers, Ill., 1871. Baltic, Ohio: B. J. Raber, 1985.

Täuferführer durch die Schweiz. Liestal, 1975.

Troyer (Treyer), David A. *Hinterlassene Schriften von David A. Treyer von Holmes County, Ohio, unter welchem sind auch mehrer Erbauliche und Geistriche Gedichte.* 1923 and reprinted. Available at Raber's Bookstore, Baltic, Ohio.

Unpartheyisches Gesangbuch. Lancaster, Pa., 1941. At Raber's Bookstore, Baltic, Ohio.

Wells, Richard D. *Articles of Agreement Regarding the Indiana Amish Parochial Schools and the Department of Public Instruction.* Bloomington, Ind.: Indiana Department of Public Instruction.

Wittmer, Joe. "Homogeneity of Personality Characteristics: A Comparison Between Old Order Amish and Non-Amish." *American Anthropologist* 72 (1970): 1063-1068.

_____, "The Amish Schools Today." *School and Society* 99 (1971): 227-230.

Wolkan, Rudolf. *Die Lieder der Wiedertäufer.* Berlin, 1903.

Yoder, John H. *Täufertum und Reformation in der Schweiz.* Karlsruhe, 1962.

Yoder, Joseph W. *Rosanna of the Amish.* Rev. ed. Scottdale, Pa.: Herald Press, 1973.

Yoder, Paton. *Tradition and Transition: Amish Mennonites and Old Order Amish, 1800-1900.* Studies in Anabaptist and Mennonite History, no. 31. Scottdale, Pa.: Herald Press, 1991.

Yoder, Peter. *Der Taufe-Spiegel.* Scottdale, Pa.: Herald Press, 1951.

Young Companion. Monthly. For youth. Aylmer, Ont.: Pathway.

Index of Persons

401

Voltaire, 191

W
Waglers, 358
Wagner, George, 165
Wagner, W. R., 47
Waldi, tanner, 169
Waldo, Peter and Waldensians, 68,
    78, 164, 311, 384
Waltner, Gary, 25
Weavers, 147, 159
Wenger, Christian, 104
Wengerd, Daniel, 24
Wengers, 236
Weynken, Claes, 165
Wickey, Solomon J., 24, 218-219
Widmers, 329, 332
Wilhelm, Count, 167
William, King Frederick I, 232
Willich, Colonel August von, 335
Wimpfeling, 179
Wycliffe, John, 68

Y
Yoder, Bennie C., 25
Yoder, Jacob, 333
Yoder, Joseph W., 377
Yoders, 25, 30, 70, 147, 159, 179, 198,
    236, 320, 329, 335, 345, 371, 389

Z
Zehr, Amos, 25, 38, 42, 220
Zehr, Henry, 137, 308
Zehr, Jacob, 308
Zehr, John, 17-18, 22-24, 33-35, 129-
    130, 132-133, 144, 194, 223, 347,
    365-370
Zehrs, 30, 70, 94, 198, 247, 291
Zimmerman, Christian, 97
Zimmermann, Verena, 188
Zimmermanns, 330
Zooks, 147, 236
Zug, 236
Zwingli, Huldrych, 53, 57-58, 60-63,
    65, 67, 70, 74, 79, 164, 167, 169,
    177, 215, 346, 384-386

Index of Places

407

411

Rotenburg, 165
Roth Road, 322
Röthenbach, 175, 330
Rotterdam, 65
Rüderswil, 175
Rüfenacht, 339
Rumpapump, 180
Russia, 104, 122, 174, 232, 332, 340, 345
Rütli meadow, 193

S
Saint Louis, France, 329
Saint Louis, Mo., 104
Sainte Anna, 180
Salm, 189
Salzburg, 166, 385
Sarasota, 320, 358, 389
Saxony, 72, 180
Schaffhausen, 68, 70
Schärding, 165
Schipfe, 59
Schleitheim, 68, 79, 165, 385
Schlettstadt, 180, 190, 333
Schüpbach, 175
Schwäbisch Hall, 74
Schwartz, Karl, 141
Schwartzenburg, 330
Schwartzenegg, 330
Schwaz, 166
Schwyz, 64
Scotland, 52
Sembach, 185, 389
Seppois-le-Bas, 25
Shipshewana, 24, 27, 181, 192, 313, 360
Siberia, 233
Signau, 175, 227
Silesia, 66
Simmental, 184, 186-187, 331
Sitter River, 71
Slovakia, 174, 344
Smucker Valley, 159
Sodom, 216, 317
Solothurn, 71
Somerset County, 245, 335, 342-343
Soudersburg, 245

South Dakota, 25, 332, 342
South Tirol, 386
South Whitley, 299
Soviet Union, 346
Spencerville, 145
Speyer, 62, 167, 386
Spiez, 186
St. Gallen, 59, 70-71, 166, 178, 385-386
St. Goarshausen, 185
St. Joseph County, 389
Stark Co., 27
Steffisberg, 169, 322, 330
Steinselz, 215, 341, 388
Stock, 339
Strasburg, Ontario, 247
Strassburg (Strasbourg), 69, 74-75, 126, 179-180, 215, 227, 318, 349, 385
Sugarcreek, 27, 147
Sumiswald, 59, 175-176
Susquehanna River, 244, 246
Sustenpass, 170
Swabia, 385
Switzerland, 19, 23, 25, 28, 31-32, 42, 46-47, 52, 57, 59, 61, 67, 69-70, 79, 127, 134, 141, 162, 166, 169, 172-173, 175, 179, 181-185, 187-188, 211, 239, 298, 330, 338, 340, 377, 385-388

T
Taiwan, 197
Tannental, 175
Täufergässl, 341
Taylor County, 389
Tennessee, 27, 389
Teufen, 178
Texas, 344, 389
Thun, 184
Thuner See, 186
Thuringia, 73, 385
Tiber River, 178
Tirol, 41, 66, 166, 179-180, 385
Todd County, 389
Topeka, 335
Toronto, 125

Trachselwald, 59, 172, 174
Trubach, 338
Trubtal, 46, 338
Turkey, 64
Tuscarawas County, 27, 245

U
Überbalm, 25
USA, 19, 21, 26-28, 32, 34, 38, 40, 42, 52, 96, 100, 149, 172, 175, 202, 206, 216-218, 220, 226, 236, 241, 243, 246, 248-249, 292, 294, 332, 341, 344, 363-364, 389
Unterhof, 231
Upper Mill Creek, 387
Utrecht, 76

V
Venice, 31
Versailles, 189
Vienna, 133, 229, 234, 332, 385
Vistula River, 232
Volhynia, 332, 342
Vosges Mountains, 180, 330

W
Wabash, 104
Wadena County, 389
Wädenswil, 168
Waldeck, 28, 245, 342, 388
Waldheim, 332
Walensee, 69
Walnut Creek, 363
Wangen, 71
Wappenswil, 166
Wartburg, 384
Washington County, 388
Washington, D.C., 210, 249

Waterloo County, 246
Waterloo, Ind., 105
Waterloo, Ont., 247
Wayne County, 27, 319
Weierhof, 25, 104, 185, 389
Westphalia, 74-75, 79, 230, 240, 386-387
White County, 389
Wiesbaden, 342, 389
Wilmot District, 247
Wimmis, 187
Windstein, 341
Wisconsin, 25, 27, 344, 371, 375, 389
Wismar, 318
Witmarsum, 76
Wittenberg, 166, 180
Wittgenstein, 342
World, 44
Worms, 342, 384
Worms-Ibersheim, 343
Württemberg, duchy of, 32, 190, 331, 335

Y
Yellow Creek, 335

Z
Zaire, 346
Zäzlwyl, 182
Zoar, 233
Zofingen, 69
Zollikofen, 330
Zollikon, 59, 70, 385
Zurich, 59-61, 64-66, 70-71, 74, 164, 166, 168, 170, 174, 180, 231, 235, 237, 247, 384-387
Zweibrücken, 180, 189-190, 231-232, 342-343, 387

414

The Author

Bernd G. Längin is a native of Karlsruhe, in the southwest of Germany near the Black Forest. In 1963-64 he worked as a foreign correspondent in the Middle East; and in 1965-69 he was the editor of the *Allgemeine Zeitung* at Windhoek, Namibia. He was in Vietnam as a journalist for six months in 1967.

During 1969-83 Längin was editor-in-chief of the *Courier* newspapers, North America's largest group of German-language weeklies, published in Winnipeg (Manitoba, Canada). For 1980-83 he was also editor-in-chief of the *Amerika Woche* (week), a national weekly published in Chicago, Illinois. In 1983-86 he was editor and foreign correspondent for the bimonthly *Globus* (globe) of Bonn, Germany, then editor-in-chief of that magazine in 1986-91.

From 1992 Längin is a roving freelance journalist and author. He works with print media, radio, television, and photography. His books in German include *Germantown: Auf deutschen Spuren in Nordamerika* (Germantown: on German tracks in North America; Westkreuz, 1983, 1984), *Die Hutterer* (Rasch und Röhring, 1986; Goldmann, Verlagsgruppe Bertelsmann, 1991), *Deutsche Bilder* (German pictures; Weltbild, 1989, 1990), *Die Amischen* (List, 1990), *Die Russlanddeutschen unter Doppeladler und Sowjetstern* (Germans in Russia under double eagle and Soviet star; Weltbild, 1991, 1992), and *Aus Deutschen werden Amerikaner* (From German to become American; Eckart, 1993).

The author has also published books on the remembered homeland of Germans in Silesia (Weltbild, 1993), the Sudetenland (Weltbild, 1993), East Prussia (Weltbild, 1994), and Pomerania (Weltbild, 1994). He has edited *Rumäniendeutsche zwischen Bleiben und Gehen* (Romanian Germans between staying and leaving; VDA, 1987, 1990, 1992) and *Die Deutschen in Russland: Gestern und heute* (Germans in Russia: yesterday and today; VDA, 1989, 1990, 1992).

Längin takes special interest in searching the world for groups that maintain significant traces of German culture and then writing about them. His books are liberally illustrated with his own photographs.

In 1990 he traveled through Europe with New Order Amishmen David Kline and Atlee Miller. He is in demand to show his slides on Amish life.

Bernd is married to Christiane, and they have a daughter, Marion Längin-Bueckert. When he is not traveling, he lives in Winnipeg while maintaining an apartment in Karlsruhe. He is a member of Grace Lutheran Church of Winnipeg.